Anonymous

Miscellany of the Scottish History Society

Volume 3

Anonymous

Miscellany of the Scottish History Society
Volume 3

ISBN/EAN: 9783337239213

Printed in Europe, USA, Canada, Australia, Japan

Cover: Foto ©ninafisch / pixelio.de

More available books at **www.hansebooks.com**

PUBLICATIONS

OF THE

SCOTTISH HISTORY SOCIETY

SECOND SERIES

VOLUME

XIX

MISCELLANY

(*Third Volume*)

OCTOBER 1919

MISCELLANY OF
The Scottish History Society
(Third Volume)

DUNDEE COURT-MARTIAL RECORDS, 1651

THE BISHOP OF GALLOWAY'S CORRESPONDENCE, 1679-1685

THE DIARY OF SIR JAMES HOPE, 1646-1654

INSTRUCTIONS FOR THE TRIAL OF PATRICK GRAHAM, 1476

THE SCOTTISH CONTRIBUTIONS TO THE DISTRESSED CHURCH OF FRANCE, 1622

THE FORBES BARON COURT BOOK, 1659-1678

EDINBURGH
Printed at the University Press by T. and A. Constable
for the Scottish History Society
1919

CONTENTS

DUNDEE COURT-MARTIAL RECORDS, 1651,
   Edited by GODFREY DAVIES, M.A.

 INTRODUCTION, . . 3
 COURT-MARTIAL RECORDS, . 9

THE BISHOP OF GALLOWAY'S CORRESPONDENCE, 1679–1685, *Edited by* WILLIAM DOUGLAS

 INTRODUCTION, . . 71
 THE BISHOP OF GALLOWAY'S CORRESPONDENCE, 74

THE DIARY OF SIR JAMES HOPE, 1646–1654,
 Edited by SIR JAMES BALFOUR PAUL, C.V.O., LL.D.

 INTRODUCTION, . 99
 DIARY OF SIR JAMES HOPE, 126

INSTRUCTIONS FOR THE TRIAL OF PATRICK GRAHAM, 1476,
   Edited by ROBERT KERR HANNAY

 INTRODUCTION, ... 171
 INSTRUCTIONS FOR THE TRIAL OF PATRICK GRAHAM, 176

THE SCOTTISH CONTRIBUTIONS TO THE DISTRESSED CHURCH OF FRANCE, 1622,
   Edited by D. HAY FLEMING, LL.D.

 INTRODUCTION, . . . 181
 THE CONTRIBUTION OF HADDINGTONSHIRE . 190
 THE CONTRIBUTION OF ST. CUTHBERT'S, EDINBURGH, . . . 193

CONTENTS

THE FORBES BARON COURT BOOK, 1659-1678,
Edited by J. MAITLAND THOMSON, LL.D.

	PAGE
INTRODUCTION,	205
APPENDIX A,	218
APPENDIX B,	220
APPENDIX C,	221
THE FORBES BARON COURT BOOK,	224
INDEX	323

DUNDEE COURT-MARTIAL RECORDS

1651

Edited by

GODFREY DAVIES, M.A.
Late Scholar of Pembroke College, Oxford

A

INTRODUCTION

CROMWELL was besieging Perth when the first rumours reached him that Charles II. and his forces had begun their march towards England. On 2nd August, 1651, Perth surrendered and Cromwell proceeded at once to divide his troops, leaving one section under Monck to complete the subjugation of Scotland, and leading in person the more numerous body in pursuit of the Scottish army.

Monck had no organised enemies to face him in the field and his task was to subdue the towns which still resisted. For this purpose he had under his immediate control three regiments of horse, commanded by Colonels Okey, Alured, and Grosvenor, and three of foot, his own and those of Ashfeild and Reade, together with ' troopes of dragoones . . . and the greatest part of the trayne of artillery, with the 2 companies of firelocks '—in all about four thousand men, to which may be added another two thousand in garrisons.[1] The force was small, but its ample supply of guns and mortars eminently fitted it for the work in hand.

On 6th August Monck summoned Stirling, which surrendered eight days later. On 26th August he appeared before Dundee, to receive a proud defiance from its governor, Sir Robert Lumsden.[2] The next few days were

---

[1] C. H. Firth, *Scotland and the Commonwealth*, pp. xvii, 1. I prefer the smaller number, since it is obvious from Monck's letters of the period that his army was wasted by sickness (cf. Mackinnon, *Coldstream Guards*, 1833, vol. i. pp. 40-5). Hacker's regiment was left with Monck, but was ordered a few days later to join Cromwell, and fought at Worcester.—*Merc. Pol.*, 4-11 September.

[2] Original letter of Lumsden to Monck among the papers at Welbeck (*Portland MSS.*, vol. i. p. 615). The garrison was eight hundred soldiers, aided by townsmen and strangers, who sought refuge at Dundee on account of the reputed strength of its fortifications.

spent in preparations, bringing up the artillery and awaiting the return of the horse who captured the Committee of Estates at Alyth. About 4 A.M. on 1st September the guns opened on the town, and after seven hours' firing, breaches were made and the signal to attack was given.[1] The storming party was composed of cavalry, sailors, and the infantry regiments of Monck and Ashfeild, about seventeen hundred men.[2] At first a fierce resistance was encountered, but once this had been broken, success was easy.

Some of the inhabitants took part in the defence[3] and were slain, and others in the streets were involved in the slaughter which followed the forcing of the breaches. When, however, the victors reached the centre of the town, quarter was freely granted, and there was no deliberate massacre of non-combatants.[4] The casualties of the conquerors were six officers and about twenty soldiers,[5] and the vanquished lost not more than eight hundred,[6]

---

[1] *Scotland and the Commonwealth*, pp. 11-12; Nicoll, *Diary*, p. 57.

[2] *Scotland and the Commonwealth*, pp. 11-12. In his letter to Cromwell announcing the capture of Dundee, Monck mentions that he had only twelve hundred foot fit to march. The two regiments engaged in the storm would thus number roughly four hundred apiece. Cf. letter of Okey, 1st September, quoted by Mackinnon, vol. i. pp. 43-4.

[3] Nicoll definitely states that 'the townsmen . . . stood stoutly to their fortune, and defended themselves.' Monck's despatch to Cromwell and the narrative printed in *Scotland and the Commonwealth* imply the same. Lamont (*Diary*, pp. 34-5) says that 'the town people were secure [*i.e.* careless] and surpresed at unawares.' Balfour (iv. 315) suggests that they failed to defend themselves since they were drunk, but Clarke asserts in his letter to the Speaker (Cary, *Memorials of the Civil War*, vol. ii. pp. 366-7) that the enemy had fifteen hundred men 'upon the line.' As there were only eight hundred soldiers in the garrison, the rest must have been civilians.

[4] The highest estimate of the slain is ten or eleven hundred (Nicoll, p. 58). This is decisive against the theory of a general massacre. I attach no importance to Clarendon's sweeping assertion that 'persons of all degrees and qualities were put to the sword for many hours after the town was entered.'—*Rebellion*, vol. xiii. §. 138.

[5] These figures are those of Monck.

[6] On 5th September Clarke wrote that 'now we come to bury the dead (which is not yet fully done) we find there was near eight hundred killed.' Probably there

among whom may have been some women and children.[1]

'The stubbornness of the enemy,' wrote Monck, 'enforced the soldiers to plunder the town.' In other words he granted his men the licence allowed by the usage of war after a successful storm. A rich booty was secured. According to Nicoll the English army 'had gotten above two hundred thousand pound stirling, partly of ready gold, silver, and silver work, jewels, rings, merchandise, and merchant wares and other precious things belonging to the town of Edinburgh, by and beside all that belonged to the town and other people of the country, who had sent in their goods for safety to that town.' Clarke told the Speaker: 'The spoil is like to prove very great; were you here, you would not know a private soldier from an officer, divers of them having got gallant apparel.' After twenty-four hours order was restored, and no further plundering was tolerated.

Having rewarded his soldiers, Monck had now to face the harder task of reconciling the inhabitants of Dundee, and indeed of all Scotland, to the rule of their conquerors. Of all the lessons of the previous ten years of civil strife none was plainer than that indiscriminate plundering both rendered permanent the hostility of enemies and irreparably damaged the morale of any army allowed such licence. The military leaders, in whose hands the government was temporarily placed, sought to obtain the acquiescence

---

was an enumeration of the corpses, and Clarke's official position would secure him access to such information. His figures are confirmed by Balfour, by *Mercurius Scoticus*, 2-9 September, and by Whitelock, *Memorials*, 1853, iii. 351. Monck gives five hundred, but he wrote on the day of the storm before the losses of the enemy could have been accurately ascertained. Cf. Lamont, pp. 34-5, and *Scotland and the Commonwealth*, p. 12.

[1] Nicoll speaks of 'seven score women and young children,' and Balfour of two hundred women, as being slain. The only accounts of eyewitnesses were written by Englishmen, and they do not mention any female victims, although Whitelock states that eighty women were killed.—*Memorials*, vol. iii. p. 353.

of the Scots by the impartial administration of justice and to secure their own supremacy by the maintenance of strict discipline in the forces under their command. The two objects were interdependent—both concerned the relations of an alien soldiery with a subject population. The instrument which regulated the intercourse of soldiers and civilians was the court-martial, which adjudicated disputes between victors and vanquished, enforced the articles of war, and issued proclamations as occasion demanded.

The only complete records of the proceedings of any courts-martial which have survived from the Puritan Revolution are contained in the following pages, and even these documents only cover a period of four months. They apply solely to Dundee and its immediate vicinity, but it is clear from fragmentary notices and casual references in contemporary diaries and newspapers that these accounts may be taken as a fair sample of similar judicial activities elsewhere.

The records of the courts-martial held at Dundee from 17th September 1651 to 10th January 1652 are preserved in volume xxi. of the Clarke MSS. in Worcester College, Oxford. The extracts here printed comprise about five-sixths of the original: the omitted portions often merely duplicate the statements in the text. In selecting which of several similar depositions should appear I have tried to retain all evidence which illustrates the social and economic life of the citizens of Dundee, and which reveals their sentiments towards the English quartered upon them.

Of the trials some only concern the army itself—as swearing, quarrels among soldiers, disobedience to officers or changing from one regiment to another without permission. There are three examples of the sin common to all armies in all ages, and the severe punishment inflicted upon the offenders proves the abhorrence of immorality felt by Cromwellian officers. The presence of moss-troopers in the neighbourhood caused the despatch of small bodies of cavalry in pursuit, and if they went far afield they had to be quartered upon the landowners outside the town. One of the most interesting cases deals with the refusal of Lady Airlie to quarter the troop of Lieutenant Greene. After a long dispute between the lady and the lieutenant, the doors were burnt down and the contending parties agreed upon the delivery of her house on condition that its occupants should be prisoners and its contents deemed the lawful prize of the soldiers. After hearing many witnesses on both sides, the Court ordered that Lady Airlie should receive the money raised by the sale of her goods and the property still unsold, except materials of war, together with '50 boules of oates allowed to her in consideracion of the eating of her corne.'

Equally noteworthy is the petition of two soldiers that James Glage should be compelled to pay them the hundred pounds he promised them the day Dundee was stormed to save his life, for they alleged that they guarded him all night and thus missed their share of plunder—statements which were contradicted by their captain and another witness. Since no judgment is mentioned the claim probably failed. Of general interest was the decision that the price of two horses of a quartermaster was not chargeable upon the town of Kirkcaldy, whence they were stolen. The value of the horses, sixteen pounds and twelve pounds, shows how well the cavalry was mounted.[1]

It was natural that the liberty allowed the soldiers after the storming of the town should have an aftermath. Some petty larceny went on under the pretext of searching for concealed arms, and there was some robbery with violence. A proclamation [2] was issued by Monck on 15th September against plundering, and the proceedings herein recorded illustrate the sentences passed upon those guilty of disobeying their general's orders.

---

[1] These sums are much higher than the usual rates paid for horses. Vide, *Cromwell's Army*, pp. 242-8.
[2] Printed in *Scotland and the Commonwealth*, p. 325; cf. *ib.* p. 324.

The perusal of these documents conveys two clear impressions. The first is the impartiality of the courts-martial and the evident determination of all officers to protect the Scots from any oppression or violence at the hands of the English soldiers. The absence of complaints in diaries and annals of the period proves that there was no serious miscarriage of justice. The second is the heterogeneous character of Monck's army. Although the conduct of the majority was excellent, there were some black sheep in the ranks. There is no sign among the common soldiers of the religious enthusiasm which is so marked in some of the officers.[1] Puritanism does not seem to have permeated the classes from which recruits were raised. On the other hand, offences which are to-day regarded as venial were severely punished in 1651. A sterner vigilance was kept upon moral delinquencies then than now. In spite of occasional lapses the conduct of the army in Scotland was superior to that of the forces Marlborough or Wellington led to victory.

A transcript of these papers, which I have carefully compared with the original manuscript, was placed at my disposal by Professor C. H. Firth. He also lent me some manuscript notes, and allowed me to draw freely upon his inexhaustible knowledge of the period. In addition I have often had recourse to his volumes, *Scotland and the Commonwealth,* and *Cromwell's Army.* Mr. R. K. Hannay has also assisted me in attempting to identify place-names mentioned in the text, and in other ways. For these obligations my best thanks are due.

G. DAVIES.

13*th August* 1917.

---

[1] The last trial recorded is that of John Dodd for manslaughter. Before sentence was passed a passage from Numbers treating of accidental homicide was 'debated att large by all the officers.'

DUNDEE. COURT MARTIALL. September 17, 1651.

Present.
Colonel Ashfeild.
Lieutenant Colonel Goughe.
 „   „   Brayne.
Major Dorney.
Captain Lee.
 „   Boone.
 „   Dawborne.
Captain Morgan.
 „   Groome.
 „   Heyrick.
 „   Lingwood.
 „   Baynes.
Lieutenant Powell.
Adjutant General Dennis.

Thomas Edgecouf committed by Lieutenant Colonel Goffe. Accus'd for bringing 6 cowes about 3 miles off.

Pleads, his Ensigne went along with him. The Ensigne sent for. Ensigne to Lieutenant Colonel Gough.

The Ensigne says, that hee came with them from the house where the Generall quarter'd.

Elias Bleaton committed by Lieutenant Colonel Brayne. Accus'd, that hee went 6 weekes before Christmas from Colonel Daniell's regiment to Captain Fenwick's troope in Sir Arthur Heslerig's regiment. Hee had bin a souldier 11 yeares. Hee was farrier to the troope. Pleads hee did itt for the good of the army.

Question. Whether hee should bee tryed uppon the Article for death,[1] or noe? Resolved in the negative.

Question. Whether Elias Blaiden shall bee tryed uppon the Article of Misdemeanour or noe? Resolved in the affirmative.

Question. What punishment hee shall sustaine being found guilty by the testimony of Lieutenant Colonel Brayne and his owne confession.

---

[1] Articles of War, printed in *Cromwell's Army*, App. I. pp. 409-22.

Adj. Gen. Dennis.	To ride the horse [1] before Col. Daniell's regiment with his fault uppon his brest.
Lt. Powell.	The same.
Capt. Baynes.	The same.
,, Heyrick.	The same.
,, Groome.	To run the gantelop.[2]
,, Morgan.	The strapadoe.[3]
,, Boone.	To ride the horse an houre with a muskett att each heele.
,, Lee.	
Major Dorney.	To ride the wooden horse 2 dayes where his regiment is, an houre each time with a muskett att each heele and his fault uppon his brest.
Lt. Col. Brayne.	The same.
,, ,, Goughe.	To ride the wooden horse an houre att the time of parade.
Col. Ashfeild.	To ride the wooden horse an hower one day.

Sentence: To ride the horse an hower att S. Johnston's att the head of Col. Daniell's regiment with his fault uppon his brest.

George Scutter
Laurence Milton } of Capt. Lee's troope.

Accus'd about the killing of a boy.

George Scutter. That they went from their colours about half a quarter of a mile to shooe their horses, and afterwards followed their colours, that a dragoone tooke the boy, and carried him behind him, threw him off and falls a cutting of the boy; they being gone away, Col. Okey's men following us laid itt to us. Laurence Milton to the same purpose.

---

[1] Described in *Cromwell's Army*, p. 290.
[2] An example of running the gauntlet is given pp. 289-90 of *Cromwell's Army*.
[3] *I.e.* 'Hanging up by the Thumbs, so that only the Delinquents' Toes can touch the ground.'—*Cromwell's Army*, p. 289, note 4.

Commanded to withdraw in regard the third man was nott there and noe newes of the boy, whether kill'd or noe.[1]

Thomas Peirson and Adam Knight, two of Capt. Dawborne's troope, committed by Col. Ashfeild for meeting with a boy neere the towne, forcing him to discover goods that were hid neere the sheepens in a chest.

Adam Knight, confes't, that the boy look't to his horse, that going into the feild they ask't him where any armes were hid, hee said hee could tell where there was a sword, a muskett, and a chest in the sheepepens, that they went to itt, and one carried one pack and the other another, and there came a man and said the goods were his, and hee would give them mony for them, for they were his.

The Scotts boye sayes hee was sheering corne, that they inquir'd for armes, that hee brought them to the chest, that they gave him cloathes.

Question. Whether Thomas Peirson and Adam Knight bee alike guilty and to bee tryed uppon the Article of Misdemeanour? Resolved in the affirmative.

Adj. Gen. Dennis. Guilty of a sharpe reproof.
Lt. Powell. Reproof.
Capt. Baynes. Ride the horse with his fault uppon his back an hower.
Capt. Lingwood. Ride the horse an hower with a muskett att each heele and writt uppon his back: 'For searching for armes without order, and for taking of plunder.'
Capt. Groome. The same.
„ Morgan. The same.
„ Lee. The same.
Major Dorney. To ride the wooden horse and after that to bee taken downe and receive ten stripes.
Lt. Col. Brayne. The same as Capt. Lingwood.
„ „ Gough. The same.
Col. Ashfeild. The same.

---

[1] Acquitted 23 September, no evidence being offered.

Sentenc't : Thomas Peirson and Adam Knight, being found guilty by their owne confession of searching for armes without orders and taking of plunder, are sentenc't : To ride the horse an hower with a muskett att each heele, and the fault writt uppon their backs, ' For searching for armes without orders, and for taking of plunder.' [1]

DUNDEE COURT MARTIALL.[2] SEPTEMBER 19, 1651.

Eight souldiers that were taken out of their quarters after the tattoo beaten.

Order'd, that noe man should bee out of his quarters, nor sitt uppe drinking in their quarters after the tattoe beaten.

A sharpe reproof given them, which was done by the president.

Order'd, that noe souldier draw beere without orders.

Information of Major Dorney against Henry Sparkes, corporall to Major Rede in Col. Fenwick's regiment, David Pew and John Humphries. Read as followeth : The information of Major Henry Dorney taken upon oath in the Court Marshall, Sept. 19, 1651.

That yesterday, being Thursday the 18 instant, haveing newly given out orders on the churchyard at Dundee, he heard a souldier whose name is David Pew (as he cals himself being with them that play'd), swearing in a grosse manner, which to his remembrance was ' by God's bloud and wounds ' ; that afterwards about 11 of the clock att night, walking to view the guards neere the Lt. Generall's quarters in Dundee, he heard much swearing amongst a company of souldiers, and amongst the rest hee looked in at a window and tooke particular notice of 2, whose names are (as hee is since inform'd), John Humphryes and Henry Sparkes, to be more emenently

---

[1] This is the case referred to by Whitelock.—*Memorials*, vol. iii. p. 354-5.

[2] The lists of officers present at this and all subsequent courts-martial have been omitted, but their names are given in the table on pp. 66-7.

swearing 'by God,' or 'as God shall judge mee,' with other oathes and execrations to that effect.

HEN: DORNEY.

Question. Whether to proceede against Corporall Henry Sparkes, being of another garrison? Resolved in the affirmative.

Uppon debate by the testimony of Major Dorney and others, Henry Sparkes, David Pew and John Humphries were found guilty of swearing, and theruppon sentenc't: To bee gagy'd (sitting uppon the horse) for an hower, with their faults written uppon their backs, vizte. For swearing.

Wm. Wells call'd in about striking of Capt. Lee, who hindred him from carrying away of bookes.

Left to Capt. Lee to take his submission.

Francis Mencour of Capt. Fitche's company in regiment, inform'd against by Capt. Dawborne, who mett him with 3 seamen carrying a sayle of a shippe. Seamen's names Geo. Maners, Jo. Mason, and Wm. Hamonds, belonging to Capt. Wheeler, sayes, that they fetch't itt out of an house where noe body dwelt. Souldier sayes that itt was in his Landladyes house. That hee knew nott that the plunder of the towne was done.

Dismis't with a sharpe reproof.

DUNDEE. COURT MARTIALL. SEPTEMBER 20, 1651.

The information of Henry Crosse, corporall to Capt. Lingwood, against Francis Paulett and Phillip Parker, souldiers in Coll. Ashfeilde's regiment, taken upon oath the 20 day of Sept. 1651.

That upon Wednesday the 17th instant being drinking with the said 2 souldiers and other company in Mother Picket's seller, and, haveing paid his parte of the reckoning, being goeing forth of the room, the candle was of a sudden put out, and a souldier rushed upon him and fell beating of him, wherupon this deponent struling with him, the rest fell upon him, and in the busle his purse (wherin there was about 14s. and 10d.) was taken from him ; which this deponent missing, caught hold of the above named Francis Paulet and Phillip Parker who were next to him, all the rest haveing escaped : that he verely beleved that Francis Paulet, who was in a gray cloake, had his purse.

The marke + of Henry Crosse.

DUNDEE. COURT MARTIALL. September 22, 1651.

Peter Thorne and Eliz. Anderson brought in, being found in bed together.

Tho. Baldwin brought in the guard and found them in bed together ; and Margaret Anderson and Thomas Robson, a backster, together in another bed.

Uppon the whole they were found guilty both by the information of Corporall Potter and Tho. Baldwin, who found them in bed together and sentenc't : To bee whip't from the Westgate to the Eastgate att the time of the parade, having fourty stripes each man and each woman coupled together in irons, and the women to bee turn'd out of towne till they shall give security to the Governour of their good or better behaviour.

DUNDEE. COURT MARTIALL. September 23, 1651.

The information of Phillipp Rakeham, corporall to Capt. Lingwood in Col. Ashfeild's regiment, taken the 22th of September 1651. Read, vizte. saith, that on Friday the 19th instant about 3 or 4 of the clock in the afternoone being at Mr. Robert Hayes' house in Droneley, and standing in the gate, saw 2 troopers about halfe a mile off driving 2 Scotchmen with their swords drawen before them, the one being upon a greene coate, upon a browne bay nagge, and the other upon a black horse, one of these troopers haveing knock't one of the Scotchmen downe with his pistoll 3 severall times. Therupon the deponent goeing towards them, upon which they rode over the lands towards St. Johnston's, and goeing into a land, tooke a browne horse out of the feild which was tedder'd, and the owner cutting corne neere it, who (as he told this deponent) durst not question them for feare of farther trouble; and afterwards the deponent perceiving them to send towards Dundee, being got before them, left worde att the port, where they were apprehended upon the discovery of one of the countrymen who knew them to be the men who had beaten and rob'd them.   PHILLIPP RACKHAM.

The informacion of Andrew Tindall taken upon oath the 20 of September 1651. Saith, that on Friday the 19 instant, this deponent and his guid father James Terry, haveing bin bringing peats and fowles to Dundee and returning towards their home at Newtile about 4 of the clock in the afternoone, were mett neere Droncley by 2 troopers, whose names as hee hath since heard are Henry Brigges and Brian Carter, the one of which (being a short black man) set his pistoll to this deponent's brest and said, 'you Scotch roge, give's your mony,' and said he would pistoll this deponent if hee would not deliver it presently; and held this deponent and put his hand into his pocket; but missing the mony made the deponent give itt him: which hee did, being a doller, a shilling and a six pence in a clout, after which the troopers rode away, and this deponent and his guidfather went to their homes.
                          The marke × of And: Tindall.

The informacion of James Terry taken upon oath this 20th day of September 1651. That yesterday being the 19 instant this deponent and his son-in-law And: Tindall, haveing bin bringing in peate and fowles for the use of the garrison of Dundee and returning to their homes at Newtille, were met neere Dronley by 2 troopers, one of which (being the tallest of the 2) whose name he since heers is Brian Carter, said 'haye give mee your siller,' and then drew his sword and struck this deponent severall times over the head; and then, litting from his horse, took away a 1s. and 6d. in boddles out of his pouch and then they both rode away.

The marke of James × Terry.

Henry Brigges uppon examination confesses, that hee tooke mony of the man about 5s., but none of the old man, that hee struck the old man severall times.

Question. Whether Brian Carter, and Henry Brigges shall bee tryed uppon the Article of Life, or uppon the Article for Misdemeanour? Resolved, that they bee tryed by the Article of Misdemeanour.

Tryed and found guilty by testimony and their owne confession of plundering and offering violence to the persons of two countrymen. Resolved that Brian Carter and Henry Brigges bee brought from the prison, with ropes about their neckes, and their faults uppon their brests, to the gallowes att the time of the parade, and being tide uppe by the neck receive 30 stripes appeece uppon their bare backes. Afterwards to aske forgivenesse uppon their knees for the injury done to the poore men and the army. And after that to bee kept with bread and water till they have restor'd fower fold to the countrymen for what they have taken away.[1]

Richard Peacock of Col. Ashfeild's regiment examined concerning a trooper taking a sheepe from a countryman.

James Oddey, of the troope late Capt. Savile's in Col. Alured's regiment, sayes, that hee was nott att the man's house att all, nor did see any proteccion hee had. That hee did nott take the sheepe, but itt seemes the souldiers paid lesse then the countryman expected.

The countryman to bee sent for, and such of the guard as tooke him.

---

[1] Cf. Whitelock, *Memorials*, vol. iii. p. 356, and *Scotland and the Commonwealth*, pp. 15-16.

William Wells of Capt. Bayne's company in Col. Ashfeild's regiment examined about opposing and affronting Capt. Lee, and striking of him.

Resolved, that hee bee dismis't uppon asking forgivenesse of, and submitting to the Captaine.

DUNDEE. COURT MARTIALL. 8° October 1651.

Robert Scupham and John Wood of Capt. Parker's companie, brought in for taking away a rundlett of strong waters of about 8 gallons from Phillipp Cooper, sutler.

Robert Scupham acknowledges his fault, that itt was the first and hopes itt shall bee the last. Jo: Wood sayes, that hee brought itt to him in the streete and desir'd him to helpe to carry it.

Question. Whether they shall have any punishment or noe? Resolved in the affirmative.

Sentenc't: To ride the wooden horse for half an hower with a muskett att each heele.

The informations of Isabell Alexander and Isabell Rankin concerning Marian Gurdon read.

Thomas Peacock and Marian Gurdon.

Sentenc't:[1] To bee whip't from Eastgate to the Westgate to have 60 stripes each att a cart's taile. After that both to bee duck't att the Key.

Agnus Askin to bee led along with them from the Eastgate to the Westgate and soe to the Key, and there to bee duck't with them, and the women to bee boated over into Fife.[2]

Tho: Price of Capt. Gardiner's company call'd in. Serjt. Tho. Sewell saith, that hee commanded Thomas Price to goe to the centry, that hee went towards the centry, but would nott releeve the centry, but came back againe. The reason was there was another man uppon the centry

---

[1] For fornication: Agnes Askin was present.
[2] Cf. Whitelock, *Memorials*, vol. iii. p. 360.

then hee expected, which hee would nott releive. That theruppon hee commanded him to goe along with him to the guard, who scorn'd, drew off, and struck the said Sewell a blow with his arme.

Jo: Hind sayes, that hee saw Tho: Price and the Sergt. of the guard strugling together and lying uppon the ground together, and that hee did pull them asunder.

James Guderick sayes, that hee being standing centinell, Thomas Price was to releive him, sayes hee, 'I am nott sent hither to releive you, neither will I,' and refused to stand civillie uppon the centinell's duty. That Price laid his hand uppon his sword but did nott draw itt.

James Tolson, that hee, standing centinell when his Landlord came by, hee desir'd James Guderick to stand for him, in the meane time Mr. Price came to releeve him, but refused to releeve Guderick. That hee saw the sergeant draw his sword and follow after Price, and after that hee saw Price take hold of his sword and draw itt out a little way.

Tho. Price sayes, The sergeant commanded him to releeve James Tolson: who said 'you are a saucie Jack-an-apes that would nott releeve mee before now.' The corporall did give him abusive words, that hee told him hee was as good a man as himself, uppon this hee giving him one punch or two hee clos'd with him, etc.

Uppon proof of the whole, Thomas Price had sentence: To ride the horse an hower with one muskett crosse under the horse to keepe his legges wide.

DUNDEE. COURT MARTIALL. OCTOBER 15. 1651

Order'd, that before the rising of each Court a President bee named for the next Court day.

Order'd, that such officers who shall have due warning given them by the Major or Marshall of the regiment, and shall nott appeare att the hower appointed (vizte. nine in the morning) shall forfeit the 4th parte of a dayes pay, to bee presently laid downe in Court, and dispos'd of from time to time as the Court shall thinke fitt.

The examination of Christian Bell, servant to Sir John Lesley, read, saith, that uppon Tuesday last there came 2 souldiers, the one a trooper and the other a foote souldier (whose names shee since heares are Wm. Custwick and Robert Bell, trooper,) to Sir John Leslie's house att Newton[1] in Fife, and demanded beere, and being told by this deponent there was none, they fell to breaking open of the house, and notwithstanding shee told them there was noe body there nor any goods therin, they broke open the gate and 2 other doores, but tooke nothing away. This deponent further saith, that the next day in the evening there came 5 souldiers (amongst which the 2 before named) and after they had bin a while there went forth and fetch't in 2 sheepe of some poore folkes, neere the house and having kill'd them tooke them away raw in their knapsacks the next day.

The marke × of Christian Bell.

The examinacion of Christian Ramsey, saith, That shee dwelling about a quarter of a mile from Sir John Leslye's house at Newton, there came on Wednesday last a foote souldier (whose name shee since hears is Wm. Custwick) and askt her for eggs, and being told shee had none, hee went up and downe the house to search, and passing by severall clothes and other goods at last finding a cloak of her guid man's, said, 'This is for mee,' and soe brought it away, that shee followed him neere Sir John Leslye's house and then left him, not dearing to demand it. He draweing his sword strucke her and threatned to kill her, and threatned her the like with oaths, when shee came afterwards to the house.

The marke of × Christian Ramsey.

The examinacion of Janett Patrick saith, that on

---

[1] ?=Newport. Sir John Leslie would seem to be a mistake for Sir James Leslie, knight.

Wednesday last sitting besides her owne house doore shee saw the foote souldier above menciond carryeing a cloke out of her neybour Wm. Weems' house which belonged unto him.

The marke of Jan × Patrick.

The examination of John Lumsdall saith, that having heard the above written examination of Christian Bell, hee knowes the same to bee true and affirmeth the same in all particulars.

The marke × of John Lumsdall.

Wm. Custwick, souldier in Lt. Col Goughe's company, examined about his going into Fife, said hee went to fetch an horse hee lent one. That for the cloake itt was restor'd, that the trooper wore itt.

Robert Bell of Col. Alured's troope;
Marmaduke Haselwood }
Wm. Padley } of Capt. Morgan's company;
Hamilton of Col. Okey's regiment; all these were in Fife.

Marmaduke Haselwood examined saith, that hee staid in Fife one night, that hee went over with a trooper, that hee had noe passe or leave from his officer, and thought to come presently back againe.

Robert Bell examined, saith, that hee had noe meate for his horse, and that his horse had the farcie, that hee was with them when itt was broken open twice, that the trooper had bin there twice, that Wm. Custwick broke open 2 doores, himself tooke a stone and threw against the doores.

Wm. Custwick examined saith, that the woman followed him that night, but that hee told her that hee would give itt (the cloake) her on the morrow morning.

Sentenc't. To bee led from the prison with ropes about their neckes round about the parade, and to receive ten stripes there, and then to bee tide uppe to the gallowes and receive 20 stripes a peece. Something of their faults to bee written and sett uppe uppon the gallowes.

Marmaduke Haselwood. To ride the wooden horse an hower with 2 musketts att each heele, and to give satisfaccion with the rest for the sheepe.

To pay two shillings apeece each of them to the country people who lost the sheepe.

Phillipp Powell of Lt. Col. Goughe's company.

Capt. Lt. Powell informes against him for swearing and cursing. That being asleepe in the highway Lt. Col. Brayne and himself coming to wake him, hee said, a pox of God take them, why did they raise him?

Question. Whether hee shall have any further punishment then his ten dayes imprisonment? Carried in the negative. A sharpe reproof given him by the President. Order'd, that noe prisoner bee detayned above 24 houres by the Marshall Generall without an order under the officer's hand unto the Marshall Generall, expressing the cause of his committement, or information given to the Judge Advocate.

DUNDEE. COURT MARTIALL. Octob. 20, 1651

The examination concerning the differences betweene the Lady Arley [1] and Lt. Greene by order from Lt. Generall Monke, taken by Capt. Kirkby and Capt. Kingwell, this 11th of October 1651.

Read:

1. The Lady Arley deposed and examined, saith, that two men came unto her gates to demand quarter, shee said there used none to bee quarter'd there, yet shee asked them for their order, and said shee would obey

---

[1] Isabel Hamilton, a daughter of Thomas, first Earl of Haddington, was now a woman of fifty-five. Her husband, the first Earl of Airlie, died in 1666. Lady Margaret and Lady Isabel, mentioned below, were her daughters. The former, wife of Patrick Urquhart of Lethintie and Meldrum, contrived the escape of her brother, afterwards second earl, from St. Andrews Castle in 1646. *Scots Peerage*, vol. i. pp. 124-5.

order, and hee held out a red booke and said, there was his order, and did nott take out the order out of the booke. And further shee saith, that shee desired to come downe and see the order, and they would nott suffer her to come downe, because they would nott goe some distance from the gate fearing least they might breake in uppon her servants ere the gate had bin shutt after her coming out unto them, and they alwayes called for the opening of the gates.

2. Further shee saith, that Lt. Greene came into the back garden with some souldiers, and soe came into the close. And hee did call unto her severall times being in an upper window three storyes high, and the water did make such a noyse, shee said shee did nott well heare what hee said, and yet shee saith shee thinketh hee did desire her to come downe to speake with him. And yet shee further saith, they did throw stones and hold out 3 carbines towards her, and the Lieutenant did reprove them for throwing stones, but shee doth nott know that the Lieutenant was there when the carbines were holden uppe. And further shee saith, that the souldiers did come over the wall in a violent way, and threatned to open the doore and offer'd to open the gates with trees and stones, giving unto her hard language before the Lieutenant came.

3. And further shee saith, that shee did call and aske if there was any that would goe call the Lord Melgan.[1] And hee came in a short time, and all this time shee satt on her knees in the window. And shee saith, shee doth beleive the gates were on fire before the Lieutenant came, and att the same window in the same close, shee spake unto the Lord Melgan, and the Lord Melgan said, 'Alas. Madam, how falls this out? This is contrarie to your resolution two dayes agoe, for you said then you would open the gates when they came, there must needs bee a mistake for the gentlemen are mightily displeased.' And further

---

[1] James Maule of Melgund was the eldest son of Henry Maule of Melgund, and married about this time Marion Ogilvie, daughter of Sir John Ogilvie of Innerquharity (or Inverquharity).—*Reg. Mag. Sig.*, x. 55. For his connection with diving and the Tobermory wreck, see *Hist. MSS. Com. Rep.*, vi., pp. 625, 627.

shee saith, that the Laird of Melgan desired her to throw over the keyes, for hee said, hee had much adoe to save their lives. 'And I have promised, Madam, you shall come out.' And further shee saith, the Laird of Melgam did desire her to come downe unto a lower window that hee might speake unto her, and shee came unto a lower window, but did nott see nor speake unto the Lord of Melgam.

And further shee saith, after the gates were open'd the Laird of Melgan said, 'Madam, what will you doe? I am sorry this hath hapned,' and shee saith shee said, shee would goe back to the place whence shee came, for shee said shee had noe other place to goe unto. And further shee saith, that Lieutenant Greene asked where there was any gold, monie, and jewells, and said, there could nott bee soe many ladies, but there might bee such thinges amongst them. And shee answered there was none. Then hee asked for watches, and shee did cause the ladies and gentlewomen to deliver their watches, which watches were restored againe.

4. Shee further saith, that Lieutenant Greene hath taken divers goods out of her house, part of them are restored and parte of them are nott yet received by her nor restored by him.

To the Ladies charge, Lieut. Greene by way of answer, saith, that hee had order for the drawing of his men into the Houses of Invernheritie and Cortochye.[1] That hee marched the troope first to Inverheritie, and while hee was viewing the house there a messenger came to him from his Quartermaster, signifying to him that Cortochye House stood out against them, wheruppon hee marched the troope thither, and after using all the civill meanes hee could, which taking noe effect, hee with the officers considering the danger of the place, being in the edge of the Highlands, where were many armed men. The Lord of the house being one of their head men as alsoe the time of the day (which was then almost spent) and

---

[1] Cortachy.

resolved to attempt the subducing of the house by force, and in prosecucion therof set fire to 2 severall dores which was backed with iron gates, and after the dores were burnt throw, the lady and himselfe (by the Lord Mellgam's messages to and from both) came to agree upon the delivery of the house upon these condicions, viz. that both men and women be prisoners, and the armes and goods at the disposure of the souldiers, upon which uppon entring the house the souldiers seised on the armes, powder, shot, cullours and other goods, beds and women's apparrell excepted, which guiedes they seized upon as lawfull prize according to the agreement. All which with other materialls circumstances he offers to prove by severall oathes. Signed by mee

HENRY GREENE.

The examinacion of Quartermaster Medley taken upon oath.

This examinant saith, that hee was comanded by the Lieutenant to take a party of horse and the orders for their quarter with him alsoe, and to goe to Invernherity Castle and Cartockwhee House, a place at the Highland (where by Coll. Okey's order the troop was for some time to abide), and that before the Lieutenant came thither with the troope the quarter might bee readye for them and this examinant saith that he being with his party att Invernheritye saw severall horsemen aboute Cortoche house to the number of 7 or 8 to whome hee sent upp Law: Innchoyce, Sam: Saker, and Rich. Clarke who pursued them, but could not overtake. After whose returne he saw them, went to Cortoewhe and knocked at the gates, and that the Lady Arley looked out at a window and demanded what hee would have there; and this examinant saith that he answered, 'Madam, I have an order for a troope of horse to quarter heere,' and the lady replyed, heere used none to quarter there, hee tould the lady, his order was to quarter there and withall desires herr either to come downe and looke upon the order, or that shee would permitt him to show it her. Wherupon he pul'd the order out of his pockquett, and shee not lookeing downe but shee refuseing to oppen the gates, this examinant with others went over the wall into the court where hee opened the order and held it uppe in his hand before the lady, desiring her to looke upon it at a low window. The lady replyed shee would not come downe except hee would put the souldiers out of the court, which this examinant saith hee did twice upon her desire, and yet shee would not looke upon it notwithstanding a woman who was below in the hearing of this examinant sayd, 'Now, Madam, the gentleman hath put all the souldiers out,' and after all these and others civill meanes was used and it produced nothing, this examinant seeing the aforsaid horsemen with divers other footemen about the hill conceived some danger in d'laying and sent to the Lieutenant who was then with the troope, giveing him an account of what a proposicion was made, who thereupon drew the troope thither.

2. Unto the second this examinant saith that when the Lieutenant came hee drew up the troope at a distance, and himselfe with some others came into the court and comanded sylence, which was obeyed, and then the Lieutenant spake to her Ladyshipp, letting her know that he came thither by order and desired her with his hat in his hand to come downe and open the dore, and promised that noe violence should be offered either to persons or goods, and this or the like the Lieutenant did severall times, but how oft hee knowes not, and alsoe that hee desired the lady to speake with him at a lower window, but that after much desiring and long wayting shee would not come to speake with him, soe that the Lieutenant and Cornet consulting togeather, and, as they sayd, conceiveing danger from the hills whilest the troope was in that distracted condicion and the day being spent, resolved to enter by force, seing other meanes would not take, and to that end attempted to breke downe the dore, which when it was done there was an iron dore behind it soe that they gave orders to fire the wood, which was done.

And to the 3d. this examinant saith, that when the dores

were almost burnt throw, the Laird Melgan came into the court and call'd to the lady, and shee spoke to him and desired that Melgan might speake to her at a back window, which was granted, from whence he brought the condicion of the surrender and reported it openly in the court amongst the souldiers.

4. To the 4th this examinant saith that upon the opening the gates the souldiers entred upon many of the goods, all of them by their condicions being in their power, and this examinant saith that almost all the goods were restored again, although they belonged to malignants openly soe knowen. This examinant further saith that there was fower barrells of powder, 2 little ones and 2 greate, some musquetts and other guns and bulletts and stones in the windowes, and 9 foote collours; and this examinant saith that hee knowes not of any goods the Lieutenant tooke out of the house except armes and powder, and that the goods disposed of was inventred by Robert Bird and call'd in by that paper.

JOHN MEDLEY.

The examinacion of Law: Gunthorne taken upon oath.

1. To the first this examinant saith that he being with the quartermaster was one of them whome hee sent out in pursuite of some horsemen, which was armed, but could not take them, and comeing to Chortawhee with some others, the lady bid the said examinant keepe of if hee loved himselfe, and further saith that the quartermaster in his sight and hearing pul'd out an order and desired the lady to looke upon itt, and upon her desire put all the souldiers out of the Court 2 severall times, and notwithstanding the lady would not come downe to see, and not let him in.

2. To the second this examinant saith, that after the Lieutenant came hee spoke to the lady severall times letting her know hee was ordered thither and desired her to open the dores, and that neither person or goods should be stirred, but for all that the lady would not open the dores nor come to speake with him.

3. To the 3 this examinant saith when Melgan came into the court and had spoke to the lady, hee desired to know what termes shee would offer to them in the house; which was answerd that both men and women to have their leaves (but be prisoners) and the goods at the souldiers' disposure as prize; to which Melgan, after hee and the lady had spoke togeather at a back window, hee returned answer in the name of the lady [and] promised these, viz., that if the men and women might have their livies as prisoners the goodes should be at the souldiers' disposure.

4. To the 4th this examinant saith, that the souldiers seized on the goods according to the condicions made, and upon the Lieutenant's comand most of the goods was restored to the lady, and hee conceives all that could be procured, which goods at their takeing forth of the roome where they were lay'd was set downe in writing by one Roberte Bird. LAWNCE GUNTORNE.

The examinacion of Roberte Bird taken upon oath.

1. To the first this examinant saith, hee being one of the party that came along with the Quartermaster, that in his sight and hearing the Quartermaster pulled forth his orders out of his red booke and held it upp in his hand, and desired the lady that shee would bee pleased for to looke on it severall times.

2. To the 2d. this examinant saith that the Lieutenant came into the court and comanded sylence, which was obeyed, while hee spoke unto the lady, desiring her that her Ladyship would bee pleased for to come downe and open the gates, and promised her that noe violence should be offered neither to persons nor goods; this being done severall times yet shee refused for to open the dores.

3. To the 3. this examinant saith that the Lord Melgan came into the court and spoke unto the lady, and presently hee desired that he might have liberty to goe to the back window for to speake unto the lady which was granted. And further this examinant saith that the Lord Melgan came presently from the lady and brought

word from the lady, that shee desired that those that were in the house might have their lives as prisoners, and that all the goods that were in the house should be at the souldiers' disposure.

4. To the 4th this examinant saith, that according unto the condicion of the surrender, the souldiers presently seized on the goods, wherof a greate parte of them was restored by order from the Lieutenant unto the lady, and he conceives all that could be got againe. And this examinant saith that hee did take an account of the goods in writing, and that the greatest parte of goods were bedding and woman's apparrell, which was not stir'd; and a greate parte of the rest of those goods were malignants', which were in actuall armes against us; and farther saith that there was much powder and shot ready in the house and bulletts and stones in the windowes.

ROBERT BIRD.

October 11th, 1651.

The examination of James Mauley, the Lard of Melgun, Junr, examined upon oath saith, that hee meeting a messenger from the Lady Arley nere unto the gate, comeing on did find the gates shut and the garden gate and the inner gate both on fire, and then he found the souldiers with their swords and pistolls in their hands, with this word: 'noe quarter to man, woman or child.' He first did intreate for their lives from the Lieutenant and souldiers, and seeing the lady in an upper window lookeing towards the court, did extremly regrate the unexpected accident. After he desired her might speake at a back window on the other side where he might heere her better. After he came unto the said window, and that he spoke with the Lady Arley at that window, and he said unto her, 'Madam, all that I can doe is to save your lifes, and the souldiers will have the goods,' which condicions were desired by the officers and souldiers, and propounded to the said lady by the said examinant, and the lady answered and said, 'doe as you thinke fitt.' Hee desired that shee would make hast to throw over the keyes. After hee, the said examinant, came into the court and told the Lieutenant the keyes should presently bee had, and ' you will save their lives as you have promised.' Then againe the Lieutenant said, ' the goods are the souldiers.' Hee the examinant answer'd all was at his disposall. Imediatly the fire was removed from the gate, and the keys throwen over. This is disposed of me.   JA: MAULE.

The examination of John Makeney.
To the 4th this examinant saith that it was the old lady herselfe which spoke to Melgam, and that the examinant with some others stood before the back window and playnley saw that it was onely the lady Arley that spoke with him, and that upon comeing back into the court the keys, as shee had promised him, was thrown downe with their owne hands, all which the examinant saith he beleiveth Melgam cannot deny if put upon his oath.   JOHN O. MAKENEY.

The examination of the Lady Margret taken *viva voce* in court, saith, that when the Quartermaster came first, the Lady Arley was willing to speake unto him and the rest, and desired them to withdraw from the gates and shee would give them content. After the Lieutenant came shee was still content, intreating them earnestly to retire and shee would obey any order they should bring, that shee knowes not that they withdrew. That hearing the Lord Melgam had bine in the inclose where some windows look't over, I did desire to speake with him; when he came to the window, he said, ' Madam, I am very much greeved for this busines and am sorry that the gates were not open'd.' This deponent answer'd, ' truly my lady was willing to open the gates,' soe hee onely spake some few words, that they were very violent in their discourse, after which the lady threw the keys out of the window. That shee never herd the lady say that Melgam should make the best condicions hee could.

The examination of the Lady Isabell, that shee was in

the roome with the Lady Margrett but does nott know what shee said.

The examination of Christian Fife, that the lady offer'd all reason to the Lieutenant, if hee would retire to the Duckett, etc.

Question. Whether uppon what hath bin heard the goods in the Lady Arlie's house are prize or noe?

Resolved in the negative.

Question. Whether uppon what lies before the Court, Lt. Greene bee worthy of blame in taking away of the goods of the Lady Arley or noe?

Resolved in the negative.

Memorandum. That, the last resolution of the Court wherby Lt. Greene is nott found blame worthy, though the goods were before adjudged nott to bee prize, was for that the Lady Arley refused to permitt his souldiers to enter in to her house to quarter uppon order, as alsoe for that Col. Okey, uppon reading Lt. Greene's letter the next day concerning the businesse, said, ' Itt was well done, much good may itt doe them.' Testified in Court by Lt. Marsh and Cornett Reames. Alsoe a parte of Col. Grosvenor's letter of the 25th of September, wherin hee termes itt prize.

The words in the letter are, ' And to lett all civillity bee showne to the lady that such as are not dangerous may freely come to her, and for the prize in the house to have respect to the poore.—I remayne, Your assured frind

E. GROSVENOR.'

September 25, 1651.

Resolved, that the Lady Arley shall have the monie, which was raised uppon sale of the goods taken in her house, and such of the remayning goods (except materialls of warre) as can bee found restor'd unto her by the souldiers in whose custody they are. And that Capt. Kirkby and Capt. Skelton are order'd to see this result putt in execution. Alsoe to see that shee have 50 boules of oates allowed to her in consideracion of the eating of her corne.

DUNDEE. COURT MARTIALL. Oct. 22, 1651.

The petition of Thomas Maurice and Wm. Wynne souldiers under Capt. Gardiner read, being produced in Court by Adj. Gen. Dennis.

The humble petition of Thomas Maurice and Wm. Wynne, souldiers under the command of Capt. Gardiner in the Lt. Generall's regiment, Humbly sheweth, that itt was your petitioners' fortune that our army entred Dundee to goe into the house of James Glaze junior, and going into the chamber found him under the bed, wee bad him come forth, and when hee came forth, sayes hee, 'Gentlemen, if you will give mee quarter for my life I will give you 100¹ sterling,' which wee granted unto him, and did nott touch any parte of his clothes, nor any thing else about him, neither did wee suffer any man else to use any violence to him, but stayed with him all the evening, and the night besides untill the souldiers were setled into the towne, that hee might suffer noe wronge in regard of his engagement to us, and our promise to him for his securitie; and neglected seeking after any of the plunder of the towne with the rest of my fellow souldiers, which might have bin more beneficiall to us then that which hee promised us. But hee being soe earnest with us, wee, being the first that found him, to stay with him and secure him, and hee will give us as is before mentioned, which now hee refuseth to doe, or to come to any composition with us att all unlesse your Worshippe bee pleased to stand our freind to putt us in what way to use to come by this mony.

And your petitioners shall ever pray for your Worshippe's health and happinesse.

Capt. Gardiner informes the Court, that wheras the petitioners alleadge that they kept this man all night and did forbeare plundering, that they had gotten as much plunder as others before they were sent for the man.

Tho. Maurice saith, that hee came to James Glaze's

quarters about the duske in the evening, and stayed with him about half an hower, and then they brought him to his Captaine's quarters, that the Captain sent for him. That hee lay with Capt. Gardiner all night. James Glaze saith, that hee was standing by the fire in his father's house, that Maurice ask't, which was the man?

Deferr'd to another Court.

The examination of Alexander Anderson, October 16, 1651, read, saith that hee being servant to Mr. John Graham, and there being stolne out of his Master's stable in the Mains on Tuesday night last an oxe, which was intended to bee fell'd the next day. And being sent by his Master with Thomas Henderson to search after itt, hee came to James Watt's house att Bonnett Hill, where after search hee found the head of the oxe, which hee knowes to bee his Master's. That there was 2 souldiers immediately before in the house which hee saw run away.

ALEX. ANDERSONE.

16° 8^{bris} 1651.
Jur. coram me. W[illiam] C[larke].

The examination of Tho: Henderson Oct. 16, 1651, saith, that on Wednesday morning last hee was sent by his Master, Mr. John Grahame, to looke after an oxe that was stolne out of the stable the night before. That, comeing to the Captain of the guard at Murraygate, hee upon complaint sent an Ensigne and 4 musketeers with him to goe to Bonnett hill to search, and comeing to James Watt's house, where hee herd an oxe was kill'd, hee enquired of the said James Watt, who told him that the 2 souldiers were just then fled away, wherupon goeing to the out house and finding the head and hide of the oxe, which hee was inform'd to belong to his master, the said James Watt said that hee would be responsable for the hide till the next morning, and notwithstanding which hee saw the same hide this day which was sold to one Robertson, as hee heerd, by 2 English men.

the marke × of Tho. Henderson.

Richard Wright, sentenc't, to ride the horse under the gallowes with a rope about his neck and the hide uppon his back an hower with 2 musketts att each heele.

James Watts, the countryman, to have a sharpe reproof.

Found guilty uppon the oaths of 2 witnesses, James Grahame: Sentenc't, to bee whip't from Bonnett Hill to Westgate with 60 lashes, and to bee imprison'd, afterwards during the Lieutent. Generall's pleasure.[1]

DUNDEE. COURT MARTIALL. Oct. 31, 1651.

The examinations of Sergt. Wood, Corporall Bond, and Sergt. Clarke[2] concerning Abr. Randall, and John Browne read.

The examination of Sergt. Wood, sergeant to Capt. Parker, taken upon oath the 27 of October 1651, saith, that uppon Wednesday last Capt. Parker's company being with others of the Lt. Generalls' regiment drawen up in the Church at Dundee, Abraham Randall of the said company, being playing and abuseing his fellow souldiers, this deponent told him if hee continued in it hee would strike him. To which Randall said, 'Doe an you dare, I will strike againe,' whereupon this deponent struck him a box in the eare, upon which Randall struck him againe severall times, till hee was parted by Corporall Bond, but afterwards this deponent being lighting a pipe of tobacko Randall fell upon him againe.

The marke of × Sergt. Wood.

The examinacion of Corporall Bond upon oath, Oct. 30, 1651, saith, that on Wednesday the 22th instant, Abraham Randall souldier in the said company, being playing and justing the souldiers, Sergt. Wood told him that if hee play'd the foole soe he would strike him, wherupon the said Randall said, that if the sergt. strooke him,

---

[1] Sentenced, on the information of Margaret Paterson and Elizabeth Mitchelson, for an attempted rape.

[2] Confirmatory evidence of Sergeant John Clarke omitted.

hee would strike him againe. and strooke the sergeant divers times, this deponent at last parting of them, and the said Sergt. Wood snatching the stick out of this deponent's hand hee strooke the said Randall. John Browne, of Capt. Gardiner's company, comeing in said if it had beene his case as it was Randall's hee would have broke the stick over the deponent's head, to which the deponent saying, 'what would you surrah?' the said John Browne said hee would cut the deponent's pate if hee would not hold his toung, and said hee had knowen the deponent of old, and tooke the deponent by the bandaleers and bid him come to the dore, and said hee would have the deponent in another place.

Tho. Bond.

Question. Whether Abr. Randall shall bee tryed uppon the 5th Article of Duties to superiours, etc.? Resolved in the affirmative.

Question. Whether Abr. Randall bee guilty of the breach of the 5th Article of Duties to superiours? Resolved in the affirmative (*nemine contradicente*).

Question. Whether Abraham Randall being found guilty and soe to suffer death according to the article shall bee hang'd or shott to death? Resolved, that hee shall be shotte to death.

John Browne examined, confessed that hee spake some words which hee is sorrie for.

Question. Whether John Browne shall bee tryed uppon the 8th Article of Duties to superiours or noe?

Resolved to try him uppon the Article of Misdemeanour.

Question. Whether John Browne bee guilty of the breach of the Article of Misdemeanour or noe?

Resolved, to bee guilty of high-misdemeanour.

Sentenc't. To bee led with a rope about his neck

through the parade and receive 20 stripes there, and after that to have 20 stripes tide uppe to the gallows.

DUNDEE. COURT MARTIALL. Nov. 3, 1651.

Francis Pouncer call'd in.

The information of Lt. Knowles read, vizte., Uppon Wednesday the 29th of October, Lieut. Col. Symonds' company being drawne uppe att the parade, Francis Pouncer souldier in the same companie giving reproachfull words to his fellow souldiers, calling them rogues and the like, his Lieutenant commanded him to hold his peace, hee said hee would nott, uppon that his Lieutenant gave him 2 or 3 strokes with his caine, and commanded him to hold his peace, and going from him hee began as afore. His Lieutenant going to him againe strucke att him with his kane, and hee letting his pike fall towards him, the Lieutenant taking hold of his pike with the one hand struck att him with the other with his cane. Then the said Pouncer closed with him and gott hold of his cane, and as Robt. Deale, John Parker and the Marshall Mr. Tite saith, that they saw him strike att the said Lieutenant, before the said Pouncer went to the ground, then the Lieutenant tooke him by the shoulder, hearing a noyse amongst the souldiers, and thrust him into the guard where hee gave reproachfull words and said, that hee might speake in prison what hee list.

WILL. KNOWLES.

The examination of Sergt. Robert Dale, sergeant to Lt. Col. Symonds' company in Col. Ashfeild's regiment saith, that uppon Wednesday the 29th of October, the Lieut. Colonell's company being drawne uppe att the parade, Francis Pouncer of the said company refused to lett a souldier lately entred to march in the file before him, wheruppon Lieutenant Knowles said, hee should march before him. Pouncer said, hee should nott. The Lieutenant said, if hee would nott hee would make him bee quiett. Then the Lieutenant striking him the said Pouncer began to handle his pike, and the Lieutenant striking him againe hee lett fall his pike, and closed with the Lieutenant, and struck him, and att last both fell uppon the ground, and the said Pouncer tooke the cane which the Lieutenant had in his hand.

The marke of O Robert Dale.[1]

Marshall Tite examined *viva voce* uppon oath saith, that Lieutenant Knowles commanding Pouncer to stand in his place, hee would nott because there was such a file-leader putt in, wheruppon the Lieutenant strikes him; going from him againe, Pouncer gives him some language, uppon that hee bends his pike att him, whether itt was to warde his blowes or strike att him hee did nott know. Att last the Lieutenant strikes him againe, and then they grapled together, and then hee was forced to carry him into the guard by maine strength the souldiers shouting as hee was carried into the guard.

Question. Whether Francis Pouncer shall bee tryed uppon the 5th Article of Duties to superiours or noe?

Resolved, to try him uppon the Article for Misdemeanour.

Question. Whether hee bee guilty of the breach of the Article of Misdemeanour? Resolved in the affirmative.

Sentenc't. For refusing to obey the commands of his officer. To bee brought from the prison with a rope about his neck to bee led through the parade, and there to have 30 stripes, after that to receive 30 more tide uppe to the gallowes. After that to make his acknowledgement of his offence to his Lieutenant att the head of the company, or else to bee continued in prison 7 dayes with bread and water.

DUNDEE. COURT MARTIALL. Nov. 13, 1651.

Evan Owen souldier in Col. Cobbett's owne company call'd in.

---

[1] Similar deposition of John Parker omitted.

The informations of Sergeant Westley, Ens. Scoble, and Corporall Scaithe read.

Rooke Westley sergeant in Col. Cobbett's owne company sworne and examined, saith, that uppon Thursday last the deponent being commanded by the Captain Lieutenant to goe fetch provisions, and to take some men alonge with him for that purpose. That as hee was going alonge and seing Evan Owen of the said company passing by, hee commanded him to goe along with him, who said, hee scorn'd to goe for him or any sergeant in the regiment to fetch provisions. Wheruppon the deponent tooke him by the shoulder and said hee should goe. Wheruppon the said Owen struck the deponent with his fists, endeavouring att his face. That afterwards strugling with the deponent, hee drew away his scabbard from his sworde, struck the deponent's hatt off from his head, and stamp't itt in the dirt.

ROOKE WESTLEY.[1]

Thomas Scoble, Ensign to Col. Cobbett's owne company, saith, that hee saw Evan Owen above named strike Sergt. Westley with his fists, and that being scuffling together the deponent parted them, and committed Owen to the guard.

The marke of × Thomas Scoble.

Evan Owen denies that hee strucke the Sergeant, saies, hee was hurt and soe could nott carry any provisions.

Jo: Warne saith, that hee was by when the Sergeant commanded Evan Owen to carry biskett, that hee said hee was disabled, that the officer drew and struck him with his sworde in his scabbard, and theruppon the scabbard fell off, that closing with him hee struck him with the pummell of his sworde.

Question. Whether to try Evan Owen uppon the 5th Article for Duties to superiors, or noe?

Resolved, to try him uppon the Article for Misdemeanour.

Question. Whether hee bee guilty of misdemeanour?

---

[1] Confirmatory evidence of Corporall John Scaith omitted.

Resolved in the affirmative.

Question. What punishment, hee being found guilty of the breach of the Generall Article for Misdemeanour in refusing to obey the commands of his officer and resisting him giving him correction?

Sentenc't. To ride the horse an hower with 2 musketts att each heele and a rope about his neck, tide to the gallowes with his fault written uppon his brest.

John Johnson call'd in.

Thomas Scoble, ensign to Col. Cobbett's owne companie, examined uppon oath, 8 November 1651, saith, that uppon Thursday last marching to the guard in Dundee with the Colonell's company, John Johnson, a souldier in the said companie, march't out of ranke and file, striking of a Scotchman and abusing others. The deponent wish't him to bee more civill in his carriage or else hee would correct him. Notwithstanding the said Johnson with a stick hee had in his hand struck his fellow souldier, wheruppon the deponent gave him a blowe with his sworde in his scabbard, uppon which the said Johnson used many reproachfull speeches and said, that if hee had the deponent half a mile out of towne hee would deale with him well enough, or words to that purpose. That hee swore by his Maker severall times uppon his march.

The marke of ✗ Thomas Scoble.

The examination of Wm. Norman taken uppon oath, Nov. 8, 1651, read, saith, that hee saw John Johnson above named strike one Webb of the Colonell's companie with a sticke hee had in his hand, that uppon the Ensigne's correcting him hee swore by his Maker if hee had the Ensigne half a mile out of towne hee would give him as much.

The marke of ✗ Wm. Norman.

Found guilty of the breach of the Generall Article for Misdemeanours in threatning his officer and swearing.

Sentenc't. To bee tide to the limbers of a peece of

ordnance, and to receive 30 stripes from the Westgate to the Eastgate, and afterwards to stand half an hower under the gallowes with a gagge in his mouth.

DUNDEE. COURT MARTIALL. IN DUNDEE, Nov. 28, 1651.

Wm. Westoc sworne and examined saith, that his wife was very sick and hee was faine to entertaine Jane Robinson to helpe her in this her sicknesse uppon their march to Dunbarre, and some two houres before day in the morning the said Jane Robinson went away with all his wive's wearing clothes, some of which shee hath on her backe att this present, vizte. one black gowne, one red petticoate, one paire of boddice and neckcloath and apron.

The marke of O Wm. Westoc.[1]

. . . . . .

Resolved that Jane Robinson for her theft shall bee whip't from the Murray gate to the water side, and thence to bee conveyed from constable to constable, till shee come to England, her number of stripes nott to exceede 30. And if the said Jane Robinson bee found in the quarters of the army, that then shee shall bee imprisoned againe.

Resolved uppon the question, that the mony that was found about the said Jane Robinson shall bee given to Wm. Westoc's wife towards the losse of her clothes.

Resolved, that William Westoc shall take away the gowne and red petticoate from Jane Robinson, provided, that the said Westoc doe give her some other to cover her nakednesse, and what else is his.

DUNDEE. COURT MARTIALL. DEC. 2, 1651.

The information of James Haliburton and John Miller in relacion to the robberies of Robert Bell, read.

---

[1] Confirmed by Ralph Ratcliff, Allen Stillen, and Robert Baker.

The information of James Haliburton of Cowper in Angus,[1] taken uppon oath the 1st day of December, 1651, saith, that uppon Friday night last being in bed in his house att Cowper, one Robert Bell with 6 more came into the deponent's close and calls for him, but his wife denying him the said Bell said, hee was commanded by the Lieutenant Generall to search for all Englishmen, and to bringe them uppe to the rest in regard the enemy was risen in the north, to the number of 14,000. Wheruppon (this deponent being rising) they entred his chamber with their swords and durkes drawne and pistolls cock't, and inquired, saying, 'Where's our men that's heere?' To which this deponent said, there was neither English nor Scotchmen in the house more then himself. And this deponent going with them the said Bell demanded of him to give him a gill of hott waters, and when the said Bell was drinking the strong waters hee told the deponent that hee was a Captaine and had warrant from the Lieutenant Generall to deliver 300 marks to beare the charges of 24 horse till they came to Aberdene, and itt should bee allowed in the sesse, which this deponent denying that hee had mony to doe, the said Bell and the rest threatned to kill him. That they carried the deponent a mile and half taking along with them severall country men till such time as this deponent had borrowed ten pounds sterling to pay them, uppon which the said Bell gave him a receipt that itt should bee allowed in the sesse. J. HALIBURTON.

The information of John Miller of Kinlogh, taken uppon oath the first day of December, 1651, saith, that uppon Friday last one Robert Bell with six more in his companie came to Blaire and entred the house of one Mr. Walter Rattray with swords drawne and pistolls cock't, where there were some gentlemen with one Wm. Rede collector, whom they tooke alonge with them to Kinlogh, where they found Mr. James Rattray, collector, and tooke away his sworde. Of which Lt. Col. Andrew Gray of Droneley

---

[1] *I.e.* Cupar Angus.

having notice desir'd this deponent and other neighbours to pursue them, which they accordingly did, and when they came to the Boate of Cowper this deponent and the rest heard that they had taken Mr. James Haliburton of Cowper out of his bed demaunding mony of him, and carrying him alonge till hee should pay the monie. This deponent and the rest pursued them till they found the said Bell with 6 more att Alexander Flemyng's house in Banevee,[1] where Lt. Col. Gray entring the close and firing uppon one of them the rest came out and fired their pistolls, but made their escape by the darkenesse of the night. The next day Lt. Col. Gray with this deponent and others being inquiring after the said Bell and the rest, the said Bell came and demanded his horse wheruppon the Lt. Colonell apprehended him, that the said Bell after hee was taken said, that hee would stab all the comm[and]ers and that before six dayes were att an end hee should take this deponent and David Kinlogh out of their beds.   Jo: MILLER.

The information of Mr. James Rattray, taken uppon oath in Court Dec. 2, 1651, saith, that on Sunday last in the morning being in Cowper in the chamber with Robert Bell, this deponent amongst other discourse heard the said Bell say, that last Winter hee went out of his quarters into the west with 3 or 4 more with him, and kill'd 7 Englishmen, that after they had cutt 5 of their throates, two of them crying for mercy, hee bid them kill them.   J. RATTRAY.

    Question. Whether Robert Bell shall bee tryed uppon the 8th Article of Duties in Generall as a spie, and uppon the 4th Article of Duties Morall for theft and robbery?
    Resolved in the affirmative.
    Question. Whether uppon what lies before the Court Robert Bell bee guilty of the said 8th and 4th Articles? Resolved in the affirmative (*nemine contradicente*).

---

[1] *I.e.* Benvie.

Sentenc't. To bee hang'd by the neck uppon the gallowes in the Markett place in Dundee till hee bee dead.

DUNDEE. COURT MARTIALL. December 9, 1651.

The information of David Thompson concerning Geo: Burton and Wm. Langley, read.

The information of David Thompson of Strackmortin, taken uppon oath the 5th day of December, 1651, saith, that the last night about sunsett, George Burton and Wm. Langley of Lt. Col. Sawrey's company with 2 souldiers more (whose names hee knowes nott) came to his house, where coming they said they had orders to quarter, and beate the deponent's servants for shutting the doore against them. Afterwards this deponent coming home, and his wife asking if they had any order, one of them who had a pistoll said, there was his order. That George Burton and another of them went to the Brewsters neere his house, and returned about ten houres being both full, in the meane time Wm. Langley (being the least of them) staid in the house, and all of them having att supper 5 pintes of ale and a pinte they had before. The deponent said, they should have noe more, wheruppon they broke open the chamber doore and being going to draw the drinke, his wife resisting them, one of them struck her with a pistoll, that they satt uppe and sange, drinking till about midnight. DAVD. THOMSONE.

Question. Whether Geo. Burton and Wm. Langley bee guilty of misdemeanour? Resolved in the affirmative.

For stragling from the garrison and demanding of provisions contrary to order.

The sentence of Geo. Burton. To ride the wooden horse an hower with his fault uppon his brest, and to receive 20 stripes being led to the parade.

Question. Whether Wm. Langley shall bee continued in prison till Friday and have noe other punishment? Resolved in the affirmative.

Information of John Wright concerninge Rich. Walton, read.

The information of John Wright, servant to Mr. Alex. Seaton, Laird of Thornton, taken uppon oath the 3d. day of December, 1651. saith, that on Munday night last being in the Master's house att Thornton, there came into the house one Richard Walton a dragoone with 6 others to quarter. Where after they had supped the said dragoone (being full of drinke) sent the servants out for drinke, and afterwards beate severall of the servants, insomuch that they durst nott stay in the house, but were forced to quitt itt. By which meanes wanting fire and other accomodacions, the said dragoone caused the locks of the doores and other wood about the house to bee burn't. JOHN WRIGHT.

Question. Whether Richard Walton uppon what lies before the Court bee guilty of misdemeanour?

Resolved in the affirmative.

Sentenc't. To ride the wooden horse an hower with 2 musketts att each heele, and two pint stoopes about his neck with his fault uppon his brest, For being drunke and abusing his quarters.

The information of Wm. Fergison, Scotchman, and Thomas Backe, Wm. Wilburne, David Shawe and Henry Bowman in Capt. Sharpe's company, read.

The information of Wm. Fergison taken uppon oath the 6th day of December, 1651, saith, that the last night about 6 or 7 of the clock this deponent being abroad and coming home found, that 4 of the souldiers which quarter'd in his house had bin disorderly, and one Thomas Barke had throwne coales out of the fire uppon his Mother who lay sick in bed, that this deponent reproving them they gave him ill language and hee return'd the like to them againe. That his Mother told the deponent that they abused her and call'd her old witch and old jade.
WM. FERGESSON.

The information of Thomas Barke, souldier in Capt. Sharpe's company in Col. Cooper's regiment, taken Dec. 6, 1651, saith, that the last night about 6 of the clock his Landlord Wm. Fergison coming in drunk, and this deponent and his fellow souldiers sitting by the fire, hee came and scattred the fire abroad with his feete. That this deponent and the rest desiring him to bee quiett hee call'd them rogues and said hee was as good a man as any was in the towne, that hee would have falne uppon some of them to have strucke them had nott the maid of the house held him in.

The marke × of Thomas Barke.

The information of Wm. Wilburne in Capt. Sharpe's company as abovesaid taken Dec. 6, 1651, saith, that the last night about 6 of the clock his landlord, Wm. Fergison coming in drunke and this deponent sitting in the roome asleepe, his Landlord with his railing language wak't him, saying : ' What rogues are these that abuse my Mother ? any one of you all come out to mee. Yee are all rogues and beggers and dogges.' And further saith nott.

The marke of × Wm. Wilburne.

The information of David Shaw in Capt. Sharpe's company aforesaid taken Dec. 6, 1651.

That the last evening this deponent being in his quarters setting uppe meate, his landlord Wm. Fergisson coming in drunke (as hee beleeves) came and pull'd the deponent by the arme, and ask't what rogue was that that had abused his Mother, and said, wee were all rogues and beggerly rogues, and if there were noe more souldiers then there were townesmen they would soone have done with them. And further said, that if there were noe more ill to come after hee would cutt some of their throates before morning.

The marke × of David Shaw.

The information of Henry Bowman in Capt. Sharpe's company aforesaid, Dec. 6, 1651, saith, that yesterday in the evening his Landlord, Wm. Fergison, coming in drunke when this deponent and his fellow souldiers were sitting by the fireside, ask't if they had their suppers. And they saying noe, then hee bid them tarry while they gott itt, and said, any three of the best of them turne out for they were all beggerly rogues that were in the towne. That if there were noe more souldiers then townesmen they would quicklie dispatch them. And further said, that if all the Scotchmen would bee of his minde hee would shutt us out of towne soone.

     The marke of × Henry Bowman.

David Shaw examined further in Court, sayes, That the night before speaking with his Landlord, hee said, that if noe ill would come after itt, hee would cutt some of our throates before morning.

 Question. Whether uppon the information that now lies before the Court Wm. Fergisson bee guilty of speaking the dangerous words mencioned in the severall informacions? Resolved in the affirmative.

 Sentenc't. To bee whip't from the Westgate to Eastgate att a cart's taile, and to receive 35 stripes, and soe to bee turn'd out of towne and never to returne to the garrison without leave first had from the Governour, uppon paine of being proceeded against as a spie.

 This ensuing proclamacion was then agreed uppon by the Court.

 Wheras divers disorders are committed by the souldiers stragling, and lying out of their quarters by abusing the country, and extorting of victualls to the dishonour of the army and great prejudice of the country. These are to require all souldiers whatsoever belonging to this garrison, that they doe nott goe half a mile from the garrison without leave from their officers uppon paine of severe punishment.

 To bee proclaim'd by beate of drum.

DUNDEE. COURT MARTIALL. Dec. 17, 1651.

The information of Quartermaster Warde, etc., read.

The information of Quartermaster Warde, quartermaster to Col. Berrie's troope, taken the 9th day of December, 1651, saith, that about 3 weeks since a souldier belonging to the said Colonell's troope, whose name is Wm. Hawy, had his horse taken out of the stable in Kirkaldy, valued att sixteene pounds sterling, but nott since heard of. That on Munday was fortnight last this deponent had a mare stolne out of one John Dick's stable in Kirkaldy aforesaid which was worth twelve pounds.

Math. Warde.[1]

. . . . . .

David Fergison, bayliff, examined, saith, that they had stronge stables, that they had the keyes in their owne hands, soe that the horses could nott bee kept by the towne, neither did itt appeare that any of the towne tooke itt. That one of them was the next doore, that they satt uppe till 12 of the clock att night and the horse was stolne betweene 12 and 3.

That when Wm. Hawey's horse was taken they heard on't by 6 in the morning. They sent uppe and downe to stoppe all the ports, that they could nott heare of itt.

Uppon debate of the thinge whether the towne of Kirkaldy should pay for the horses taken away, there appearing nothing of blame in any of the townesmen.

Resolved. That itt bee offer'd to the Lieutenant Generall to appoint some other way of satisfaccion for the souldiers, but that they see noe reason why the towne of Kirkaldy should bee particularly charged with the horses.

Information of David Ferguson, bayliff, concerning the horse of Capt. Robinson's souldiers which was stolne there, taken uppon oath before the Court.

Wheras I am informed, that Capt. Robinson of Col.

---

[1] Confirmed by James Graves and Joseph Barriclowe.

Berrie's regiment hath obtayn'd an order for causing the Bayliffs of Kirkaldy to make their appearance before the Martiall Court of this garrison being Friday next. Therfore being call'd hither before this Court by order from the Lieutenant Generall, my desire is to declare concerning that horse for which I suppose that order is for the Bayliffs to appeare.

Fower troopes of the said regiment being quarter'd uppon us for the space of 7 dayes (uppon free quarter) uppon their removall were left behinde 16 sick men with their horses, without any order from a superiour officer (as I suppose), uppon the particular charge of towne and parish, some of them belonging to Capt. Robinson, of which one horse of his was taken away (by whom wee know nott) though hee was in a sufficient stronge stable and 2 doores broke open before they came att the stable doore, but noe intimacion made to us by the said Captaine, nor the owner of the said horse till five weekes after. DAVID FERGUSONE.

Tho. Scoler of Capt. Skelton's company examined, saith, that a souldier was buying mutton, that hee offer'd her half a crowne but shee would nott give change, wherefore hee brought itt away with him.

Marshall Tite, informes that hee ran away uppe a paire of staires, said hee had noe mutton, att last pull'd out an whole quarter of mutton out of a cupboard in straw.

Referr'd to the Captaine to give the woman satisfaccion, and what punishment hee will inflict uppon the souldier.

DUNDEE. COURT MARTIALL. DECEMBER 19, 1651.

The informations of Edward Groves quartermaster to Col. Grosvenor's troope and the 2 troopers, concerning the taking Lt. Stuart, etc. And the examinacions of Lt. Stuart and the rest of the gentlemen with him, read.

The information of Edward Groves quartermaster to

Col. Grosvenor's owne troope taken the 9th day of December, 1651.

That uppon Friday night last having intelligence that a partie of the enemy were abroad under the conduct of one Steelhand,[1] and some of them came within half a mile of Glame's, march't forth the next day to Killimure, where hee heard Steelhand was with about 60 horse. When this deponent with his party came there they heard hee was gone, wheruppon they returned back to the garrison. And the next morning, being Sunday the 7th instant, this deponent went forth with a partie of 14 horse, and hearing att Killimure, thatt here was a partie of about half a score that march't that way by breake of the day, they pursued to Ellit,[2] where this deponent hearing that they were in the house where Lesly[3] was taken, this deponent sent in 3 before him uppon whose alighting and going into the house where 6 men and 4 youthes were drinking hee heard a pistoll goe off which was shott by one of our men, and wounded one of the Scotts, wheruppon the rest cryed for quarter. That the deponent heard nott of there passes till they were come out of Ellitt. EDW. GROVES.

The information of Thomas Pitt, trooper in Col. Grosvenor's troope of horse, taken uppon oath, Dec. 8, 1651, saith, that yesterday morning being commanded out by Qr. Mr. Groves together with one Quintayne Moore to enter into Ellett, where they heard that a partie of Scotchmen in armes were. This deponent went into the house, and seing about half a dozen of them in a roome hee bid them call for quarter and deliver their armes. To which one of them said, that they would nott for wee were deceived, they were nott Englishmen and theruppon began to draw his tuck, uppon which the deponent firing his pistoll att his bodie, hee struck itt downe and the deponent shott him into the thigh. Notwithstanding which they would nott part with their armes, till the

---

[1] Cf. *Scotland and the Commonwealth*, p. 28. [2] *I.e.* Alyth.
[3] Alexander Leslie, Earl of Leven.

deponent fell to cutting of them, and then they call'd for quarter.

The marke of × Thomas Pitt.

The information of Quintayne Moore, trooper in Col. Grosvenor's troope of horse, taken uppon oath, Dec. 8, 1651, saith, that this deponent entring the house att another doore distant from that where Thomas Pitt was, who was commanded with the deponent to goe as a forlorne into Ellitt, and finding Thomas Pitt engag'd with half a dozen Scotchmen who were making to their armes, the deponent offered to fire uppon one of them, vizte. Lt. Mathew Stuart, but his pistoll nott going off hee advis'd them to call for quarter, wheruppon they submitted and the deponent and Tho: Pitt brought them forth to the Quartermaster who staid without with the partie. That the deponent heard nott any of them speake of their passes till they were brought to the Quartermaster and ready to mount.

The marke of × Quintayne Moore.

Thomas Pitt further saith, that just after they were disarm'd one of them said hee had a passe but nott before, and asking him who itt was from whom hee had itt, hee said from Col. Overton.

The marke of × Thomas Pitt.

The examination of Mathew Stuart, late Lieutenant to the Lord Blantire,[1] taken uppon oath. Dec. 8, 1651.

That this deponent, being disbanded with the rest of Marquesse Huntley's forces,[2] came to Aberdeene on Friday last, and quarter'd that night with one Quartermaster Ryburne, a quartermaster in the English army in New Aberdeene, with whome hee chang'd an horse for a mare and had five pounds in mony to boote. That there quarter'd with him Quartermaster Stuart, quarter-

---

[1] Alexander Stewart, fourth Lord Blantyre.

[2] Lewis Gordon, third Marquis of Huntly, agreed to disband his forces on 21st November 1651.

master to the Lord Blantire's troope to which this deponent was lieutenant, Mr. John Walkinshaw who alsoe rode in the same troope, Roger Mackgill, Wm. Baskett, and Archibald Patterson all of the same troope. That on Saturday night they quarter'd att one Mr. Levingston's house att Memuss neere Killimure, and from thence went out about breake of day to Ellitt where they came before morning sermon, intending to have brake their fast there and soe to have gone to the Ferry of Kinclaven, and soe homewards. That while they were sitting att breakefast there came in one Moore a Scotchman and another trooper, and bid them render and then demanded their monie, that shewing their passes one of the troopers tooke away his passe, and said hee would shew his passe to him that commanded the partie, that this deponent being told by the landlord where hee was that Steelhand was there the Friday before, thought when hee heard the Scotchman's voice itt was hee, for that hee was told that Steelhand had threatned to meete some of those that were disbanded and take away their horses, that hee was going with the rest to the sheriffdome of Renfrew beyond Glasgowe where they all live except Roger Maghill and Wm. Baskett, that this deponent lived in Argowan when hee was leavied with the Lord Blantire and the rest. That hee never saw Steelhand in his life. That there was none of the Gentlemen with him had any armes besides the deponent, Quartermaster Stuart and Mr. Baskett, only his boy carried a sworde before him.

MATHEW STEWART.

The examination of Quartermaster Mathew Stuart taken uppon oath the 8th day of December 1651, saith, that this deponent with Lt. Stuart and 4 more of the Lord Blantire's troope coming from Strathbogy where they were disbanded with resolutions to goe to their homes in the west, came on Thursday night to the new kirke of Minicaboek[1] about 7 miles from Aberdene on the north side, where there being a troope of English

---

[1] ? Menie House.

horse quarter'd and a quartermaster of the English, gave them quarters. That on Friday night they quarter'd att Drumlethee, that they mett divers of the English foote that day but noe horse. That on Saturday they came within 2 mile and an half of Killimure and lay there that night, that the next morning they came to Ellitt a little before sermon was beginning. Alighting there to breake their fast, there came in an Englishman (a little man) and one Moore and another or two, and cryed, 'Yeeld, yee rogues, take quarter or else you'le all die.' The Lieutenant cryed, 'Hold your hands for wee 'le doe you noe wronge, heere's my passe.' That Baskett said to his remembrance seeing Moore, 'Wee are Scotchmen,' thinking they had bin Mossers. That the little man demanding this deponent's mony hee gave him fower pounds sterling, and eight shillings. That this deponent to his knowledge saw nott any of the company offer to draw a sworde or oppose them. That the last night Moore and the rest told this deponent and the rest, that the Marshall would take away their mony, and theruppon desir'd this deponent and the rest to deliver their monies, wheruppon there being thirty shillings and sixpence left this deponent, which they promis'd to give him, hee gave itt to them and they gave itt to Moore. That the deponent had a passe from Col. Overton which hee lost in giving out his money att Ellitt. That the deponent had 2 horses and a boy, Lt. Stewart 3 horses and 2 boyes, and Mr. Walkinshaw had one horse and a boy, and the rest had each of them an horse and amongst them all 5 portmantuas with their clothes and linnen.

The marke of × Mathew Stuart.

The examination of John Walkinshaw taken uppon oath the 8th day of December, 1651, saith, that the deponent belonging to the Lord Blantire, being disbanded with the rest of the Marquesse Huntley's forces was goeing with Lt. Stuart and some other gentlemen of the troope to his home in the west neere Paisley from whence hee was rais'd as of Middleton's regiment imediately after the Scotts' armies going for England. That they quarter'd on Thursday last neere Aberdeene, where an English quartermaster procur'd them quarters. That on Friday night last they quarter'd att Drumlethee and on Saturday night neere Killimure from whence they went for Ellitt yesterday by breake of day. And intending to breake fast there, there came into the towne about 6 of the English horse, and 4 or 5 of them into the roome, and one of them caught hold of Wm. Baskett's sworde, who was going for Ireland but intended to goe with them into the west and soe for Port Patrick. That the English troopers when they came in ask't whether they would have quarter, to which Baskett said, 'Noe, Gentlemen, you are mistaken. Wee are Scotchmen' (thinking they were Mossers), that the rest with him desir'd them to heare them, but they would nott, but brought them away prisoners to Dundee. That they tooke 2 or 3 dollars from the deponent att Ellitt, and the rest when they came to this towne, telling them, that if they kept their mony the Marshall Generall would take itt away when they came into the prison doore.

Jo: WALKINGSHAW.

The examination of Roger Magilgan taken uppon Oath, December 8, 1651, saith, that this deponent, after his being disbanded with the rest of the Marq. Huntley's forces, being going with Lt. Stuart and some other gentlemen of the Lord Blantire's troope (wherin hee rode) towards the west, from whence hee was raised imediately after the Scotts armies going for England, hee then serving the Laird of Arrankeble[1] to whom hee now intended to returne. That they lay on Thursday night att the Kirke of Municabbock beyond Aberdene and on Friday lay 16 miles on this side Aberdene, and came on Saturday neere Killimure, from whence they went the next morning to Ellitt, where they intended to refresh themselves and horses. That being att break-

---

[1] Probably Ardincaple.

fast with the rest of his companie, there came in three troopers belonging to the English, and bad them, take quarter, and the gentleman who was shott through the thigh thinking them Mossers (seing a Scotchman with them), said, 'you are mistaken wee are noe Englishmen.' That the deponent had a passe from Col. Overton which hee gave the last night to the quartermaster who commanded the partie that tooke them. That they having taken away seaven shillings from this deponent hee was mounted and brought to this towne.

The marke of × Roger Magilgan.

The examination of Archibald Paterson taken uppon oath the 8th day of December 1651, saith, that hee riding in the Lord Blantire's troope, and being disbanded with the rest, was going with Lt. Stewart and others of the troope westward towards his home in Lenoxshire att Banesailide [1] from whence hee was raised, when the Scotch army marched for England. That being resolved to goe homewards they quarter'd on Thursday night att the New Kirke of S. Kabon 5 miles beyond Aberdeene where Lt. Stuart chang'd an horse with a quartermaster of the English. That they came on Friday night to Drumlethe. That they mett divers of our foote souldiers that day but noe horse. That on Saturday night they came to a gentleman's house call'd Mr. Levingston neere Killimure. That yesterday morning they went to Ellitt intending to goe over the ferry neere Skoone. That being att Ellitt refreshing themselves and horses, there came into the house a trooper in greene clothes and black skarfe about his neck and gray cloake, with one Moore a Scotchman. That one of the company knowing Mr. Moore said, 'Oh, Mr. Moore, you are mistaken. Wee are Scotchmen, wee are nott Englishmen,' thinking him to bee a Mosser, having knowne him in the Lord Brechin's [2] regi-

---

[1] It seems impossible to identify the name of the place hidden by this grotesque spelling.

[2] George, son and successor of Patrick Maule, Earl of Panmure, Lord Brechin and Navar.—*Scots Peerage*, vol. vii. pp. 19-22.

ment. That the English bid them take quarter, which they were willing to doe nott opposing, but were taken away prisoners. That this deponent had noe passe being by reason of his spraine in his thigh nott able to goe for one. That hee knowes nott nor to his remembrance ever saw Steelhand, alias Gurdon.

The marke of × Archibald Paterson.

Question. Whether John Walkinshaw, Wm. Basken, and Roger Magilgen have done any thinge prejudiciall to the Commonwealth of England, wherby they should loose the benefitt of their passes? Resolved in the negative.

Question. Whether uppon what lies before the Court Lt. Mathew Stuart should have the benefitt of the passe, which hee alleages to have bin taken from him, but not produc't to the court?
Resolved in the affirmative.

Question. Whether Quartermaster Mathew Stewart should have the benefitt of his passe which hee alleages to have lost, till itt bee made appeare that hee had a passe? Resolved, that hee have nott the benefitt of the passe till itt bee made appeare.

Question. Whether Archibald Paterson shall bee dismissed to passe home (notwithstanding hee had noe passe)? Resolved in the affirmative.

Question. Whether Lt. Stewart, Quartermaster Stewart, Wm. Basken, Roger Mackgilgan, John Walkinshaw, and Archibald Paterson shall have libertie with their fower servants, boyes, horses, armes, and what belonges to them to goe to their homes? Resolved in the affirmative.

Memorandum. That the Court was afterward satisfied, that Quartermaster Stewart had a passe, by the testimonie of Archibald Paterson who heard itt read.

DUNDEE. COURT MARTIALL. December 20, 1651.

The information and examinacions of Robert Wylde, Geo. Cutter, and John Dodde concerning the killing of Henry Thompson of Col. Berrie's troope, read.

The informacion of Robert Wylde of the troope late Capt. Lee's in Col. Berrie's regiment, taken December 20, 1651, saith, that on Sunday night last about 10 of the clock this deponent being in bed in his quarters in Cowper (where hee had layne from 8 of the clock that night) there came into the roome John Dodd and George Cutter of Capt. Lee's troope to goe to their beds, that there followed them uppe one Henry Thompson (of the Colonell's troope) and the 2 former of them quarter'd in that roome with the deponent, where having staid discoursing till about 2 in the morning, and, falling out one with the other, fell to blowes, and Henry Thompson tooke off a pistoll from off the table and broke John Dodd's head with itt. Uppon that Geo. Cutter coming uppe and this deponent rising out of his bed parted them, and being parted they fell againe to crosse words, and imediately John Dodd snatched forth his dagger which hee had by his side and stabbed the said Henry Thompson.

The marke of O Robert Wilde.

The examination of Geo. Cutter of Capt. Lee's late troope, taken uppon oath the 20th of December 1651, saith, that on Munday morning last about 3 of the clocke, Henry Thompson of the Colonell's troope came into their quarters aforesaid, and after a little while Henry Thompson and hee fell into discourse about the changing of their horses, soe presently they agreed and hee was to give Henry Thompson six pounds sterling to boote, which the said Thompson received and was satisfied. Hee further saith, that there was a race made betwixt him John Dodd and Henry Thompson for 40^s of each side to bee run the next day, but hee saith that Henry Thompson would nott bee satisfied but would have itt run in the night, and being run Henry Thompson having lost, John Dodd demanded the monie which hee had won by the race, but Henry Thompson refused itt. Soe the deponent went to putt uppe his horse into the stable, and John Dodd went into the chamber where Robert Wylde was in bed, and half an hower after Henry Thompson came uppe, the deponent coming in found them together by the eares, and Henry Thompson had broke John Dodd's head with a pistoll, soe hee coming uppe parted them and pulled Henry Thompson from John Dodd and Robert Wylde. That presentlie after the deponent had parted them they fell into words againe, and John Dodd snach't a dagger from his side and stabb'd him.

The marke of × Geo. Cutter.

The examination of John Dodd, taken December 20, 1651, saith, that about 3 or 4 of the clock on Munday morning last this deponent, George Cutter, and Henry Thompson being att this examinant's quarters in Cowper, Henry Thompson and Geo. Cutter having chang'd horses, and afterwards Henry Thompson challeng'd Cutter to run with him in the morning which they did agree to for 40^s a side, and this deponent was to beare share with Cutter, but the said Thompson being in drinke would needs run then, which being yeelded unto this examinant beate him thrice. Afterwards this deponent coming to his quarters and putting off his clothes with intention to goe to bed, the said Henry Thompson came into this examinant's chamber, and call'd him rogue and rascall, and after punching him brake his head with a pistoll, and after that had one hand in the examinant's haire, and the other att his throate. That Cutter came in and parted them, the said Thompson having throwne this deponent downe and Robert Wylde uppon him (who was then risen to part them). That being parted they fell againe to blowes, the said Thompson pulling the examinant by the haire and clos'd with him which occasion'd him to strike att the said Thompson with a pockett dagger.

The marke × of John Dodde.

The examinante John Dodde confesses the fact wherof

hee was accused, that hee never saw Thompson before, that hee knew nott whether hee was a married man or noe.

That they were about an hower scuffling before hee struck with the dagger, that hee gave him but one stroke with the dagger and drew itt out againe, that hee did nott fall downe uppon itt.

That the examinant hath a wife in Edinburgh. That hee putt his handkercheif about his head, that Henry Thompson said, 'thou hast kill'd mee.' That the examinant was in service with Col. Ponsonby in Ireland, and that his brother was alsoe in the service.

Uppon producing of the discharge of Cornett Ferrett dated December 13, to John Dodd as one of the 20 disbanded by order from Major Generall Lambert, and Corporall Singleton, declaring to the Court, that Henry Thompson was alsoe disbanded out of Col. Berrie's troope, soe that none of them being att present members of the army was resolved:

That in regard itt appeares to the Court, that neither John Dodd nor Henry Thompson were att the doing of the fact members of the army, nott to proceede further therin, but to referre itt to the further direceion of the Lieutenant Generall or Major Generalls.

The examination of Wm. Lambe, and James Donaldson, read.

The examination of Wm. Lambe, late trooper in the Lord Blantire's troope under Marquesse Huntley, taken uppon oath the 20th day of December 1651, saith, that about a month since this deponent and five more came away from the Marquesse of Huntley intending to come to the English forces att Aberdene and staid 4 or 5 nights att Forden[1] about 16 miles from Aberdene. That there staid with him Robert Hamilton who had sold his horse, that the rest went away towards the west where hee and others were leavied imediately after the armies goeing

---

[1] Fordoun.

for England. That hee stay'd att one Archibald Grey's a change house in Forden, to sell his horse. That hee was in a widdowes house in Forden parish when hee was taken where hee had noe armes with him, there being none in the house but women, but uppon his taking hee told the dragoones that tooke him where his armes were, being a case of pistolls and a sworde. That hee having sold his horse intended to goe on foote to Sterling where his friends are.   WILL. LAMB.

The examination of James Donaldson, taken uppon oath the 20th day of December 1651, saith, that about 2 monthes since coming from his sister's, Marian Donaldson, in Edinburgh to see his brother, George Donaldson, a shoemaker in Elgan in Murray, that coming to Tulleroy,[1] and being acquainted with Wm. Seaton a chamberlain of Fife, who gave him horse and armes and maintayn'd him 10 dayes att his owne charges, and afterwards hee was entertayned in the Lord Blantire's troope. That imediately after the capitulation hee came away without a passe intending to have gone for Edinburgh after hee had gotten mony for his horse, which hee brought away for feare that Capt. Peter Gurdon should have taken itt in regard hee was first raised under him, that hee lay but one night att Fordon where hee intended to have sold his horse to one Commissary Faulkenor. That being in an house in the towne taking his breakfast, and his horse, being in Wm. Faulkenor's house, there came 2 dragoones, vizte. one Mr. Lenox Skeldon and Wm. Todd, and Skeldon asking if hee would have quarter which hee tooke, yet afterwards the said Skelton cutt this deponent over the head. That Wm. Todd hath taken his horse before. That hee never saw Steelhand in his life.   JAMES DONALDSONE.

Resolved. That there having noe charge bin brought in against Wm. Lambe and James Donaldson that they

---

[1] Tillery House (six miles north of Aberdeen).

bee sett att liberty, but that James Donaldson's horse is prize to the souldiers who tooke him, in regard hee came from the enemy into our quarters without a passe.

DUNDEE. COURT MARTIALL. December 23, 1651.

Jane Kid of Dundee, examined, saith, that yesterday in the afternoone being in the shambles selling meate, there being a gathering together of souldiers, and amongst the rest, Rich. Bolter tooke a legge of mutton from her and was carrying itt away, but that the Marshall stay'd him, and made him give itt her againe. That after the Marshall was gone hee and others fell uppon the Markett folkes, took away store of meate from her and others, and some of them cutt her purse and tooke away her monie.

The marke of × Jane Kid.

The information of Provost Marshall Tite.

That this deponent going towards the Murraygate saw many souldiers in the shambles, in a disorderly way, crying, 'All, All'; and amongst the rest Rich. Bolter, who had a legge of mutton in his hands of one of the women, which hee made him restore to her. That hee was one of the first that came in when they cryed, 'All.' That having perswaded them to goe out and going to the Mayne guard for a guard they came in againe and plundred the markett. That this deponent asking why hee tooke itt, the said Bolter answer'd they must nott starve.

The marke of O Robert Tite.

Question. Whether Richard Bolter shall bee tryed uppon the Article of Mutinie or disorder, or of theft, and offering violence to those that bringe victualls to the campe where the penalty is death, or uppon the Article of Misdemeanour?

Carried to try him for misdemeanour.

Question. Whether Rich. Bolter bee guilty of misdemeanour in being present att the mutiny and disorder of the souldiers in the shambles?

Resolved in the affirmative.

Found guilty, For being present att and pertaking in the late disorder of the souldiers in taking away meate from the butchers in the shambles.

Sentenc't. To ride uppon the horse an hower with a muskett att each heele and to bee whip't from the Maine guard round the shambles, and to receive 30 stripes.

DUNDEE. COURT MARTIALL. DECEMBER 27, 1651.

Tho: Robinson call'd in. The charge taken by Lieutenant Bagge read before him and the witnesses.

Munday, Dec. 22, 1651.

Thomas Robinson that doth quarter att younge Sandy Sommers his house in the Overgate, of Lt. Col. Sawrey's company, did say as followeth,

That if they had nott monie before Christmas they would plunder the towne of Dundee and make itt a blewer day then that was when the towne was stormed, and that they had consultation therof the last night on the guard. This hee spake att Margret Rankin's house the same night, as alsoe if that were the quarters hee would putt the little childe in the house on the spitt and roast itt. And concerning the officers hee said, Hange all the commanders for all that hee cared for them, and that the Lieutenant Generall had like to have bin kill'd att Edinburgh, and hee should speede but little better yet; and being reproved for the same hee said, That if the officers should know of itt hee would make away for England.

Witnesses { Margaret Rankin. Katherine Piggott. Katherine Mernes.

and Richard Ives of Col. Sawrey's company that doth quarter att the said Margrett Rankin's house.

The charge denied by Tho. Robinson.

Katherine Piggott examined uppon oath, saith, That

on Munday last about 7 in the morning coming to Margret
Rankin's house and knocking att the doore, and being
lett in by a lasse, hee seem'd to bee very angry, and this
deponent standing by the fire side the said Robinson said,
that if that were in his quarters hee would garre her smart.
That if they had nott their pay by Christmas they would
make itt a blewer day then when the towne was first
taken, that hee further said, that they had consultations
of itt uppon the guard to deale with them which were
to pay their siller. That the child crying hee said, that
hee would base or spitt itt, [itt] would make good broath.

The marke of × Katherine Piggott.

Katherine Mearnes examined uppon oath, saith, That
on Munday last about 7 in the morning Thomas Robinson of Lt. Col. Sawrey's companie came to Margrett
Rankin's house where Rich. Ives quarters to warme
himself. And being lett in by Katherine Piggott after
his knocking hard, and shee reproving him for itt because
hee disturb'd the woman who was sicke in the house,
hee call'd her 'Old bitch' and 'Scotch bitch,' and said,
that if they had nott monie they would make itt a blewer
day on the Wednesday following in Dundee then that
of the storming of the towne. That the deponent reply-
ing 'God blesse the Lieutenant Generall, and your officers,'
for if itt were nott for them the souldiers would doe them
mickle wrange. Wheruppon the said Robinson said,
that the Lieutenant Generall had like to have bin kill'd
the last yeare att Edinburgh, and itt would bee little
better if they gott nott their monie yet. That seing a
little childe there hee said, hee would boyle itt, itt would
make good broath, and afterwards, that hee would roast
itt, that hee would come and drinke the sacke and plunder
the house, and kill the woman (meaning Katherine Piggott)
for reproving him.

The marke of × Katherine Mearnes.

The examination of Richard Ives taken uppon oath,
saith, that hee came off with Thomas Robinson from the

guard, on Munday morning last, that the woman being angry with him for disturbing his landlady, hee miscall'd them, that afterwards standing by the fire hee said, that if they had nott monie itt would bee worse with them before Christmas day. That they lived there and had nott monie to buy them clothes, and shoes, and that if they had nott monie before Christmas day itt would bee worse for the officers. Hee further saith, that the said Robinson and 5 others were drinking the night before about 10 of the clock their six pence a peece att an house neere the Craige Fort, that Sergeant Platt was with them, James Woodward, Barnard Davids, and Geo. Burton with one stranger more. That they were there an hower while this deponent stood centinell, and came in againe before the grand round.

The marke of × Richard Ives.

Sergeant Platt sent for with James Woodward, Bernard Davids and Geo. Burton.

Edward Everett call'd in.

Wm. Barker saith, that hee heard words spoken but did nott heare him. That hee heard them say, 'Goe all, goe all, and plunder the butchers' stalls.'

That they were saying, they would come and goe to the Colonell's to complaine.

Capt. Broadhurst sayes, that Wm. Backer told him, that hee said, that hee did reprove them for itt, and said, 'though they bee knaves lett us bee honest men.'

Wm. Barker, That the souldiers did say together that they would goe to the Governour. That hee reproved any man that hee heard speake such words.

Edward Everett's charge.

Lt. Woodward sayes, that being weighing the cheese and the souldiers thrusting them, hee said, Gett you out, to which Everett said, 'Shall wee nott see our biskett and cheese weigh'd? I hope to see such officers as you are disbanded before longe bee,' that hee hath witnesse of itt.

David Everett sayes, that hee spoke itt out of ignorance. That hee was mazed by his blowe downe the staires.

Wm. Barker sayes, that Flaskett was there and Rich. Roberts.

Adjourned till Munday morning 9 of the clock.

DUNDEE. COURT MARTIALL. December 30, 1651.

Tho. Robinson call'd for, and the disposicions against him read, vizte. the preceding Court.

Tho. Robinson denies that hee spake any of those wordes. That hee was newlie come out of sicknesse and in drinke which made him speake them. That the woman call'd him rogue which provok't him.

Lt. Lun, that hee was nott in the tumult in the Fish Markett, but was with him when hee was paying of monie in his chamber 3 houres.

Question. Whether Tho. Robinson shall bee tryed uppon the 8th Article of Duties to superioures, For seditious words, or uppon the Article for Misdemeanour?

Resolved that hee bee tryed by the Article of Misdemeanour.

Question. Whether Tho. Robinson uppon what appeare to the Court bee guilty of misdemeanour?

Resolved in the affirmative.

For mutinous and seditious words. Sentenc't. To ride the horse an hower with a muskett att each heele tide uppe to the gallowes and receive 20 stripes att the head of the parade.

The examinacions of Sergeant Neaves and Sergeant Monkes concerning Wm. Everitt read.

The examination of Sergeant Wm. Neave taken uppon oath the 29th day of December 1651, saith, that on Tuesday last this deponent being att Ens. Kent's quarters delivering out provisions, there was amongst other souldiers Wm. Everitt, who being commanded to goe downe the staires in regard that the roome was soe full they could nott have liberty to deliver them out. The said Everitt refusing, the Ensigne thrust him downe the staires, wheruppon the said Everitt said, 'Faith, wee'le rout such officers as you and the Lieutenant.'

WM. NEAVE.

The examination of Sergeant Christofer Monkes, in Capt. Broadhurst's company in Col. Cobbett's regiment, taken uppon oath, December 29, 1651, saith, that on Tuesday last as aforesaid being att Ens. Kent's delivering out provisions, the roome was soe pester'd with souldiers that they could nott stirre one by another, wheruppon the Ensigne bid some of them gett them downe staires, to which Wm. Everitt of the same company said, hee would nott, wheruppon the Ensigne gave him a blowe on the neck, and thrust him downe staires, who soe soone as hee was downe the staires said, 'Faith wee'le rout such officers as you and the Lieutenant is.'

CHRISTOPHER MONKES.

Wm. Everitt called in, saith, that the occasion of his speaking those words was, that there was a souldier struck by Lt. Woodward uppon the parade, and cutt to the scull to the very braine. That hee was nott att the mutinie of the butchers.

Lt. Woodward. That the souldiers were punching one att another with their musketts, and that hee cutt att him.

Capt. Lt. Wood. That hee saw the souldiers one against another with their musketts, and saw the Lieutenant strike att him and strike him to the braine.

Capt. Broadhurst. That the souldier is cutt to the braine and the chyrurgeon sayes very dangerous. That never any of the souldiers did complaine against the Lieutenant.

Referr'd till itt were knowne whether the souldier should die or noe for the triall of Lt. Woodward.

Question. Whether Wm. Everitt bee guilty of the breach of the Article of Misdemeanour?

Resolved in the affirmative.

Question. What punishment? Sentenc't. To ride the

wooden horse half an hower with one muskett att each heele with his fault uppon his brest. For abusing his officer.

DUNDEE. COURT MARTIALL. JAN. 10, 1651.

John Dodd call'd in,

The examinations of Robert Wylde, and Geo. Cutter, and his confession read, *ut ante* in the Court held Dec. 20.

John Dodd sayes, that hee never knew the said Thompson before, that hee struck him first, and made the bloud run about his cares.

Col. Cobbett satisfied, that hee did nott doe itt with an intention to murther him, that according to the law of England and to the law of God itt is manslaughter.

That text Number 35. 22, debated att large by all the officers.[1]

The words are, ' But if hee thrust him suddenly without enmity, or have cast uppon him any thinge without laying of any waite, or with any stone wherwith a man may die, see him nott and cast itt uppon him that hee may die, and was nott his enemy neither sought his harme, then the congregation shall judge betweene the slayer and the revenger of bloud according to these judgements.

'And the congregation shall deliver the slayer out of the hand of the revenger of bloud.'

Question. Whether uppon what lies before the Court, John Dodd shall bee tryed uppon the Article of Murther, or uppon the Article of Misdemeanour. Resolved to try him uppon the Article of Misdemeanour.

Question. Whether hee bee guilty of High Misdemeanour, or noe? Resolved in the affirmative.

Question. What punishment? Resolved, that John Dodd shall bee imprisoned for 2 monthes as punishment, and then either to pay the somme of twentie pounds or to putt in good securitie to pay itt within 2 monthes from his release to the wife or kindred of Henry Thompson who shall in that time demand the same, or otherwise

---

[1] Quoted verbatim from Numbers, chap. xxxv., verses 22-5.

to putt in securitie to the Governour of Dundee to pay the said somme of twentie pounds within 12 monthes and a day after his discharge to the wife or next of kindred of the said Henry Thompson, or their assignes who shall demand the same, and in case of default of paying the monie (or putting in securitie) to continue in prison at the discretion of the Governour.

The Court doe further declare, that in case the said monie shall nott bee demanded by the wife or kinred of the said Henry Thompson or their assignes within a yeare and a day, that then the bond to bee void.

OFFICERS PRESENT AT COURTS-MARTIAL.

Ashfeild, Colonel Richard.
Bagge, Lieutenant.
Baynes, Captain Robert.
Boone, Captain.
Bramston, Captain.
Brayne, Lt. Colonel William.
Bridges, Major Tobias.
Broadhurst, Captain William.
Butter, Ensign.
Campfield, Captain.
Charlesworth, Lieutenant.
Cheese, Lieutenant William.
Cleare, Captain Henry.
Clun, Lieutenant Joseph.
Cobbett, Colonel Ralph.
Cressett, Captain.
Crispe, Major Peter.
Daberon [or Dawborne]. Captain John.
Davis, Captain William.
Dennis, Adj. General.
Dodgin, Captain.
Dodgson, Captain.
Dorney, Major Henry.
Douglas, Captain.
Ely, Captain.
Evans, Lieutenant Peter.
Everard, Ensign Richard.
Farmer, Captain.
Fellowes, Ensign.
Fitch, Captain William.
Fox, Lieutenant.
Gardiner, Captain.
Gillott, Captain.
Gough, Lt. Colonel William.
Green, Captain John.
Groome, Captain.
Grosvenor, Colonel Edward.
Grosvenor, Cornet.
Groves, Quarter Master Edward.
Gunter, Cornet.
Harman, Ensign.
Hatfield, Ensign Robert.
Hatt, Captain.
Heyrick, Captain.
Holbrooke, Lieutenant.
Hooper, Lieutenant William.
Howard, Ensign Jerome.
Howard, Ensign Thomas.
Hughes, Lieutenant.
Iles, Ensign Arthur.
Jallott, Captain.
Jones, Captain Thomas.
Jordan, Lieutenant.
Kent, Ensign.
Kid, Ensign.
Kirkby, Captain.

Kingwell, Captain.
Knowles, Lieutenant William.
Lee, Captain.
Levett, Lieutenant.
Lingwood, Captain Livewell.
Lun, Lieutenant Edward.
Mace, Ensign.
Mayor, James, Captain.
Maplesden, Lieutenant.
Marsh, Lieutenant John.
Marvell, Captain.
Mason, Lieutenant Humphrey.
Mennere [or Munnier], Ensign
Moore, Ensign Thos.
Morgan, Captain Ethelbert.
Morris, Captain.
Newham, Captain.
Nicholas, Captain.
Okey, Colonel John.
Overton, Colonel Robert.
Owen, Ensign Richard.
Owen, Ensign Thomas.
Painter, Ensign John.
Parker, Captain George.
Peirson, Ensign.
Penkaven, Cornet.
Pettibones, Ensign.
Powell, Captain Lieutenant William.
Powell, Lieutenant John.
Powel, Ensign Thomas.

Reade, Ensign.
Reames, Cornet John.
Richbell, Lieutenant.
Robins, Captain John.
Robinson, Captain.
Rooke, Lieutenant.
Rooke, Ensign.
Sawrey, Lt. Colonel Roger.
Scuttle, Ensign.
Sharp, Captain.
Shipden, Capt.
Shockley, Lieutenant.
Skelton, Captain.
Smyth, Ensign.
Stephens, Ensign Joseph.
Sutton, Lieutenant Henry.
Symonds, Lt. Colonel William.
Tay, Ensign.
Taylor, Lieutenant.
Tew, Lieutenant.
Thompson Captain Lieutenant William.
Vanderoone, Ensign Peter.
Waite, Ensign.
Walley, Captain.
Weaver, Lieutenant Richard.
Wrenche, Captain.
Wood, Captain Lieutenant.
Woodward, Lieutenant.
Young, Major Arthur.

THE BISHOP OF GALLOWAY'S CORRESPONDENCE

1679-1685

Edited by

WILLIAM DOUGLAS

INTRODUCTION

JAMES ATKINE,[1] to whom the following letters were written, was Bishop of Galloway from 6th February 1680 to the date of his death. He died in Edinburgh at the age of seventy-four on the 15th November 1687.

It is not proposed to give here an exhaustive account of the Bishop's life, but it may be useful to record that he was born about the year 1613, and was the son of the Commissary and Sheriff-Clerk of Orkney. He graduated Master of Arts at Edinburgh in 1636, and studied divinity at Oxford from 1637 to 1638. He held the living of Birsay and Harray in Orkney from 1641 to 1649. He married Alison Rutherford of Hunthill, Jedburgh, in 1648, and had three daughters :—

Lillias, who married Patrick Smyth, advocate; Marion, who married William Smith, minister of Moneydie; Alison, who married Duncan Robertson, Sheriff-Clerk of Argyll.

After being in Holland for three years, he resided in Edinburgh from 1653 to 1660. He was minister of Winfrith, Dorsetshire, from 1661 to 1676, the Bishop of Moray from 1676 to 1679, and he became Bishop of Galloway on 6th February 1680, which office he held till the date of his death, 1687.

While Bishop of Galloway he was given a special dispensation to reside in Edinburgh, it being thought 'un-

---

[1] This name has been written in various ways. Anthony à Wood has it Etkins or Atkins, Dr. Thomas Murray as Aiken or Aitken, John A. Inglis as Atkine or Atkins, and the endorsement of one of the present documents is Aitkin.

reasonable to oblige a reverend prelate of his years to live among such a rebellious and turbulent people.' It is also recorded that during the seven years of his office he so carefully governed his diocese, ' partly by his pastoral letters to the synod presbyteries and ministers, and partly by his great pains in undertaking a very great journey for a man of his age and infirmities to visit his diocese, that had he resided on the place better order and discipline could scarce be expected.' [1]

His predecessor, John Paterson, was granted a like indulgence, but on the grounds ' that there was no complete manse or dwelling house in his diocese.' [2]

Among the Bishop's other papers, which have been lent to me, but which have not been printed here, is an inventory of his estate, evidently drawn up by some lawyer, showing that the whole amount came to 81,323 merks, ' besydes what more money the Bishop might had by him, and imbazlements that are perhaps made in the Bishop's estate upon all which the oaths of the parties Suspect will be had.' There are other curious items to be found in this document, such as ' The moveable airship, parliament robes, house furniture, Liveries, Sedan and abulyiements valued at 1333·6·8, and 200 great folios besydes many other books estimat at least to 1333·6·8.'

The originals of these letters are in the possession of Mr. Archibald Campbell, S.S.C., who has been kind enough to allow them to be printed. He tells me they were found among the papers of his deceased father, but he is unaware how his father came to acquire them.

For further particulars regarding the Bishop, see Anthony à Wood's *Athenæ Oxonienses*, Dr. Thomas Murray's *Literary History of Galloway*, and the two papers

---

[1] Wood, *Athenæ Oxonienses*, 1721 ed., vol. ii. p. 1171.
[2] Mackenzie, *History of Galloway*, vol. ii. p. 207.

which recently appeared in the *Scottish Historical Review*, by Mr. John A. Inglis, viz., 'A Seventeenth-Century Bishop' (January 1915), and 'The Last Episcopal Minister of Moneydie' (April 1916). To these two papers I have to acknowledge my indebtedness, and to their author my thanks for his kind interest and for his help in aiding me to decipher the somewhat illegible writing of the originals.

My thanks are also due to Sir Philip Hamilton Grierson for his help in identifying the writer of the third letter in this series, and to Mr. A. Francis Steuart for his note on the Marquess of Huntly.

WILLIAM DOUGLAS.

THE BISHOP OF GALLOWAY'S CORRESPONDENCE
1679-1685

I

From James Sharp, the Archbishop of St. Andrews, to James Atkine, the Bishop of Moray

St. Andrews, Apryll 21st [16]79.[1]

MY VERY GOOD LORD,—I must begg your pardon that after I had received the favour of two letters from your Lop: you have not had any returne from me, which I hope you will not mistake; your servant has told you, that last month in Edinburgh, I was necessitated to disappoynt him above thrice, and now I take hold of this opportunity from Keith, to tell your Lop: I doe reproach myself for this long forbearance I am guilty off. Tomorrow I expect word of my Lords our brethren to assist at the translations, of the Bp: of Edinburgh[2] to Ross, and Galloway[3] to Edinburgh, which is to be preformed at this place, in obedience to the King's mandat sent to me for that effect; the good Bishop of Dunkeld dyed this last week of a languishing desease which hung long upon him; we are to implore the mercy and direction of God, that the vacancies of our order may be filled with meet instruments for worth and abilities, to bear up under the pressures which doe infect this poor Church, whose condition your Lop: knowes, will be influenced much, by the disposall of providence towards that of England. The information you receive by the publick letters makes it unnecessary

---

[1] Archbishop Sharp was murdered on the 3rd of May 1679.
[2] Alexander Young translated from Edinburgh to Ross, 1679.
[3] John Paterson translated from Galloway to Edinburgh, 1679.

for me to give you account therof : your Lop: is better acquainted with sufferings for conscience sake, and the tossings of the Church of God in these kingdoms, than to remitt of your confidence in doing your duty, or to despond that our lord will order all our tryalls for a good issue ; for my part, as I am much satisfyed to hear of your prudent and steady pursuance of the dutyes of your charge, so I expect the help of your prayers, that I may be enabled to wrestle with the difficulties and opposition I meet with in my imployments, and to give assistance and encouragement to my brethren, who labour with diligence and faythfulnes in the same work, for the interest of the gospell in the way appoynted by God, and for the preserving of the body of Christ in unity and peace. My Lord, I received lately a letter from my L. Marques of Huntly [1] with a presentation for a blank person to be filled up by me to your Lop: to the Kirk of Rynie, of which I desired one to speake to his Lop: without wreating of a letter, that I may know how to order that affair ; and as I think your Lop: will see it fitt to keep

---

[1] George, fourth Marquis of Huntly, as a Catholic, had been much harassed in earlier life by Archbishop Sharp about his ' religion.' The Cortachy MSS. show this in his letters to his mother, Marie Grant, the Marchioness-Dowager, who remarried in 1669 James, second Earl of Airlie, as his second wife. In early life he 'lived with his mother at Elgin very mean,' and it was only in 1661 that the forfeiture of his grandfather (beheaded in 1649) was rescinded. Soon after this the Archbishop began his religious persecution. Lord Huntly wrote to his mother (signing the letter with crosses) :—' My Lo St Andrews did speck to me this day concerning religion, and I doe thingk I did speck to him as y^r La/ culd haue diseyred me.' Later Lord Huntly wrote on 23rd December 1665 to his mother from St. Andrews :—' I am informed that y^r La/ did hear that I was to go to the Kirk on Sunday or else on Christmas Day, but I pray y^r La/ doe not beleue it for it is a great lie. . . .' There was considerable difficulty in accomplishing the marriage of Lady Huntly—as a papist—with Lord Airlie, and the latter had to promise the Bishop of Moray by a deed signed at Bog of Gight, 4th April 1669, not to receive any priest or have Mass said under a penalty of two thousand pounds scots, before her ' excommunication' was relaxed. Lord Huntly went to France in 1668 for his education and remained a Catholic. The Archbishop evidently intended that he should not be offended needlessly, and should be treated in a politic manner as he had only returned in November 1675 from serving with the Prince of Orange in the campaign in Flanders.—[Note by A. FRANCIS STEUART, Advocate.]

as fair a correspondence with my Lord Huntlye as the
duty of your office in the Church will allow, so I suppose
you will not make use of what the Law does allow as to
the *jus devolutum*, seeing he has been prevailed with to
deferr thus to my interposing in that matter; he should
have no occasion to think, that you or I take advantages
of the present circumstances he is under; I would not
wreat this, if I had not a good opinion of your Lops:
prudence and conduct, which leads you to forbear by
speaking or acting, to give any just occasion of reception
to the Marques of Huntley, and therby consult your own
and the Churches interest in your Diocese. I must also
thank your Lop: for your favourable way towards the
Laird of Kempcairn,[1] my friend, of which he has expressed
his sense to me, and hope you will order that difference
betwixt him and others as you find conducing for the
good of that place.

I comend your Lop: to the spirit and grace of our Lord,
and desire you may be assured that I am, My good Lord,
Your very affectionat brother and servant,

J. St. ANDREWS.

[*Addressed*:]
For My Lord Bishop of Moray.

II

From Arthur Ross, the Archbishop of Glasgow, to James Atkine, the Bishop of Galloway

Glasgow, November 22 [16]81.

MY DEAR LORD,—I called in Seven presbiteries the
last week, most part of which did cheerfullie com and tak
the Test. Of the absents most wer detain'd by sicknes
which is sufficientlie attested, withe ther promise under
ther severall hands to doe the sam, how soon they ar able.
The few who hav neither com nor written to me ar the

---

[1] Alexander, son of John Ogilvie of Kempcarne, was married on the 24th April 1679 to a daughter of Sir Alexander Burnett of Leys. Was this the occasion of the difference? Vide *The Family of Burnett of Leys*, p. 76.

BISHOP OF GALLOWAY'S CORRESPONDENCE 77

most insignificent and all of them of Bishop Leightenns [1] partie and impression, without whom the churche may be better served, being influenced (as is reasonablie apprehended) by som great men who are not so well principled for the King's service as either you or I could wishe. They hav all repaired to Edinburgh to consult the matter withe Ms. Charters, Meldrum [2] and som others about Haddingtoun and Dalkeythe, thes poisoned fountains that sent forthe so many infectious streams of needless scruple, and disobedience to authority, bot I mak no doubt bot by the indefatigable care and vigilant resolutions of his Royall Highnes [3] to put the law impartiallie in operation thes ill humours may be cured, and thes factious heads may be reduced to a mor peacable and calm behaviour. We hav gott too much kyndnes show'd us to mak demurr'g. We serve a most gracious Master who is evere way represented by a most excellent prince who may justly expect the greattest signs and expressions of our gratitud. The other eight presbiteries are requyred to be heer this week and the next without faill, from whom I expect the like obedience to authority. Of whiche your Lo/ shall have an accompt by the next. They say that ther hav been som Conventicles about Crawfurd Lindsay,[4] and Crawfurd John ; on[e] also at Leshmahagow. If ther be any truthe in this I doubt not bot his Royall Highnes hath had notices befor nowe. Our Town Counsell is not full because som of our Provost's [5]

---

[1] Archbishop Leighton resigned in 1674, and was at this time residing at Broadhurst Manor, Sussex. He died in London, 1684.

[2] Lawrence Charteris, Professor of Divinity in the Edinburgh University, and George Meldrum, rector of Marischall College, Aberdeen. Their names are coupled in Grubb's *Ecclesiastical Hist.*, vol. iii. p. 267. They refused to subscribe and resigned their charges. This course was followed by a considerable number of the younger clergy, 'who revered Charteris as their teacher and guide.'

[3] The Duke of York.

[4] The old name for Crawford. It was changed before 1519 to Crawford Douglas. See *Hist. MSS. Com. Report*, 'Hope Johnstone MS.,' p. 14.

[5] For a corroboration of this statement, see p. 304 of the *Records of the Burgh of Glasgow, 1663-1690* (Glasgow, 1905). James Bell was provost of Glasgow in 1681.

friends (whom he would needs choose contrar to all advice) will not be Counsellours nor take the Test. This troubles me not a little that ther should be any thinge wantinge heer to the King's service, bot my opinion nor assistance was not required to that Electione. God Almightie preserv the King and his Royall Highnes whiche ought to be the daylie prayer of all good churchemen, whiche (with the outmost of my other services) shall never be wantinge on his part who is, My Lord, Your Lop. most affectionat Brother and servant,

ARTH. GLASCUEN.

[*Addressed :*]

Are for the right reverend father in God my Lord the Bishop of Galloway.

III

From Thomas Greirsone,[1] son of William Grierson of Bargatton, to the Bishop of Galloway

Culquha, 23 Decer 1681.

MY LORD,—I have made bold being on[e] of your lops/ vassells to give you the trouble of this lyne in favores of my freind Mr. More[2] who I heir is in termes with your lo/ anent the comissars place[3] of Wigton. Mr. McCulloch wes buried Thursday last and the place is vaccant at present, and I hope, my lord, yor lop/ will prefer him befor any other and what ye condescend on, his brother and I sall give your lop/ securitie, bot I hope, my lord, your lop/ will use him kyndly: the sooner ye dispatch the supplicing of the place so much the better. I long to have the honor

---

[1] Thomas Grierson had sasine in the lands of Over and Nether Culquha, as heir of his father. Recorded Dumfries, 22nd February 1677. He was killed by a smith named Macmillan about 1690. See *Hist. MSS. Com. Report*, 'Hope Johnstone's MSS.,' p. 202.

[2] William Moir succeeded Mr. M'Culloch as Commissary of Wigton.

[3] The Commissary of Wigton was at the disposal of the Bishop of Galloway. Its jurisdiction extended over the presbyteries of Wigton and Stranraer. The Commissar held court at Wigton every Wednesday for confirming testaments and deciding causes brought before him.—Symson, pp. 68-69.

to sie your lop/ in this country, that I may give you some
prooff of my kyndnes as a vassell. I doubt not bot Baylie
More my brother in law hes given yor lop/ notice of the
comisr's death. This with my service to your lop/ wishing
you all health and happines, is all ffrom, My Lord, Your
lops/ affect. freind and Servant,

THOMAS GREIRSONE.

IV

From Arthur Ross, the Archbishop of Glasgow, to the Bishop of Galloway

Glasgow, March 2. [16]82.

MY DEAR LORD,—I received this day from the Bishop
of Argyll an accompt of his ministers how they hav behaved themselves in order to the Test at ther last meetinge,
bot since he tells me that he hath given full notices of that
affair to my Lord primat.[1] I shall referr your Lo/ to his
Grace's information, onlie Mr. Fullertown[2] hath not
dissapointed the character and judgement I gav off him,
who hath not onlie acted contrar to all the promises and
professions he mad at Edinburghe, bot hath been the
head and Author of the mutinous section against authoritie in that Diocess. The Bishop desir'd me to interpose
withe your Lo/ that you would allow him to supplie Mr.
Fullertoun's Charge for som tym, since he could gett his
own provided by another for that space. Wherin I cannot
be positiv withe your Lo/ albeit I am readie to doe the
Bishop all the services that ar possible and proper for me.
Because I am affrayed this should raise a clamour bothe
against him and us, that he should enjoy so many bene-
fices at once as his own at Dunoon, and that of Kilmoddan,

---

[1] Alex. Burnet, Archbishop of St. Andrews.

[2] John M'Cloy or Fullerton, of Kilmodan or Glendaruell, Argyll—a pendicle of the Priory of Whithorn—was installed in this charge in 1669. He neglected to take the test in 1681, when he lost the benefice; but petitioning on 16th March, 1682, he was authorised to take it. He was transferred to Paisley before 17th September 1684.—Scott, *Fasti*.

and you say a 3ʳᵈ at Morven besydes the Bishopricke, and therfor I leav it whollie to your Lo/ consideratione if you please to advise with my Lord primat in itt. I desir not to appear further in that particular. Since I cam heer I hav gott out our former Rector [1] of this Colledge, and hav setled the Dean of Glasgow in his place. I hope the storm is now over, and that we shall liv in mor quyet for som tym to come. I need not use many arguments to recommend any of my concerns to your Lo/ since you ar mor zealous for my interest then I am my selfe, and I am sure I shall never be forgetfull of your kyndnes, bot on all occasions shall giv testimony of my sincerity and forwardnes to advance what may contribut for your advantage. The sincer respects and humble duty are tendered to your good Lady and Daughters of him who is, My Lord, Your Lo/ most affectionat Brother and Servant,

ARTH: GLASCUEN.

[*Addressed :*]

These are for the right reverend father in God my Lord the Bishop of Galloway.

V

From Hector Maclean, the Bishop of Argyll, to the Bishop of Galloway

Glas., Apryll 7, 1682.

MY LORD,—Mr. Fullerton hes given me ane order from the Counsall to administrat the test to him, and to recommend him to his patron for a presentation. I am soe farr from the law, that I am ignorant of all that I may doe in this case, but I resolve to obey what the Counsall hes enjoined. But whither he may immediatlie enter to his charge or preach without a further licence from me and befor a new presentation, or whither another presented by yor lop. will be preferable to him, I entreat yoʳ lop.

---

[1] Dr. Matthew Brisbane was rector of the University in 1681, and was succeeded on 1st March 1682 by Robert Douglas, Dean of Glasgow.—*Mun. Univ. Glas.*, vol. iii. pp. 326-7.

who is nearer the law then I am to enforme me, for altho Mr. Fullerton hes behaved both insolentlie and malitiouslie in relation to me, yet I will be determined by the primat and yor lop. in any thing relating to him. And I entreat yor lop. always to remember him who is, My Lord, Yo^r lop. faithfull brother and humble Sevt.,

HECT. LISMOREN.

[*Addressed:*]
For The Right Reverend father in God, My Lord The Bishop of Galloway, the upmost closs in the Casthill.

VI

From Hector Maclean, the Bishop of Argyll, to the Bishop of Galloway

Dunoun, May 20, 1682.

MY LORD,—Although I have judged Mr. Fullertoun his standing off so long from taking the test as the greatest impediment that hindred the rest of the Brethren from taking the same, for which and other reasons I looked upon him as the ring-leader of the recusants of my Diocesse; yet now considering that he hath procur'd ane order from the counsell to have the test administred to him and that accordingly he hath taken it this day, and that he is so very dear to the people of his paroch that the most considerable of them supplicated me to interpose with your Lordship for him and withall resolved to make their earnest application to your Lord: and councell for their having him, for these and severall other great and weighty reasons moving Mr. Fraser[1] to give up his presentation to your Lord: (which reasons indeed appear considerable to me) all which he himself shall abundantly declare to your Lord:. I humbly judge it will be most for the peace and advantage of that church of which your Lord: is patron, that ye present Mr. Fullertoun himself

---

[1] Andrew Fraser was presented by Sir John Campbell of Ardkinglas in May to Lochgoilhead, and after passing trials was installed 5th July 1682.—Scott, *Fasti*.

who I persuade myself will be observant, dutifull. and respectfull to me; and for Mr. Fraser who is greatly devoted to your Lord: service and exceedingly depending on your favour, I shall provide him mor comfortably, honourably, and profitably then this of Kilmodan wold be to him. I do not by those give order or commands to your Lord, only devolve all on your good prudence and pious judgment and expects your Lord. directions and advices relative to this particular. all which will be readily obeyed by, My Lord. Your Lordship's Affectionate Brother to serve you, HECT. LISMOREN.

[*Addressed :*]

These are ffor the Right Reverend ffather in God, My Lord The Bishop of Galloway.

VII

From Archibald Grahame, the Bishop of the Isles, to the Bishop of Galloway

Rothesay, this 22^d of May 1682.

MY LORD,—I received yours wherein your Lo:^{p} have given ane account of your favour to Master Fraser and what you have done for him in reference to Kilmoden. For my part I fullie agree to whatever your Lo:^{p} and he shall conclude to be for his advantage. albeit for the present I am destitute of ane helper to preach for me at Rothesay. I understand that the Bishop of Argyll and Master Fraser both doe judge it more fitt for Master Fraser to embrace another charge in Argyll, which now is in his offer than that of Kilmoden, and it seems the Bishop has now a better opinion of Master Fullerton than formerlie he had. so that if your Lo:^{p} will present him he is most willing to stay still at Kilmoden, whatever your Lo:^{p} please to doe in this. I am of opinion that Master Fraser will be more happie and doe more good, and will have lesse oposition in the parish that is now in his offer than in the other, besides it is ane Archdeconrie and within a short time will be a very considerable benefitt, but I know albeit it were a greater advantage to him he will be verie carefull to have your Lo:ᴾ/ consent for his injoyment of it, a person on whose favour and kyndnesse he so much depends. I shall intreat your Lo:ᴾ to inquire at My Lord primat's what is become of My addresse to the King, and whether there be any thing of it in the signatur that I hear is come downe. It will be sadd if the Bishop of Argyll and I be forgott. As for my part I declare to your Lo/ I have not seen one farthing as yet of the whole Bishoprick except a little from Calder. Commiting you to the Grace of God, I am, My Lord, Your lordship's most affectionat [*paper torn*] servant,

ARCH. SODOREN.

[*Addressed :*]

To The Right Reverend Father in God, My Lord Bishop of Galloway, This.

VIII

From Robert Paterson[1] to the Bishop of Galloway

Abd. [Aberdeen], 9 May 1682.

MY LORD,—I cannot but in graditud return your lo: heartie thanks for your favour to the bearer, Mr. Gray, my wyfes cousin, whom by your secretarie his desyre I have sent to wait your comands. I houp he shall give your Lo. all content since I have had such experience of his lyf's principles. He hes bein a student of devinitie thir ten years, and of that tym three years a preacher, so that I intreat your Lo: may doe him favour in expeding him as to his entrie to that place which thorow your kyndnesse he is to injoy. Your Lo: may tack a tryall of him yourself and remitt him to the Brethren of the exercise for the rest, but if yee would bee pleased to allow him orders befor he went for Galloway that he needed not return

---

[1] Probably Robert Paterson, brother of the Bishop of Edinburgh, and principal of Marishall College, Aberdeen, 1678-1717. He married one of the Southesk family who had relatives of the name of Gray, and Mr. Robert Gray, who was minister of Whithorn in 1684, married an Aberdeen lady.

from his post it wir a great favour to the young man and his friends. and would now much obleidge, My Lord. Your lo. obedient Son and servant, Ro. PATERSON.

Putt my dewtie to your lady and Mistresse Alison.

[*Addressed :*]
For My Lord Bishope of Galloway   These are.

IX

From Henry Walker, minr. of Whithorn, to the Bishop of Galloway

Whiteherne, Juny 19th, [16]82.

My Lo/,—Ere I could get Baldoune [1] accoasted in favors of Mr. Gray for the church of Twinhame, he had granted to Mr. Thomas Ireland [2] a presentatione thereto which if yr Lo/ shall be pleased to sustain, I hope yr Lo/ tendernes toward my interest and standing will incline yr Lo/ to see to his settlement and provision elsewhere seing yr Lo/ has other vacancies within yr Diocess, and I myself have overcome those difficulties that before restrained my obedience to the Law and am now radie to satisfie the preceptive part of the Statut and my respect also for this people and unfeigned desire to spend and be spent among them in the service of the gospel is such as preyvailed with me to decline other occasions and opportunities (as I did insinuate to yr Lo/ before) more conducive towards the advancement of a secular interest. If yr Lo/ shall be pleased to acquiesce to my first suit I must also intreat yr Lo/ would either authorize me to preach till God bring yr Lo/ unto the countrey or impower

---

[1] The gift of Twynholm Kirk was in the hands of Sir David Dunbar of Baldoon. Sir David was the father of David Dunbar, jr., of Baldoon, who married, 1669, a daughter of Lord Stair. From the traditional story of this marriage Scott drew his inspiration for the romance of the *Bride of Lammermoor*.

[2] Thomas Ireland was transferred from Kirkcolm to Twynholm about 1672, and remained there till 'outed' in 1689.—Scott, *Fasti*.

Mr. Colhun[1] or Mr. Symson[2] to tender the Test to me here seing ther has been and as yet is such a long continued silence in this place and elsewhere in this corner through the absence of some of my brethren and my wife's conditione (as being kept these severall months under ye aflicting hand of God and overtaken with a farr more violent distemper in my last absence which threatens no lesse than the worst) is such as altogether incapacitates me for any adventure abroad. Shall adde no more at prest., leaving the preymises to yr consideratione save to signifie to yr Lo/ that ye shall not be forgotten in his prayers to Almighty God who subscribes himself, Yr Lo/ Most humble and devouted Servant,

HENRY WALKER.

[Addressed :]
For The Ryt. Reverend Father in God, My Lo/ Bishop of Galloway, These.

X

From John Graham of Claverhouse, afterwards Viscount of Dundee and Lord Graham of Claverhouse, to the Bishop of Galloway

Dumfriese, 28th July 1682.

MY LORD,—The goodnes that the Clergy believes your lordshippe hes for me is the reason that they adresse themselves often to me and force me to importune you with recomendation, houever I alwayes hertily imbraice the occasion of assuring your lordshipe of my respeckts. My lord, the bearer heirof Mr. Chrystie,[3] brother to the minister of Wigton,[4] as I am informed a very discreit

---

[1] James Colquhoun, minister of Penninghame.

[2] Andrew Symson, minister of Kirkinner and author of *A Large Description of Galloway*, written in 1684 and published in 1823.

[3] James Christie, M.A., presented to Kirkcowan by John Hamilton, sub-dean of the Chapel Royal, 12th October 1682, and transferred to Kirkinner about 1686.—Scott, *Fasti*.

[4] Thomas Christie, M.A., ministe of Wigton in 1677, and transferred to Dunning, 14th December 1682.—Scott, *Fasti*.

and deserving young man hes got a presentation to the Kirk of Kirkcouan from Barnbaroch[1] who pretends right of patronag and is indutedly in possession. But Mr. Hamilton the Subden of Ed^r, I hear pretends also right. I haue writen to him in favors of this gentleman, wherfor I beg your lordshipe will countenance him and persuad Mr. Hamilton to approve what is doen or give him a nou presentation. I recomend wholly this busines to your lordshipes goodnes. My lord, you was plesed to promise that you wold wreit to me befor you cam into this cuntrey, which I beg you not to faill because I intend to cause some attend you on the rod. Their ar a duson or sextein of our men that will be in on tuysday to whom I shall give order to wait on your lordshipe and either who will be readie to pairt wednesday or wait tuo or thre dayes upon your lordshipe, but houever I pray you let me hear from you by them. I am, My Lord, Your lordshipes most faithfull and humble servant, J. GRAHAME.

XI

Contemporary copy of letter to Lord Stair from the Bishop of Galloway (after 14 August) 1682, with endorsement 'Double Mys. ffor The Lord Stairs Be Bishop Aitkin'

My Lo:—Yo^{rs} of the 14^t of August came late to my hands while I was att Wigtoun. The very day that Claverhouse went thence to Ed^r, I could promise myselfe no long tyme to speak to him of the priviledges belonging to the

---

[1] Andrew Symson in his book on Galloway (written in 1684) says at p. 54: 'The patronage of this parish-kirk [Kirkcowand] is the same with that of Kirkinner to which it is adjacent.' And at p. 40 he says: 'The patronage of this parish of Kirkinner is controverted. The Laird of Barnbarroch claims it by vertue of a gift from King James the Sixth, to his great grandfather, Sir Patrick Vaus, who was also one of the Lords of Session, and who was sent to Denmark to wait upon Queen Anne. The Sub-dean of his Majestie's Chapel Royall claims it as titular of the teinds of the said parish.'

Regalitie of Glenluce.[1] Yet took the freedom to show him that this Regalitie (though the Justice Gñall did first attach) could reprieve any person who had wronged another within the Regality as to life or goods and give out sentence and execute the same against him. He answered, he neither intended to wrong me nor the rights of my Regalitie. All the priviledges where with the Regalitie wes att first endowed he wes not to wrong it. But any power by a late law given to them equallie as to heritable Shirrefs, he reckoned his first attach to stand good as well against a Regality as against a Shirreffe. And I must say that I conceav my selfe not a little wronged that the priviledges of my Regality should be tossed with such heat and no notice given me of it, till this last week yor letter came to my hands. And it is very probable if I had been favoured with tymeous intelligence therein, this difference betwixt him and the members of the Court had never come to this height. I did lyke wise in Gñall propose to him that there might be thoughts of peace for removing that unhappie difference betwixt him and yor son S^r. Jo^n. I can not say that I found him averse or slighted the motione, but till I should first speak with S^r. John and knowe from him the state of that affaire neither descretion nor tyme would permitt to tender particulars. If I finde the laird of Claverhouse att his returne to be of the same minde as when I last left him I am not with out all hope but that differences may be removed and the affaire adjusted. For the Laird of Claverhouse as he is a Gentleman of valour, so he is of prudence and generosity which are witnes of a benign aspect and takes of[f] all despondencie from those who minde to interceed with him. I am not so vaine as to promise that I can effect this Reconciliation and settlement, yet I will assure yor Lop. I shall use my utmost endeavours for effecting it, and what I can not doe of myselfe I shall assist by my

[1] 'The whole parish of Glenluce holds of the Bishop of Galloway as Abbot of Glenluce, who hath a Regality here. Sir John Dalrymple, younger of Stair, is Heritable Bayly thereof. This office is at present exerc'd by Sir Charles Hay of Park.'—Symson, p. 56.

prayers to God to sende out fitt and select Instruments and means for their Reconciliation and peace that among other great advantages consequent thereupon,[1] yor Lo'p might enjoy ane uninterrupted quietnes and serenitie in yor recesses from the world, which is the hearty desire and shall be the true endeavour of him who is.

[*Unsigned.*]

XII

From James Gordon [2] to the Bishop of Galloway

Carletoun, Sepber 13th, 1682.

My Lord,—Harvest and such necessary lets doe stop a personall attendance, at present very requisit, yet in the meantime till the other be I request your favourable acceptance of this account anent Mr. Hasting [3] whom ye have offred minister heir. Upon the 3rd of Sept. his edict was intimat, being the first sight and knowledge that any of us had of him, after which it was desired oftner than once that he would delay his course some longer time than the Edict seemed to allow of, wherein we might endeavour to be better knowne each one to another which he refuseing once and again the parish were necessitat to entir some objections agt. him before the moderator and certain brethren with him, which was done with all respect to your concernment and reverence to your place and authority. I humbly therfor desire your Lop. not to mistake us in it, for I protest I am conscious to no by end

---

[1] The case came before the Privy Council on 12th February 1683. That body condemned Sir John Dalrymple, the Master of Stair, and acquitted Claverhouse. Sir John was deprived of his jurisdiction and office as bailie and fined £500 sterling. He was committed to prison in the Castle of Edinburgh until payment was made. The fine was paid 20th February 1683.—Mark Napier, *Viscount Dundee*, vol. ii. pp. 306, 309.

[2] James Gordon, son of Wm. Gordon and Margaret Fullerton. It was through his mother that the lands of Carleton came to him.—M'Kerlie, *Landowners of Galloway*, vol. iii. p. 190.

[3] Patrick Hastie or Hastings got the church of Borgue in 1683, and was there till 'outed' in 1689.—Scott, *Fasti*.

in it. A true desire for such a minister as wee may
benefitt by and livie peaceably and cordially with, is the
only end I know of; which if your Lo/ can believe I am
confident your goodness will encourage not Crosse so
Innocent and honnest aimes. That Mr. Patrick [Hastings]
may be suitable to such ends with another parish I shall
not deny; from these it will not follow that he must be
such to us even at first, bot farr less now; refers your
Lop. to the objections for further cleering in that point.
And humbly requests that unproven misinformations
which men upon self interest may suggest passe not for
current without exact tryall and its one of the ends of
this expresse to receave your comands ther anent being
ready to attend your Lop. if we be so enjoyned. I shall
only in one word presume to signify that this people in
Borg has been brought up under painfull and popular
ministers: to gratify them with one somewhat suitcable to
ther temper would be seasonable att this time. I hope the
stipend is not incompotent to ane able minir. bot being
persuadet that your Lops main concern is the peoples
reall good and that ye will not suffer any insinuationes to
divert you from that end, I have almost concluded that
ye will not impose upon a people a minister they have so
declared against and expecting your comands, I signe.
Your Lops humble Servant,   JA. GORDON.

[*Addressed :*]
For, Very The Reverend My Lord Bishop of Galloway.

XIII

From Alexander Young, the Bishop of Ross, to the Bishop of Galloway

Decr. 1682.

MY LORD,—This comes to testify my hearty thanks
to your lo/ for your Letter which came to me lately: and
the satisfaction I had to understand of the faire reception

you met with in your dioces.¹ I wish the people there
may long continue in that good humour, and that your
Lo/ may finde them more and more tractable. It was to
me a very great refreshment to heare of the hopefull
progress of the King's effaires in England; and that his
majestic and the Duk doe continue to owne this poor
church: I hearticly wish that all who are intrusted in the
governement of it may so acquit themselves as that the
King may never hav cause to think he hath misplaced his
Royal favour on them. I must earnestly beseach your
Lo/ to present my humble duty to my Lord primat, whom
I hav so much importuined of late that I dare not adventure to giv his Grace the trouble of a letter, unless I had
something to write that were of moment. I resolve never
to fail willingly in that duty and obedience I ow to his
Grace, and if I happen at any time to err through impru-
dence or inadverteney a very little intimation of ane
escape of that nature will reduce me. I wish all happiness
to your lo/ your family and effairs and shall ever continue,
My Lord, Your Lo. most affectionat brother and faithfull
servant, ALEX^R ROSSEN.

[*Addressed:*]
My Lord Bishop of Galloway.

XIV

From Alex. Burnet, the Archbishop of St. Andrews, to the Bishop of Galloway

Windsor, May the 19th [1683].

MY LORD,—I receaved your Lo^{ps} of the 10th, which
refreshed me very much, and imparted the good news you
sent to our friends here, to whom they were very welcome.
I intend to acquaint the King with them as soone as I
find a convienent opportunity. The little mistakes which
have beene among your great ones since I came off, have

---

¹ This refers to the only visit the Bishop paid to Galloway.

BISHOP OF GALLOWAY'S CORRESPONDENCE

made too great noise here; but I hope they are now over; if we be united among our selves we may signifie something to the King and countrey, and make both our selves and others happy; but if we divide the countrey will breake, and we will become the object of our enemies scorne and contempt. I hope so many of your Lop^s as can conveinently meet will send me such advise or instructions as you shall thinke fitt, and among the rest it will be convenient that My Lord of Glasgow and you move to have the Bp' of Brechin's [1] case recommended to me, for not only strong but strange endeavours are used to obstruct that affair,—but this must be a secret betweene Glasgow and you, of which more at meeting. The Duke and Dutchesse and Lady Anne [2] went yesterday to Oxford to visite the University and some other places in that country, and will not returne till Weddensday next, all which tyme I will be idle here. I should have beene very willing to serve Craichly [3] upon your recommendation, but I find the gentleman concerned is resolved to come downe to Scotland, to treate and transact with him there. Present my ducty and service to your Lady and daughter, and all our other friends with you, and be confident of the best services of Your most affectionate brother and faithfull servant,

ALEX. ST. AND.

[*Addressed:*]
For The Right Reverend Father in God, My Lord Bishop of Galloway at Edinburgh.   Galloway.

---

[1] Robert Douglas, Dean of Glasgow, appointed Bishop of Brechin in 1683, and Dunblane in 1684.

[2] The Duke and Duchess of York and Princess Anne visited Oxford from Friday, 18th May to 22nd May 1683.—Anthony à Wood, *Life and Times*, vol. iii. pp. 47-55.

[3] James, son of old Wm. Gordon of Craiglaw, who would not take the test, and who, with Makgie, got a safe conduct from Claverhouse (*Hist. MSS. Com. Report*, 'Drumlanrig MS.', p. 269) on 5th March 1682, and one in 1683 from the Privy Council, which is signed by 'Alex. St. And.' among others.—*Privy Council Register*, vol. viii. 3rd series, 1683.

XV

Letter from James Colhoun, minister of Penninghame, Andrew Symson, minister of Kirkinner, and Wm. Watson, minister of Wigton, to the Bishop of Galloway

Pennighame, Jan^{rie} 22, 1685.

My Lord,—Having the occasion of this bearer we have thought it both our Ductie and interest to acquaint your Lo" with the present sad state of our presbyterie within this Shire.

From the generalitie of the inhabitants of these bounds we do not apprehend anye great danger at present, they continueing as yet indifferentlie civil and orderlie since Claverhouse his ingress to this countrey; but our greatest fear, which is nether small nor groundles, proceeds from considerable parties of rebells frequentlie sculking, roving and making inrods upon our borders and within our bounds, particularlie of lait at **Castl Stuart** and **Fintilloch** within the paroch of Pennighame; and as its frequentlie reported, they have been, and perhaps are further in this Countrey. By reason whereof the ministers of this presbyterie are necessitate to desert their Dwellings and to retire to places verie uncertain, trusting to no securitie. Some of our number have not onlie deserted their dwelling places but even their churches; not daring to adventure to preach therin. Captain Leiv. Winrame[1] (our kind friend) lay with his partie at Wigton till his garison at Mauchrye-moore[2] was made readie, all which time we have some shelter in Wigton, but now he being to remove the morrow from that town, we know not what (at present) to do, being this night (tho. somewhat late) necessitate to seek our lodging elsewhere; and now, My Lord, we humbly desire your Lo" to use your outmost endeavour for our speedie securitie, or els we will be

---

[1] One of Claverhouse's men; his name appears on the tombstone of 'the Wigton martyers.'

[2] Machermore, Newton Stewart.

necessitate to desert not onlie our Charges, but the countrey. My Lord, we committ Your Lo" and ourselves to God Almightie's protection. Your Lo" most obedient servants in all deutie, James Colhoun, minister of Penighame, Andrew Symson minr. of Kirkinner, Wm. Watson min^r. of Wigton.

[*Addressed:*]
For My Lord Bishop of Galloway.

XVI

From Robert Bowis, minister of Stoneykirk; Thomas Naismaith, of Stranraer; George Young, of Kirkmaiden; James Cameron, of Inch and Soulseat; and John Innes, of Glenluce, to the Bishop of Galloway

Strar, the 27 of Jan. 1685.

MY LORD,—Since our brethreen Mr. Sommervell and Mr. Broun[1] went from us (for anie thing we know) for securittie of their lives our fears are still greater and our danger we have represented to Collonell Graham of Claverhouse and his brother,[2] our Shirref, who is readie to doe us all kyndness, so that without we have some forces or a garison at Stranrauer there will be a necessittie for all of us to leave our charges.

Trusting therfor that your Lo/ will use your endevor for the procuring us a garison for the securittie of our lives till God shall be pleased to bring order out of those confusions we presentlie lye under and remain, Your Lo/ most obedient Sonns and afflicted Servants,

    Mr. R. BOWIS.   J. CAMERON.
    T. NAISMITH.   JOHN INNES.
    GEORGE YOUNG.

[*Addressed:*]
ffor My Lord Bishop of Galloway.

---

[1] Probably Wm. Somervill of Leswalt and George Brown of Stranraer.
[2] David Grahame—afterwards third Viscount Dundee.

XVII

From Robert Bowis, minister of Stoneykirk; George Young, of Kirkmaiden; John Caldwell, of Portpatrick; Thomas Naismith, of Stranraer; John Cameron, of Inch and Soulseat, to the Bishop of Galloway

Stranrauer, 20 Febr. 1685.

My Lord,—May it please your Lordshipp We again represent to your L/ our dangerous condition, so that hitherto not with out great hazard of our Lives we have continued in the exercise of our ministrie The Rebells having come with in our bounds, and our saftie hitherto (under God) has been by the vigilancie and care of Cornet Grahame Sheriff of Wigton among us, but he now removing from us, and the insolences of the rebells still encreasing as we cannot keep our own houses so we will be necessitate to leave our charges (not with standing the regularitie of our people) if some considerable forces be not sent to defend our bounds from the inroads of the enemie, we have also represented our condition to Collonell Grahame of Claverhouse.

Trusting that Your L/ layes our sad state to heart we remain My Lord Your Lordshippes Most obedient Sons and afflicted Servants,

    Mr. R. Bowis.   T. Naismith.
    George Young.   J. Cameron.
    John Caldwell.

[*Addressed :*]
My Lord Bishop of Galloway.

XVIII

(*Endorsement*)—

Double Myssiv, ffor The Moderator of the Presbetery of Wigtoun anent Elizabeth Stewart In order of her being relaxed from the sentence of Excommunication.

Reverend Brother,—As to yor last concerning Elizabeth Stewart, the relaxatione of hir from the sentence of excommunicatione pronounced Against hir by my predicesser I judge that sentence too rigid, he being acted to it by secular powers and exasperated by the transcendent contumacie and impudencie of hir husband, which now by his death ceaseth, and the woman towched with remorse now returning is to be receaved with mercie. Ye are then not to putt hir to pennance in all the Churches of the shire, but only in one where then, and now at present she resides: nor are you to cause hir to stand first at door, and after one pilloric, but it sufficeth that she stand on the publick place of repentance, and as to duratione, ye are to contract or prorog her tyme, according as ye find hir affected with sincere greife for hir sin, and hir heart to pant after reconciliatione with God and the Churches peace, that she may not be overwhelmed with greif. And albeit 'Ἐπιείκεια be used towards her, yett that that sentance may still be terrible to others, and the nerves of disciplin not slackned, she is to undergoe hir repentance for hir offence agst. God and contempt of the Church in the habit of an excommunicated persone, in publick as I have said, solemnely acknowledging that hir sin which brought this Course upon hir. Lett her take the shame of hir sin upon [her] that God may have glory by hir humiliation: Let hir detest that sin which intercepted God's favour and countenance from hir, and earnestly contend to be restored to his favour which is better than Life. Let her witness her faith and love to her dearest Lord and Savior J: C: who have taken hir sins off hir, and laid them upon himself to free hir from the wrath to come. Lett her earnestlie beseach God by him that the divine anger may be appeased, and turned aside from hir and hir soull reconciled to God. Let hir earnestly beseach the congregatione to pray for hir that hir sin may be removed and that she obtaine these graces which may make her worthie to be receaved in the body of the congregatione againe: after all hir obtestations and performances in that ritwall (which is to be followed according as it is usuallie practissed in this Church only abstaining from words which are averse from the present goverment, for our Statut law at present binds us up from

giving new formes) ye shall proceed to absolutione and declaire that by a warrand from me yor ordinary ye are to publish the sentence of Relaxatione wherby she may be freed from the bonds of sin and of the curse due to sin, and therfor by that power and authority which ye have receaved from God as a Minister of the Gospell ye absolve hir from hir sin and relax hir from the sentence of Excommunicatione laied upon hir, and restore hir to the Church, —in the name of the father and of the Sone and of the holy Ghost ye are to end with prayers and praises and benediction of the people. The Spirit of the Almightie be with you in that solomne work, direct. assist, guide and prosper you in all your Spiritual Labours, I ever am,
Your affectionate   ORDINARY.

THE DIARY OF
SIR JAMES HOPE
1646-1654

Edited by

S<small>IR</small> JAMES BALFOUR PAUL
C.V.O., LL.D.

INTRODUCTION

The Diarist

THE writer of this Diary was Sir James Hope of Hopetoun, sixth son of Sir Thomas Hope of Craighall, the eminent Lord Advocate and Jurist, by his wife Elizabeth, daughter of John Bennet of Wallyford. He was one of a family of fourteen children, and was born 4th and baptized 12th July 1614. Like so many cadets of Scottish families at this period, he was, as a young man, sent abroad to complete his education. We get a detailed and interesting account of his starting, from the pen of his father Sir Thomas,[1] along with his next elder brother, Alexander: James was bound for the university of Orleans, where an ancestor of his future wife, James Foulis, afterwards a Judge of the Court of Session, had been ' procurator of the venerable Scottish nation ' so long before as 1512,[2] while his brother Alexander already held a position at the English Court.[3] They were well equipped with funds

---

[1] He also kept a diary which was published, though unfortunately without any assistance to the reader in the way of editing, by the Bannatyne Club in 1843.

[2] 'The Scottish Nation in the University of Orleans,' Scottish History Society *Miscellany*, vol. ii. p. 97.

[3] An application for some post for Alexander had been made on or before 1627, but owing to his youth (he was only sixteen) had not been granted. On 29th September 1627, Sir Thomas writes to the Earl of Annandale, who had had the direction of Scottish affairs, and who had evidently promised to do what he could for the boy, 'Ye hope at sum uther tyme to gif me contentment, and hope I and my sone, being Hopes, will rest upon that hope, and still hope that his sacred Majestie will not disappoint our hope.'—' Report on Laing MSS.' *Hist. MSS. Com.*, vol. i. p. 178.

by their father, who chronicles in his Diary, under date 24th February 1636, their departure from home :—

' This day my two sones Mr. Alexander and Mr. James tuik journey, the one to Court, and the other to France : and gevin to Mr. Alexander xxxvii doubill angels, quhilk, with the 13 quhilk he had, makes 50 doubill angels : and als gevin to him 5^{c}lb of rydals of gold for his journey. Item, gevin to Mr. James 50 doubill angels, with a Portugal ducat of gold. Item, to him 1 merkes of gold for his journey, with some 30 s. sterling of xii s. peeces. Item, thair mother gaif to ilk of them 2 rosnobles. Item, I gaif ather of them the buik of Imitatioun of Chryst of Thomas Kempis, with command, ilk day, in morning and evening, to reid ane cheptor thairof ; and last gaif them my blessing. God send me a happie sycht of them both.'

Notwithstanding this generous provision both for body and soul, the boys appear to have been rather greedy and did not think it sufficient, for their father adds :—

' Item, eftir they went als far as the Patter raw, they sent for x dollors, quhilk I gave, and uther ten dollors wes borrowit be Mr. James from Hary Hope, quhilk I payit.'

James was at Orleans in the beginning of October, when his father sent him other 50 double angels, and in the following January he got 500 francs sent him at 24s. (Scots) the franc, which came to 600 lbs. Scots, or about £50 sterling. On the 5th July he had started on a tour and was at Bourges, where he got a letter from his father ordering him to return home by Michaelmas, and on the 19th of the same month 500 francs were again sent him. James duly returned home on 1st November 1637, but it was rather the return of a prodigal, as he not only had spent the last 500 francs but had borrowed 300 more in Paris and £23 sterling in London. The old gentleman, however, it is fair to say, makes no complaints, and not only paid his son's debts but expended 227 merks on a new suit of clothes for him.[1] This may have been the suit he wore at his wedding, because either before or after his excursion to Orleans he had become engaged to Anna Foulis, and they were married in Greyfriars Church, on Thursday, 11th January 1639, by Mr. Andrew Ramsay.[2] The bride was the daughter and heiress of Robert Foulis, advocate, and his wife Sara Speir, and a granddaughter of James Foulis of Colinton. Robert had acquired, in 1625, the lands and barony of Crawfordmuir or Friarmuir, in the county of Lanark. These lands included what is now known as the Leadhills, still the property of Anna's descendants, the Earls of Hopetoun and Marquesses of Linlithgow. Crawfordmuir was celebrated for its gold mines, which were worked to a considerable extent and with very successful results in the reigns of James IV. and James V., though the output of gold had fallen very much by the middle of the seventeenth century. Still the property as a whole was a very valuable one : it has been stated [3] that Sir William Baillie of Lamington was the uncle and only guardian of Anna Foulis, that he had attempted to defraud her of some of the Leadhills property, that she had come to Edinburgh to take legal advice, and that the matter ended by her marrying the Lord Advocate's son. But the truth of the story is doubtful : whether or not it is true, Anna took an early opportunity of handing over all her landed property to her husband in security for her promised dowry, which amounted to £20,000.

It is doubtful whether James Hope ever followed his

---

[1] *Sir Thomas Hope's Diary*, 15th December 1637.
[2] Andrew Ramsay, born 1574, son of Sir David Ramsay of Balmain. He was minister of Greyfriars, 1634-1641. Died at Abbotshall, to which he had retired, 30th December 1659.—Scott, *Fasti Eccl. Scot.*, 2nd ed., vol. i, p. 70.
[3] *Lives of the Baillies*, p. 40.

father's profession of advocate ; there is no record of his having been admitted to the Bar. Having obtained through his wife such a valuable property, he was, not unnaturally, anxious to develop it, and had the good sense to make himself acquainted, so far as he could, with metallurgy. His knowledge of the subject was probably among the reasons of his being appointed Master of the Mint in 1641. He worked his mines with much assiduity both to his own profit and apparently to the benefit of his employees, if we are to believe Nicoll, who tells us in his Diary that he 'kepit mony pure and indigent pepill in the leid mynes and be his meanis had a lyfliehood.' Some of his workmen were obtained in a rather curious way. Sir James Balfour[1] relates that six of the followers of Montrose, among those who had been taken prisoners, 'being young lustie fellows,' were assigned to Sir James Hope 'to his lead mines.' It would be interesting to know what wages, if any, he paid them.

In politics Sir James seems to have been somewhat wobbly, and like all wobblers he did not command the full confidence of either party. He sat in the Scots Parliament for Stirlingshire, 1649-50, and for Lanarkshire, 1650. As will be seen from the Diary, he had an interesting interview with King Charles II. at Falkland after his arrival from Holland. What he said to the king, or, at all events, what he says he said, is perhaps non-committal, but he evidently wished the king to believe that he was a loyal supporter. Only a few days before the interview, however, he had voted against levying an army to resist the advance of Cromwell. He was roundly taken to task by Argyll, who denounced him as 'not only a main enemy to king and kingdom but a main plotter and contriver, assister and abetter of all the mischief that has befallen

---

[1] *Annals*, vol. iv. p. 19.

the kingdom ever since.'[1] On 7th January he was refused a pass to go out of the country unless he formally petitioned Parliament for it, giving his reasons, and a few days afterwards he got into a worse scrape. In a letter of 20th January 1651, written from Perth by one of the king's suite, the following passage occurs : ' Sir Alexander Hope (whom his Majesty at the solicitation of some of his friends, hath made Gentleman Usher of his privy chamber, and master falconer in this country) came within these two days and made his addresses to the king, to let him know that there were two brothers of his (both Lords of Session) that were much troubled *in consience* to see him take those ways he now was in ; and, perceiving his distruction if he persisted in them, they were restless till they sent his majestie their humble advice, which was, that he should speedily treat with Cromwell, quit his interest in England and Ireland, give cautionary towns for the performing of the articles, and content himself with this country, till he had a better opportunity to recover the rest. To which his majesty resolutely and discreetly answered that *he would see both him and his brothers hanged at one end of a rope and Cromwell at the other, before he would do any such thing*; and went instantly and complained of it to the Committee of Estates, but what they will do with them is not yet known.'[2] What was done with two at least of the authors of the pusillanimous advice was to send them to prison ; their detention, however, was not prolonged, as on the 21st January both Sir James and Sir Alexander were released from confinement, but ordered to reside in their country houses and not to leave the kingdom. This seclusion cannot have lasted long, and the advent of Cromwell

[1] Balfour, *Annals*, vol. iv. p. 173.
[2] Carte Collections, Bodleian Library, quoted in Lyon's *Personal History of King Charles II.*, Edinburgh, 1851, p. 163.

brought him once more into notice. He rendered indeed such services to the Parliamentarians that in May 1652 he was nominated one of the Commissioners for the administration of Justice in Scotland. He had had some experience of the duties of a judge, as he had been appointed a Lord of Session in 1649; but on a new commission being appointed two years after, his name was omitted from it. In the interval he had, on 14th June 1653, been made a Member of the Council of State in England, and he represented Scotland in the Barebones Parliament of that year. He gives a vivid account of the forcible dissolution of that body.

Nicoll in his Diary laments the exclusion of Hope from the second list of Cromwell's judges, giving him high praise as 'a very fyne judicious man,' and saying that the 'land suestnit much prejudice throw his removall for he wes a guid and upright judge.'

In March 1660, however, his gown was restored to him, but he does not seem ever to have sat again on the Bench. It is an interesting fact that of the four sons of Sir Thomas Hope who attained to mature years, no fewer than three became judges, Sir John of Craighall, Sir Thomas of Kerse, and Sir James of Hopetoun.

Sir James went to Holland in 1661 on business connected with his mines. While there he contracted 'the Flanders sickness,' which may have been influenza, or possibly the plague, which developed in such intensity a few years later. He was able to reach Scotland, but died at his brother's house at Granton, 23rd November 1661, aged forty-seven. He was buried at Cramond, where there is a monument to his memory with his 'vera effigies' and the motto *sperando superaui*.

He married 1st, as above-mentioned, Anna Foulis, who died in 1656, and 2ndly, on 29th October 1657, Mary, eldest daughter and coheiress of William Keith, seventh

INTRODUCTION

Earl Marischal: she survived him and married, 2ndly, Sir Archibald Murray of Blackbarony, baronet, the nephew of her sister-in-law Margaret, the wife of Sir John Hope, second Baronet of Craighall.

Sir James had in all fifteen children. By his first wife he had :—

1. Thomas, baptized 23rd November 1640, died 29th March 1644.
2. Robert, born 6th February 1645, died 25th March 1647.
3. Thomas (*secundus*), born 3rd February 1647, six or seven weeks before his time, and died two days after.
4. James, baptized 22nd April 1649, and died a few days later.
5. John, born 10th June 1650. He succeeded his father and made large additions to the Hopetoun property, purchasing the baronies of Abercorn, Niddry, and Winchburgh. He was drowned while coming home with the Duke of York, in the wreck of the *Royal Gloucester*. The family tradition is that he had actually obtained a seat in one of the boats, but gave it up to the Duke of York and was, in consequence, drowned. On this account Queen Anne gave his son a peerage almost immediately after he came of age. He married, 21st December 1668, Lady Margaret Hamilton, eldest daughter of John, fourth Earl of Haddington. She survived him, dying 31st January 1711.
6. George, baptized 23rd November 1654, and died young.
7. Alexander, born 6th April 1656, and died young.
8. Thomas (*tertius*). The date of his birth is uncertain. He died in London, as mentioned in the Diary, on 16th November 1653, and was buried

in St. Margaret's, Westminster, on the following day.

9. Elizabeth, born 5th September 1642, died 13th February 1647.
10. Sara, born 30th December 1643, died 30th July 1644.
11. Ann, baptized 29th February 1652, died 13th March 1653.
12. Rachel, born 13th March 1653, married in 1669 David Betoun of Balfour.

By his second wife Sir James had issue :—

13. William, baptized 1st August 1658, and died in infancy.
14. William (*secundus*), baptized 15th April 1660, became a soldier, traveller, and author. He published a treatise on the art of fencing (Edinburgh, 1686), and translated Solleysell's *Parfait Mareschall* in 1696. He was created a baronet 1st March 1698, a title which became dormant on the death of his grandson in 1763. Sir William was known first under the designation of Granton, having succeeded to that property on the death of his uncle, Sir Alexander. He subsequently acquired Kirkliston, and in 1705 he purchased Balcomie in Fife for £7500. He died in 1724, having married, in or before 1672, Elizabeth Clerk.
15. Mary, a posthumous child, baptized 7th July 1662, died young.

It is a significant commentary on the infant mortality of the period that out of these fifteen children only two sons and one daughter attained anything like mature years.

The Diary

The Diary is contained in a little leather-covered book measuring 5⅜ inches by 2⅞ inches. The binding is a little worn and worm-eaten in one or two places, and one of the two clasps is missing. It is written in an exceedingly neat and legible hand on excellent hand-made paper, and each page has a black line drawn round it at a distance of about six-sixteenths of an inch from the margin of the leaf. The number of the page is placed in the space formed by the intersection of these lines at the top outside corner of each page. The word *Memoriall*, followed by the year, forms a heading to every page. The numbering of the pages extends to 137, but, as will be seen presently, this is twenty pages in excess of the number actually written. The last entry of the Diary refers to the death of Lord Craighall, 27th April 1654: after that follow blank leaves amounting in number to about as many again as those written.

The Diary, then, is a fragment extending from 23rd September 1646 to the date above mentioned. Whether it was part of a more continuous journal it is impossible to say: not only is it in itself a fragment, but unfortunately that fragment has been grievously mutilated, and has, in addition, some blank pages in it which perhaps the writer intended to fill up at some convenient season but never did so. On page 71 twenty lines have been effectually blackened over under date 1st January 1652, so that it is impossible to read the entry. After page 74 five leaves have been carefully cut out: on the inner margins, however, can still be read the dates 22nd and 26th February (1652), 21st and 26th April, and the next legible entry begins on Monday 4th July. This has no doubt been done for a purpose by some later possessor of the Diary, though what that purpose was is inexplicable. A still more singular circumstance is that although the last page of the mutilated leaves should be numbered 84, the next page, when the Diary begins again, is numbered 105. There is no trace of the little volume ever having been rebound or altered from its original condition. The mystery of this jump of twenty pages remains unexplained.

On the inside of the board, at the beginning of the volume, and on the *verso* of the first leaf are some family memoranda, which, as they include the death of Sir James's son John in 1682, must have been added after the death of the Diarist.

After this follow eight pages containing a table of contents of the Diary, written evidently not by Hope himself but by some one into whose possession the volume came after the erasures and mutilations above mentioned. After the contents there is a note signed by John Hope, Sir James's son, to the following effect :—

'This book of my Father's memorials delivered to me by my cosin Archibald Hope at Edinburgh ye 24 Novr. 1670; wch is ye very day of ye moneth my D. Father died on, viz. at Granton, anno 1661 : and is buried at Cramond in my uncle's Isle.'

Apart from the flyleaf the Table of Contents occupies four leaves of the volume; then there is a blank page and John Hope's note is written on the *verso* of this leaf. As the Diary begins on the next page it is difficult to understand how the writer missed twelve good pages unless indeed he had a Table of Contents in view.

The cousin Archibald referred to was Sir Archibald Hope of Rankeillour, the second son of Sir John of Craighall, and the ancestor of the Hopes of Pinkie. How the Diary came to be in his possession and whether he was the mutilator of its pages we do not know.

The Diary itself begins on Wednesday, 23rd September 1646, with the narration of a dream the writer had. This is by no means the only chronicle of the kind in the Journal, and the recording of dreams seems to have been a family characteristic, as there are many similar instances in the Diary of Sir Thomas Hope. Three days after we get an account of the last illness and death of Sir Thomas himself. The details are interesting: notwithstanding his serious indisposition he seems, like a patriarch of old, to have gathered all his available posterity round his bed and to have given them severally his solemn blessing: nor were his 'servitors' or clerks, as we would now call them, forgotten. After some apparent improvement in his condition he became worse on the 30th September, but on the following day he was still able to 'take up' the twenty-third Psalm—the Psalm always so dear to Scottish hearts—and sang it to the end with the help of a little prompting from Lord Craighall. His age is not precisely known, but it is probable that he was not much above sixty at the time of his death.

Sir James was an enterprising and perhaps a rather speculative man. He took a great interest in metals and metallurgy, and frequently refers to the subject, which is not surprising seeing that a considerable part of his income must have been derived from his Leadhill mines, which he got through his wife Anna Foulis. Not long after his father's death, two Edinburgh merchants, who were interested in the manufacture of silver lace, approached him with a request that he would 'mediate' between them and the Incorporation of Goldsmiths, who stood upon their trade privileges and refused either to furnish the lace-makers with silver for their work or to allow them to melt it down and refine it for themselves. Sir James appears to have been able to bring the matter to a successful compromise. The Goldsmiths were either to supervise the refining of the silver by the lace merchants or sell to them ingots of refined silver at 5s. 9d. or 5s. 10d.

the oz. The manufacturers appear to have been so satisfied with what Sir James had done in the matter that they made an offer to him of a share in the profits. They expected to get a profit of one shilling sterling on every ounce of manufactured lace sold at 4 lbs. and 4 lbs. 4d. (Scots) the ounce. Now four pounds Scots would amount to about 6s. 8d. sterling, so that the profit would come to a quite satisfactory percentage. There were other alternative proposals put before Hope and he took them *ad avizandum*, but the Diary does not say whether he ultimately accepted the offer of partnership.

On the 3rd February Hope chronicles the birth of a sixth child by his first wife, who was baptized by the name of Thomas. It is rather pathetic to note the great desire of the son to commemorate his distinguished father by naming one of his sons after him: this was not the first Thomas in his family, as his eldest son born in 1640 had been named after his grandfather but had died within four years: the second Thomas, born six weeks before his time, only survived two days, and a third son of the same name died in London in 1653. But not only did he lose, at this time, his son the second Thomas: within the space of about six weeks the nursery was twice again devastated: on 19th February a daughter, Elizabeth, a child of four years and a half was removed, and on 25th March a son Robert. On this child an examination *post mortem* was held, the results of which his father chronicles in great detail and with much interest. The medical men who made the examination were Dr. Purves (probably a connection of the family) and Dr. Cunningham; the surgeon was James Brown, the apothecary Samuel Hunter. The case is rather a remarkable one: here was a child only two years of age, who died of stone in the kidneys; this in itself is not unusual, but to find two cases of the kind in one family—his brother Thomas, as we shall see, died of exactly the same thing at the age of six—must be very rare.¹ The child 'had calculi in both kidneys and old pleurisy with adhesions, the results of former inflammation of the lung. The data as to the symptoms are not sufficient to allow of definite diagnosis as to the cause of death but probably it arose from uræmia, *i.e.* blood poisoning, from suppression of urine through blocking of the ureter, or kidney disease. The explanation of the adhesions and lung affection from leaning on his nurse is ingenious but incorrect.'

Only a few weeks after this Sir James has to chronicle another death in the family. His sister-in-law, Helen Rae, the widow of his brother Sir Thomas Hope of Kerse and Wester Granton, had come to Edinburgh 'anent the bussnesse of Airth,' over which property the Hopes had bonds.² She had been unwell two days before and had hardly arrived before she took dangerously ill, and she had 'fittes of the mother,' or hysteria arising from some uterine affection : this 'did stricke her in ye head whereby she reaved and was distempered.' This means, according to Dr. MacGillivray, that she had epileptiform convulsions with delirium, perhaps arising from a brain tumour or brain tuberculosis ; or she may have had epilepsy and died in a 'status epilepticus.' The treatment was by 'ventoses' or cupping glasses, and later by leeches, which gave her some relief, but she died after two days' illness.

At the beginning of August 1647, Hope is much interested, along with other people of standing, on the proposal made by Christopher Visitella, probably a Venetian who

---

[1] My friend, Dr. Charles W. MacGillivray, has most kindly gone over the medical and surgical aspects of the cases of the two children and Lady Kerse mentioned in the Diary, and it is from his information that I am enabled to give the comments in the text.

[2] See *Reg. Mag. Sig.*, vol. ix. No. 1966.

was living in Edinburgh at the time with his brother or relative, Isaac Visitella, a painter, to set up glass works at 'the Pans,' probably Prestonpans. The plan was examined very carefully, and it was calculated that after a capital expenditure of about £200 for the erection of furnaces and purchase of materials, the weekly expenses would amount to £11 while the estimated sales of 900 wine glasses at 2/ per dozen and as many beer glasses, or tumblers, at 2/6d. per dozen per week would amount to £16, 17s. 6d. This seems quite a satisfactory profit, but the difficulty was to find an outlet for the sale of all these glasses. There was not, indeed, a market for so many in Scotland, and Hope shrewdly points out that they 'would make more in one weeke than could possiblie be vented in a mounth, and in one year than in three.' It would seem, too, that a certain John Joussie had already tried the manufacture, but had ultimately been compelled to give it up with a loss of 20,000 lbs. (Scots) on account of not getting a wide enough market for his goods. Whether the scheme proposed by Visitella and his friends ever came to anything is not recorded, but probably it was dropped.

In September of this year Hope had a great controversy with the assessors for Clydesdale as to the valuation of his Leadhill mines, which had been assessed at 5000 lbs. (Scots) for the year. He objected to this, but also refused to be put on oath about it: there was much debate on the whole subject, which was complicated by a curious mistake in his statement of accounts, wherein he omitted to debit himself with 6000 lbs. for workmen's wages, on which he naturally did not wish to be assessed. The end of the matter was that the valuation was put on a fixed basis of £1000 per annum, whatever might be the profit or loss in the year. The memorandum is interesting as showing the amount of wages paid to the workmen annually, and that he was willing to admit having raised about 150 tons of ore in the year.

In January 1648 there is another *post mortem* examination recorded, this time on a nephew, a posthumous son of his brother Sir Thomas. He was born, as is recorded in his grandfather's Diary, on 12th December 1643, so had not reached the age of five. He had some form of intestinal disease, but the details are not given so fully as to enable the exact cause of death to be ascertained.

After the relation on January 1648 of an unfortunate accident, resulting in the death of the only child of a widow, which occurred in the removal of some rubbish from the back of his house in the Cowgate, the Diary comes to an end for a time. Indeed it is not for two years and a half that it is again resumed. During the interval much had happened: Charles I. had lost his throne and his head, and his son had signed the draft of the Breda agreement, by which he became a Covenanted King of Scots. Sir James was much perplexed which way to turn, and he had recourse to the *Sortes Biblicae*, turning up at random 2nd Chronicles, chap. xi. v. 4: 'Thus saith the Lord, ye shall not go up nor fight against your brethren: return every man to his house; for this thing is of me.' Sir James interpreted this oracular deliverance to mean that he was to go at once to the king, and accordingly, on Friday, 15th July, he set out for Falkland, where the king was staying, having landed in Scotland on 23rd June. He had a bad crossing to Burntisland, taking five hours to it, and stayed that night and over Sunday with his brother at Craighall. On Monday both brothers proceeded to Falkland. The account of their entertainment there is rather confused: he says that after dinner they both kissed the king's hands and Craighall had some conversation with him. All this probably took place before dinner, though Sir James goes on to relate that at *supper* the king's physician intimated that the king wished to see him after supper. This interview took place, and the king thanked Hope for sending him when he was in Holland the present of a great piece of Scots gold. But Sir James goes on to say that the king (after this interview) being withdrawn with some company he 'went to supper with the Treasurer Depute to the Green Cloth.' It is impossible that he can have partaken of two suppers on the same day, and the probability is that the kissing hands took place before dinner, that Dr. Fraser gave him the king's message at dinner, not at supper, and that the conversation about the piece of gold took place after the former meal. Then comes supper with the Treasurer Depute, after which Hope says he returned to the Privy Chamber and waited for an hour till the king came out of his bedchamber, when he had an interesting conversation with His Majesty, which is as graphically described as anything in the Diary. The king at once created a favourable impression and increased Hope's self-esteem by tactfully addressing him (as he is careful to tell us) as 'my Lord Hopetoun.' The title was, no doubt, due to Sir James, as he had been appointed a Lord Ordinary of the Court of Session the year previous, but it had a specially pleasant ring when coming from the lips of his sovereign. Charles, whatever else he may have been, was a well-informed and intelligent man and particularly fond of scientific subjects. So he engaged Hope, most tactfully, on the subject of his mines and told him about the tin and silver mines in England. He then discoursed on 'ambergris' and told how a quantity had been found in a cove on the south coast of England. This is specially interesting, as amber is but a rare product in the British Isles. Before taking his leave, the king, suiting his conversation to his company, piously expressed his resolve to redeem his time and to assist in advancing the work of

God, ending by expressing a desire that Hope would befriend him in Parliament. Honoured by such condescension, the guest could only reply that 'however some of us might be represented to His Majestie, yet by ye Lord's assistance wee were resolved to approve ourselves faithfullie to all interests, and trusted his majestie's experience should find it so.' And with such loyal protestations the interview closed. Alas, the king was to find before long that the support of Sir James Hope was that of a broken reed.

After the narration of a dream which need not trouble us, Hope notes that 'this day the king came from Stirling to our camp and at the same time the English armie advanced and lay down before ours.' But this cannot have happened till some time after his interview with the king. We are told that 'on one of the rainiest nights that could be' the English army, under Cromwell, began a bombardment and that the ships 'also played from the road upon Leith.' This helps us to fix the exact date: Cromwell had entered Scotland on the 22nd July; the night of Sunday, the 28th, was spent at Musselburgh; he advanced upon Leith the next day but found Leslie's army strongly entrenched between Edinburgh and Leith, and too formidable to be tackled with safety. Cromwell himself says: 'we did find their army were not easily to be attempted. Whereupon we lay still all the said day [Monday the 29th]; which proved to be as sore a day and night of rain as I have seldom seen and greatly to our disadvantage.' So on Tuesday the English army withdrew to Musselburgh 'there to refresh and revictual.'[1] This very wet night when the Lammas floods were, as they are still very frequently, in full force, fixes the date of Hope's entry as the 29th July.

---

[1] *Cromwell's Letters*, vol. ii. p. 164.

After the recital of another dream comes the erased portion of the Diary mentioned above.[1] It is not till after the lapse of more than three years that it is resumed. On Hope's return, in January 1652, from a visit to his brother at Craighall, he finds on reaching home that a Mr. Vanhoght, who had come over (probably from Holland) on business connected with the mines, was lying dangerously ill in his house. Hope had been sent for, but the messenger could not get across the ferry, and everybody was thankful when the master of the house appeared himself at home. The patient got worse: if business affairs were to be cleared up no time was to be lost. Whether at his own request or by the insistence of Sir James, he was subjected to a close examination as to the position of the affairs which had brought him over. The whole scene is rather pathetic: the dying stranger harassed in his last hours by repeated interrogatories in the presence of witnesses—Dutch skippers, Edinburgh burgesses, and Hope's own wife and niece. He appears to have been in possession of his faculties (though Hope says that after the first night 'he was never fullie at himselfe') and makes quite coherent statements, asking that what was due to himself should be remitted to his wife.

What was the issue of this tragic occurrence we do not learn, for the Diary stops short in the middle of a sentence, and here comes that mysterious mutilation and apparent omission of thirty pages to which reference has been already made.

The next entry is made on 4th July 1652, and shows us a family council consisting, on one side, of the Diarist, his brother, Lord Craighall, and their two brothers-in-law, Lord Cardross and Sir Charles Erskine, and on the other

---

[1] P. 107.

Sir John Smith of Grote Hall, an eminent citizen of Edinburgh, and Mr. John Ellis, who was probably his brother-in-law. The business in hand concerned the settlements in connection with the marriage of Hope's niece Elizabeth, the daughter of his brother Sir Thomas Hope of Kerse, and Sir John's son Robert. The lady was to have a tocher of £1000 (Scots), and Sir John made very handsome settlements on the couple and their prospective children. The Hopes were determined that Elizabeth should be well provided for, and they succeeded in getting Sir John to give two chalders of victuals more than he had been originally prepared to offer. Matters were satisfactorily arranged, and the marriage took place on the 12th of August in St. Giles, though whether the Hopes were altogether pleased with the match is doubtful, as Sir James notes that none of their friends attended outside the immediate family circle.

Hope was now tempted by Thomas Henderson, an advocate,[1] to purchase the estate of Tulliallan, but the price was evidently much beyond what Sir James considered its value and the negotiations came to nothing.

Another marriage now claimed the attention of Hope, who seems to have acted as adviser to his relatives on such occasions. The bridegroom in this case was Sir George Mowat of Ingliston, who had by this time been knighted, and who was ultimately to be created a baronet in 1664. The lady was another niece, also of the name of Elizabeth, a daughter of Lord Craighall. The course of true love had not been running altogether smoothly, and Sir James evidently asked the young man what his intentions were and how matters stood between him and the lady.

---

[1] His family had some business connection with the Hopes as being at one time part proprietors of the lands of Southside, in the lordship of Newbattle, part of which belonged to Hope's wife as heir of her father Robert Foulis (cf. *Reg. Mag. Sig.*, vol. x. No. 1515).

'Wherein he exprest a resolutione' [to marry her if she was agreeable], but like an honest and sensible man, 'would not meate with her till she should first expresse the removall of ye former prejudice and a present consent.' All this Elizabeth must have done, as they were duly contracted within little more than a month from this interview, and the marriage ceremony took place on the 28th October.

After this no less than nine pages of the Diary are taken up with chronicling several weird and fantastic dreams of the writer, but these need hardly claim our attention.

The next real item of news is yet another marriage of a niece, also a daughter of Lord Craighall, Anna Hope. Her husband was William Cochrane of Rochsoles in Lanarkshire, son of James Cochrane, a merchant burgess of Edinburgh. The details of the settlements are not, in this instance, given, but the marriage took place on 24th March 1653 in the East Church or Choir of St. Giles. It is perhaps worthy of note that all the marriages mentioned were celebrated in churches, and not at the house of the bride as afterwards came to be the custom. Lady Hope was probably unable to be present at the ceremony, as she had just had her eleventh child a few days before. She was called Rachel, after Lord Craighall's second wife Rachel Speir, who was in all likelihood a relative of Lady Hope's mother Sara Speir, the wife of Robert Foulis.

It is a singular coincidence that three consecutive entries in the Diary at this period chronicle a wedding, a birth, and a death. The death was that of Sir James's daughter Anna, a child of little more than a year old, who died from teething exactly a month after the birth of her sister Rachel.

Three weeks after this event Sir James had an experience which plunged him into the very vortex of politics.

All his professions of loyalty to the king, which had been made so dutifully if not fervently, were forgotten, and he was to identify himself with the Parliamentary party of the extremest type. On the 5th of May 1653 he was on his way to Leadhills, and had nearly reached his destination when he was overtaken by one of his clerks, hot with riding post haste after him, bearing a letter from Colonel Lilburne, the Commander-in-Chief of the English forces in Scotland, desiring Hope to meet him in Edinburgh. He accordingly returned to town, but found Lilburne had gone to Dalkeith, where his headquarters were. He accordingly followed him there and had an interview of some importance. Lilburne sounded him as to his willingness to go to London ' to be assisting there,' as Hope puts it, but what exact form the assistance was to take is not mentioned. He told Lilburne that while he had no objection to act under Cromwell in Scotland, he did not desire to go out of Scotland or to meddle with State affairs. Lilburne advised him to write to the general himself to that effect, which he forthwith did. Not only so, he kept the draft of the letter, but unfortunately did not extend it in his Diary, which is rather aggravating for us, as it would have explained what it was he was to do. After having written his letter he started immediately for the Leadhills, where he arrived next day. How long he stayed we do not know, but he utilised a Sunday on which to ride home. Arriving at the Wrightshouses, in the vicinity of Edinburgh, where his children were then staying, he found awaiting him a letter from Lilburne enclosing another from Cromwell. This could not have been an answer to the one he had just sent, which was still on its way to London. The letter he now received contained a peremptory summons from the general to be in London on 4th of July following. It was probably the second week in May when he got it. The summons was, as Hope puts it, 'to the effect therein contained.' There is no doubt what this was: it was a summons to the Little (or Barebones) Parliament, for which Hope was to be one of the nominees of Cromwell who were supposed to represent Scotland in it. It consisted of a hundred and forty persons, such as Cromwell thought he could manage, and was to assemble on the day mentioned, the 4th of July. Hope resigned himself to the circumstances, and the Diary gives no indication whether he did it willingly or unwillingly. Just before his departure, he had the misfortune to lose his sister Lady Cardross, who died rather suddenly, having taken 'a kinke of a cough after supper and went away with it.'

After an interview with Lilburne at Dalkeith, Hope, on the 22nd June, caught a coach at Haddington and proceeded south. He had for company one of his fellow-members, John Swinton, going to London on the same errand as himself, his servant: his own nephew, a son of Lord Craighall, in all probability the eldest son who was to become the third baronet within the next year in succession to his father, and who was now, as a young man of twenty, going on his travels abroad; and Sir James's 'servitor' or clerk, Peter Barbour. The dates in the Diary are not always quite clear, but it would seem that he left Edinburgh on the 22nd June and arrived in London on the 3rd July, having ridden post the last fifty-eight miles in one day in order not to be late. The next morning he and Swinton went to Whitehall, where they met the rest of their fellow-members to the number of about a hundred and forty. They were all given chairs and sat round a long table. To them entered Cromwell and his suite of officers, and took up his position on the embrasure of a window opposite the centre of the table, 'leaning on the back of a chair' Hope is careful to tell us. He then delivered a speech 'of an houre,' though probably longer,[1] and presented to them their commission as a Parliament and also one nominating fourteen persons as a Council of State. This done, Cromwell and his officers withdrew, and his audience, after some discourse, adjourned till the next day, 'with resolution to set the day apart to seek the Lord.' It was proposed to have the assistance of a minister to help them in their prayers and meditations, but the great majority of members thought themselves quite as fit as any minister to conduct the devotions of their brethren, and the proposal was 'cryed doune.'

Hope does not appear to have taken a prominent part in the business of Parliament. His name occurs only on two committees, both in connection with Law.

Except for the recital of some of his dreams, there is no entry in Hope's Diary from the 4th of July to the 10th of November. It would have been interesting to hear, instead of these, his remarks upon the proceedings in 'the Little Daft Parliament,' as Row calls it.[2] On the last-mentioned date it is not any political incident that is mentioned but one of family interest. His son Thomas, the third of that name in his family, shared the ill-luck which befell his brothers, and died. It is evident, therefore, that by this time his family had joined Hope in London. Poor little Thomas's ailment was of the same nature as that of his brother Robert, and as in his case a *post mortem* examination was made. The cause of death was quite clear (I quote from the medical authority previously mentioned): 'he had calculi in the kidneys with blocking of right ureter. The left kidney had previously been affected with partial blocking of ureter; leading

---

[1] The speech itself is given at length in Carlyle's *Cromwell's Letters and Speeches*, vol. ii. p. 337.
[2] *Life of Robert Blair*, p. 311.

to hydronephrosis, *i.e.* distention of kidney with retained urine, destruction of organ and obliteration of ureter. The child then depended only on the right kidney, the ureter of which became suddenly completely blocked with entire suppression of urine and uræmia.' He was buried in St. Margaret's, Westminster, two yards to the right of the pulpit.

And now we come to the end of the Barebones Parliament. On 10th December the Diarist notes that all the week had been spent in discussing a Report from the Tithes Committee. Carlyle's account of this Report agrees with Hope's, and is described in his characteristic style. The Report, he says, recommended 'that ministers of an incompetent Simoniacal, loose, or otherwise scandalous nature, plainly unfit to preach any Gospel to immortal creatures, should have a Travelling Commission of chosen Puritan Persons appointed, to travel into all Counties, and straightway suspect them and eject them and clear Christ's Church of them.' The Report was keenly debated, and Hope gives some of the objections to it. On Saturday, 10th December, the matter was put to the vote, approve or not approve. Those for approval went out of the House to the number of fifty-four, while the dissentients sat still to the number of fifty-two, which included all the Scots members save one. Cromwell was indignant at the Report having been thus treated, and the members of the minority, having met early on Monday morning before the usual hour of sitting and in the absence of the other side, passed a resolution, after five speeches had been made, that they should resign their powers into Cromwell's hands. This resolution, however, was not passed without some dissent, two members at least openly protesting against it. But the majority of those assembled were convinced of their incompetency to carry on any longer, rose as one man, and made for the door: 'old

Speaker Rouse' came out of the chair and went with them, and the Sergeant-at-Arms carried off the mace. A few members, however, to the number of between twenty and thirty, remained behind and called on the Speaker to come back to the chair, and to the Sergeant to bring back the mace. No notice was taken of them, and they then closed the door and were about to pray for guidance in their difficulties. But in those days Parliamentary events were treated with less ceremony than they are at present. While they were considering the question of prayer, the door opened and entered to them stout Colonel Goffe, a devoted creature of Cromwell and one who would stand no nonsense. The name of the officer who accompanied him is left blank in the Diary, but it was Colonel White, who had been with Goffe, as major, at the battle of Dunbar. The historic scene of the dissolution of this somewhat preposterous Parliament, or remnant of a Parliament, is described so graphically that Hope must have been one of those who did not withdraw with the Speaker, but remained in the House.

Goffe said to them : ' Gentlemen, there is no house here [which was quite true, as there were neither Speaker, mace, nor quorum], be pleased to remove.' It was explained to him that the members were about to seek direction in prayer ; but Goffe would have none of it. ' You may go,' he said, ' to any other place, but we must have this room cleared.' They then attempted to argue the matter, whether he had authority for his procedure or if he was acting at his own instance. When he said he only was responsible, one of the members plucked up sufficient courage to tell him that they did not think it expedient to remove yet. No answer was given to this note of defiance : Goffe turned on his heel, and strode to the door. To a hasty petition by Hope himself and Alexander Jaffray, another of the Scots members, that he would at all events allow them to close with prayer, the Colonel, by this time at the door, answered 'By no means in this room,' and made a sign whereupon a clash of arms and tramp of feet were heard and twelve musketeers filed into the room. The company saw the game was up and 'removed peaceablie.'

All this historic scene Hope saw himself, and he adds from hearsay that the majority who had gone out first went to the Horse Chamber at Whitehall, and there subscribed a paper resigning their powers. The manner of signing is heard of from other sources: how they did not wait to subscribe the document one after the other, and how each man wrote a name on a slip of paper, which was wafered on to the deed of resignation and so presented to Cromwell.

On Friday the 16th December Cromwell assumed the dignity of Lord Protector of the Commonwealth, and was installed in the Court of Chancery in Westminster Hall, thereafter being sworn in by the judges and conducted back to Whitehall in a State procession, the Lord Mayor carrying the sword before him, and all going bareheaded, the Protector himself only being covered. All this, however, Hope, for some reason or another, did not himself see, though he records it in the Diary.

Hope must have returned to Edinburgh shortly after these events. The last entry in the Diary records the death of his brother Lord Craighall on 27th April 1654. He seems to have faded away more from general exhaustion than anything else: at least no specific disease was diagnosed and Sir James, to his disappointment, perhaps, did not get the opportunity to have a *post mortem* examination. He was only fifty at the time of his death.

It is, of course, impossible to say why this journal was not continued. The little book in which it is written is only half full and there is plenty of room for a continuation. Hope survived his brother more than seven years, and lived till after the Restoration, on which it would have been interesting to have his comments. He died when he was forty-seven : the Hopes were not a long-lived race.

The Diary is printed exactly as it is in the manuscript. It has evidently been hastily compiled at odd moments of leisure, and its style and composition leave much to be desired. The punctuation has been revised, and the use of capital letters somewhat modified.

I have to acknowledge with grateful thanks the kind assistance given me by my colleague in the Register House, Mr. R. K. Hannay, who has been always helpful. Professor Firth of Oxford and Dr. W. A. Craigie of the *Oxford English Dictionary* have also been good to me, and I have obtained considerable information from Mr. H. A. Glass's book on the Barebones (or more correctly the Barbone) Parliament.

J. BALFOUR PAUL.

Christmas, 1918.

THE MEMORIALL OF SIR JAMES HOPE

[*Inside front Cover of Volume.*]

Sr Tho.	Octr 1. 1646
Ld. Hopton .	Novr 24, 1661
Jo. Hope	May 5, 1682

[*Fly-sheet of front Cover.*]

Sr Tho. Hope of Craighall, King's Advocate, was born , dyed Oct. 1, 1646.

Sir James his son Ld. Hopetoun, born Jully 4, 1614, dyed Novr. 24. 1661.

John, his son and heir, born June 10, 1650, drownd May 5, 1682.

[*On the eight following (unnumbered) pages.*]

TABLE

1646

	MS. PAGE
An accompt of a dream on 23 Septr 1646 a litle before his Fathers death, wch was on 1 Octr 1646 . .	1
An accompt of his Fathers sickness and death; his blissing to his children, and others; particularlie on condition to his son Sr Alexander that he should fear ye Lord and adhere to ye Covenants	3

1647

Jan^{ry} 16. A discourse wth some, who were prosequoters of ye working of silver-lace, anent wch they give him some information, haveing offered him a proportional part in it	16

	MS. PAGE
Mines of Lead, copper and iron in Glenorchie's lands; also a storie of a weightie yellowish substance came out of burnt turfes there	20
Of a reddie grained whitish stone, found at Maxwellheugh near Kelso	22
Y^e Birth, Christning and buriall of a son of his named Thomas	25
Proposition anent Lead mines of Glenlyon and a wood of ye Laird of Closeburns	26
The death of his daughter Eliz. as also a litle after of his son Robt, and an accompt of his being opened .	27
My L. Cardross brought to bed of a child in ye 7. month, but it lived not; also ye L. Kerses sickness, death and buriall-place wch is hard by her husband's, etc. .	30
Aug. 2. A meeting betwixt himself and others wth one Visitella, anent getting up of Glassworks at ye panns: for ye first erecting of ye work about £. st. 200: weeklie charge £.11: weeklie income about £.17: ye great impediment would be no vent for ye glasses: of Barilia, Magnes and Saphire and other things relateing to this work	35
The same day a discourse wth Cap. Tho. Lindesay for buying of charcoall	41
Sepr and Octr 1647. Severall passages anent paying maintenance money for ye Leadworks: at last agreed by way of valuation at a certain rent, viz. £.1000 communibus annis	43
Novr. I parted from Leadhill to Ed^r . .	56

1648

Jan^{ry} 3. Y^e death of his br. Kerses 2^d son: and Jan^{ry} 17 an accident of a child killed by one of his own carts .	57

1649

1650

Jullie 5. Upon what occasion he accidentallie fell upon 11 Chap. at ye begining and 4 verse of ye 2^d of ye Chronicles	61

	MS. PAGE
Moond. 15 Jullie. haveing gone to salute ye King at Falkland, how he spoke to him particularlie and of several things .	63
An odd dream	66

1651

August 25. another dream some days before Worcester fight, wch was on ye 3 Sepr being Wednesday 1651 .	70

1652

There are severall lines blotted oute page 71 . .	71
Master Vanhocht fell sick page 72 but from page 74 to page 105 there are severall leafes torn out, whither by himself or some else in who'^{s} hands it has fallen since his death	74
Meeting anent his neice'^{s} marriage on Mr. Robt Smith: they maried Thursday 12 Aug. 1652 . . .	105
Aug 18. anent Tullialane to be sold: Sir George Monat'^{s} comeing to him: Octr 1. anent Sir Georges contract and Octr 28 mariage	107
Octr. a Dream anent a great many ships: Novr. a Dream anent Cromwell	110
Novr. another Dream anent his being saluted for one of ye Judges: Decr 29. another Dream anent his goeing to ye Gouffe.	112

1653

Jan^{ry} 12. a Dream anent sproutings of pure silver growing out of cuttings of trees: at ye same time another anent one came to him and bid him eat etc., and gave him a printed paper, etc. . . .	113
March 24. Mr. Wm Cochran'^{s} mariage	119
March 13. his d. Rachel born .	119
Aprill 13. his d. Anne'^{s} death . .	119
May 5. anent a letter from Lilburn to him	119
June 20. My L. Cardross her death .	121
June 22. his taking journey to London . .	121
Jully 4. what past at a meeting etc. at London . .	122

THE DIARY OF SIR JAMES HOPE

	MS. PAGE
Novr 10. (1653) a Dream	124
Novr 15. a Dream	125
Novr 16. his son Thomas died of ye gravel at London	128
Decr 10. what passed at a meeting etc. . .	129
Decr 10. what passed etc.	132
Friday Decr 16. Cromwell declared protector	136

1654

Aprill 27 his br. Craighalls death . . .	137

[*On page opposite to Page* 1 *of the* '*Memoriall.*']

This book of my Fathers memorials delivered to me by my cosin Archibald Hope at Edinburgh ye 24 Novr 1670, wch is ye very day of ye month my D. Father died on, viz. at Granton, anno 1661, and is buried at Cramond in my uncles Isle.

Jo. HOPE.

[MEMORIALL, ANNO 1646]

Wednesday. I dreamed y^t comeing in to ane house I *Sept. 23.* found all y^twer in y^t house mourning, and when I asked for what, they told me y^t my father was dead and shewed me his Corps wch I could not be persuaded of, bot lookeing about me I apperceaved about ane inche long of ane small wax candle lyeing besyde the corps; and y^t I said [*page 2.*] that it was throw evill usage y^t he had dyed for there was lying by him ye candle wch he should have burnt, bot y^t they had putt it out; wch I would needs goe to the fyre and light againe bot they thoght it impossible and leugh at me yett (thogh w^t difficultie) I did it, and wee thoght it burnt more cleirlie yⁿ of before; bot while wee expected y^t it should have burnt out the wholle litle wax candle, I thoght it died out in my hand upon a suddaine so I awoke.

Saturday. May father haveing beene all y^t day well as *Sept. 26.* he used to be; at night he tooke a drusinesse and havi- [*page 3.*] nesse w^t which he went to bed; and about midnight tooke a paine in his backe, wch tormented him sore, so y^t he

Sept. 27.

[*page 4.*]

[*page 5.*]

could not rest ; whereof wee did know nothing untill y^t the nixt morneing being Soneday wee came up to goe to church w^t him according to our coustome bot found y^t he was lyeing, and my mother said y^t shee thoght he was fallen upon a litle rest, so wee went to Church fearing nothing, bot w^n wee returned wee found him fallen in a kynd of Lethargie, so y^t he could nather move nor speake bot only discontinuat words w^t difficultie ; presentlie wee sent for doctors Kinked [1] and Purvis,[2] who caused give him a cleister [3] and about 4 a clocke apply ventoses [4] by James Browne chyrurgian, whereby hee was much restored ; so y^t about 10 a clocke he called first for my Lord Craighalls sone Thomas,[5] and gave him his blessing, then to my brother Craighall [6] himselfe and to his Lady [7] and ye rest of his Children who wer at Grantoune nameing them orderlie by y^{re} names ; [8] then called up^n my wyfe [9] and me ; and beginning to give us his blissing he tooke

---

[1] Alexander Kincaid, doctor of medicine, Edinburgh ; died 1649 ; married Marion Mawer.

[2] Henry Purves, surgeon, Edinburgh, married Margaret Thomson, 12 October 1631.

[3] Cleister=clyster, an injection *per rectum*.

[4] Ventoses=cupping glasses.

[5] Thomas (afterwards Sir Thomas) Hope, eldest son of Sir John Hope of Craighall ; born 11 February 1633 ; married Elizabeth, daughter of Sir John Aytoun of that Ilk ; died before 26 March 1663.

[6] Sir John Hope of Craighall, second baronet, eldest son of Sir Thomas Hope, admitted an Ordinary Lord of Session 27 July 1633 ; one of Cromwell's Committee of Justice, May 1552, and President thereof ; died at Edinburgh 27 April 1654.

[7] 'His Lady.' This was his second wife, whose existence has hitherto been unknown to genealogists ; but both the preliminary arrangements and the marriage itself are chronicled by Sir Thomas Hope in his Diary. She was Rachel Spier or Spiers, widow of Sir James Skene, second baronet, of Curriehill. The marriage with Hope took place 7 December 1643.

[8] Sir John had only one other son, Sir Archibald Hope of Rankeillour, who was baptized 9 September 1639. He was a Lord of Session, 1689 ; married Margaret Aytoun, a sister of his brother's wife, and died 1706. He was ancestor of the Hopes of Pinkie. Sir John had at least six daughters, Elizabeth, Margaret, Mary, Agnes, Anna, Bathia, Helen, and another Agnes.

[9] Anna, only daughter and heiress of Robert Foulis of Leadhills, a wealthy goldsmith in Edinburgh, and grandson of James Foulis of Colinton. She married Hope 14 January 1638, and died in 1656. It was through this marriage that the valuable property of Leadhills came into the Hopetoun family.

him selfe, and upon my head he gave it first to my sister Kerse [1] and her children who for ye tyme wer all in ye Kerse; Therefter he gave his blissing upon my head, also [*page 6.*] to my brother Sr Alex^r,[2] who for ye tyme was at Newcastle attending his Majies service the tenor of y^ls blissing because it was speciallie recomended by him to me to wrytte it to my brother, I have sett doune (so neere as my memorie could serve me to remember it) in a paper apart; only y^ls much it was conditionall y^t he should feare ye Lord and adheare to ye 1st and second Covenant. Then he gave his blessing to my sister Cambuskenneth [3] [*page 7.*] and her houseband who was at London and her sone Charles,[4] then to my sister Cardross [5] and my Lord. Then to my mother [6] to whom he made ane apologie y^t he did not begin at her; then to Eliz.[7] my brother Craighalls doughter, then to my Couzine Harie Hope [8] and his wyfe of whom he tooke promise y^t when it pleased God to blesse him, he would give some consideratione to

---

[1] Sir Thomas Hope of Kerse and Wester Granton, second son of Sir Thomas; born 1606; knighted 1633; Lord Justice-General 1641; died *vitâ patris* 1643. He married, before 30 December 1630, Helen, third daughter and co-heiress of Adam Rae of Pitsindie. They had a son, Sir Thomas, born 1637; created a baronet 1672, and died the following year, and at least two daughters, Elizabeth and Louisa, of whom hereafter.

[2] Sir Alexander Hope of Granton; born 1611; became Cup-Bearer to Charles I.; married, 1642, Anna Bell, and died *s.p.* 13 February 1680.

[3] Mary Hope, baptized 13 June 1620; married, 5 February 1639, to Charles Erskine of Bandeath, son of John, Earl of Mar. He is generally known as Sir Charles Erskine of Cambuskenneth, having succeeded his brother Alexander as commendator of the temporalities of that abbey in 1640.

[4] Charles was the third son of his parents; born 1643; created a baronet 30 April 1666; married about 1670 Christian, daughter of Sir James Dundas of Arniston, and died 4 June 1690.

[5] Anne Hope, the youngest daughter of Sir Thomas, was baptized 9 April 1625; married, in 1645, David Erskine, Lord Cardross, who had succeeded his grandfather, John, seventh Earl of Mar, in that title. Her sister Mary had, as above mentioned, married her husband's uncle.

[6] Sir James's mother was Elizabeth, daughter of John Bennet of Wallyford; she married Sir Thomas Hope in or before 1602.

[7] Elizabeth would appear not to have been at Granton with the rest of her sisters.

[8] Henry Hope, eldest son of Henry Hope, Sir Thomas's eldest brother, by his wife Jacqueline Tott.

Margarett Seatoune d. Gourlay's relict [1] anent some debt wch had been owne to them by harie's brother James.[2] Thereefter to Mr. Th. Veich [3] to whom he gave a varie great testimonie and comendatione and recomended him to us to befreind him and contribut our helpe to his furtherance and advancement in his calling. Thereafter he gave his blessing also or rather ane exhortatione to his servit^rs Mr. George Norvell [4] Martine Crawfurd [5] and Johne M'gachen; All y^is he did in a most eloquent and poureful straine above my expressione. From y^t tyme fourth he bettered by degrees untill tueseday at 10 a clocke, at wch tyme he was so well come to himselfe, y^t he punctuallie dicted ansuers to lettres of great concernment, w^h he did w^t y^t acuitie so y^t wee conceaved good hopes of him; bot efter y^t his fiever did incresse upon him untill Wednesday y^t his paine came to him againe, and his judgement was not so posed and setled; bot he had in all y^is tyme his owne dilucide intervalles in ye wch he did most comfortablie expresse himselfe in ane eloquent and most elevat straine. Efter Wednseday at night he spoke litle, only Thurseday in ye morneing he did take up himselfe the 23 psalme, and w^t a litle helpe of my brother Craighall for ye lettre he sung it out to ye end and closed w^t a litle prayer, efter ye w^ch, except some ejaculatorie words, he spoke almost nothing; and about 12 a clocke he lost his speech altogether; and efter y^t sensiblie

---

[1] Perhaps the relict of David Gourlay, the son of a burgess of Edinburgh who married a daughter of Gilbert Primrose, surgeon, Edinburgh, by his wife Alison, daughter of John Graham of Claverhouse and Margaret Beaton, a sister of the Cardinal.

[2] James Hope, writer, Edinburgh, the progenitor of the Hopes of Amsterdam.

[3] Sir Thomas in his Diary mentions a nephew, Thomas Veitch, the son of a sister; he died at Dantzig 17 December 1644. Sir Thomas had a godson of the name, perhaps a son of the other Thomas Veitch, who graduated at Edinburgh University 9 April 1645.

[4] George Norvell was with Sir Thomas as a clerk at least as early as 1634, and is frequently mentioned in his Diary. He is probably identical with that George Norvell of Boghall who was admitted advocate 2 June 1647; married Margaret Elphinstone, and died in December 1672.

[5] The testament of Martin Crawford, writer, Edinburgh, was confirmed 23 December 1656.

decayed untill betuixt 9 and 10 a clocke at night y{t} he dyed peaceablie. The same night my brother Craighall and I searched for his lettre will to see if y{r} was any order for his buriell, wee found nothing bot y{t} it should bee w{t}out any kynd of ceremonie, and y{t} he desyreed to be layed in such a place as y{t} his bonnes might not be exhumat whereupon presentlie wee gave ordor for his buriell upon Teuseday y{e} 6 of Oct{r}.

Teuseday in y{e} efternoone my father was buried in y{e} Grayfriers besyde ye wester dyke yreof betuixt it and ye stonne y{t} stands at D. M. M.[1] y{e} Lady Craighalls head. My brother Kerse lyes close by his right hand, bot not so deepe by the thickenesse of my fathers wholle chest, for so deepe caused I his grave to be digged expreslie to satisfie (so much as in us lay) his lettre will. Freidday wee looked his papers, and found my mothers provisione to be to y{e} house in Ed{r} and to Grantoune and y{e} house y{r}of, and the maines of Craighall and y{e} house y{re}of; bot shee is ordeined to quitte one of y{e} tuo at her owne optione, and his aires ordeined to make up w{t} y{e} other w{ch} shee keepes y{e} summe of 2500{mks} by ycire, y{is} is besydes y{e} tenement in Ed{r}. My brother in the test{t} is left sole exequutor and universall legatar; and in his test{t} he has some wonderfull profeticall expressions concerning y{e} tymes whereof I ame promised a double.

[Oct. 6. [Page 12.]
Oct. 7.
[Page 13.]

[*Page 14 is blank in the manuscript.*]

Saturday. This efternoone came to me Patricke Crightoune[2] and Johne Flint[3] partiners and prosquutters for y{e} present of ye working of Silver lace w{t}in y{is} kingdome; and efter regraite how they wer hardlie used by y{e} Gold smithes, who would nather furnish y{m} silver for y{r} worke, nor suffer y{m} to molt doune and refyne for y{m}selfes,

[Page 15.]
1647.
Jan{le} 16.

---

[1] Dame Margaret Murray.

[2] There were several Patrick Crichtons living in Edinburgh at this time. This may have been the Patrick Crichton, merchant, whose testament was confirmed 11 March 1679.

[3] John Flint, son of John Flint in Merchiestoun, was apprenticed to Ronald Robieson, wobster, 24 October 1610. The testament of John Flint, merchant, burgess of Edinburgh, was confirmed 14 September 1655.

pretending it to be ane privilege of ye Gold smith trade, desyred me yett further to mediat betuixt y^m (for I had been dealling betuixt them of before) and I broght y^m at last to be content either y^t ye Gold smithes should have ane locke and kye of y^r melting and refyneing chambre not to be made use of bot at y^e sight of one of ye trade of y^e Gold smithes, or vtherwyse the Goldsymthes to undertake to furnish them Ingottes of utter fyne silver casten and forged reddie for y^e draught; and they to pay for y^e ℥ $y^r$of so prepared 5/9^d or 5/10^d sterling as I could aggrie y^m; and y^e Gold smithes to be obleiged to furnish y^m so betuixt 4 and 12 lb. weight a month; whereunto nather syde should be tyed any longer y^n ye dollers runne at y^e rate of 58/ and y^e realls at 56/ y^e peice. Therefter they made a motione to me y^t if I would imbrace it, they would willinglie lett me have a propor°nall part of y^e worke. And for my informatione of y^e estaite $y^r$of, they told me y^t y^{re} stocke for y^e present would be about 500 lb. sterling $w^{re}$of 600^{mk} Mr. Crightounes and the rest Mr. Flints. That they reckoned y^t all charges payed selling ye ℥ of made work at 4 lb. and 4 lb. 4/ they would and might have a twelvepense st. of benefite upon everie ℥; that they would entertaine some 20 workfolkes, and make some 50 ℥ of lace a weeke that to 5 ℥ of silver y^{re} will goe ordinarlie in y^r worke about 3¼ or 3¾ ℥ of silke that to ye gildeing of ye Gold worke they will bestow ordenarlie ane ½ ℥ of gold to 36 ℥ of silver, wch is done thus, they cast ye silver in to ane Ingot, forges it round, smoothes it, beattes the Gold ass thinne as may be, and fittes it round about the ingot, and puttes it to ye fyre, where it festnes, y^refter hammers it and douces[1] it, and it will draw so as ye silver does and still keepe ye gilt.

They proponed y^t seing they wer to be in attendance and trouble about y^e worke, they behooved to have a consideratione above y^r proportionall p^t of y^e stocke, at least so long as y^e one does undergoe y^e charge of a greive and y^e uther of a clerke for y^e wch they demanded each

---

[1] Douces = strikes.

of y^m ane shilling sterling a day ; or uther wyse y^e wholle stocke being 700^lb, each of y^m to pay in 200 ; and I to pay 300^lb ; and all three to share a lyke benefite ; wch they remitted to my optione and consideratione. And I tooke all to be advysed upon.

Tewseday. In discourse w^t ye Laird of Glenorchie [1] he [Jan^ie 19.] told me that y^r wer severall mynes in his boundes both of lead, copper and yron and y^t he has abundance of wood he told me particularlie that in a mure called [*page 21.*] [*blank*] ye yron oare is found w^tin halfe a foote of the turfe wch will wall [2] togither lyke oscment [3] yron ; Then he told me a storie y^t in his owne house of Glen Lyon he, one winter, being skarce of elding,[4] a boy of the house broght in some old turfes from ane coatchouse, and laying y^m or ane harth fyer wch had ane wind hole under it (as is the custome of the north) the fyer being great the turfe did sueett out of it an yallowish substance [*page 22.*] weghtie as any mettall bot brickle wch he caried in to Ed^r w^t him, and shewed it to ye Goldsmithes and ye officers of the Mint bot none of them could tell him what it was nather could they all melt it againe.

I receaved ane pound weight or y^rby of a reedic grained [Jan^ie 25.] whyttish stonne from one Johne Scotte marchand holding booth on ye south syde of the heigh streit of Ed^r, who said he had caused bring in some of it to whytte y^rw^t [*page 23.*] his plaisterred housses ; he said it is to be found in Maxwellheugh overforgainst the boatt of Kelso where y^re is ane large vaine of it. It is a kynde of gypsum called comonlie plaister and in Holland by the drogesters Spade ; and I take it to be y^t kynd of Gypse wch is called Lapis

---

[1] The Laird of Glenurchy. Sir Robert Campbell, second son of Sir Duncan of Glenurchy, succeeded his elder brother Sir Colin in 1640. He was now seventy-two years old : for a large part of his life he was in financial difficulties, and from what is related in the Diary was probably a sanguine speculator. He married in 1605 Isabel, daughter of Lachlan Mackintosh of Dunnachton, and died in 1657.

[2] Wall=amalgamate.

[3] Osement (osmund) iron : a superior quality of iron formerly imported from the Baltic regions in very small bars or rods.

[4] Elding=fuel.

Arabicus for it represents broken Ivorie. When I was of late in Fyfe haveing of before beene informed y^t y^r was of this spade to be found in the Craiges neire Brunt-Island I went and searched and in y^e heigh craige neire y^e end of Brunt Island sands towards Kinghorne wch is a rotten weather beatten Craige, I found severall litle vaines of a whytteish litle stone, of about ane skarce inche thicke at most, somewhat resembling the trew spade in ye graine; bot harder a great deall, and if it be of y^t kynde, it is a bastard sort of it. It is reedie and brakes bricle as does Lapis Hematitis proprie Schistos dictus.

[page 24.]

Feb^r 3.
[page 25.]

Wednesday. About a quarter before 10 a clocke at night my wyfe was broght to bed of her sixth chylde being a sone; who (because he was wake and as wee apprehended borne 6 or 7 weekes before ye ordinrie tyme thogh he had nailles and some haire), was baptized ye nixt morning in ye west called Mr. R^t douglas's churche [1] be one [blank] Annane [2] minister in [blank]. And efter my father was named Thomas; witnesse Cardros, Craighall his sone and Humbies sone.[3]

Feb^{re} 5.
[page 26.]

Freidday. My sone Thomas dyed about ¼ houre efter one in ye day.

Feb^{re} 6.

Saturday this day at tuo a clocke efternoone he was buried betuixt my father's head and ye wall, one the west syde of ye Grayfreeres yaird.

---

[1] This was the west portion of St. Giles's church nearest the Tolbooth, from which it took its name. Mr. Robert Douglas was minister from 1641 to 1649, when he was translated to the High Kirk.

[2] Annane: this cannot have been the well-known dean of that name as he was only a boy at the time, nor can it have been his father, the whilom minister of Ayr, who was now the rector of an English parish. It may perhaps have been that John Annand who graduated at St. Andrews in 1618, and was minister of the second charge at Inverness 1624: minister at Kinore 1627 to 1640, when he came back to his former charge at Inverness. He was presented to the first charge in 1645, and to one of the charges in Edinburgh in July 1647, but this apparently was not carried out, as he died minister of Inverness in 1660. He may have been in Edinburgh in connection with his proposed presentation in February 1647.

[3] Humbie's son: probably Thomas Hepburn, eldest son of Sir Adam Hepburn of Humbie, one of the senators of the College of Justice.

This day young Glenorchie [1] proponed to me the prosequutteing of y{e} Lead mynes of Glenlyon; w{ch} I said I should advyse upon, if wee should have peace. This day also Mr. R. Blacke [2] minister at Closeburne proponed to me the buying of some wood, belonging to the Laird [*page 27.*] of Closeburnes [3] y{re}, w{ch} I said I could not doe unlesse he would obleige himself y{t} it should be caried at such a rate as he and I could aggrie upon. He desyred me howsoever to think upon it, and he would come to me againe about it, more particularlie instructed; he said y{t} it is almost all oaken timbber, and y{t} I would gett a greatt bargane of it.

Saturday. This day about ii houres in y{e} forenoone my douchter Eliz. dyed. Feb{r} 13.

Suneday. In y{e} efternoone my doughter Eliz.[4] was buried. Feb{r} 14. [*page 28.*]

Thurseday. About 2 a clocke in y{e} efternoone my sone Rob{t} [5] dyed, and I caused open him about 4 a clocke; present D{rs} Purves [6] and Cunigahame, and Sam. Hunter Apothecarie,[7] James Broune, Chirurgean, my selfe and others. There was a great disproportione in his noble parts, ane hudge bigge livver, ane small splen, bot both of them of a reasonable good substance; his kidneyes bigge also bot varie good, only he had a numbre of stonnes in both of them, parte in cute [8] parte in y{e} concavities and some of them prettie bigge. There was one or tuo also [*page 29.*] March 25.

---

[1] Young Glenurchy: Sir John Campbell, son of Sir Robert above mentioned; born 1606; married, first, Mary, daughter of William (Graham), Earl of Airth and Menteith; second, Elizabeth, daughter of Patrick Dow More Campbell of Edenchip; and third, Christian, daughter of Robert Mushet of Craighead. He died in June 1686.

[2] William Black, graduated at St. Andrews in 1638; was appointed assistant and successor in the parish of Closeburn in 1647.

[3] The Laird of Closeburn, Robert Kirkpatrick, third but eldest surviving son of Thomas Kirkpatrick and his wife Agnes Charteris. He married Grizel, daughter of Sir William Baillie of Lamington; died about 1664.

[4] Elizabeth, born 5 September 1642.   [5] Robert, born 6 February 1645.

[6] Dr. Purves. See note 2, p. 130.

[7] Sam. Hunter, apothecarie, married Helen Johnston, 28 February 1633.

[8] Parte in cute: this may refer to the outer part of kidney (*cutes*=skin) in contrast to the inner part, *cavitas*.

in ye mouth of his ureters, his lungs wer a litle consumed and growen to his right syde w^t leancing upon his nurse in her armes, his hart had much water in pericardio, and some varie blacke mater lyke lappered [1] blood in y^e right concavitie. Wee opened also his head, bot wee found nothing a misse y^{re}, only y^r was a litle water in ye backe croune of his head.

He was buried besyde my father on ye morrow y^{r}efter.

Apr. 12.
[*page 30.*]

Monday. About [*blank*] a clocke in ye morneing my sister Cardros was broght to bed of a daughter some tuo mounthes before her full tyme; the chyld lived bot some [*blank*] houres and was buried ye same day about tuo a clocke in ye efternoone.

June 11.

Freidday. At night my sister Kerse thogh shee had beene somewhat unwell tuo dayes before, yett haveing appointed a treist [2] at Ed^r anent ye bussnesse of Airth shee came to toune; and tooke bed y^t same night; shee presentlie apprehended death thogh wee did not. Her seecknesse incressed upon her, her Physiciane Dr. Purves, finding it proceede from ye interruptione of her courses and motioned y^r by fittes of ye mother, wch did stricke her in ye head whereby shee reaved and was distempered. Efter advyce and approbatione of Dr. Sibbett caused apply ventoses to her thighes neere her birth this was done on ye Thurseday at night whereby shee recovered for y^t night some more sense and spirits bot y^r efter grew worse againe whereupon upon Saterday at night being in a senselesse lithargicklyke dispositione the D^r caused apply Loch leaches to her hemerhode vaines; whereby shee was also that night a litle broght to sense and speache againe; bot ye nixt day shee fell waker and so decayed still untill 11 of clocke at night being Soneday y^t shee dyed. At ye begining of her seekenesse shee apprehended death and did leave her doughter Eliz. to my mother, Anna to my sister Cardrosse, Marie to my sister Cambuskenneth, her sone Johne to my brother Craighall, and Alex^r to me, for my brother Sr Alex^r all ye rest being y^r Godbairns.

[*page 31.*]

[*page 32.*]
June 19.

June 20.

[*page 33.*]

---

[1] Lappered = coagulated.   [2] Treist = tryst, appointment.

She intreated me to make the thousand merkes left be my brother to y^e poore or for a burserie to y^e college of K. J.[1] to make it out a thousand pounds, wch I promised to doe.

In her seecknesse shee had greatt fittes of y^e mother and untill her dyeing houre continuall trembling and shakeings specially of her hands and startings and panting of her hart.

Teuseday. At 2 a clocke in ye eftornoone my sister Kerse was buried closse by ye right hand of her houseband, who lyes at ye right hand of my father, who lyes closse by the second tree under G. Foulis's Tombe upon ye west syde of Grayfriere yaird. And because her sone Thomas had been layed in y^t place where shee now lyes, I caused rease his chist wch was nowyse consumed, and digge a place for it just under her so farre doune as y^t shee might lye at ye ordinarie deepnesse abone him. *June 22.* [page 34.]

Moneday. Ther was a meetteing w^t ye Generall of ye Artillerie Sr Alex^r Hamiltoune,[2] Sr Jame Balfoure, Ld. Lyon,[3] Johne Mille, Mr. Maissone and my selfe w^t Christopher Visitella[4] Glasse maker anent ye setting up againe by us foure of the Glasse workes at the pannes. *Aug. 2.* [page 35.]

---

[1] The College of King James VI., now the University of Edinburgh. The Hopes were great benefactors to the College of Edinburgh. Sir Thomas of Craighall had in 1625 built two 'chambers' or studies for the students, under the provision that his own children and descendants should always have a preferable claim to them.—Grant's *History of the University of Edinburgh*, vol. ii. p. 186.

[2] Sir Alexander Hamilton, fifth son of Thomas Hamilton, a senator of the College of Justice, under the title of Lord Priestfield, and brother of the first Earl of Haddington. Alexander served under Gustavus Adolphus, was an enthusiastic Covenanter, and a popular and able general of artillery. He constructed some light guns of tin and leather, bound round with ropes, which were called 'dear Sandy's stoups.' He married, first, the eldest daughter of Thomas Dalzell of Binns; second, a lady of the name of Cochrane; and, third, Elizabeth, daughter of Sir David Crichton of Lugton. He died 26 November 1649.

[3] Sir James Balfour of Denmylne, baronet, Lord Lyon King of Arms, son of Sir Michael Balfour of Denmylne; born 1600; made Lyon 1630; created a baronet 1633; deprived of office by Cromwell, 1654; author of *Annals of the History of Scotland*, and other works on antiquarian and heraldic subjects. Died 1657.

[4] Probably a brother or other relative of Isaac Visitella, a painter, who lived in Edinburgh at this period. They may have originally come from Venice, which would account for Christopher being interested in glass making.

He gave up his accompt for erecting and entertaineing of a worke for tuo workemen and tuo serviteurs thus—

[page 36.] The dressing of the workehouses, building of ye fornaces, ye makeing of brickes for y^t effect and pottes £80 stlg. that is for the first erecting of ye worke.

Foure tunne of 2000 wg^t of Barilia [1] or soda at £25 st. a tunne is £100 sex hundreth weight of Magnes at 15/ st. p^r 1 [cwt] is £4 10/.

Ane hundreth weight of saphire [2] £2, 10/ st.

Tuo dozen of Hollow yrons or blowers £3 st.

For some moulds for makeing of Glasses £5 st.

All wch will be w^{t}in or about £200 sterling for ye first erecting of the worke.

[page 37.] That ye aforesd̃s Barilia being mixed w^t about tuo part sand, they will use of y^t compositione about 400 weight a weeke whereof tuo fitters w^t y^r tuo serviteurs wil be able to make 1800 glasses a weeke either beare or wyne or halfe of ye one and halfe of the uther. That the weekelie charges for tuo workemen wil be . £4 0 0

There tuo servit^{rs}	.	.	.	.	£1	10	0
The Consor	.	.	.	.	£0	15	0
The Materi	.	.	.	.	£3	0	0
Coalles 3 Cartfull	.	.	.	.	£0	10	0
Three labourers	.	.	.	.	£0	15	0
packeing and yrons mending	.	.	.	£0	10	0

Sum̃e weekelie Ch	.	.	.	.	£11	0	0
The 900 wyne Glasses at 2/ p. dozen is	.	.	£7	10	0
The 900 beare at 2/6^d	.	.	.	.	£9	7	6

Sum̃a weekalie proceed . . £16 17 6

[page 38.] That he could be able to boylle up his mater to als great puritie as ye Venice glasses, bot that then of three hundreth of Barilia he will have bot 100 or at most 105 of y^t mater

---

[1] Barilia—an impure carbonate of soda made from certain plants growing in salt marshes or other places near the sea: most of it at that date came from Spain. As soda can now be got from common salt the use of barilia is given up. [2] Saphire—perhaps some blue colouring matter (cf. p. 141).

for Glasses. That this Barilia is nothing els bot y^t salt wch is called Soda, called barilia because it comes from such a Toune, or because it comes in barrilles. That it differs from Pott Ashes or cineres clavellati, that it is made of a certaine herbe, these of any wood or herbe almost; that w^{t}out a lixive [1] and these w^t one.

That he hes seene a glasse made wch would hold 40 [page 39.] English Gallouns.

That window glasses and drinking glasses can not be made in one fornace because those requyre a great deall stronger heatt then these; That the fornace for those is y^{r}for long vauted; and for these round bot however y^t he could not make window glasse, nather possiblie could find workemen who have skill of both, so wee needed not thinke of makeing both sort glasses in one fornace [page 40.] wch was my ouvertur to him because wee wer informed that ye greatest impediment in ye worke would be the vent [2] of ye glasses in y^t they would make more in one weeke then could possiblie be vented in a mounth, and in one yeere then in three, wch wee wer informed of be Johne Joussie [3] who w^t in these few yeeres had sett up these warkes at ye pannes, and as he s^d for the same reasone, was forced to quitte them with 20000^{lb} of losse. That the saphire is to give colour to the glasse lyke it selfe; and ye magnes to make ye glasse transparent and p^{r}lucide.

The same day also Cap. Th. Lyndsay[4] spoke to me anent [page 41.] charcoall, he sayed y^t by ordor from the Thesawrare he had boght in England and was a cutteing of a greatt wood for repaireing of the Kings houses here; that of the small of the wood he intended to make Charcoall

---

[1] Lixive=lye, water impregnated with alkaline salts extracted from the ashes of wood.

[2] Vent=sale.

[3] John Joussie of West Pans, merchant, Edinburgh; married, 19 September 1633, Catherine Morison; testament confirmed 17 July 1669.

[4] Captain Thomas Lindsay, a Leith skipper; appointed H.M. shipwright in Scotland 11 August 1646. Along with his son John he had a grant of giving and sealing the cockets (or customs certificates) of all goods exported from the Port of Leith.

whereof he thought he would have foure or fyve hundreth chalder; whereof everie chalder according to his aggriement w^t the coallmen should consist of 12 seckes, and everie secke to be tuo elles long and one in diameter, y^t is to conteine three elles about, for the Chalder whereof to be delyvered to me at Leith he asked first 40/ st. I offered him 20/; by degrees he came to accept of my offer bot herein wee differed, y^t he would have me to advance and ansuer mony upon his lettres, before the delyverie of the charcoall, wch he would not undertake to delyver befor the nixt spring, wch advancement I would not condiscend to, so wee parted w^{t}out any formall closure.

Sept. 17.

Freidday. The Comitté of ye shirreffdome of Clidsdaille haveing, w^{t}out citeing of me, ordored me to pay for my leadworkes maintenance mony according to fyve thousand pounds for this yeere, I went upon Wednsday last w^t my Lord Craufurd[1] to Hammiltoune to ye buriall of my Lady Marques of Hamiltoune,[2] who was buried yesterday, and this day a frequent Committé of the Shyre being mett y^{re} I gave in a petione to y^m that they would appoint some of y^{re} numbre to meette. They first pressed y^t they would take my oath wch I ansuered was ane hard measure seing no mans oath was taken w^{t}in ye shyre for y^{re} land rent, yett if they would lay it upon me, I would be content to give my oath y^r anent, if so be they would allow to me in yis yeere my superexpences in my former valuatione found and declared by y^r owne act of date ye 15 of Septr 1646, wch they absolutlie refused bot said they would have everie yeere to be valued per se w^{t}out compensatione of former depursements, whereupon they appointed 5 of y^r numbre to meette, take tryell of my Compts and report

---

[1] John Lindsay, son of Robert Lord Lindsay of the Byres and first Earl of Lindsay, succeeded his brother Ludovic as seventeenth Earl of Crawford in 1644.

[2] Anna, daughter of James (Cunningham), Earl of Glencairn, married in 1603 James, second Marquess of Hamilton. In 1639 she raised a troop of horse for the Covenanters, and rode at its head in opposition to her eldest son who was on the king's side.

to y^m upon the 5 of Octr being a meetteing appointed at Lanark for choyceing of Comissionaires for the parlt. This sub comitté mett at Lanarke upon ye 28 of yis Sept. 28. instant.

Efter reviseing of my compts, and takeing the oath of [page 46.] my servants toucheing what lead oare I had caried this yeere, they called upon my selfe and desyred me to rebait als much of everie article of my depursements as well I might, so to this purpose it behoved me to wrytte the summes of everie article over againe in ane uther columne, bot when wee came to ye article of the worke- [page 47.] mens wages extending to £6000 (because I would not rebait anything y^rof) it was forgott at first to be written doune in ye new margine, wch made me to be a benefiter, wch I would not condescend to, and so keeped us in debate be ye space of tuo houres, bot besydes that mistake they posed me what lead oare I had above ground wch I knowing myselfe be my compts to be farre superexpended [page 48.] and remembering that they had refused to allow super-expences, and y^rfor thinkeing ye more leadoare I declared to be aboveground it would be the better for me the nixt yeere, whereupon I declared that I thoght y^r was not above fyfeteine yett I should admitte y^r wer 25000 stonne ; wch togither w^t ye former omissione, and some articles of my compt wch they refused altogither to allow (as ye pryce of my worke lowmes from Holland and ensurance [page 49.] mony because I would not positivelie declare I had payed any) made me to be a benefiter by varie neere als much as y^t article omitted, for I had forecast things so before-hand y^t I might runne neere, bot could not at first con-ceave where ye errour was. whereupon they would have had me to pay according to 3000^lb wch I absolutelie refused, bot finding y^t they went varie strictlie and narrowlie about [page 50.] the tryell of my compts, I said y^t thogh I be confident if my compts be rightlie calculat I shall be found to be no benefiter this yeere, yett to be free of trouble and that both the shyre and I might be at a certaintie, I would be content to give them tuentie peices by yeere, wch they said they had no poure to accept of, bot would report it to y^e

[*page 51.*] Comitté ye 5 of Oct^r, whereupon they parted. So soone as they wer out at doores, I went to revize my compts a part and at first vew I discovered ye mistake whereupon I presentlie followed them, and did shew it to some of y^m who did acknowlege it bot could not move y^m to meette againe y^t night bot they promised to meette a litle sooner upon ye 5 of Octr and take a word of it before
[*page 52.*] the Comitté should meette, wch they did.
Oct. 5.   Thursday. The Gentlemen of ye Shyre mett at ane head shirreffe Court and did choose y^re Comissionares to ye parlt, my Ld Ley[1] and Lamingtoune.[2] The doeing whereof spent the haille day so y^t I could have no heareing that day, bot my businesse was continued untill ye nixt
Octr 28. meeting appointed to be At Hamiltoune ye 21 Octr. This
[*page 53.*] meeting did not hold, bot ane uther upon the 28 Octr where the report of my Compts being heard, and what had passed in ye tryell y^rof, thogh nothing could be justlie demanded of me for this yeere, yett they insisted upon my offer, and pressed me to more; And I being willing to setle and to be at a certaintie, I adhered still to my offer to beginne from yis tyme furth, bot they
[*page 54.*] chused to have it by way of valuatione to a certaine rent according to ye wch I should pay as ye rest of ye Shyre and y^reupon they putt it to ane thousand pounds according to ye wch I should pay *communibus annis* whither I wer a greater benefiter or a losser—whercunto I condiscended, and y^rupon presented to y^m ane act wch I had in reddinesse (foreseeing there purpose) to be past in my

---

[1] Sir James Lockhart of Lee, senator of the College of Justice, under the title of Lord Lee: a Royalist, he was imprisoned in the Tower in 1651, but reinstated in his offices at the Restoration; Lord Justice-Clerk 1671; married, first, Helen, daughter of George Fairlea of Braids; and second, Martha, daughter of Sir George Douglas of Mordington; died May 1674, aged seventy-eight.

[2] Sir William Baillie of Lamington, son of Sir William Maxwell *alias* Baillie of Lamington, born 1600. It is said that Sir William was the uncle and only guardian of Anne Foulis, daughter of Robert Foulis, and that he had attempted to defraud her of some of her Leadhills property, and that she came to Edinburgh to consult Sir James, who thereupon married her, and got a decreet against Sir William (*Lives of the Baillies*, p. 40). He married Grizel, daughter of Sir Claud Hamilton of Shawfield, and died 8 March 1668.

favours. To ye same sence they had resolved, bot it being [*page 55.*]
late, efter they had heard it red they cast it of untill y^e
nixt meetteing, bot in ye meane tyme ordeined ye clerke
to make ane note of what was condiscended unto, and y^e
Act to be past at nixt meetting, and my payment according to this valuatione to beginne from ye 10 of Oct^r
instant, whereupon I delyvered the forme of my Act unto
ye clerke, who promissed to have a care of ye passing of it. Novr 9.

Teuseday. I w^t my wyfe by Coatch parted from y^e [*page 56.*]
Leadhill for Ed^r, wee came to Englstoune brigges[1] y^t
night, and ye nixt day about 2 a clocke to Ed^r. Cornelius
Vizitelli[2] Glesse maker who had beene w^t me in the
Leadhill some 7 or 8 weekes came w^t us.

[*One-third of p. 56 left blank at the end of this last entry
in 1647.*]

Moneday. My umquhile brother Kerse's second sone, Jan^{re} 3, 1648.
and posthume, efter ten or tuelve dayes seeknesse dyed, [*page 57.*]
was opened, bot wee could remarke no considerable defect
bot y^t y^r wer severall obstructtiones and glandulles in
his mestericke vaines; he was buried on ye nixt day
y^{r}efter at his mothers feete.

Moneday. I haveing some three weekes before entered Jan^{re} 17.
tuo cartes w^t one horse a peece to ye out caricing of the
red[3] at ye backe of my house in ye Cowgate and conduced[4] one Johne Clerkesone to dryve one of the Cartes,
he drove on reasonablie well all that tyme w^t these horses [*page 58.*]
wch came immediatlie from my waggones, bot this day
one of my spare waggon horses haveing come from y^e
Kerse and given to him to putt in ye Cart, the horse being
wanton and lustie, he being a sillie wake old body could
not command him, whereupon comeing doune ye Societie
wynde and being overmaistered w^t the horse, he lett him
goe the horse finding himselfe free and y^e Cart ratleing
upon the calcay[5] behind him made doune the wind y^e [*page 59.*]

---

[1] Englstoune brigges: now Ingraston, near Dolphinton, as Mr. H. R. G. Inglis informs me.
[2] He has called him Christopher before, see p. 130, unless he may have been another member of the family.
[3] Red = rubbish.   [4] Conduced = hired.   [5] Calcay = causeway (*Fr.* chausée).

K

harder untill comeing forgainst niere the well some children being in y^e way thereabout he overrunne ane of them w^t one of y^e wheeles wch went directlie over the chyldes head and killed it. It was a last chyld belonging to a websters weiddow called [blank][1] Dicke her only chyld about 7 yeeres old. This greived me extremlie thogh I had this satisfactione, y^t ye horse had beene a peaceable drawing horse in my waggons 6 or 8 monthes before.

[*Page 60 blank in MS.*]

Freidday
[5 Julie]
[*page 61.*]

Haveing for a long tyme before this had great doubtings with my selfe, anent ye treattie [2] w^t his Majie not seing a clearenesse how y^t ye worke should be caried on y^t way; and now after a full relatione of ye treattie from some of our Comissionares and great testimonie given be y^m of ye kings douce nature and good naturall parts my mynde begineing to compose it selfe, and close with ye same, and so not to doubt bot y^t ye Ld was probablie yett to restore him to his kingdomes, whereof I had

[*page 62.*]

conceaved some doubts of before; and y^rupon debateing with my selfe what should be my cariage in relatione to a warre against England for his Majies restitutione, wch I did presage would be ye upshott and effect of our present livvees, thogh pretended for defence allanerlie. this morneing before I was privat, casting up at adventur [3] a chapter to reid, I fell upon the 4 v. and begineing of ye 11 ch. of ye 2de of ye Chron [4] wch did amuse [5] me exceddinglie; I pray ye Lord direct me, y^t as I ame zealous in dutie to man, so I be not found fighting against ye Lords decrees. This day ye approbatione of ye treattie

---

[1] Probably Bessie Pringle, widow of Harry Dick, weaver, burgess of Edinburgh, whose testament was confirmed 24 June 1674.

[2] The Treaty of Breda which made Charles II. a 'covenanted King of Scots' (*Charles II. and Scotland in* 1650, by S. R. Gardiner, Scottish History Society, p. xx).

[3] The 'Sortes Biblicae'—an adaptation of the Sortes Vergilianae of Pagan times—was frequently resorted to by doubting souls at this time.

[4] 'Thus saith the Lord, ye shall not go up, nor fight against your brethren; return every man to his house; for this thing is of me.'

[5] Amuse = bemuse, puzzle.

and his Ma͡Jies entrie to y^e exercize of his government wer solēnlee proclamed and y^e parlt rose.

This day I went over to BurntIland intending for Falkland to salute the king; wee wer 5 houres up^n y^e sea w^t a varie crosse wind, did cast 8 boords. That night w^t my brother Craighall to Craighall, upon Mooneday to Falkland where imediatlie efter dinner wee gotte a kisse of ye kings hand and my brother had discourse with him. At supper by Doct^r frazer[1] he desyred me to attend efter supper, wch I did, he called for me and gave me thankes for ye peece of Scots gold I sent to his Ma͡Jiee to Holland w^t Will. Murray[2] of ye Bed chamber; It was ye great peece of 10^dr weight wch I gott from Mr. Wilsone.

Satday, Julie 13. [page 63.]

The king being withdrawen with some companie; I [page 64.] went to supper w^t ye Ther deput to ye greene cloath. Efter supper returned to ye Privie chambre and attended ye kings comeing out of his bedchamber ane houre, when he came out he called me againe (My Lord Hoptoune) and enquyred of me some quastiones anent mynes and publicklie discoursed anent ye tinne and silver mynes in

---

[1] Dr. Fraser, son of Adam Fraser of Finzeauch; born about 1610; appointed Court Physician in Ordinary to Charles I. in 1645, and continued in the service of Charles II. in that capacity both during his exile and his visit to Scotland in 1650, and afterwards at the Restoration. He re-purchased his grandfather's estate of Dores, which had been sold, and was created a baronet, 2 August 1673, and died 1681, having married, first, Elizabeth Dowchly of Bristol, and second, Mary, daughter of Sir Ferdinando Carey and widow of Dudley Wylde of Canterbury. He was skilful in his profession, and was one of the founders of the Royal Society. He was a Fellow of the College of Physicians, 1641, and an 'Elect' thereof 1666. Notwithstanding the strictures passed on him by some contemporary writers, he seems to have been an able and faithful servant of his royal masters, and Walter Macfarlane, the antiquary, who was an intimate friend of his son, Sir Peter, styles him a 'noble fine gentleman.'

[2] William Murray, son of William Murray, parson, of Dysart, and a cadet of the Dollerie family. He was page and 'whipping boy' to Charles I., and a great favourite with that monarch. He was with Charles II. at the Hague in 1649, and was sent to Scotland with letters for Argyle. He is said both by *The Complete Peerage* and the *Scots Peerage* to have been created Earl of Dysart in 1643, but Lamont in his Diary gives the date as 1651. Bishop Burnet says he never took the title on himself, and that it was not recognised by any authority. He died before 22 May 1651.

England; and then anent ambergreise [1] whereof he told ye storie of ye great quantitie y^rof found accidentallie in a cove whither ye sea flowed on ye south coast of England; efter all y^is discourse, my brother tooke his

[*page 65.*] leive of him. And when I was takeing my leive, he expressed him selfe, y^t howbeit he had beene long out, yett now being come in, he was resolved to redeeme his tyme and to be assisting to the advanceing of ye worke of God, and withall desyred me y^t I would befreind him in parIt or committees in anything concerned his interest. My ansuer was, That however some of us might be represented to his Majie yett by ye Lords assistance wee wer resolved to approve our selves faithfullie to all interests, and I trusted his Majie in experience should find it so. So I tooke my leive.

[*page 66.*] This night I dreamed that (our armee being lying betuixt Leeth and Ed^r, and the English about Resterrig) there arose a litle fyre in our campe lyke a bonne fyre, but in a suddaine it overrunne our wholle campe and consumed it, and I fell y^reupon in a rapture of praiseing of God, and to my apprehensione was for a short tyme in such a heavenlie conditione as I was never in the lyke wakeing, so that throu the passione thereof I awaked.

Nota. This day the king came from Stirling to our Campe, and at the same houre the English Armee advanced and lay doune before ours, and begoud to play w^t their cannon, it being on of the rainiest nights that could be, the shippes also played from ye road up^n Leith.

[*Three blank pages at this point in MS.*]

Aug. 25 [1651]. This night I dreamed that goeing doune to some of
[*page 70.*] the workes (wch I imagined to be about the Water [2] head) I was sett upon by a beast, wch at first seamed to be a fox or a dogge; and after it made a mint [3] at me but did

---

[1] Ambergris is a morbid secretion found in the intestines of the sperm whale; but as the king mentions a quantity found on the south coast of England, where the presence of spermaceti whales is unlikely, he more probably referred to what is known as amber, a resin found principally on the shores of the Baltic.

[2] Waterhead is at the head of Glengonner, near Leadhills (cf. *Exchequer Rolls*, 1634-39, f. 204).

[3] Mint = an aim, attempt.

me no harme it fled from me, but I would needs follow to see what it was whereup^n at a full discoverie I found it to be a Lyon; who seekeing a place to escape but finding none turned backe up^n me againe w^t ane open mouth, whereup^n I caught him by the jawes and cutt off his head. And I keeped his body in my neive thinking it should have dyed (meane whylle my sister Cardross and uthers in my heareing s^d to my wyfe, This presages your husband will be a great man and come to some preferement for he has cut off a lyons head) but it retained lyfe and strugled so long in my hand y^t being wearie w^t it I gave it to Willm Hunter Steuart bystanding. Compare this with Worcester defaict.

1 Jan^{re}. I was in Craighall haveing upon the teuseday [*page 71.*] before ye 29 Decr gone ouer the water at my brothers desyre to beare him compannie.

[*The next twenty lines have been carefully and effectually erased.*]

Freidday to Brunt Iland and lay their that day and 2 [Jan^{re} 1652]. Saïday for passage, and went over on ye Sunneday afternoone.

At my returne I found that Mr. Vanhoght who (had Jan. 3. arryved in Scotland about the mater of lead oare upon [*page 72.*] the 13 Oct^r, and had come to my house to abyde upon ye 29, thereof) had ye day before I parted taken a litle fitt of seeckenesse, was become dangerouslie seecke and they wer drawing blood of him at ye emeraud veines: when I came in, he caused send for me, but the massager could not gett ye ferrie croced, and was exceeding glad when I came but after that night he was never fullie at 12 [Jan^{re}]. himselfe. He desyred me to cause wrytte over our compt y^t it might be sub^d, and after a litle debate anent the interests questionable he called for Ha. Hope and bid him writte it over in mundo^1 (y^e wch I had given him in) and leive out the interests upon both sydes, wch was done, but he was never y^{r}after in a capacitie to subscryve them. Being posed ^{2} be Johne Wallace anent some moneyes wch 15 [Jan^{rie}].

---

^{1} *In mundo, i.e.* a fair copy. ^{2} Posed = questioned.

[*page 73.*]
12 Janr¹⁹.

he had receaved from George Jardin [1] for Jacob Keene skipper, in the presence of the s^d Johne, Vincent Verbest skipper in Midleburgh, Alex^r Tait, my neece Eliz. and my wyfe, he declared y^t he had receaved from the s^d George in name of y^e s^d Jacob foure hundreth sextic nyne lb stling 18/, according to the note thereof amongst his papers, and that the s^d money was to be payed be him in Camphere to James Weir factor; but y^t their is dew to him selfe and to be reteined theireof the particular summes following wch he ordered to be given to his wyfe, first £28 stling for ordinarie, and 20 lb stling for ordinarie [*sic*] charges, in all 48 lb. stling wch he had depursed for the s^d Jacob Kien, in the trouble he was broght to be ye English commissionaires at Lieth anent the confiscatione of his shippe and goods: 2^dlle that y^re is to be reteined 2½ p c. for his pro-

[*page 74.*]

vision in remitting of y^ls s^d money, wch he was to remitte from this to Mr. Tirens at London and from thence to ye s^d James Weire in Camphere at ye easiest exchange he could aggrie for. He declared further that he had receaved from the s^d Alex^r Tait the summe of sexteene lb. 2/ stling as for the pryce of 1340 lb. weight nett tobacco comitted be Jacob Cornelius the bouer [2] skipper in Maeslan and Sluys to the s^d Alex^r Tait to be sold at 24/ st. the hundreth weight, and the pryce ordered to be given to him ye s^d Mr. Vanhoght, whereof he acknowleged the receat. Thereafter the s^d Mr. Vanhoght being interrogat if this declaratione as it is afore sett doune (after reading thereof to him) was according to his mynde, he then declared y^t he would have no more but 50 lb. stling for his provision charges and all; so that the wholle charges of that businesse comes (as he declared) to ane hundreth and

[*Thirty pages cut out of MS. at this point, of which the margins of ten pages remain, with dates*] 22 feb., 26 feb., 21 Apr.

[*page 105.*]
Mooneday. Mett in y^e Chambre my brether Cardros,[3]

---

[1] George Jardine, younger, merchant burgess, married Violet Hilstoun, March 1639.
[2] Bouer = boor, Dutch farmer.
[3] David Erskine, Lord Cardross, who had married his sister Anna.

Craighall[1] and S{r} Charles;[2] with Mr. Johne Elis[3] and [4 Julie [1652]. S{r} Johne Smith[4] anent the mariage of his sone Mr. Robt[5] up{n} my neece Eliz. Hope of Kerse: my brother Craighall after opening of the case was necessitat to goe to Lieth. After long debate wee resolved thogh not positivelie in thir conditiones; That S{r} Johne should provyde the bairns of the mariage to his lands in Cramond paroch (Grottall excepted, w{ch} is provyded to his 2{de} sone) estimat to 24 Chalders of victuall and to the wodset he hes upon Northberricke for 30,000 lb. and to als much money or bonds as will make up fourtie thousand pounds, and to his ludgeing in Ed{r} w{t} the uther adjacent thereto late boght in; and to this to be joyned 10,000 lb. of tocher [*page 106.*] to be payed with my s{d} neece; that they shall be provyded to threttie thousand pound and the tocher for their subsistance dureing S{r} Johnes lyfetyme, that shee shall have tuentie chalders of victuall of conjunct fie if their be no aires of the mariage (they offered only 18) or dureing her widdowhead untill the aire be 16 yeares of age, shee intertaining the aire untill that age: And fyfeteene * [* words one above the thereafter to have onely sexteen chalders victuall the rest other, but to be quitte to the bairnes. And if their be onely aires neither delete.] female, they offer that the doghter being but one shall at her s{d} age have 20,000 m̃ks, if more 20,000 lb. amongst y{m} to be divyded at sight of freinds.

---

[1] Sir John Hope of Craighall, at this time one of Cromwell's Committee of Justice; died 27 April 1654.

[2] Sir Charles Erskine of Cambuskenneth, another brother-in-law.

[3] John Ellis, admitted advocate 1634, son of Patrick Ellis, merchant, Edinburgh; married, first, Rebecca, daughter of John Scott of Scotstarvet; died 1642; second, 1645, Margaret, second daughter and co-heiress of James Scott of Clonbeath, died 1646; third, in 1655, Marion Sandilands, died 1662. He died 1680.

[4] Sir John Smith of Grotehall and Kings Cramond; only son of Robert Smith, merchant, Edinburgh. An eminent citizen of Edinburgh and provost of the city 1642-43; was one of the commissioners sent to negotiate the Treaty of Breda with Charles II.; married, 1616, Jonet Ellis, probably aunt of the John Ellis mentioned above.

[5] Robert Smith of Southfield, Cramond, eldest son of the above. Born, 1631; married, 1652, Elizabeth, daughter of Sir Thomas Hope of Kerse.

Julie. The contract was subscryved in the substance litle differing from what is above.

Aug. 12. Thurseday betuixt 1 and 2 in the day they wer maried be Mr. David Dicke[1] in the east church of Ed^r. At the mariage wer none of our freinds at it but briether and sisters and y^{re} childrene.

Aug. 28. Mr. Th. Hendersone[2] came to my chambre and broke
[*Page 107.*] off if I had yet a mynde for Tullialane that he would interpose him selfe, and that it would be also a great inducement to him to goe on in the buying of the Blaire which is offered to him. I told [him] I was not able, but still willing; may yee not be tempted said he if a varie good bargaine much under that wch it stands the partinares (to witt a 100,000 lb.) wer offered; I ansuered none in Scotland would now give a 100,000 mks. for it; for me at no rate I was hable for it. So Sr George Mowit[3] came in upon us to whom I moved my neeces businesse Eliz. of Craighall; wherein he exprest a resolutione, but would not meete wth her till she should first expresse the removall of ye former prejudice and a present consent.

Octr 2. This day being Freidday my neece Elizabeth Craighall
[*Page 108.*] was contracted up^n Sr George Mowalt, Mr. Roger would not contract any of his estaite with him nor condiscend upon any lands but what was of necessitie to be specified for her conjunct fie, wch is 3000 ch. victuall free of all publick impositiones out of Bochollie and Drumbrecke and the house of Bachollie dureing her widdowhead or untill the aire of the mariage be of yeares of age,

---

[1] David Dicke, apparently a mistake for David Dickson of Busby, minister of the second charge of St. Giles, 1650-62 ; born, 1583 ; son of John Dickson, a wealthy Glasgow merchant; minister of Irvine, 1618 ; Moderator of Assembly 1640, and again in 1652 ; Professor of Divinity in the Universities of Glasgow 1640-50, and in Edinburgh 1650-62 ; married, 1617, Margaret, daughter of Archibald Roberton of Stonehall ; and died 1662.

[2] Thomas Henderson, or Henryson, son of Patrick Henryson ; admitted advocate 1635 ; married, 1641, Jean Murray.

[3] Sir George Mowat of Inglestoun, son of Roger Mowat of Dumbreck, advocate ; created a baronet 2 June 1664, having been previously knighted ; married, 28 October 1652, Elizabeth, daughter of Sir John Hope of Craighall, second baronet.

at wch tyme shee is to quitte it to the heires of the mariage only, they payeing her £133 6s. 8d. yearlie for a duelling elswhere reserving to her sillarage for the girneling of her victuall. Onely Sr George is bound to provyde what ever estait he shall succeede to be his father to the heires male of the mariage and failzieing of male the daughters are [*page 109.*] provyded if but one to £20,000, if tuo to m̄k 40,000, viz. m̄k 25,000 to the eldest and m̄k 15,000 to the 2de, if thre m̄k 50000 viz. m̄k 20,000 to the eldest and m̄k 15,000 to each of ye uther tuo, or if more then m̄k 15,000 m̄k to the eldest and the rest amongst them with this provisione, that in respect Mr. Roger has summe untalzied lands, it shall be in their optione either to take themselves to the s^d respective provisions or to the untailzied lands at there owne optione, but so that if they make choyce of the sumes theye shall enter to the lands and resigne them in favours of the neerest aire males of taylzie, they fraing the daughters of all danger throw their entrie; my brother on the uther p^t contracted m̄k 18,000 payable at Mart. 1652.

Thursday they wer maried be Mr. R^t Traill [1] in Ed^r. Octr 28. I dreamed that I saw a great many shippes up^n the firth [*page 110.*] and that from those that wer Westmost, wch I conceaved to be our's arose a great smocke lyke the shootting of many gunnes, with which they evanished.

I dreamed that heareing that Ld. G. Cromwell was Novr. come to Scotland and was in my brother Craighalls gallarie chambre in Ed^r, I went to see him and found him in bed varie secke, who tooke kyndelie with me and I expostulated much with him that this land found not so kynde usage as wee expected. After that a litle space I thoght his head appeared to me in the floore up^n a platte or table sueeming in blood and pale lyke death. It appeared as if the head had beene cloven in tuo, and the face halfe onely sueeming in the blood; and when wee wer lookeing

---

[1] Robert Trail, born 1603, son of Col. James Trail of Killcleary, Ireland; minister of Old Greyfriars, Edinburgh, 1649-62; married, 1639, Jean, daughter of Alexander Annand of Auchterallan, Aberdeenshire; and died 1678.

[page 111.]

he was gone. I thoght he gott up and putt one his cloathes, and went out, and that in the utter roume wer many officers attending, and that both he and his officers wer all in blacke, that my brother Craighall, Sr Charles and I followed him doune staires being of intentione to goe to Church being a fast day, that I lighted a wax candle to shew light doune, and that I caried it to the closse head lighted; that Cromwell was formest, my brother Craighall nixt him, and S^r Ch. and I behind desyrous to follow them, but whilst I halted at the close head (to putt out the candle whereof I toght there was then no more nead) and immediatlie followed I could see none of them before me, but lookeing up the gate and doune the gette, I saw many lights as it wer people repaireing to church wth candle in ther hands with much zeall and rejoiceing thogh in darknesse; at the which so suddaine disapeareing of the L. Għl and my brother, amazed I awaikned.

[page 112.]

I dreamed that one mett mett me up^n the streets and saluted me with a joy to be one of the numbre of the judges, and would needs have me returne to sitt doune with them, who I thoght wer siting about a table foregainst my owne gate at the long stairefoot, and when I came neere, that judge Owen [1] and Moseley [2] rose to give me place but that my brother and rest cryed that there was there a voyde chaire for me at my brothers right hand where I satt doune; but I thoght they wer all in mourning and there table covered wth blacke about which they satt, and the streets solitarie; and when I admired why it was so, I thoght there was some exequutione at the croce.

Decr 29.

I dreamed I was with my brother Craighall and Moseley in plaine smoth litle feeld goeing to the gouffe; and the feeld was so fyne and pleasant that for feare it should be

---

[1] Andrew Owen, one of Cromwell's commissioners for the administration of justice in Scotland appointed in 1652, and one of the visitors of the universities and schools. The appointment was recalled in 1653, and his name does not appear in the Commission of 1654.

[2] Edward Moseley, a commissioner for the administration of justice in Scotland, 1652; and a visitor of the universities; he was re-appointed in the new commission of 1654.

spoiled with horse feett (for it was close by the heigh road- [page 113.]
way wee wer projecting to inclose of purposs to preserve
it for our selves alone, and to take our full of sport in it);
it being for the tyme a sueett cleere day but whilst wee
wer thus resolveing that it fell doune a darke closse night
on a suddaine before ever we entered to our sport, at the
wch I was so amazed, that I awaked, troubled.

  I dreamed I was in a roume with my father, mother 12 Jan^{ir} 16:3.
and uther freinds. I looked towards the window, and
behold before it, as it wer amongst and above heapes of
earth I saw some cuttings of trees, one about a foott long
another not so long and about the greatness of my shekell
boune, whereout of I perceaved growing as it wer sproutings of pure silver, and the lesser peece I tooke up in my
hand and broke a litle of it, and it appeared bright silver
colored within polished lyke ; and I weighed it in my [page 114.]
hand and withall it was ponderous ; I called my freinds to
see it and did declare unto them that that was a pure
rich silver myne ; and considdering how of a long tyme
I had beene projecting for the mynes of Hilderstoune,[1]
and could not copasse them ; I said to the bystanders,
Yee may see what it is to rest up^n providence, for behold
a silver myne is come to my hand when and where I was
not lookeing for it ; then I begoud to inspict the earth
about it, and I thoght it lay all in litle heapes, as if it
had beene new coupped out of hurlebarrowes, just as my
pryon [2] does about the Schacht [3] mouths when first taken
out ; And when I looke to the walles I thoght the seemes
betuixt the stones was stiking full of sproutings and litle [page 115.]

---

[1] There is now a coal mine at Hilderston Hills to the west of Bathgate,
Linlithgowshire, and silver mines were worked there in 1609.

[2] Pryon or Prian (a mining term) = a soft white clay (*English Dialect Dict.*).
Probably used here to denote the 'spoil' taken out in wheelbarrows at the
opening of a mine shaft. It is a Cornish word, and probably Sir James had
Cornish miners working at the Leadhills. They certainly were employed at the
Hilderston mines (cf. Cochrane Patrick, *Early Records Relating to Mining in
Scotland*, p. 144).

[3] Schacht. Jamieson gives schacht as meaning property, possession, or land ;
but there is no foundation for this. Hope evidently uses it to denote a mine
shaft, having got the form from some of his Dutch or German workmen.

plates of pure and rude silver and the earth was full of peices of the oare; whilst I was admireing all I awakened. And recollecting what had appeared whilst I was considdering what this might portend as to the silver mynes of Hilderstoune, whereof I was now about to gett the right. I fell a sleepe againe and dreamed that being in my brothers Craighalls house in Ed^r, and being about to cause dresse a chambre for my nephew Thomas [1] his sone in my laigh duelling in the Cougate I went doune, and after I had viewed the house and given orders there anent I begoud to forethinke that ever I had gone out of it unto Speeres tenement because of the charges it had cost me, and was now too large and deare a duelling for my straitned conditione   Thus thinking I offerred to goe out to returne to my brothers I see some wyne and bunne bread standing for me at the doore and behold one came to me and bid me eatt, and withall desired me to prepare, for this summer the K. would be at my house to eat, but great expectacion of trouble would be in the land before, and then I thoght he would not continue nor come but evanished; the same Messag^{er} presented to me a printed paper lyke to ane Act or proclamatione wherein he said I was ordeinned to rule in his stead; at which I was much astonished; and when I had red the paper, being desyrous to know whence it had flowed, thinking it to be but a fancie of some, I walked up the yaird varie sad and pensive, at wch my mother and uther freinds wer much astonished, not knowing the cause; at last I went foreward to the messager who was goeing before them and tooke him foreward a part (meane while the printed paper wch I had putt in my pockett fell out and they tooke it up and red it). I posed him, Are yee or this mesage from man or from God; he answered, from God, at wch ansuer all my body growed; [2] but then (drawing him asyde to the inner closse) said I, from whom hes this businesse its

[*page 116.*]

[*page 117.*]

---

[1] Sir Thomas Hope of Craighall, third baronet; born 1633; married Elizabeth, daughter of Sir John Aytoun of that ilk; and died 1633.
[2] Growed = groued, shuddered, shivered.

ryse, for the heads of the people doe not lyke me so well;
he ansuered from the people who crye out that now in
their destitute conditione, after so many tryells they will
have no uther, for that they have seene yo{r} upright
walkeing; and y{t} thereupon when the heads are at there
meetting consulting what to doe, the commone people
come to the windowes, and throw in papers to this purpose
significing their desyres; at w{ch} relatione I fell first in
an passionat admiratione of the dispensations of God;
and then into a doolefull sorrow and greeffe, because of
such a thing w{ch} my heart served me not to; so leveing [*page 118.*]
him I went in to the hall; where I saw the long table
covered with great cheere, at w{ch} moved with indigna-
tione, I threw away a litle fasciculll (w{ch} I thoght was
lyke a brush or litle cheeffe of wheate) which the messager
had given me in token of my electione and badge of my
government; then I went fumouslie benne to the chambre
(as I conceaved at the east end of the hall lyke the Lead
hill chambre to be retired) wher I did also see great
abundance of meatt standing befor the fyre and throw
the roume; and whilst I was walkeing some turnes throw
the chambre, sadlie bewailing with teares my conditione
in that behalfe, throw the extreame passione of my
greeffe I awaked, and found indeed my body in a passionat grievous distemper. The Lord keepe me closse
in his wayes; that whatever beefall, I may be found
in him. [*page 119.*]

My neece Anna[1] was contracted upon Mr. Will{m} 24 March.
Cochrane[2] upon the [*blank*] and maried this day
24 March being Thursday be Mr. Geo. Hutchesone,[3] in
the east church of Ed{r}.

The threttenth of March Sunneday about 7 in the 13 March.

---

[1] Anna, daughter of Sir John Hope of Craighall; born 1634; married, 1653, William Cochrane of Rocksoles. (He is incorrectly called Alexander in the Edinburgh Marriage Register.)

[2] William Cochrane, son of James Cochrane of Rocksoles, Lanarkshire, merchant burgess of Edinburgh. He succeeded his father.

[3] George Hutcheson, minister of Tolbooth Parish, Edinburgh, 1649-62; 'indulged' minister at Irvine, 1669; died 1674.

morneing my wyfe was broght to bed of her eleiventh chyld being a daught^r named Rachell (aft^r my brother Craighalls Lady)[1] baptized the same day be Mr. Robt Lowrie[2] in the Pālt hall.

13 Ap^r.

The 13 Aprile My daught^r Anna[3] dyed betuixt 3 and 4 in the afternoone; her seekenesse had beene long contracted throw breeding of teeth and defluxtione and buried the morrow thereaft^r in the Grafrieres neere my fathers grave.

5 May.

The 5 May I tooke journey to the Leadhill, but be I was 6 myle off, I was overtaken be Mart. Crauf^d with a letter from Cõll Lilburne[4] desyreing me to meett at the Lady Hoomes yairds[5] haveing some businesse of great importance to impart to me; whereup^n I returned but he not keepeing in respect the messager had returned ansuer y^t I was gone, I went out to Dalkieth, where his residence is, being commander in Cheeffe And haveing long attended his ryseing from a Counsill of warre, he at lenth tooke me apart, and shewed me a letter from my Ld. Gñll Cromwell, wherein after love remēbred, he desyred him to sound my freedome to come up to London to be

[page 120.]

---

[1] His second wife, Rachel, widow of Sir John Skene of Curriehill.

[2] Robert Laurie, son of Joseph Laurie, minister of Perth : minister of Perth, 1641-43; of Trinity Parish, Edinburgh, 1644-48; and of the Tron, 1648-62, when he was translated to St. Giles, and made Dean of Edinburgh. He subsequently became Bishop of Brechin ; died 1678.

[3] Anna, baptized 29 February 1652.

[4] Colonel Robert Lilburne, son of Richard Lilburne of Thackley Puncherdon, Durham; born 1613; one of Cromwell's colonels; took a prominent part in the second civil war and the Scottish campaigns, but was not quite in the first rank as a military commander; signed the death warrant of Charles I., and at the Restoration was formally sentenced to death, but the sentence was commuted into imprisonment for life ; died 1665.

[5] Lady Home's Yairds : what is now Moray House in the Canongate of Edinburgh was built by Mary, wife of Alexander, first Earl of Home, and daughter of Edward Sutton, ninth Lord Dudley, some years before the coronation of Charles I., and became the property of Margaret, Countess of Moray, her daughter, in 1645. She advanced £70,000 in aid of the Covenanters, and it was in this house that Cromwell and Lambert had their headquarters in 1648. It was probably here or in some place closely contiguous that Lilburne made the appointment to meet Hope. He himself was quartered at Dalkieth, where what is now the ducal residence was taken possession of by the English commissioners.

assisting there; whereunto I presentlie as it lay upon my spirit declared my freedome to owne them, or even to act under them in Scotland, but not to goe out of the Scotland, nor to medle in state affaires, whereupon at his desyre I immediatlie wroat a Letter to the Gñll to the same purpose whereof I have a scroll; which done I immediatlie tooke horse and went that night to ye 7 myle house, and frō thence ye nixt day to Leadhill.

I returned from Leadhill to Ed^r Suneday at 8 at night. [*page 121.*] I receaved at the Wrightshouses (whither I had gone to see my childreen) a letter from Cōll Lilburne, with another lyke a lettre inclosed within it directed to (Sr James Hopetoune, Knight) me as he wreat from the Geñll, wch opened I found it but a cover to a summonds directed from the Gñl to me to be at London 4 Julie 1653 to the effect therein conteined.

Thurseday. At 4 at night when goeing to take coach 21 [May]. from Ed^r for London, wee receaved notice of my Sister Cardros[1] death wch had beene Wednesday about 10 a clocke at night; have supped before as well and chearefullie as of a long tyme, but takeing a kinke of a cough after supper went away with it.

Freidday. I went journay by Dalkieth spoke wth Lil- 22 June. burne, overtooke the coach a^t Heddingtoune where my nephewes Smith[2] and Cochrane,[3] and Cousin Harie[4] and [*page 122.*] uthers tooke live; and wee went that night to Barwicke. There wer in the coach Judge Suintoune[5] goeing up upon the same score, and his servant, and my nephew Craighall

---

[1] See p. 131, note 5.   [2] See p. 151, note 5.
[3] See p. 157, note 1.   [4] See p. 131, note 8.
[5] John Swinton, eldest son of Sir Alexander Swinton of that ilk; joined Cromwell's party after the battle of Dunbar, and ultimately became 'the man of all Scotland most trusted and employed by Cromwell.' In 1655 he was a member of the Council of State for Scotland, and in 1656 one of the commissioners for the administration of justice; became a quaker in 1657; imprisoned at the Restoration, but was apparently freed in 1667; went to England, where he married, as his second wife, Frances White of Newington Butts, a widow, sister of John Hancock of Wallyford, East Lothian. He had married, first, in 1645, Lady Margaret Stewart, daughter of William, Lord Blantyre; she died, 1662, when in prison with her husband. Swinton himself died at Borthwick, 1679.

(goeing about his travells) and my servit^r Peter Barbour [1] wth me.

23 June. Suneday at night wee aryved at London, haveing ridden post 58 mylles that day, that wee might fetch the apoint-
[24.] ment. Mooneday wee mett in the Counsill Chambre, Whytehall, where the Lord Geñll Cromwell after a speech of ane houre sheweing the grounds of the dis-solutione of the last Partt, and why this meeting so extraordinarlie called, he presented them with a comissione wch was red. It was word by word according to the
[page 123.] summonds particularlie sent to each member, onely omitting ye sůonding words; when it came to the impowering words it constitute them (nameing all that wer summoned by their names with out any additione relateing to natione or countrie) and impowered them with the supreme authoritic of England, Scotland and Ireland and Dominions y^rof. He presented to them also a Commissione granted be him to 14 persones as a councell of state till they should appoint uthers; wch both being red (those summoned being sitting all the tyme and the Gñll and M. Gĥl Lambert standing in the bosse window leaneing upon the backe of a cheire) he delyv^d both to Sr Willm Rob^ts [2] in name of the rest and so he and the remanent officers removed. Those summoned, after some discourse, adjourned till the nixt day, with resolutione to sett the day a parte to seeke the Lord, and when moved to have the assistance of some minister it was cryed doune. Place of meetting was appointed the Old Partt house.

10 Novr. I dreamed I was goeing by where tuo workemen wer
[page 124.]

---

[1] Peter Barbour, writer, Edinburgh, was buried in Greyfriars, 21 December 1662.

[2] Sir William Roberts, Baronet of Willesden, second son of Baron Roberts of Willesden; born 1605; knighted by James I. in 1624, and served under Charles I. in various minor local posts. He joined the Parliamentarians and was employed by Cromwell, and was a useful though not distinguished public servant. He was one of Cromwell's House of Peers, 1657. After the Restoration he was created a baronet in 1661, and died the following year. He married Eleanor, daughter and heiress of Robert Atye of Reburn. On the death of the fourth baronet the title became extinct.

THE DIARY OF SIR JAMES HOPE

sinkeing a ditch, and because there came water in to it from some parts about, there was a pompe neereby, and some workers to draw out the water as it came in. I thoght I stood still and was hudgelie pleased to see the workemen worke, and while I was lookeing on there came of a suddaine in up^n them a great flood of water wch overtopped them both, I was hudgelie troubled at it, and called to the pompers to pumpe; but they wer out of the way; and it was some tyme before they could be had. And when they came and wer about to pompe, the pompe staffe was broken or somewhat els out of order, that it would not worke. They righted as well as they could, and drew vigourouslie, whereby they made the water to fall [*page 125.*] so farre as that wee wer once almost at a sight of the workemens heads; but the water incresced so fast that they could not bring it further doune; wch wee by-standers seing, putt in a tree to helpe him out in whome wee thoght there was most lyfe (for by this tyme they seemed both almost dead) but he was not hable to hold it. So in great passione for their losse I awaked.

I dreamed againe that being at dinner with my brother [Nov^r] 15. Craighall in the hall of his ludgeing in Ed^r, there fell doune a stone from the inner pend of the window up^n the table but hurt none; wee looked up and immediatlie after there fell another; I looked to the stone wall behind the table and I observed it to beginne to ryve, and the whole walls of the house to shake; I bid them ryse and advysed them to pull doune the partitione wall; which [*page 126.*] wee went about, and did it without any hurt, the whole walls of the house shakeing in the meane tyme. I thoght so much fell that the jeesting [1] seamed to hang in the aire, so that wee wer forced to under-prope them; this done whilst wee wer goeing out to the closse, behold Kerses ludgeing was all a faling; wee called for workemen to helpe to take it doune, who went cheerefullie about it. Nothing of it (I thoght) stood but that quarter where the staires enter up; and when gathering our

---

[1] Jeesting = joists, beams.

[page 127.]

spirits and resolutione again to goe about the rebuilding y^rof, my mother and I wer vieuing if the stones and timbre wer anything wronged by the doune takeing. I thoght severall of the carved worke and best hewen stones were a missing, stollen away by the workemen; and that they had sawen in tuo the jeasts, and taken away the one halfe and left the uther. Yet after long and serious deliberatione what to doe wee resolved the rebuilding and for a passage went to repaire an old passage which was strait, darke and unpleasant, out of wch I made a varie sueett entrie with a plote at the head to take off to severall roumes wch promised a farre more excellent building then the former: with wch I was hudge well pleased, blissing the Lord, who was lykelie to make good the losse, but finding it beyond my present capacitie to pefyte the building ansuerable to such an entrie, and thereat troubled. It was borne in upon me that these to come after me should perfact it, wth passione whereof I awaked.

16 Nov^r.
[page 128.]

Wednsday betuixt 6 and 7 at night my sone Thomas[1] died haveing 12 dayes before not urined; upⁿ the 11 Octr apprehending the stope to be from the stone in his blather, wee caused sound him with a cathetre (one Mr. Edward Mullins a chyrurgeon did it, immitting the cathetre at his yaird, and his finger at the fundament) but found he had no stone; nor that there was any urine in his blether. Thus being to seeke in the cause of the stope of his urine, for tho one of the kidneyes or uraturs might be obstructed,

[Nov^r] 17.

wee could not conceave how both could fall to bee togither. Whereupon we caused open him and found all his noble parts whole and sound and lyvelie beyond expectatione; but his right kidney a stone as bigge as ones litle finger at the small end y^rof and as almost my thumb at the great end; and by the small end it had fallen in into the

[page 129.]

orifice of the uritour and stoped it exactlie from all passage; the stone at the small end wch had entered the

---

[1] This was the third son whom Sir James had named after his father: none survived infancy.

uritour was hard but the great end soft and mullerie; besyde it in another cavitie of the same kidney was a numbre of small gravell: his left kidney had no flesh in it but ane emptie skinne or bagge into wch all the urine had diverted, and had distended it and the neighbouring veines to the biggenes 5 or 6 inches over, and 8 or 9 inches long, the uritur had no passage, but was wissend and runne togither lyke a nerve; there was above a Scots pynt of urine in it. He was buried the same night in Margarets, Westminster, before the pulpitt (closse by the ends of the pewes) some 2 yairds to the right hand. vide my dreame 10 Novr page 124.

Satureday. All this weeke haveing beene spent in the house in debate upon a report frō the Committé of tythes, broght in in countrepoide of a bill presented for abolishing of Patronages, wch had beene ordered to a vote the weeke before. This report did runne to this sense; That they offered it to the house as the best way for removeing of scandalous Ministers, That a Comitté of 18, three to each of the 6 circuits, and with them 6 honest men of each Counté w^thin the severall Counties respectivelie should be impowered to eject all scandalous, ignorant, and ungifted ministers, given to filthie lucre or erroneous in their doctreene, and to place hable and honest men in their roumes; and where they should see cause to unite paroches, so the furthest inhabitants should not be above 3 mylles distant; This Report being spoken to all this weeke, wherein many honest men had expressed their dissatisfactione; as the Majistrates too much medleing in things of Religione; wishing eather it might runne in expressiones of withdrawing or giveing of incouragement and maintenance, not of ejecting and placeing; uthers that it was a owncing of the present parochiall ministrie upon that foot of accompt; from whom rather all maintenance should be withdrawne, that that antichristiane constitutione might once be unhinged and thogh not any thing inacted against it imposeinglie; yet withdrawing all Civill acts owning it; and that such of them as wer honest men might have the States encourge-

10 Dec^r.

[*page* 130.]

[*page* 131.]

ment for preaching the Gosspell whether Ministers of Churches under any forme, or not; The House seamed once they should have come to some agg^t in this; but at lenth it being putt to ye vote this day the house was divyded up^n it; those for aproving of the report went out and wer 54, those against satt in, and wer 56, and it was observed that the English in this vote wer aequall and the Scots did cast it for of us foure onely Coll. Lock [1] went out. This vote put all these uthers and my Ld. G. in a great chaffe. These for the report in former vote mette in the house somewhat tymelie before the uthers where it was first moved be S^r Ch. Wolselie,[2] seconded by Alderman Tichburne,[3] thirded by Major Geñll Disborrow,[4]

[margin: *page 13?.*]

[margin: 12 [Dec^r].]

---

[1] Coll. Lock. This must refer to Sir William Lockhart. He is evidently one of the four Scots members: Swinton, Jaffrey, Lockhart, and Hope. Alexander Brodie of Brodie, who was the fifth member nominated for Scotland, did not take his seat. He was the son of Sir James Lockhart of Lee; born 1621; at first a royalist, he entered into Cromwell's service a few years after the battle of Worcester; governor of Dunkirk 1656-60, when he gave up the keys to Charles II. He was Cromwell's ambassador at Paris 1656-58, and held the same office under Charles 1673-75. Appointed Lord Justice-Clerk in succession to his father 1674, but as he was in France he never took his seat on the Bench, and died the following year. Married, first, Margaret, daughter of Sir John Hamilton of Orbiston, and, secondly, Robina Sewster, whose mother, Anne, was a sister of Oliver Cromwell.

[2] Sir Charles Wolseley, son of Sir Robert Wolseley of Wolseley, Staffordshire. When only eighteen he married, in 1648, Anne, youngest daughter of William Fiennes, first Viscount Saye and Sele. He was a member of the Barebones Parliament of 1653 and was an ardent, though not an infatuated, Cromwellian. He was pardoned at the Restoration, but got no employment, and he lived in retirement to the close of a long life, occupying himself with gardening and writing pamphlets.

[3] Alderman Tichbourne, son of Robert Tichbourne; he was a linen draper in London. A colonel in Cromwell's army, but according to contemporary accounts he was a very poor soldier. In religion he was an extreme Independent; signed the death warrant of Charles I.; sat in the Barebones Parliament; and was one of Cromwell's House of Lords. He was one of the Sheriffs of London in 1650, and Mayor in 1656. At the Restoration he was sentenced to imprisonment for life, and after being confined in Holy Island and Dover Castle died in the Tower in July 1682.

[4] Major-General Desbarrow or Desborough, son of James Desborough of Ettesley, Cambridgeshire. Born 1608; originally a lawyer and farmer he, in 1649, became a major-general in the army of Cromwell, whose sister, Ettesley Jane, he had married in 1636. A rough and blustering revolutionary; he was, however, more laughed at for his ill-breeding than respected for his sense, of

fourthed be Coll Sydenhame,[1] and fifted be S[r] Anthony Ashlie Coupper [2] to this purpose that it was there expectationes that the Lord should have done great and good things by this present power, yet had they observed that never any good thing had beene done, but on the contrarie many expressiones uttered tending to the dissolutione of all bonds, and shakeing the varie fundationes, as by the takeing away of tythes, voteing a new body of the Law, takeing away of Patronages, and everie way brakeing in upon the proppertie of the people and now this last of brakeing the whole ministrie at a blow, to the drawing of the whole natione to confusione. That therefor each of them for themselves, and they trusted uthers would doe the lyke, wer resolved to goe and resigne their power to him who gave it. Sueet Mr. Th. S[t] Nicolas [3] [page 133.]

---

which he had little. Scott describes him in *Woodstock*, chap. xi. At the Restoration he went through various experiences, but in the long run he died peaceably at his house in Hackney in 1680.

[1] Colonel William Sydenham, eldest son of William Sydenham, Wynford Eagle, Dorset; born 1615; served with distinction in the Parliamentary army; a member of the Barebones Parliament in 1653, and of the Council of State of that year. He was also one of Richard Cromwell's Council. After the Restoration he was one of eighteen persons perpetually incapacitated from holding any office. He did not long survive, dying in July 1661. His wife, Grace Trenchard, whom he had married in 1637, died about a week later.

[2] Anthony Ashley Cooper, born 1621; son of John Cooper of Rockborne in Hampshire. At first an adherent of Charles I. he went over to the Parliament side in 1644, and did valiant service as an officer in that army. He took a leading if sometimes an inconsistent part in the politics of the Protectorate time, but was one of the committee deputed to go to Breda and invite Charles to return. After the Restoration he was, at the Coronation in 1661, raised to the Peerage as Baron Ashley of Wimborne St. Giles, and eleven years later he got a further step by being created Earl of Shaftesbury and Baron Cooper of Pawlet. His career was a wholly political one, but in that sphere he proved himself one of the ablest and most excellent men of his day. This did not, however, prevent his star setting in obscurity, as in 1681 he was, as the result of his political intrigues, indicted for high treason. He fled to Holland, and died at Amsterdam, 21 January 1683.

[3] Thomas St. Nicholas of Aske, Steward of the Court of Chancery, 1651; a commissioner for the approbation of 1654; member of the Council of State; commissioner for Westminster militia 1659, and for Kent 1660; Recorder of the city of Canterbury 1659; appointed Clerk of the Parliament 1659. He is probably called 'sueet' because his theological opinions agreed with those of Hope.

(after Ald. Tichb.) declared his dissatisfactione with that resolutione, and that he would protest against for that things wer not at that distance but that in meekeness, love and mutuall condiscensione they might be composed, and called the Lord to witnes they wer reddie to applye

[*page 134.*] them selves to all meanes of unitie; that thoghe he had his summonds from my Lord Generall yet he looked upon his call as from God; and cd not be so unfaithful to it as to give up his trust and opportunitee putt in his hands to doe good things for the Glory of God and good of his people. After Sr Ant. Ashlie Coupers speech w^{ch} (as most of them) was varie short these of that judgement rose all up as one man and went to the doore. The speaker came out of the chaire and went with them, and the Sergant caried also the mace away: some that wer resolved to sitt, betuixt 20 and 30, not the 3^d p^t of the house nor a quorum, called the Speaker backe to the Chaire and the sergant to bring backe the mace; but none of them would ansuer; these that sitt still caused close

[*page 135.*] the doore (Mr. Moyer [1] and Mr. Anlibie [2] withdrew, pretending wee wer not a house) and wer about to resolve what to doe, but first proposed to pray in order either to resolutione or dissolving. Whilst Mr. Squibbe [3] was speaking to this purpose came in Coll Goffe [4] and [Col. White] and said, Gentlemen, there is no house here, be pleased to remove. It was ansuered we wer about to seeke direc-

---

[1] Samuel Moyer sat for London City in the Barebones Parliament. A London citizen with a great financial reputation; member of the Council of State; Master of Trinity House and member of the East India Company.

[2] John Anlaby sat for York in the Barebones Parliament; one of the king's judges, 1648; member of the Council of State; married Dorothy, daughter of Sir Matthew Boynton of Baronston, York.

[3] Arthur Squibb sat for Middlesex in the Barebones Parliament; Teller of the Exchequer 1650; commissioner at Goldsmiths' Hall 1652.

[4] Colonel William Goffe, son of Stephen Goffe, rector of Stanmer in Sussex. He became a captain in the model army in 1645, and was a staunch supporter of Cromwell, commanding his regiment at Dunbar, and having command of another at Worcester; signed the death warrant of Charles 1. He assisted Colonel White in the ejection of the Barebones Parliament; one of the Protector's House of Peers. At the Restoration he fled to Massachusetts, where after a somewhat adventurous life he died in 1679.

tione what to doe. No, sayes he, yee may goe to any uther place, but wee must have this roume cleered. He was demanded if that was his privat desyre or if he had any order for it;[1] he said it was his privat desyre, then s^d Mr. Courtnay[2] wee doe not find it expedient to remove yet; whilst he was makeing to the doore as to bring in a partie br. Jaffray[3] and I desyred him onely to close with a prayer, but he ansured, by no means in this roume, so gave a signe and there came in 12 musketeres, where upon wee removed peaceablie.

These who withdrew (as wee afterwards understood) [*page 136.*] went altogither directlie to the Horse chambre in Whyte hall where they sub^d a paper resigneing their power, wch was sent to my Ld. Gñll. Our brothers Suintoune and Lockart, wer not in the house, but in comeing to it mett the withdrawers and returned: C. Lock went and sub^d the resignatione. It is the Lord.

Freidday. Cromwell was conducted in great state from 16 [Dec^r]. his owne house to Westminster, and their suorne protector of the Commonwealth of England, Scotland and Ireland, according to a parch^t exhibited to him be M. G. Lambert, entituled The Government of the Commonwealth of England, Scotland and Ireland. He was suorne be the judges, and y^{r}after conducted backe to Whytehall the L. Maire carieing the suord before him [*blank*] carieing [*page 137.*] the Parlt and [*blank*] the Councell maces; all the Com-

---

[1] The words, as reported in a letter of Mansell to Pritchard (*Thurloe*, i. 637), were as follows: 'We are here by a call from the general and will not come out by your desire unless you have a command from him.'

[2] Colonel Hugh Courtney. Captain of militia in Carnarvon and Anglesea 1650; commissioner for the propagation of the Gospel in Wales; member of the Council of State; disapproved of the Protectorate; afterwards recommended to be Governor of Beaumaris. Banished after the Restoration.

[3] Alexander Jaffray, son of Alexander Jaffray, Provost of Aberdeen; born 1614; M.P. for Aberdeen 1644-50; one of the commissioners for the Treaty of Breda; Provost of Aberdeen 1651; member of the Barebones Parliament; Director of Chancery 1652; became a quaker in 1662; and after suffering imprisonment for his opinions died at his estate of Kingswalls in 1673. Married, first, 1632, Jane Downe; and, second, in 1647, Sarah, daughter of Andrew Cant. His Diary, edited by John Barclay, was published in 1833, and reprinted in 1834 and 1856.

1654.
[Aprile] 27.

panic bare headed and he onely covered. This I could not be spectator off but heard it by report.

Aprile. My brother Craighall dyed about one after midnight; wee knew no disease to him, but that his spirits wer spent, an indispositione in his stomacke, and generall dibilitie and defect of naturall heat throw his whole body.

[*On fly-sheet at end of volume.*]

Cap: Th. Lindsayes offer of Charcoall. C. Th. Ly, 12 Seckes in a chalder everie secke 2 yairdes long consisting of 3 yairds about, wch is a yaird wide. Ane hundreth chalder betuixt and Whyts. 1648. For the chalder . . .

INSTRUCTIONS FOR THE
TRIAL OF PATRICK GRAHAM

A.D. 1476

Edited by

ROBERT KERR HANNAY

INTRODUCTION

IN the Biblioteca Vittorio Emanuele at Rome Dr. Maitland Thomson found a seventeenth-century copy of the document which is now printed.[1] It is important owing to the mystery attending the life, character, and fate of the first Archbishop of St. Andrews. Buchanan wrote an eloquent and pathetic story, which is alarmingly incorrect where it can be tested by documentary evidence, and which must fall under grave suspicion of misrepresentation—not, indeed, because he wished to deceive, but because he took no trouble to ascertain the actual facts or to put them in their true relation.[2] His tale has coloured many subsequent narratives. Tytler followed Spottiswoode in reproducing Buchanan with additions and modifications derived from Ferrerius and Lesley. Hill Burton, who writes of 'Robert' Graham, ignores the difficulties, and dismisses him, with some not very illuminating comment, as probably a madman. Hume Brown says that 'in view of all the circumstances, as they are known to us, there is no improbability in the statement of Buchanan that Graham was an honest reformer, and the victim of a rapacious court and a purblind clergy.'[3] Hill Burton was probably right in seizing upon Buchanan's incidental remark that a coadjutor was found for Graham *velut mentis parum compoti*. The suggestion was adopted by Andrew Lang, who exposed some of the errors in Buchanan's narrative, and was inclined to the opinion

---

[1] Fondo Gesuitico, 151, c. 198.
[2] *History*, xii. 32 ff.
[3] *History of Scotland* (1911), i. 213.

that Graham's troubles might be traced to a megalomania which ended in complete mental alienation.[1] Whatever be the truth of the matter, the successive versions of this story illustrate the dangers to which our historians expose themselves by placing too much confidence in the literary tradition, and forcibly recommend the advisability of beginning with solid documentary evidence, when it is to be had.

Buchanan need not be quoted at length. In spite of corruption, he says, there remained in the Church some show of the old *gravitas*. Bishops and abbots were chosen by chapter election; but courtiers, with an eye to their own profit, urged James III. to assume the right of nomination and aggrandise the royal power. The court was turned into a market. Patrick Graham, 'the only drag upon a church going headlong to ruin,' had sought refuge in Rome from his enemies. Learning how things stood, he determined to return, armed with legatine powers. This was a shock to the whole mercenary crew, who raised an outcry against 'Romanists.' Ultimately there was an appeal to the Pope against the newly created archbishop. Then the court astrologer, William Schevez, appears upon the scene, Archdeacon of St. Andrews and the bitterest of Graham's foes. He conspires with the Rector of the University, is appointed by the King to be coadjutor, and finally becomes judge in the Archbishop's case. What hope for the unfortunate man? Compelled to resign, he sees Schevez supplant him by papal authority, and pines away, first on Inchcolm—*scopulus verius quam insula*—then at Dunfermline, last of all in Lochleven Castle.

Not only are the facts of Buchanan's narrative very often inconsistent with the documentary evidence and

---

[1] *History*, i. 341-2.

with one another : the general significance of the story is hard to reconcile with what we know of ecclesiastical conditions in the fifteenth century. How he produced so distorted a result is a mystery. He had seen at least one or two of the documents still in our hands. Possibly he assumed, or accepted a St. Andrews myth, that Graham must have been a reformer because he was deposed, and proceeded on that basis. Or, as Dr. Maitland Thomson suggests, he may have desired to pay a tribute to a man from his own countryside.[1]

Under James I., Bishop Cameron took the part of the Crown, because he resented papal interference with what he regarded as the rights of the national church. He may have hoped that the Council of Basel would secure reform and adjust the competing claims. His career did not end in tragedy, but, apparently, in a somewhat factious obscurity.[2] James Kennedy, the next great churchman, was no anti-papalist. Government at home taxed all his resources, and he had need of what support interest at Rome could offer. When his biography comes to be written, it may appear that he adapted himself to the system of reservations which was leading inevitably to collision with the Crown. In the time of James I. the export of money for the Roman traffic was the ostensible ground of contention :[3] under James III. we have a period in which the conflict came to centre round nomination to the prelacies and the question of external interference with the appointment of men who were lords of Parliament. It is this fact which Buchanan, along with many other historians, fails to grasp. The suggestion that free chapter election was on a sudden superseded by royal appointment is a travesty. In reality, papal reserva-

---

[1] Patrick was son of Robert Graham of Fintry, and was nephew, not brother, of Bishop Kennedy (*Archbishops of St. Andrews*, i. 12).
[2] *Scot. Hist. Rev.*, xv. 190 ff.   [3] *Ibid.*

tions had killed chapter election, and had concentrated in the hands of the Pope powers which the Crown must regard as a danger to unity of control. About a decade after Graham's fall, James III. obtained what was almost a right to nominate to prelacies.[1] The significance of Graham's career, apart from his personal misfortunes, was that it raised a question which was finally settled by severance from Rome.

It is vain to inquire whether the Catholic Church might have maintained itself in Scotland if it had been permitted to select its own leaders : it is certain that the conduct of Crown and Papacy wrought irretrievable ruin. Patrick Graham was no reformer. He identified himself with the *Romanenses*, as Buchanan styles them ; he accepted favours from the Pope which were themselves illustrations of current abuse : he returned to Scotland as the Pope's man.[2]

It was recognised that Buchanan's account of Graham's trial was unfair in respect of the part played by Schevez, a scholar and book-collector, with a feeble record in public life. We knew that Sixtus deputed a special emissary to collect information for the consideration of three cardinals and final judgment by himself.[3] It seems to have been supposed, however, that the elaborate procedure only deepened the darkness of injustice. On a broad view of the case, the papal authorities were not likely to depose their man unless he had become a traitor to the Church, or was, for some other reason, incapable of governing. Now, in the present document, we have the instructions delivered to the nuncio Herseman—or

---

[1] *Archbishops of St. Andrews*, i. 157.
[2] Robertson (*Statuta*, i. 112) quotes the *Annales* of Raynaldus, where it is said that Sixtus *metropolitano solio ecclesiam Sancti Andreae ornaverat studiis Parisii*—the last word a strange blunder for *Patricii*.
[3] *Archbishops of St. Andrews*, i. 60 ff.

Huseman—for the conduct of the inquisition, showing clearly that there was no desire to crush hurriedly a dangerous heretic and reformer or yield too readily to the animosity of the royal court. A recent historian has asserted that 'in his trial there was barely a show of impartiality.'[1] That position, at least, does not appear to be tenable.   R. K. H.

---

[1] MacEwen, *Hist. of the Church in Scotland*, i. 349: where an attempt is made to rationalise the story on the assumption that Graham was sane.

INSTRUCTIO PRO DOMINO JOHANNE HERSEMAN NUNCIO APOSTOLICO IN SCOTIAM ITURO

Primo conferat se ad serenissimum dominum regem Scotiae, et impertita sibi nomine Supremi Domini Nostri salute et apostolica benedictione exponat causam sui adventus, et cur sit nuncius, et maxime quod S D N pro satisfactione ipsius domini regis et cleri Sancti Andreae, et ut bene consulatur ecclesiae Sancti Andreae, ne ex defectu et mala gubernatione sui pastoris praesentis detrimentum patiatur in spiritualibus, ipsum mittit ad inquirendum et informandum super his quae obiciuntur domino Patricio archiepiscopo Sancti Andreae, ut veritate cognita possit sua sanctitas secundum Deum et justitiam prout intendit super hoc negocio deliberare et providere.

Item eligat locum tutum et liberum, in quo constituat judicium suum, et citato legitime ipso domino Patricio archiepiscopo, et aliis qui fuerint evocandi, ita judicium agatur quod cesset omnis violentia et suspitio et metus, tam ratione loci quam personarum quae in eis intervenient.

Item informet se diligenter, et inquirat super irregularitate, simonia, blasphemia, scandalo, dilapidatione bonorum ecclesiae et aliis excessibus qui praedicto domino Patricio objiciuntur, habeaturque informatio ipsa a personis gravibus, fidedignis, probatis, non suspectis, et maxime ecclesiasticis et Deum timentibus, a quibus medio juramento et servatis aliis requisitis a jure super objectis veritas intelligatur.

Item in citatione quae fiet domino Patricio archiepiscopo praedicto, assignetur terminus competens ad comparendum et nihil fiat praecipitanter, set mature, graviter, juridice, et servata aequa lance, nec habendo principaliter respectum nisi ad Deum et justitiam et veritatem, servando semper gravitatem et dignitatem judiciariam.

Item quod admittat omnes et singulas defensiones, testes et jura quae dominus Patricius archiepiscopus producet ad defensionem suam, omniaque intelligat patienter, et cum humanitate.

Item quod omnia et singula quae testificabuntur et producentur tam contra ipsum Patricium archiepiscopum quam pro ipsius defensione faciat fideliter redigi et sincere in scriptis per notarium seu notarios legales integros et merito non suspectos juxta id quod in hujusmodi causis arduis jura fieri volunt et debet.

Item quod ubi de praemissis plenam habuerit informationem, eamque in scriptis ut praemittitur redigi fecerit, processum ipsum factum et scripturas omnes claudat et sigillet, et sic clausum et sigillatum quantocius reportari curet ad supremum dominum nostrum juxta id quod in litteris et in commissione continetur.

Item quod in omnibus et singulis praemissis ita semper se habeat et gerat quod nulla merito suspitio interveniat, et servetur apostolicae sedis dignitas, et optima supremi domini nostri voluntas executioni demandetur.

[(1) He is to see the King, convey to him the greeting and blessing of his Holiness, and explain the causes which have brought him and why he is nuncio, dwelling especially upon the fact that the Pope is sending him to satisfy the King and the clergy of St. Andrews and to consult the interest of that church, for fear that it may suffer spiritually from the failure and maladministration of its present head. His object is to ascertain fully the charges against Archbishop Patrick, in order that his Holiness may know the truth and make his decision in the matter as in the eye of God and according to justice.

(2) He should select for his court a place safely and freely accessible, and issue lawful citation to the archbishop and others who ought to be called. Proceedings ought to leave no room for force, suspicion, and fear in respect of the place or the persons concerned.

(3) He is to inquire carefully regarding the irregularity, simony, blasphemy, scandal, dilapidation of church property, and other excesses in the charge, obtaining the facts from persons of character, worthy of confidence, of established repute, and not open to suspicion, especially ecclesiastics and God-fearing men, from whom the truth about the accusations may be elicited under oath and with all the formalities required by law.

(4) In the citation the archbishop should have a competent term to put in an appearance. Nothing is to be done in a hurry; but deliberately, gravely, in form of law, and with perfect fairness. Regard is to be had, above all, to God, justice, and truth, with unwavering observance of judicial seriousness and dignity.

(5) He should admit every possible defence, witness, and claim of right which the archbishop may bring forward, listening with patience and in a spirit of humanity.

(6) All evidence against the archbishop and in his favour should be faithfully recorded and honestly written out by a lawful notary, or notaries, of unblemished repute, whose character is above suspicion—as the rules of law require in so difficult a case, and as ought to be done.

(7) When he has obtained full information, as above, and has caused it to be reduced to writing, he must close and seal the process with all the relative papers, and see that it is conveyed to his Holiness as soon as possible, according to the letter of his commission.

(8) He will be sure to regulate his conduct throughout so as to exclude any plausible ground of suspicion, maintain the Apostolic dignity, and give effect to the disinterested will of his Holiness.]

THE SCOTTISH CONTRIBUTIONS TO THE DISTRESSED CHURCH OF FRANCE IN 1622

I

THE CONTRIBUTION OF HADDINGTONSHIRE

II

THE CONTRIBUTION OF ST. CUTHBERT'S, EDINBURGH

Edited by
DAVID HAY FLEMING, LL.D.

INTRODUCTION

THE Edict of Nantes, granted by Henry IV. on the 13th of April 1598, has been described, despite its many restrictions, as the Huguenot Magna Carta. Paul de Félice has said that it 'was really never observed either in letter or in spirit,' although, in the first half of the seventeenth century, 'the numberless violations were only trifling ones.'[1] When Clement VIII. heard that the less liberal Edict of 1577 had been received by the Parliament of Paris he changed colour.[2] So Cardinal D'Ossat reported in March 1597. In the previous month he wrote: 'The Pope . . . then added what he had said to me before in the former audience, that kings and other sovereign princes permitted themselves everything which turned to their own profit, and that the state of matters was that no one blamed them or was displeased with them for this; and he quoted a saying of Francesco Maria, Duke of Urbino, which meant that if an ordinary gentleman, or a nobleman below the rank of sovereign, did not keep his word, he would be dishonoured and blamed by every one, but that sovereign princes, for reasons of state, could without any great blame make treaties and not fulfil them, make alliances and abandon them, lie, betray, and all such other things.'[3]

It is hardly surprising, perhaps, that the enemies of the

[1] *Tercentenary Celebration of the Edict of Nantes*, 1900, p. 105.
[2] *Lettres de Cardinal D'Ossat*, Paris, 1624, p. 276.
[3] *Ibid.*, pp. 248, 249.

Protestants set themselves to enervate the concessions of the edicts. In 1621 the irritation, and the fear of worse to come, led many of the oppressed to defend themselves and their liberties. Several of the cautionary towns were surrendered, but others held out valiantly, notably La Rochelle. John Welsh, Knox's son-in-law, was one of the ministers of St. Jean d'Angely, and he distinguished himself by his courageous conduct during its siege and also after Louis XIII. entered it.[1] A few weeks after the capitulation of that town, the magistrates, ministers, elders, and deacons of the kirk-session of Aberdeen appointed 'a publict fast and humiliation' of all the inhabitants of the burgh, to begin in the middle of July and to continue all the week with the Sabbath day immediately thereafter following, ' as the lyk is indicted be the bishop throchout the haill kirks of this diocie, be reasone of the great impietie abounding in this land, and of the distrest estate of the Kirk of Chryst in France, Germanie, and Poleland.' And, on the 23rd of September, another fast was ordered on account of 'the persecution of the Kirk of God in France, Germanie and Pole, and the present imminent danger of the wracking of the cornes be thir extraordinarie weittis.'[2]

On the 18th of December there was laid before the Privy Council in Edinburgh 'Ane missive from his Majestie concerning a voluntair contributioun for releif and supporte of the people in France distrest for religioun.'[3] This missive, dated 8th November 1621, was brought before the kirk-session of Aberdeen on the 10th of the following February, along with a copy of a letter from the Lords of the High Commission to the ministry of

---

[1] Young's *Life of John Welsh*, 1866, pp. 395-401.
[2] *Selections from the Records of the Kirk-Session, etc., of Aberdeen*, Spalding Club, p. 98.
[3] *Register of the Privy Council of Scotland*, vol. xii. p. 620.

every diocese, and a letter from Bishop Forbes, who was then in Edinburgh. From the royal missive, it is learned that, by reason of the troubles in France, 'a verie great number of people professing our religioun have left thair fortunes in that kingdome, and for thair saiftie have fled, with thair wyffis, childrene, and famelies, into this, having no other meanes of mantenance saiffeing the charitie of weill disposed people.' Moved by his 'royall commiseratioun,' his Majesty had permitted a voluntary contribution to be levied in England, 'from suche as out of thair christiane charitie sal be disposed to contribute to thair releiff'; and, although 'not ignorant of the small store of money presentlie' in Scotland, yet, in so pitiful a case, he had yielded to the humble suit of the deputies of the French Kirk, who had besought him that the voluntary help of well-disposed Scots might also be craved and collected. As the High Commission is usually associated with acts of tyranny, it is all the more pleasant to find that in this matter it was deeply moved by compassion:—

'Thair hath laitlie come hither ane of the chois ministers of the Reformed Churche in France, who hath bene heir before us, and declarit to us the lamentable estate of that Churche, and withall schawed unto us ane ampill commissioun from the same, togidder with a warrant from his Majestie to come into this realme, and to seik such relief for the afflicted state of that Churche as may come by the voluntarie contributioun of devott charitable people; thairfor, we—having considderit that the professioun of the Gospell there is in great danger evin to be exterminat and rooted out of that most floreshing kingdome, to the unspeakable hurt and detriment of the whole Reformed Churche, whairof we are a pairt—have thought good, as feilling memberis of one body with thame, earnestlie to recommend thair present cace to all weill affected professoris of religioun. And to the effect that quhilk shuld be done heirin, may be performed with

expeditioun, ordour and some good effect, we have thocht
it meit that in everie presbyterie thair be appoynted one
of the ministrie thairof, and tuo or thrie of the gentillmen
of best creditt within thair boundis, assuming to thame
selffis in everie paroche the minister thairoff, to gadder
the voluntar benevolence of all that are abill and weill
disposed within the landwart paroches of that presbyterie;
thairfor, we entreatt yow, in the bowellis of the Lord
Jesus, that ye, tacking with yow the minister of ilk paroche,
will be pleased to tak the paynes to go throw all the
landwart paroches within the precintis of your presbytrie,
addressing your selffis to the gentillmen and utheris that
ar abill, and efter a trew declaratioun of the great necessitie
of our poore afflicted brethrene, to receave and collect
what it shall pleas God to move thair hartis to bestow;
and that ye wald have ane booke whairin the particular
contributioun of everie one may be set doun, . . . which
roll or booke we desyre yow subscryve with your handis,
and to send it to the bishop of your diocie, together with
your contributioun, that it may be tymouslie delyverit
to the forsaid commissionar who presentlie attendeth the
end of this bussienes at Edinburght.'

The kirk-session found the desire to be most reasonable,
and were willing to contribute according to their power,
and to give orders that a voluntary contribution be craved
to that effect from such inhabitants of the burgh as are
able to give the same, 'efter they have hard what course
is taken thairanent be the burrowis in the south pairtis of
this realme.' [1] So far as the Spalding Club volume of
selections from the ecclesiastical records of Aberdeen
shows, nothing more was done there in the matter.
Glowing reports from the burghs in the south of Scotland
may have led the Aberdonians to the conclusion that
contributions from the north were unnecessary. The

[1] *Selections from the Records of the Kirk-Session, etc., of Aberdeen*, pp. 99-101.

DISTRESSED CHURCH OF FRANCE IN 1622

French commissioner intended to visit Aberdeen, but changed his mind. James Roberton, a regent of Glasgow University, writing to Boyd of Trochrig, on the 4th of April 1622, says : ' Monsr. Basnage, the commissioner from France to gather contributions for the Protestants, has writt to you. I wonder what holds him so long at Edinburgh. He has given over his journey to Aberdeen, and said to me he was going to Perth and Stirling and thence to you. What I saw in him I shall show you at meeting. Our ministers, that came home from Margaret Wallace assize and burning [at Edinburgh], say he is to be here yet. Our town has contribute 5000d. merks, the bishop's thousand will make it six ; I think he will produce it for his promise sake.' Apparently the contribution of the town was not included in that of the presbytery of Glasgow, which only amounted to £1040 Scots.[1]

From Basnage's double receipt (in French and in the vernacular) which I have transcribed from the original (belonging to the Trustees of Sir William Fraser, K.C.B.), it is seen that the sixteen churches of the presbytery of Haddington raised £2305 Scots. The names are arranged in conformity with their liberality, Haddington heading the list with £666, 13s. 4d., and Morham, Barra, and Garvald closing it, each with £13, 6s. 8d. It will be noticed that Keith-Marischal and Keith-Humbie, which Scott says were united in 1618,[2] are entered separately, the former having given £200 and the latter £15, 6s. 8d. When the items are added together they amount, not to £2305, but to £2304, 13s. 2d. No doubt some one in charge had given the necessary 6s. 10d. to make the money even. Basnage signed the discharge, in presence of four witnesses, on the 23rd of March 1622. The first of the four, N. Wduart,

---

[1] Wodrow's *Collections upon the Lives of the Reformers*, Maitland Club, vol. ii., part i., pp. 167, 168.

[2] Scott's *Fasti*, 1866, vol. i. p. 339.

may safely be identified as Nicol Uddart, Udward, or Udwart, merchant burgess of Edinburgh.[1] Of the other witnesses, James Speir is designated in the St. Cuthbert's voucher as a merchant burgess of Edinburgh, and James Macmath is probably the merchant whose son Edward drew up one of the receipts.

After referring to events of 13th January and 6th February 1622, Calderwood says : ' About this time there was a collection through the countrie for the Kirk of France. It began in Edinburgh upon the twelf, and endit upon the twentie-sixt of Februar. The Nonconformitanes exceedit all others verie farre in their liberalitie. The servants, maids and boyes were not behind for their part, for they contributed foure thousand merks. The summe of the whole amounted to threttie-five thousand merks. The ministers were forced to confesse that the Nonconformitanes were the honestest men in their flockes.' [2] By Nonconformitanes, Calderwood means those who objected to the Five Articles of Perth Assembly, which had been ratified by Parliament in August 1621. Their interest in the collection may have been quickened by the fact that such exiles as Andrew Melville and John Welsh had found refuge among the Huguenots.

Zachary Boyd, writing to Trochrig in February 1622, states that ' the [presbytery ?] of Edinburgh have been very liberall in their contributions for the distressed Presbyterians in France, and even the very servants have given largely.' [3] The liberality of the servants and of the working classes, as well as those of higher rank, is most

---

[1] *Register of the Privy Council of Scotland*, vol. xiii. pp. 120, 176, 324. There was at the same time a Mr. Nathaniel Udwart, son of the deceased Nicol Udwart, late Provost of Edinburgh. This Nathaniel obtained a monopoly of soap, but was deprived of it in 1624 (*ibid.*, vol. xii. pp. 106, 516, 519 ; vol. xiii. pp. 294, 295).

[2] Calderwood's *History*, Wodrow Society, vol. vii. p. 543.

[3] Wodrov's *Collections*, vol. ii., part i., p. 167.

amply borne out by the fourth volume of the *Register of St. Cuthbert's Kirk-Session*, to which volume I obtained access through the kindness of Mr. Lorimer (one of the original members of the Scottish History Society, and author of *The Early Days of St. Cuthbert's Church, Edinburgh*); and Mr. A. B. Campbell, W.S., session-clerk. I have copied its long list of subscribers, the formal receipt, and the relative minutes. There are in all 265 contributors. Sir William Nisbet of the Dean gave £100. Sir George Touris, Sir William Fairlie, and the Laird of Wariston each gave 100 merks, or £66, 13s. 4d. The interest of the list is enhanced by the occupations and places of abode. To give some idea of the value of money in those days a few notes of prices are here added from documents in the Register House. In 1614, 'a muchkin aquavytie,' 8s.; 'a pound of fegis,' 5s.; 'a pound succour,' 32s.; 'a pair broune glufis,' 6s. 8d.; 'a pair dry leder schone,' 30s.; 'a pair wemenis glufis,' 5s.; 'a blak sowrd belt,' 13s. 4d.; 'a kist,' *i.e.* a coffin, 50s.; 'a winding scheit,' 48s. The following rates of wages were paid, in 1622, for work at Holyrood and the Castle, for six days: the master wright, £4; three other wrights, 53s. 4d. each; one mason, £4; another, 53s. 4d.; other two, £3, 12s. each; one slater, £4; another, 36s.; three barrowmen, 36s. each. These prices and wages, like the contributions, are in money Scots, then a twelfth of money sterling.

On the 23rd of April 1623 a complaint was brought before the Privy Council ' by William Dick, William Speir, John M'Math and Alexander Colvill, " commissioneris nominat be Mosure Bosnage for ressaveing of the contributioun voluntarlie grantit be the subjectis of this kingdome for support and releiff of the distrest people of the Protestant Kirkis in France," as follows: There was collected within the bounds of the presbytery of [*blank*]

£115, 6s. 8d., and that sum was delivered to Mr. Alexander Home, minister at Aytoun, upon his promise to pay the same to the said "Monsure Bosnage" or to the complainers, commissioners. It was expected that Mr. Alexander Home " sould have faithfullie keipit his promeis and nowayes abstractit the benevolence and cheritie of the people so frielie and willinglie grantit be thame to so goode and necessair a caus" ; but he still retains the money.—John M'Math appearing for himself and the other pursuers, and the defender not appearing, the lords decern the defender to make payment to the pursuers, and direct the usual horning against him.'[1]

Benjamin Basnage is said to have been born in 1580 at Carentan in Normandy. He became pastor there and took a prominent part in several synods of the Reformed Church of France.[2] Robert Blair, in speaking of the time when he was a regent in Glasgow University, says : ' In the sixth year of my profession in the college, many faithful ministers being put to suffering for Perth Articles, . . . I conceived that suffering might also be my lot, whereof I got special warning by a grave and gracious French minister whose name was M. Basnage. . . . This gracious man, coming to Glasgow to receive the contributions gathered there, took me aside and told me he had carried himself indifferently towards the parties that were in our Kirk, lest he should have marred the errand he had come for ; but now, having done his work, he might and did more freely declare what and whom he liked and misliked. He told me he had heard well of me, and did believe it to be so ; but withal assured me that the bishops and their faction were sore displeased with me, and that, in his

---

[1] *Register of the Privy Council*, vol. xiii. p. 213.
[2] Quick's *Synodicon in Gallia Reformata*, 1692, vol. ii. pp. 75, 100, 119, 259. He was moderator of the Synod of Alençon in 1637. He was then designated ' pastor of the church of Ste Mere ' in Normandy (*ibid.*, pp. 322, 323).

judgment, ere a year were turned about, I would see the effects thereof (as it came to pass indeed); but withal, he encouraged me not to fear what they could do; exhorting me that, when I was troubled by them, I would come to France, where I would be very welcome.'[1]

The gratitude of Basnage was no doubt increased by the knowledge of the fact that the Church of Scotland had, in 1587, raised about ten thousand merks for the French Protestant exiles then in England.[2]

D. H. F.

---

[1] Blair's *Life*, Wodrow Society, pp. 20, 21.
[2] Melville's *Diary*, Wodrow Society, pp. 264, 265.

I

THE CONTRIBUTION OF HADDINGTON-SHIRE

JE, soubsigné, recongnois avoir receu, selon le pouvoir et commission qui m'a este donnée par l'Assemblée Generalle des Eglises Reformées de France, et Souveraincté de Bearn, de Maester Jacques Carmichaell, Mr. George Greer, pasteurs de l'Eglise d'Adington, Mr. Jean Ker, pasteur en Preston, Mr. Robert Balcanquall, pasteur en Tranent, George Hepburn, ballif d'Adington, deputes du Presbitere d'Adington, la somme de deux mil trois cents cinq livres, Escossoises tout en bon or et argent courant au païs, provenante de la colecte qui a esté faite es eglises dudit presbitere ; Assavoir de Hadington 666ll. 13s. 4d., de Preston 333ll. 6s. 8d., de Tranent 318ll., Keith Marschall 200ll., Salton 151ll. 2s. 8d., Gullan 147ll. 8s. 6d., Bothens 113ll. 6s. 8d., Aberladie 101ll. 5s., Norberrick 88ll. 14s. 4d., Pencatland 74ll. 15s. 4d., Bolton 40ll., Keithumbé 15ll. 6s. 8d., Elsinfurd 14ll. 14s., Morrame 13ll. 6s. 8d., Bara 13ll. 6s. 8d., Garuat 13ll. 6s. 8d. ; par la volunté et permission de sa Majesté de la Grande Bretagne. Laquelle somme sera (Dieu aydant) seurement et promptement transportée à la Rochelle, ou emploiée selon que ladite Assemblée Generalle jugera plus-apropros pour le bien des affaires et necessités de noz Eglises. Au nom desquelles (attendant un plus ample tesmoignage de recongnoissance de la part de ladite Assemblée Generalle), Je remercie tres-affectueusement les freres et fidelles des dites Eglises de ceste leur charitable et voluntaire assistance, laquelle nous estant un gaige de nostre mutuelle communion nous sera aussy une saincte et estroicte obligation à prier Dieu pour la longue paix et prosperite des Eglises de ce Royaume, lesquelles nous supplions tres humblement vouloir continuer selon les occasions et pendant qu'il plaira à Dieu nous tenir soubz l'espreuve de la persecution presente, leur Chrestïenne affection. Pour en cela avoir ce tesmoignage devant Dieu et les hommes d'avoir esté des utilles instruments de sa providence en la delivrance de son Eglise. Fait à Edimburth, le 23 jour de Mars, mil six cents vingt deux.

    BASNAGE deputé de l'Assemblée Generalle des Esglises Reformees de France vers sa majesté de la Grande Bretaigné.

        N. WDUART, tesmoin.
        JAMES SPEIR, witnes.
        JAMES MAKMATH, wittnes.
        JOHNE HAMILTOUN, witnes.

 I, underwrittin, grantis me to have reacevit, according to the pouer and commissioun givin to me be the Generall Assemblie of the Reformed Churches of France and Souveranatie of Bearn, from the handis of Mr. James Carmichaell, Mr. George Greir, ministers of Hadingtoun, Mr. Johne Ker, minister of Preston Pannes, Mr. Ro^t Balkanquall, minister at Tranent, George Hepburne, baillife of Hadingtoun, deputed from the presbyterie and counsaill of Hadingtoun, the sowme of tua thousand thric hundreth fyve pundis, guid and usuall money of the realme of Scotland, all gold and greatt silver, quhilk is the totall sowme of the collectioun maid in the churches of the said presbyterie ; to wit, in Hadingtoun sex hundreth thrie score sex pundis threttein schillingis foure pennyis, in Preston Pannes thrie hundreth threttie thrie pundis sex schillingis auchtein pennyis, in Tranent thrie hundreth auchtein pundis, in Keith Marscall tua hundreth pundis, in Salttoun ane hundreth fyftie and ane pund tua schillingis aucht pennyis, in Gullen ane hundreth fourtie and sevin pundis aucht schillingis sex pennyis, in Bothens ane hundreth threttein pundis sex schillingis aucht pennyis, in Aberladie ane hundreth ane pund fyve schillingis, in North Bervick four scoir aucht pundis fourtein schillingis four pennyis, in Pencatlaine thrie scoir fourtein pundis fyftein schillingis foure pennyis, in Boltoun fourtie pundis, in Keith-humbie fyftein pundis sex schillingis aucht pennys, in Alschenfoord fourtein pundis fourtein schillingis, in Morame threttein pundis sex schillingis aucht pennys, in Baraw threttein pundis sex schillings aucht pennys, in Garvat threttein pundis sex schillingis aucht pennyis ; be the favoure and permissioun of his Majestie of Great Britane. The quhilk sowme schall be, God willing, saflie and spedelie transportit to the Rochell, or els imployed as the said Generall Assemblie sall think fittest for the guid of the affaires and necessiteis of our churches. In the name of quhilk churches (in the meine tyme untill thair cum ane more ample testimonie of acknawledgment from the said Generall Assemblie) I give most hartlye thankes to the brethrein and faithfull of the said churches, for this thair charitable and willing assistance, the quhilk being ane pledge of our mutuall communioun sall also be to us ane holy and strait obligatioun to pray unto God for the continuance of the peace and prosperetie of the churches in this kingdome, the quhilkes we intreate most humbly to contenue thair Christiane affectioun according to the occasines and so long as it sall pleas God to hauld us under the tryell of the present persecutioun. In so doing ye sall have this testimonie before God and men to have bein profitable instrumentis of His providence in the delyverie of His Churche. In witnes of all the premisses thir presents, writtin be Edward MacMath, sone to James MacMath, merchand, are subscryvit as followis : at Edinburgh the tuentie thrie day of March, ane thousand sex hundreth tuentie and tua zeires,

     Basnage, deputè de l'Assemblèè Generalle
      des Esglises Reformeès de France, vers
      sa majeste de la Grande Bretaigne.
       N. WDUART, witnes.
       JAMES SPEIR, witnes.
       JAMES MAKMATH, wittnes.
       JOHNE HAMILTOUN, witnes.

[*Indorsed.*] Discharge of the collectioun for the Frensche Kirk.

II

THE CONTRIBUTION OF ST. CUTHBERT'S, EDINBURGH

Thuirsday, the 21 Februarii 1622. . . . The quhilk day, the sessioun, being frequentlie convenit for the tyme, ordanit Edward Cuningham, Thomas Lowrie, George Broun, Johne Dickiesoun, Thomas Zoung, Alexander Symsoun, and James Johnesoun and Mr. William Arthour to mak intimatioun upoun the Sabboth nixt to the parrochinneris to be beneficiall to the distressit Kirk of France, betuixt or efter the sermones, or upoun Tysday at sevin houris quhill tuelf, and to that effect ordanes the haill collectouris to be present.

Thuirsday, the 9 Maii 1622. . . . The sessioun ordanes the catologue of these persones that contribuittit to the Kirk of France to be insert in the Sessioun-buik with thair names particularlie, and particular sowmes and dyet of the delyverie of thair money, as also of the discharge subscrivit be the Frensche commissioner of the ressait of the sowme of aucht hundreth pundis delyverit be the minister and Edward Cuningham, thesaurer and collectour of the said money, to be also registrat in the said Sessiounbuik *in perpetuam rei memoriam*. . . .

These are the names that contribuitit to the distressit Kirk of France with thair particular sowmes that everie ane of tham hes gevin :

Sir George Touris of Gairnttoun,[1] knycht . 66li. 13s. 4d.

---
[1] Now *Garleton*.

Sir William Nisbit of the Deane,[1] knycht	100li.
Sir Archebald Napeir of Edinbellie, knycht	26li. 13s. 4d.
Sir William Fairlie of Brunsfeild, knycht	66li. 13s. 4d.
The Laird of Wareistoun	66li. 13s. 4d.
Mr. William Arthour, ordiner minister	13li. 6s. 8d.
Mr. Robert Cheislie	3li. 6s. 8d.
Thomas Zoung in the Craig of Inuerleyth	6li. 13s. 4d.
Alexander Symsoun in the Quhythous	5li. 6s. 8d.
Johne Stevinsone in the West Port	3li. 6s. 8d.
Thomas Miller, meikmaker [2]	36s.
Archebald Ingilis, weavir	20s.
William Craig in Minthulie	6s.
Robert Howiesone in the Potteraw	6li. 13s. 4d.
Johne Dickiesone, there	6li. 13s. 4d.
Robert Stevinsone, there	6li. 13s. 4d.
Charles Hog, there	6li. 13s. 4d.
Richard Howiesone, there	5li.
Johne Chalmeris, West Port, tailzeour	33s. 4d.
Thomas Ker, wrycht, there	24s.
James Rid, tailzeour, there	30s.
James Wilkie in Sauchtounhall	13li. 6s. 8d.
George Broun in Eleis mylnis	8li. 3s. 4d.
Walter Bell in Sauchtounhall	6li. 13s. 4d.
Thomas McQuorne in the Seins	5li. 6s. 8d.
Thomas Syme in Sauchtounhall, tailzeour	12s.
George Lowrie, merchand	3li. 6s. 8d.
Robert Wilsone in Sauchtounhall	6s. 8d.
Robert Leaseris in Bonitoun	40s.
Mongo Andersone in the Watter Leyth	12s.
Alexander Zoole, West Port	3li. 6s. 8d.
Alexander Gray, maltman, there	3li. 6s. 8d.
William Wallace, kirk-officer	53s. 4d.

---

[1] Until the autumn of 1845 there stood about the centre of what is now the Dean Cemetery 'a large, venerable, old mansion-house, the seat of the now extinct family of Nisbet of Dean, a family long of great local influence.' The village of Dean 'has always had a peculiar population of its own, quite distinct from that both of Edinburgh and of the country' (Cockburn's *Journal*, 1874, vol. ii. pp. 139, 140). It was doubtless a tiny village indeed in 1622, for only seven of the contributors are entered as 'in the Deane.'

[2] *Meikmaker* is a clerical slip for *meilmaker*.

DISTRESSED CHURCH OF FRANCE IN 1622

William Mathie, brouster, West Port	40s.
Jeane Hineschaw,[1] maidin, there	20s.
George Aitkin, massone, West Port	30s.
James Hill, cordoner, Potteraw	20s.
Walter Scot in the Deane	4li. 7s. 6d.
George Smaill, cordoner, West Port [2]	12s.
Thomas Fairholme, West Port	3li. 6s. 8d.
Adame Bar, there	53s. 4d.
Robert Jacksone, there	53s. 4d.
Alexander Hislope, beltmaker, West Port	12s.
Robert Thomsoun, West Port	20s.
Mr. James Watsoun of Sauchtoun	4li. 6s. 8d.
Edward Cuningham, baillie of the West Port	5li. 6s. 8d.
Robert Broun in Sauchtounhall	40s.
Johne Howiesone, West Port	3li.
Johne Crawfurd, tailzeour, there	30s.
Johne Zoung in the Deane	40s.
James Johnesoun, portioner, there	13li. 6s. 8d.
George Dewar, meilmaker, West Port	30s.
Alexander Cairnis, meilmaker, there	30s.
John Lowrie, maltman, there	3li. 10s. 8d.
James Johnesoun, maltman, there	24s.
Peater Moffet in Sauchtounhall	6s.
William Wyshart, meilmaker, West Port	16s.
Robert Dykis in Sauchtoun, meilmaker	16s.
The Laird of Braid, elder	20li.
Thomas Russell, cordoner, West Port	12s.
Johne Broun, zounger, in Dalry-millis	13li. 6s. 8d.
Johne Wast in Sauchtounhall	4s.
Andro Gudfollow, brouster, West Port	30s.
Helene Johnesoun of the Craighous	3li. 6s. 8d.
Nicoll Adamsone, baxter, West Port	18s.
Margaret Broun, wedow, there	53s. 4d.
George Ramsay, smyth, West Port	30s.
Johne Ros in Bellismill	40s.

---

[1] May be read *Hindschaw*.
[2] *Samuell, smyth in Dalrye*—deleted, and *Smaill, cordoner, West Port*, interlined.

William Cleghone,[1] West Port		12s.
Adame Purves, baxter, there		24s.
Thomas Syme, tailzeour, there		40s.
Thomas Purves, baxter, there		30s.
James Bigar, maltman, there		48s.
Johne Wyshart, meilmaker, there		18s.
Cristian Fiffe, wedow, in Quhithous		3li. 6s. 8d.
Archibald Andersone, belt maker, West Port		3li.
Johne Dowgall in the Seins		3li. 6s. 8d.
Mr. James Drummond, West Port		13li. 6s. 8d.
Johne Don, Brigend		20s.
James Meinzeis, Watter Leyth		20s.
Gawin Pollok, there		40s.
Johne Pollok, there		30s.
Johne Bell in Bellismill		6li.
Gawin Porteous, Watter Leyth		12s.
Piter Ros, Potteraw, baxter		12s.
William Forrester, there		20s.
Henrie Heriot, there		22s.
Thomas Gray, there		24s.
Cristian Mitchell, maidin		3li. 6s. 8d.
Charles Cosche, pultriman		18s.
Robert Gray, cordoner, West Port		20s.
George Linlythgow, there, smyth		12s.
Alexander Elder in the Deane		40s.
William Pirie, there		30s.
James Alexander, Watter Leyth		6s. 8d.
Thomas Gray		6s.
James King		4s.
Robert Mudie, Watter Leyth		10s.
Johne Crystesoun, walker in Bellismill		48s.
Alexander Broun, zoung man		33s. 4d.
Walter Brok, West Port		6s.
Barbara Alane, there		6s.
Robert Mowbray, armorer, there		12s.
Johne Patersone, brouster, there		12s.
Johne Finlasoun, smyth, Potteraw		20s.

---

[1] *Cleghone* is probably a clerical error for *Cleghorne*.

DISTRESSED CHURCH OF FRANCE IN 1622

Peater Zoung, merchand	42s.
Alane Boriland, West Port	40s.
Issobell Fairholme, there, maidin	24s.
Agnes Hodge, wedow, there	10s.
James Aitkin, Quhithous	9s. 4d.
James Broun, meilmaker, West Port	9s.
James Broun, tailzeour, there	24s.
Thomas Cummyng, there	12s.
Alexander Robesoun, Watter Leyth, cowper, there	20s.
Patrik Bowie, Watter Leyth	24s.
William Quhyt, Potteraw	12s.
Patrik Dowglas, there	12s.
Walter Bell, chopman, there	7s.
James Mowbray, smyth, West Port	20s.
James Sandelandis, baxter, there	4s.
Robert Phinnie in Gorgie	52s.
Mr. Robert Naper in Merchesoun	6li. 13s. 4d.
Dauid Law in Sauchtounhall	16s.
Johne Fribairne, smyth, West Port	20s.
Alexander Fribairne, smyth, there	20s.
Thomas Williamsoun, cutler, there	22s.
William Jemisone, weaver, there	6s.
William Scowlar, weaver, there	6s.
William Sinclair, Cannomillis	36s.
Harie Listoun, Backraw	53s. 4d.
Johne Broun, elder, in Gorgie Mill	13li. 6s. 4d.
Robert Johnesoun, brouster, West Port	18s.
Jonet Neilsoun, wedow, Watter Leyth	18s.
Alexander Symsoun, zounger	12s.
Dauid Wilsoun, brouster, West Port	33s. 4d.
Dauid Hodge, smyth, there	12s.
Johne Steill, Borrowmure	3li.
Daniell Cook, sheithmaker, West Port	30s.
Jonet Cook, his dochter, there	4s.
James Craw, Cannomillis	24s.
Alexander Moore in Multers in the Hill	36s.
Walter Flemyng, meilmaker, Watter Leyth	40s.
Richard Aikman, there	12s.

Thomas Lamer, there	6s.
Johne Gairdner, there	3s.
Dauid Nisbit, West Port	12s.
Johne Melros, tailzeour, there	12s.
Johne Napeir, tailzeour, there	24s.
William Dickiesoun, tailzeour, there	24s.
William Nicoll, tailzeour, there	24s.
Dauid Bigar, skinner, there	12s.
William Bellendene, Cannomillis	3li.
Johne Blak, stanman,[1] West Port	12s.
George Marteine, tailzeour, there	12s.
Margaret Robesoun, wedow	4s.
George Samuell	20s.
Barbara Sandie, Inuerleyth, wedow	36s.
Johne Hog, hir gudsone, there	10s.
Johne Crawfurd, cordoner, Watter Leyth	12s.
William Chalmeris in Brouchton	40s.
George Bartilmo, stanman, there	12s.
Robert Wilsoun, beltmaker, West Port	40s.
Alexander Weir, meilmaker in Sauchton	12s.
Alexander Weir, his sone, there	4s.
James Hadden, there	3li. 6s. 8d.
Johne Craig in Dalry	12s.
Robert Saurle, in Sauchtounhall	6s.
James Andersone	12s.
Cuthbert Eisoun,[2] maltman, West Port	53s. 4d.
George Wast, tailzeour, West Port	12s.
Robert Gordoun, meilmaker, in the Deane	30s.
Johne Corrie, tailzeour, Watter Leyth	6s.
James Mathie, meilmaker, West Port	6s.
Margaret Guyld in Edinburgh	24s.
Jeane Guyld, there	20s.
Margaret Crawfurd in Brochtoun	13li. 6s. 8d.
Clement Gordoun, Watter Leyth	30s.
Margaret Crawfurd, West Port	6s.
James Heriot, there	20s.
James Kennoche, Watter Leyth	12s.

---

[1] Probably *tinman*. [2] May be read *Eistoun*.

DISTRESSED CHURCH OF FRANCE IN 1622

William Bradie, Brigend	24s.
Marioun Murray, wedow, West Port .	20s.
Daniell Cowtis in the Deane . . .	40s.
Thomas Symsoun, tailzeour, West Port .	24s.
Thomas Bell, Watter Leyth . .	30s.
William Huntar, there . . .	18s.
William Broun in Plelandis . .	6li. 13s. 4d.
Dauid Scot in Blakfurd .	40s.
George Thomsone	10s.
Robert Porteous, Watter Leyth .	10s.
Thomas Kilpatrik, there . . .	6s.
Alexander Wrycht, there . . .	6s.
Johne Lamb, there . . .	6s.
John Lyell in Plesance . .	53s. 4d.
Johne Ros, maltman, there . . .	50s.
Thomas Bennet, glaissin-wrycht, there .	30s.
Jonet Pacok, wedow, there, brouster .	3li. 6s. 8d.
Williame Barrone, stanman, there .	4s.
Richard Scot, there	12s.
Johne Hammiltoun, there . . .	12s.
Johne Dowglas in St Leonardis .	30s.
Issobell Meyne, wedow, there . . .	3li.
Agnes Robesone, there	4s.
Johne Henrysone, there	30s.

SERVANDIS

Elspet McMariage, West Port . . .	12s.
Issobell Cranstoun, Kirk-styll . . .	12s.
Jeane Traquhane, there	6s.
James Cockburne, there	6s.
Ewphame Symsone, there . .	6s.
Robert Gibsone, West Port . .	8s.
Johne Hill	6s.
James Henrysoun	6s.
Alexander Forrester . . .	6s.
Alexander Clyd	6s.
Marioun Smyth	12s.
Agnes Dunlope	5s.

Agnes Murray	4s.
Johne Hodge	4s.
Alexander Galbrayth	4s.
Agnes Moore	12s.
Marioun Hanna	10s.
Robert King	6s.
Johne King	4s.
Nicoll Lowis	4s.
Elspet Wast	6s.
Bessie Nimok	6s.
Bessie Murdoche	4s.
Catherene Gluiffer	12s.
Johne Johnesoun	4s.
Elspet Rid, maidin, West Port	14s.
Johne Fischer	4s.
Johne Gib	12s.
Archibald Quhyt, officer	4s.
Jeallis Wast, West Port	9s.
Cristian Cooke, there	4s.
George Wilkie	12s.
Alane Boirlandis servand	4s.
Issobell Pennicook	4s.
Agnes Park	12s.
Jonet Hangitsyd	24s.
Bessie Mar	6s.
Issobell Cairnis	6s.
Jonet Ormisoun [1]	4s.
Margaret Marschell	6s.
Alexander Donaldsoun	4s.
Thomas Haistie	6s.
Thomas Drummond	6s.
Johne Hanna	4s.
Johne Beg	8s.
Alexander Robesoun	4s.
Thomas Lyoun	4s.
William Park	3s.
Johne Wod	9s.

---

[1] May be read *Ormistoun*.

DISTRESSED CHURCH OF FRANCE IN 1622

Agnes Dauidsoun	2s.
Agnes Adamsoun	4s.
Bessie Gibsone	4s.
Niniane Denholme	2s.
Patrik Bischope	6s.
Alexander Burnet	6s.
Andro Thomsoun	6s.
Johne Huntar	4s.
Robert Rodger	4s.
Mr. Johne Cant of the Grange	35 [?][1] li.
James Crawfurd in Plesance	6li. 13s. 4d.
Mathow Hodge, West Port	13s. 4d.

Followis the discharge of the ressait of the foirsaid money gevin be the Frensche commissioner callit Benjamin Bannage, ordanit and directit be the Generallie [sic] Assemblie of the Reformit Kirkis within the kingdome of France and soveranitie of Beeren.

I, Benjamin Bannage, commissioner appoyntit and direct frome the Generall Assemblie of the Reformit Kirkis within the kingdome of France and Soveranitie of Beern, to the kingdomes of Ingland and Scotland, to sute and requyre thair cheritabill helpe and willing supplie for releiff and support of the present distres of the saidis Reformit Kirkis; and haveing obtenit to this effect the power, gud will, and permissioun of the rycht michtie and potent prince King James, his majestie, King of Great Britane, etc.; be the tennour heirof grant me to have resavit fra Mr. William Arthorr, minister at the West Kirk, outwith Edinburghe, and Edward Cuninghame, collectour appoyntit of the sessioun of the said West Kirk for the ingaddering of the money underwrittin, the sowme of aucht hundreth pundis usuall money of Scotland, for the weill, utilitie, and profeit of the said Frensche Kirk. Off the quhilk sowme of aucht hundreth pundis money foirsaid, I, the said Benjamin Bannage, in name of the said Generall Assemblie of the Reformit Kirkis of France and soveranitie of Beern, hauld me weill content, satisfeid

---
[1] The first figure has been altered. If £35; then the total is £826, 12s. 2d.

and pleasit. Quhilk sowme of aucht hundreth pundis abonenamit, I faythfullie promeis (with the helpe of God) sal be surelie and with all possibill diligence exchangit to the Rotchell, or sal be imployit according to the ordorr sal be gevin be the said Generall Assemblie, for the weill and utilitie of the said Frensche Kirk; as also oblissis me to report ane sufficient generall discharge and acquittance of the said Frensche Kirk to the Kirk of Scotland, quherin speciall mentioun sal be maid off the ressait of the foirnamit sowme of aucht hundreth pundis money abonwrittin. For the quhilk cheritabill affectioun and loveing kyndnes of the minister and parrochinneris of the said West Kirk, I, the said Benjamin, in name of the said Frensche Kirk and Generall Assemblie abone specifeitt, randeris most humblie and hartlie thankis. Quhilk being ane singular pledge of our mutuall communioun in ane bodie, quherof Chryst is the Heid, dois most firmlie bind and obleis us in all our kirkis to pray and mak daylie supplicatiounes unto God for the long peax and prosperitie within the kingdome of Scotland and utheris his Majesties dominiones; requeisting them lykwyis most humblie to contenew this thair Cristiane affectioun and love to us under the tryall of the present persecutioun, sua lang as it sall pleas God to keipe us under the samyne; quhilk sal be ane sufficient witnes befoir God and man that zow have bene good and furthering instrumentis off the releiff and delyverie of the distrest sanctis of God, His Kirk in these partis; Be this my acquittance and ressait of the money abonnamit, thir presentis, writtin be James Downis, *sic subscribitur* the samyne with my hand, at Edinburgh, the xxiiii day of Apryll, the zeir of God i m.vi c. and tuentie twa zeiris, befoir thir witnesses Johne McMath, William Dick, and James Speir, merchandis, burgessis of Edinburgh and conjunct ressaveris of the money abonwrittin, etc.

      Basnage, depute from the Generall Assembly
       of the Reformed Churche of France to
       his Majestie of Great Britanny [*sic*], etc.

THE FORBES BARON COURT BOOK
1659-1678

Edited by

J. MAITLAND THOMSON, LL.D.

INTRODUCTION

THE records of Manorial Courts in England go back to the reign of Henry III., are preserved in great numbers, and are most valuable sources of information as to details of social life in the Middle Ages. That similar records were kept at an equally or almost equally remote time in Scotland is probable : that heritable jurisdiction in all its grades was granted and exercised at least as widely here as in England is certain. But our existing records are, judged by the English standard, late : prior to the sixteenth century I know of only two examples, cited by antiquaries and possibly still extant, though not at present traceable. One of these is a roll of proceedings in the Baron Court of Fowlis in Gowrie, recording how the heirs of Gifford of Yester were deprived of certain lands which they had held of the Grays of Fowlis, in 1385-6.[1] The other, a roll of the Baron Court of Camnethan, Lanarkshire, is quoted by Andrew Stuart [2] for proof of a point of pedigree. The earliest Baron Court Book preserved in the Register House is that of Carnwath, A.D. 1523 to 1542. At Drummond Castle there are records of the Baron Courts of Auchterarder, 1514 to 1520, also of those of Drummond, Drummond in Lennox (now Drymen), and Kincardine in Menteith, between 1536 and 1540.[3] When we come to the seventeenth century, the material becomes more

---

[1] *Hist. MSS. Com. Rep.*, iii., App., 410.
[2] *Genealogical History of the Stewarts*, p. 96.
[3] Information from Mr. W. C. Bishop.

abundant, but little of it has been published or (so far as I know) examined. Two Court Books, those of the baronies of Urie, Kincardineshire, and Stitchill, Roxburghshire, have been published by the Scottish History Society ; the Barony Court Book of Corshill, Ayrshire, forms part of one of the volumes issued by the Ayrshire and Wigtonshire Archæological Association ; and short extracts from other Baron Court Books have been included in the Spalding *Miscellany,* vol 5, and in the *Transactions of the Banffshire Field Club,* vol. 24. These last, as well as the Urie book, refer to the north-eastern counties. But examination will show that this fact does not affect the value of the present publication, which in subject matter and procedure differs materially from the Baron Court Book of Urie as well as from its other predecessors in print. However, they are its predecessors, and the editors of the two Scottish History Society publications have prefaced them with learned and laborious introductions. The present editor, therefore, might hold himself excused from going deeply into the antiquities of the subject, even if he were qualified for such a task.

In England, from the earliest days of feudalism, every manor had a right to hold its Court Baron, held (in legal theory) not by the lord of the manor but by the suitors, that is, the tenants ; an arrangement which gives some colour to the theory that in older times the land had been divided not into manors under a lord but into townships consisting of free tenants. At all events, the manor court had jurisdiction *qua* manor court, apart from any royal or other grant. But it could not exercise any franchise, that is special jurisdiction other than the pettiest, unless by special grant or by immemorial possession : in which case, the court was not a *court baron* but a *court leet,* or view

INTRODUCTION

of frankpledge.[1] In Scotland, so far as the evidence goes, there is nothing to show that any court held any inherent right of jurisdiction apart from grant by the feudal superior. If a barony were granted *cum curiis*, the baron could hold courts similar to the English Court Baron; if *cum furca et fossa* (and the other antique words of style which accompany them in charters), he had power not only to punish but to put to death, if the offence was a capital crime and was not one of the 'four points' reserved to the Crown; in which latter case jurisdiction could only be conferred by a grant of regality. In the Baron Court of Carnwath (*temp.* James v.) offenders were tried for minor capital crimes, and presumably if convicted sentenced to death.[2] But in the seventeenth century we find that even where the baron by his charter had the right of pit and gallows, he had ceased to exercise it; it was in desuetude. According to Stair, this was largely due to the action of the Court of Session, which had and freely used the power of Advocation, that is, of removing any cause from any court, civil or criminal, which the Judges regarded as unsuitable for its trial, and transferring it to the appropriate tribunal. Thus at the period to which this record belongs, Baron Courts, including the Court of Forbes, retained only the power of dealing with minor civil actions and petty breaches of the peace, the most important being those which had resulted in effusion of blood, for which a 'bloodwit' not exceeding £50 Scots was inflicted.[3] The baron retained

---

[1] 'It is, to say the least, doubtful whether the system of frankpledge extended to any part of the ancient kingdom of Northumbria' (Pollok and Maitland, *History of English Law*, vol. i. p. 569, and authorities there quoted).

[2] I have not noticed any case in which the verdict or sentence on a capital charge is recorded.

[3] In the Carnwath record the offence is described as 'fylin my lordis grund with violent blude.'

also the right to incarcerate an offender, if he had a prison available : the laird of Urie had a prison,[1] but Lord Forbes apparently had not ; at least there is no mention in this record of any prison, unless we reckon as such the stocks, in which an offender might be sentenced to sit four days if he disobeyed the ground officer and could not afford to pay the prescribed fine.[2]

It is possible that the restriction of the powers of the Baron Courts had had the effect of causing a number of them to be discontinued. But it is also possible that Cromwell and his English advisers, when in 1654 they issued their Ordinance for the Establishment of Baron Courts in Scotland,[3] had a different object. The Courts they had in view were to be on the English model ; held every three weeks, held not by the lord of the barony but by the suitors, that is the tenants, jurisdiction restricted to petty civil causes, the agenda determined by juries who were to make presentments to the Courts like the English grand juries. These provisions were calculated to assist in the accomplishment of two objects which Cromwell certainly had in view, viz. the diminishing of the power of the Scots landed aristocracy, and the assimilation of the Scots law to the English. But none of these modifications seem to have been adopted by the authorities in Scotland who were expected to carry them out. The Baron Court of Stitchill bears to have been established with an eye to the Ordinance of 1654, if not by authority of that ordinance ; yet its sittings were not held at regular intervals but from time to time as required ; it was held not in name of the suitors

---

[1] *Court Book of the Barony of Urie* (Scot. Hist. Soc.), p. 164. Is this prison to be identified with 'the theefs hole at Stonhyve'? (*ibid.*, p. 109).
[2] P. 232.
[3] Reprinted for reference, below, Appendix B.

but of the baron's factor; and the jury, so far as appears from the minutes, did nothing but put in an appearance at the opening of each Court, and did that only till 1658, after which there is no further mention of them. Juries, it may be added, were part of the machinery of our Baron Courts long before 1654; at Carnwath they in 1523 and onwards were present at every sitting and gave their verdict on each case; their regular form of finding an offender guilty is, they *cannot quit* him, which suggests a reminiscence of the ancient form of compurgation. In the court of Forbes the Bailie trying those accused of breaches of the peace regularly refers the question of fact to the jury; but in the minutes of the courts held at Tolmauds (see below) there is no mention of them. It is quite probable that different courts followed different practices in this matter.

Before going into further detail as to the Baron Court of Forbes, it will be convenient to describe the MS. of which its minutes form the greater part.

That MS., preserved in the Forbes charter chest and liberally put at the disposal of the Scottish History Society by the present Lord Forbes, consists of 146 leaves (not counting blank leaves), viz. 66 leaves containing rentals of the Forbes estates, and 80 leaves containing proceedings of the Baron Court. The earliest rental, epitomised in *Antiquities of Aberdeen and Banff* (Spalding Club), and noticed at some length in Innes's *Scotch Legal Antiquities*, is dated 1552, and deals with the baronies or estates of Kearn, Forbes, Alford, Abergardin (parish of Glengairn), Tough, Cluny, Tolmaads (parish of Kincardine-O'Neil), Fodderbirs (parish of Birse), Fiddes (parish of Foveran), and some lands in Buchan; the leases being in every case granted for five years. In 1557 there is another rental comprising the same lands, and some teinds and other possessions of the priory of Monymusk. Then comes a rental dated 1597, of which the MS. gives the title only, and leaves eight pages blank for details. Then another rental dated 1617, bearing to include all Lord Forbes's lands within the sheriffdom of Aberdeen; but only the rental of the barony of Fiddes is actually engrossed. This is followed by notes of leases renewed in 1623 for another five years, ' in ane fencit court of the baronye of Fiddes.' The next item is a scheme of division of the work of thatching of the 'laich bigging' of Fiddes among the tenants of that barony, which is printed as Appendix A to this Introduction. The concluding part of this division of the MS. consists of tacks of Puttachie and other lands in the parish of Keig, dated between 1623 and 1632. One leaf of this section contains copies of the records of the admission of Arthur Lord Forbes as burgess of Edinburgh in 1617 and of Aberdeen in 1622, and a notice of the death of King James VI. Eight blank pages divide the Rental from the Baron Court Book, which begins 1659 and ends 1678. Whether similar Courts were held for the Forbes estates at earlier or later dates does not appear, unless an inference can be drawn from the above cited notice of a 'fencit court' of the barony of Fiddes in 1623. In the MS. the proceedings of 58 Courts are minuted, of which 48 were held for the principal Forbes lands, in the parishes of Forbes, Keig, Auchindoir, Clatt, and Kearn, or for specially designated parts of them. Of these, the Keig lands had belonged before the Reformation to the Archbishop of St. Andrews, and in the seventeenth century were held by Lord Forbes of the Marquess of Huntly; the lands in the other four parishes were ancient Forbes property, and in the Rentals comprise

INTRODUCTION

the baronies of Kearn and Forbes.[1] Two other Forbes baronies, those of Fiddes and Alford, had before 1659 passed into other hands.[2] The other ten Courts were held for a detached property, Tolmaads, also held of the Marquess of Huntly, and in the Court Book styled the Barony of the Braes of Tolmaads. One Court, in 1668, is held for the lands of Tillykerrie in the parish of Tough.[3] Apparently all the remaining lands comprised in the rentals had by 1659 ceased to be Lord Forbes's property. In 1665 two Courts are held for the parishes of Forbes and Kildrummy; how Lord Forbes had an interest in Kildrummy I have not ascertained.

The Baron Bailie of Forbes, like his brethren elsewhere, was first and foremost concerned to enforce payment of his lord's rents in money and victual [4] and next to that, to compel the tenants to do their duty by the millers to whom they were thirled, and the millers to do their duty by the tenants. The getting in of the minister's teinds is also a prominent object in this and other Court Books;

---

[1] The 'List of Pollable Persons within the Shire of Aberdeen, 1696,' shows that in that year Lord Forbes was the sole heritor in the parishes of Forbes and Kearn, and an heritor also in Keig, Auchindoir, and Clatt.

[2] Fiddes was acquired in 1626 by James Crichton of Frendraught, who had a Great Seal charter in 1627, and sold it in 1635 to John Udny of Newburgh, whose family still owned it in 1696. The barony of Petflug or Balfluig, part of the Alford estate, belonged in 1648 to Forbes of Leslie, who in that year held a Baron Court, the minute of which is printed in the Old Statistical Account of Alford Parish. The barony of Auchintoul, also a part of Alford, appears in 1677 and 1678 among the lands for which the Forbes Baron Court was held; possibly it was in nonentry, and so in the hands of Lord Forbes as superior; or he may have been exercising the conjoint jurisdiction of which a superior did not and could not divest himself though he granted the right of holding courts to a vassal. In 1696 the owner was Mr. Arthur Forbes of Auchintoul.

[3] Tillykerrie is included in the Forbes rentals of 1552 and 1557. In 1696 it belonged to Leslie younger of Kincraigie.

[4] There is no victual rent mentioned in the proceedings of the Tolmaads Courts. In 1552 the rents did not include any victual, but in 1557 one of the farms, Tornaveen, paid 4 bolls malt.

and so was the performance of the carriages to which the minister was entitled, though at Forbes it was not judged necessary, as at Stitchill, to interpone the Bailie's authority to the acts and sentences of the kirk session. Encroachments on the lord's policies and his woods and moors, crops, grass and brooms, were constantly being forbidden by enactments and punished when detected, and the attempts to enforce the long series of Acts of Parliament enjoining planting of trees in the yards of the tenants as in those of the landlords were repeated in Court after Court, probably to little purpose, being as yet unsupported by public opinion. Burning heather at forbidden seasons was another offence constantly reprobated; its advantages were imperfectly understood, and though the public law at this date allowed it up to 15th April, the Baron Courts at Forbes and elsewhere endeavoured to enforce the old law which prohibited it after the end of March, which law was reimposed by Parliament in 1685.[1] In these matters the Forbes Court did not differ much from other Courts. The same remark applies to the numerous Acts enjoining good neighbourhood among the tenants. Trespassing upon one another's crops, excessive and injurious cutting of peat, turf and broom, were practices everywhere reprobated and everywhere indulged in. More peculiar to the Forbes properties were breaches of the peace. The author of the valuable and very interesting description of the old-fashioned methods of cultivation, contained in the Old Statistical Account of the parish of Alford, observes that the inhabitants in his day had 'laid aside that quarrelsome temper which once prevailed, without adopting in its stead the spirit of litigiousness that has succeeded it in many places.' The Forbes record, a hundred years earlier, shows

---

[1] *Acts of the Parliaments of Scotland*, viii. 475.

the ' quarrelsome temper ' in full vigour. A tenant finding his neighbour's sheep in his corn promptly exercises his legal right to ' poind ' them ; the owner comes ' and his servand and ane trie in his handis, and said he should mak patent doris and tak forth his sheip.' A woman salutes her neighbour as ' perjurit and miswaron carll,' and the repartee is a blow : brought into court, she fails to prove the allegation of perjury, so her husband for her slander, and her neighbour for his assault, are each condemned to pay £5 Scots to the master of Forbes. Cases of this sort form the staple of the record, so far as it relates to litigation, though usually not the origin but the circumstances of each scuffle are described, sometimes with some gusto ; the ordinary conclusion is the binding over of the parties to keep the peace—except when the other party is resisting the law, when intervention becomes a no doubt agreeable duty. In short, Cromwell intended his Baron Courts to be small debt Courts, and the Corshill Court, for instance, was largely occupied with work of that sort ; whereas the Forbes Court more resembled a modern police court. Its proceedings required less formality, but it enjoyed in practice more independence. The lands lay in a remote district, their owner was a powerful baron ; the inhabitants were uneducated ;[1] there was no neighbour tribunal from whose rivalry loss of prestige and of court fines was to be feared—at Corshill the inhabitants when they went to law with one another had to be discouraged by fines from preferring to settle their differences before the bailies of Irvine ; nothing of that kind was to be feared at Forbes.[2] The

---

[1] At Urie and at Stitchill the schoolmaster was much in evidence. The *List of Pollable Persons* mentions no schoolmaster resident on the Forbes lands.

[2] Note the permission granted in 1668 to some tenants of Puttachie to sue each other at any court in the sheriffdom, p. 274.

Courts were held by the Baron Bailie, attended and recorded by the Court Clerk; the only other necessary official was the ground officer. The dempster is always mentioned in the minutes, but his name is always left blank; there was no need to appoint him, for the Bailie exercised his functions. The birliemen indeed could not well be dispensed with, but the consent of the tenants to their appointment was evidently a mere form, so that as a rule they are described as chosen by the Bailie,[1] sometimes as chosen by the Baron himself.[2] The procurator fiscal, who in theory ought to have prosecuted whenever a fine was claimed on behalf of the Baron, is never mentioned in this record; in cases of assault the complaint usually bears to be made by the injured party, who is sometimes awarded a sum of money as compensation, but always a much smaller sum than that of the Baron's solatium for the 'fylin of his grund vith violent blude.'[3] It is not surprising to find that sometimes the assaulted party prefers to make common cause with the assailant, and deny that the 'blood' was shed at all.[4]

The record provides a certain amount of information as to the then state of the country. The phrase 'taieth and ewell corn'[5] indicates that the system of husbandry in use was the same as that so clearly described in the Old Statistical Account of Alford: there is no sign of the dawn of modern and less wasteful methods.[6] The frequent prosecutions for trespass upon the yards, orchards, and

---

[1] P. 237.
[2] P. 245.
[3] See p. 207, note 3.
[4] See p. 267. The practice of producing a bloody cloth in court as evidence that blood had been shed (p. 268) savours of antiquity.
[5] See Glossary, Appendix C, below.
[6] Lime is mentioned twice; no doubt it was used not for the land but for building purposes (pp. 278, 314).

INTRODUCTION

garden dykes of Druminnor and Puttachie (the ancient and modern Castle Forbes), and the green and park of Puttachie, prove that those houses were already beginning to surround themselves with 'policies,' though doubtless on a very modest scale ; [1] and the ordinances for protection of the tenants' yards show that the Acts for planting trees round farmhouses were not absolutely a dead letter (note especially the prosecution of a tenant for cutting down a tree in his own yard). But the woods and bogs (the terms seem to be synonymous) of Forbes or Druminnor, Bithnie, Balfour, and Kirkton of Forbes in Forbes parish, the woods and the *arnes* (alders) of Bogieside, the birks of Windseye in Kearn Parish, the saplings of Logie in Auchindoir parish, and the wood of Puttachie, must have been not plantations but natural wood, such as, under less unfavourable conditions, covers parts of the same ground still.[2] In one moss, that of Towie in Clatt parish, there were trunks of ancient fir and oak trees imbedded, the *holling* (digging out) of which by a tenant was a punishable offence. We read that 'thin splits of fir taken off logs that had been dug up in mosses, and twisted into a sort of rope, because they stood wet well without rotting, were preferred above all others for tethering horses in the field, as well as for draught purposes. These ropes of a proper length were sold ready made under the name of fir tethers : and when

---

[1] The condition of a neighbouring estate, Monymusk, about 1716 is thus described : 'At that time there was not one acre upon the whole esteat enclosed, nor any timber upon it, but a few elm, cycamore, and ash about a small kitchen garden adjoining to the house, and some straggling trees at some of the farm yards, with a small copswood, not inclosed and dwarfish and broused by sheep and cattle' (*Notes and Sketches Illustrative of Northern Rural Life in the Eighteenth Century*, by the Author of Johnny Gibb of Gushetnook, p. 84).

[2] The 'Saplings of Logie' are still marked on the Ordnance Map. According to the New Statistical Account there are 378 acres of natural wood on Lord Forbes's estates in Keig parish.

no longer fit to be used as a tether they were employed as candle fir.'[1]

The enactments that ' no unfamed person shall be resset in the land of Tammadis, nor no skandalous person shall duell in the saides landis without famed testimoniallis,'[2] and ' that no laborer within the forsaid barronrie sall recett nor give any hadin to ani soroner nor idle persones nor non quo mack nor travill for kaill and fyr bot tacks and stealls quhair they can have them,'[3] are illustrated by the description in *Notes and Sketches* before cited, how vagabonds ' would get temporary housing on some doubtful form of tenancy, stealing kail and peats from the neighbours quite freely and almost openly.'[4]

The allusions to State affairs are few. In 1664 the tenants are charged to obey the ground officers as to public dues and cess.[5] In 1678 the tenants of the barony of Auchintoul are required to pay their share of public burdens as provided in their leases ;[6] and it is enacted that ' His Majesty's new supply for this term ' shall be cast on the tenants proportionally, they getting relief in the shape of a fixed contribution from their subtenants, cottars, grassmen, and domestics; the Bailie ordaining that this stent shall be only for this term, and noways to be ' ane

---

[1] *Notes and Sketches*, as above, p. 36. Dr. R. M. Wilson writes : I have seen some magnificent oak trees in a splendid state of preservation dug out of peat mosses, some of them 20 to 30 feet long and set up for flag-poles about a large farm or near a proprietor's mansion-house. Then again the fir trees were cut and used not only for fuel but for lighting, being split into long narrow strips, each of which would burn for a considerable time. In my grandfather's young days (over a hundred years ago—he was all through the Peninsular War) the *Aberdeen Journal* (a weekly paper then) was read in the evenings by the light of these fir *caules* (candles), and as the poor were always with them, it devolved upon the beggar man to hold and keep up these lights one after the other. In process of time a stand was made with a metal spring to hold these burning strips of fir, and these stands are called ' puir men ' to this day.

[2] P. 231.   [3] P. 299.   [4] *Notes and Sketches*, p. 165.
[5] P. 246.   [6] Pp. 316-17.

INTRODUCTION 217

preparateiv' in time coming.¹ In 1670 it was enacted that the tenants in the parish of Forbes (following the Militia Act of 1669) must pay their soldiers for this present militia 'ane constant fie in land and money,' and that 'ewry shoulder of the militia within the pariochin of Forbes sall hav after Witsonday nixt and als long as the militia sall happin to continow yeirly ten markes money.'² In 1671 there is reference to the distribution of arms for the militia, and the exaction from tenants, cottars or grassmen of 'sojours fies, clothing, money or vages for the randiwowes.'³ In 1677 there are two Acts, one for the principal properties and the other for Tolmaads,⁴ that each inhabitant according to his social position is to bear arms for his own defence, the arms appropriate to each class being specified; which reads like a revival of the legislation of fifteenth-century Parliaments on this head.⁵

Of duties exigible from tenants, there is one seemingly not recorded elsewhere, viz. carr meall,⁶ which Dr. Wilson interprets carr mail, payment for the right to rear calves.

Of unfamiliar measures of capacity, we should note the *Haddish* of meal, exigible by an ordinance of 1670 :⁷ it is quoted in dictionaries from a legal document of 1814, but is now obsolete. It is said to have meant in some places one third, in others one quarter, of a peck. Dr. Wilson suggests that it is a corruption of *half-dish*. The *Muttie*, ordered in 1676 to be kept and precisely measured along with the mill peck, of which it is declared to be a quarter, in each of Lord Forbes's mills,⁸ is said in the *Dialect Dictionary* to contain half a stone of meal. The *moudefow*,

---

¹ Pp. 320-21.   ² P. 279.   ³ Pp. 282-83.
⁴ Pp. 313, 315.
⁵ *Acts of the Parliaments of Scotland*, ii. 10, 45, 226.   ⁶ P. 234.
⁷ P. 279.   ⁸ P. 304.

the under-miller's fee ' for ilk boll of shilling,' [1] is also a strange word.

My thanks, and the thanks of the Scottish History Society, are due to Lord Forbes for his liberality and patience in allowing me the use of the manuscript for a prolonged period ; and to Dr. R. M. Wilson of Tarty, Ellon, for several valuable notes on points as to which I ventured to consult him.

APPENDIX A

The minnett off the forme off the theaking off the laich bigging off Fiddes within the clos. Ilk tennentis pairt quhilk they sould wphald *pro rato* for ther awin pairtis att Fiddes the fyftein day off Julij.

1624

Item in the first Allexr. Forbes for Davies hill & Arthour Jafray for Davies hill theakis the for syd off the kitchin & geilhouse to the syd off ye brewhous dore neirest the zard zett ;

Item Arthour Forbes in Kinknockie & the pluche off the Hill of Fiddes ar iust anent them in theaking, on the baksyd off the kitchin and geilhouse, als far fordvard on the baksyd, & als neir the zard zett, as ye oyeris on the forsyd ;

Item Thomas Grege for Auchinderg theakis the brewhous iust to ye zard zett on the forsyd theroff neirest the close ;

Item David Aikin theakis the baksyd off the brewhous to the zard zett for the pluche off Blaircheillie, als far fordvard as Thomas Grege does ;

Item Jhon Cragehead for ane pluche off Fiddes beag, theakis the owne house within the zard zett, on both sydis ;

And this is for the east quarter off the laich bigging within the close off Fiddes ;

---

[1] P. 300.

APPENDIX A

Item Thomas Grege for the milne off Fiddes, theckis the stabill neirest the zard zett on both sydis;

Item Jhone Mitchell for the ailhous off Fiddes, theackis the forsyd off the mid house, on the south syd off the close, callit the old girnell house;

Item Jhone Crageheid for ane pleuche in Fiddesbeag, theakis the baksyd off the said mid house neirest the zard, als farr as Jhone Mitchell does the oyer syd;

Item the twa pleuches off Munkis hill theakis the lymhouse on both the sydis theroff:

> And this for the south syd neirest the zard off the laich bigging within the close off Fiddes, quhilk is iust anent the hall doire;

Item Robert Forsye fore ane pleuche off Fiddes beag theakis ye forsyd off my lordis staibill neirest the close;

Item the tenent off Allexr. Couperis tak, off the Hill off Fiddes, theackis the oyer syd off my lordis staible, nixt to the ail house on the west syd theroff;

Item George Beang & Andro Beang his sone, for the pleuche off Pettimucke, theackis the Womanhouse, quhilk is neirest to my lordis stable, on both the sydis theroff;

Item Gilbert Jafray for Cultercullen theakis the schoole house callit the scholleris chalmer, & that pairt yat is abowe ye zett;

Item Arthour Couper for ane pleuche off Muttonbrey theakis the oyer syd off the schoole house callit the scholleris chalmer, that syd theroff, quhilk is neirest the close, & lykwayis he theakis abowe the zett, als far as Gilbert Jafray does;

Item Thomas Jafray for his twa pluchis off Cultercullen the ane was Wm. Smythis, & the oyer occupieit be him selff, he theakis the nuik chalmer, callitt the new girnell hous on both the sydes yeroff;

> And this for the west syd off the laich bigging within the close off Fiddes.

Item the north syd is all sklettitt.

Nota. The haill tennentis, theakis the chappell or girnell houss off Fiddes, quhilk is att the hill off Fiddes, ilk ane for ther awin pairtis, *pro rato* amongis them all;

Nota the haill tennentis wphaldis ther awin pairt off off (*sic*) the laich bigging within the close off Fiddes, wnder thack and raip, zeirlie *pro rato*.

APPENDIX B

Cromwell's Ordinance for the Establishment of Baron Courts in Scotland (*Acts of Parliament of Scotland*, vol. vi., pt. ii., p. 816).

Wednesday, April 12, 1654.

Be it Declared, Established and Ordained, by his Highness the Lord Protector, by and with the advice and Consent of his Councill, That in every place or Circuit of land which really is, or hath commonly been called, known, or reputed to be a Manor, within the Nation of Scotland, there shall be one Court, which shall be in the nature of a Court Baron, or Court of a Manor here in England, to be holden every three weeks : which Court shall have power, order and jurisdiction of all Contracts, debts, promises, and trespasses whatsoever, arising within the said Manor or precincts thereof: Provided that the matter in demand exceed not the value of forty shillings Sterling, and that in any such action of trespass the freehold or title of the land be not drawn into question : And it is farther declared and Ordained, that every the said Court Baron shall be held in manner following, That is to say, the Stile of the Court shall be, the Court of A B held the   day of   one thousand six hundred   by K. D. C. Sutors of the said Court, and the homage or Sutors to be named in the entry, then after three *O yes* made, the Sutors, or their Clerk or Steward, shall say, If any will be assoigned or enter any plaint, let them come in, and they shall be heard : then the Jury are to be impannelled and sworn, and then a short charge is to be given concerning the several matters and things to be done there, and after presentment and enquiry made, the Sutors shall proceed in the several matters presented, and give order and relief as the case shall require, and make execution by attachment upon the goods of the party within that Manor.

And it is hereby further Declared and Ordained, That the Sutors in every the said Court Baron may, from time to time, as there shall be occasion, make By-laws for the publique weal, rule, and government of the Persons within such Manor, and all and every such By-Law shall be binding to every party within the Manor : And the said Sutors shall have power and authority to amerce such persons as infringe any of the said By-Laws, and may give warrant to the Baylif of the Manor to distrein for such amercement by attachment upon the Goods of the party offending. Provided that such By-Laws be not extended to bind the Inheritance of any person who is not party to the same, and agrees not thereunto.

   Ordered by his Highnesse the Lord Protector, and his Councill, that this Ordinance be forthwith Printed and Published.

    Henry Scobell, Clerk of the Councill.

Confirmed in Parliament, 17 Sept. 1656
 (*Ibid.*, p. 848.)

APPENDIX C

Glossary of Archaic and Provincial Words

Abefor, before.
Arnes, alders.
Awell (Ewell) fields, fields bearing a crop of corn a second year in succession.
Bink, press down and crush.
Blood, make to bleed.
Bondage (Bonnage), agricultural service done by tenants and their dependants to the proprietor.
Bordes, bourds, mocking words.
Brew tallon, tallow paid by brewers for the privilege of brewing; also called brew taugh, and brew creisch.
Brok, break up into small parcels.
Cess, public burden laid on the shires.
Cook an enclosure, to fence it; literally, to hide it.
Cows, tufts of heather.
Daach, a davoch, ancient measure of land. The only *daach* mentioned in the Forbes record is that of Towie in Clatt parish.
Dowett, a flat turf, thinner than a *fail*.
Eard dyke, wall made of earth.
Eir, plough.
Fail, turf.

Flachter spade, a long two-handed spade for casting turfs.
Flyting, scolding.
Fogitch, foggage, rank grass on which stock feed in winter.
Futeit compts, balanced accounts.
Girsschman, tenant of a cottage with no land attached.
Grethstings, poles for making hoops.
Haddish, a measure of grain. See Introduction.
Hadin, a holding; it might be either land or a house.
Haining, enclosure.
Hainit girs, enclosed grass.
Handigrips, close grappling.
Hearring, harrowing.
Holling fir and aik, digging up trunks of fir and oak buried in a moss. See Introduction.
Hucle, heckle, torment.
Hunied corn, damaged corn. Dr. Wilson suggests that the word ought to be read 'humid'; but at p. 287 it seems synonymous with 'sweit.'
Kail, cabbage.
Knaveship (also written 'kenship'), a small duty in meal paid to the under-miller.
Leg dollar, a Dutch coin, having the impression of a man in arms with one leg and a shield covering the other leg. In 1670 its value in Scots money was reduced by Act of the Privy Council from 58 to 56 shillings Scots. (See *Reg. of Privy Council*, third series, vol. iii. p. 136.)
Mailing, farm for which mail (rent) is paid.
Mein dykes, march dykes, common to two adjacent farms.
Merciment, fine imposed by a judge, *amerciamentum*.
Midden hird (zeird), heap of earth mixed with manure.
Mill swyne, swine paid by a miller as part of his rent.
Miswaron, mansworn.
Mossgreiv, overseer superintending the casting of peat.
Moudefow, small fee paid to the under-miller.
Muck-fail, heap of turf mixed with manure.
Muirburn, burning heather. In old days it was followed by stripping the surface of the moor.
Muttie, quarter peck. See Introduction.
Nolt, black cattle.
Opposit, questioned.
Pickiman, the under-miller.

APPENDIX C

Plantins, small trees intended for planting.
Raiff, reave, carry off.
Resting, owing arrears of rent.
Rey, rye; heavier than oats, and therefore used for adulterating the 'ferm.'
Rot tres, fallen and decaying trees.
Rugeing, tearing.
Sepleines, saplings.
Sess, same as cess.
Shilling, grain freed from the husk.
Stryk oxin, yoke oxen together in a plough, in token of 'good neighbourhood' between their owners. The word 'strike' used in the same sense as in the phrase 'strike hands.'
Sucken, territory bound to grind corn and pay multure exclusively at a certain mill.
Syss, assise, jury.
Sysseres, jurymen.
Tach (taieth), and ewell (awell), corn; corn off field which had had crops taken off it in two successive years, after manuring.
Taw, tumble about.
Tirr a house, strip the roof off it.
Tost, torment.
Tulyeing, scuffling.
Unlaw, onlei, a fine.
Wands, long shoots of willow.
Weet or Bloodwit, fine for shedding blood.

THE FORBES BARON COURT BOOK

The Court of ye landis and leiwing of Forbes, haldin at Castell Forbes vponn the sewint day of October 1659 zeiris Be Williame maister of Forbes, Arthour Dilgarno of Tollie his baillie, George Andersone notar publict clark of court, Patrik Taviotdaill, Johne Milne, officeris, and [blank] damnatour.

The Court lauchfullie fensit and affermit.

The said day ye haill tennentis within ye grund ar ordanit to pay to ye maister thair haill resting byrune dewteis of silver, victuell and malt conforme to yair futeit comptis, within terme of law, vnder ye pane of poinding.

The quhilk day ye haill tennentis in ye grund ar ordanit to vphold such biging as they resauit at yair entrie and to leiwe yaim in als guid estate as they fand yaim quhensoeuir they remove, and quhat they better yame they salbe satisfeit yairfoir.

The said day it is statute and ordanit that no tennentis within ye grund cast faill nor dowett within medowis nor hainit gers nor midding hird within proper haning in tyme cuming, quhairin gif ony failzeis, they sall pay tuentie pundis vnlaw for ilk fault *toties quoties*.

The quhilk day it is statute and ordanit that no tennentis nor induelleris within ye grund cast nor leid moir peittis zeirlie in tyme cuming nor may convenientlie serve yair awin vses, quhairin gif ony failzeis he sall pay tuentie pundis *toties quoties* for ilk fault.

The said day it is statute and ordanit to tuo (? that no) tennentis within ye grund kendle nor fyir muires nor hedder in forbiddin tyme, vnder ye pane of tuentie pundis for ilk breck.

The quhilk day it is statute and ordanit that ilk tennent within ye grund pay yair ministeris stipendis of Forbes and Keirne for yis crop 1659 zeiris and byganes, vnder ye pane of poinding.

The said day ye haill tennentis within ye grund ar ordanit to send in yair servandis to such work and service as they salbe requyred, and yat tymouslie about sone rysing.

The quhilk day it is ordanit yat no inhabitantis within ye grund of Puittachie loup nor cast doun ye garden dykis, vnder ye pane of ten pundis.

The said day ye haill cotteris, croftmen and girsmen ar ordanit to help and contribute with ye rest of ye suckin for carying and transporting of stane and tymmer heirefter according to yair halding.

This court continouit to ane new day and lauchfull wairning.

G. ANDERSONE, notar publict, clerk of court.
ARTHOUR DALGARNO, Bailzie.

[Court held in Castle Forbes as above, 27 March 1660. Suits called, &c.]

The quhilk day ye haill tennentis within ye parochines of Forbes, Keig, Auchindoir, Clatt and Keirne ar ordanit to pay yair ferme bollis resting be yame for crope 1659 betuix and ye thrid day of Maij nixtocum, and quha failzeis at ye said day ar ordanit to pay tuelf pundis for ilk boll meill and sextein pundis for ilk boll malt they salbe resting ather of yair fermes [1] or multur victuell or teind victuell, vnder ye pane of poinding.

The said day ye haill tennentis forsaidis ar ordanit to pay yair resting silver dewteis preceiding yis day within fyftein dayes, quhairin gif they failzie they ar ordanit to pay tuentie schillingis for ilk mark resting be yame within terme of law vnder ye pane of poinding.

The quhilk day in corroboratioun of ane former act it is statut and ordanit that no tennentis, induelleris nor removing tennentis cast faill, douett nor miding zeird within

---

[1] *Ferme* means rent paid in corn or meal; *mail* is money rent; *customs* are rents paid in kind, such as poultry or sheep; *due service* is farm work, including carriage.

proper haning, nor eir nor labour hauch nor medow zeird yat hes nocht bein labourit abefor, quhairin gif ony failzeis, they sall pay tuentie pundis vnlaw for ilk fault *toties quoties.*

The said day ye haill tennentis in Forbes, except Blakhillok and Sillivathie and Stralunak and Knowheid and Walkmylne, ar fund giltie in cutting, distroying, and away taking of tymer out of ye bogis of Bithny, Balfour and Kirktoun of Forbes, and ye tennentis of Barflett and Bogiesyid ar fund lykwyis giltie of cutting of grein wod in ye arnes of Bogiesyid, and als ye tennentis of Edinbanchrie ar fund giltie of cutting and distroying of greind uod, and yairfor conforme to former actis ilk man is stent to tuentie pundis vnlaw.

The quhilk day it is inactit that quhatsumewer tennent in ye grund refuiss to obey ye command and chairge of ony officer lauchfullie to be vsit aganis yaim for ony dewtie or service salbe imposit vponn yaim, the pairtie disobedient sall pay ten pundis for ilk fault.

The said day Johne Gellan in Eister Glentoun, James Jamesone in ye wod of Puttachie, ar appointed birlamen for ye parochin of Keig; William Grein in Blakhillok, Patrik Jamesone in Stralunak and Johne Mitchell in Balfour, Arthour Mitchell in Culhay, for ye parochin of Forbes; Robert Mitchell in Logie, Johne Mitchell in Edinbanchrie, for ye parochin of Auchindoir; James Walker in Wasthillis, Johne Glas in Barflett, James Oliver in Tollie, Robert Wricht in Talzeach, ar apointit birlamen for Clatt and Kerne, and they ar ordanit to convein vponn adverteisment and dischairge such dewtie as salbe incumbent to yair office of birlamen.

The said day it is statute and ordanit that no inducller within ye grund teder zewis besydes yair neighbouris cornes or gers in no tyme cuming, and quha hapnis to failzie sall pay fourtie schillings for ilk fault.

The quhilk day it is statute and ordanit that all cotteris and girsmen within ye grund keip fouldis with such gudis and scheip as they haue vnbrokin ordour till ye ending of ye harvest.

[Court continued as above.]

[Court held as above, 27 February 1661. James Thomson, notary public, clerk of court. Suits called, &c.]

The said day the haill tennentis within the parichones of Forbes, Kearn, Keag, Clet, Auchindoir according to former actis ar heir ordained to mak peyment of yair rest silver dueties and yair wictuall dueties and that vithin term of law, vnder the pane of poindeing. quhilk is relateing both to silver and victuall duetie.

The said day John Layng haueing controvenit former actis, he is ordained to pey sex [deleted and *fyv* substituted] poundis vithin terme of law.

The said day the haill tennentis of ye afoirsaid parishes ar ordained vithin terme of law to mak peyment of yair Mertimes silver dueties for crop sextie and ye victuall bethe meill and malt, to vit yair meill betuixt this and Pase,[1] and yair malt against ye tent of May, and incaice of faillie at the affoirsaid dayes ten pound for ilk boll, and that vithin terme of laue, the termes of peyment being first com and bypast.

The said day Bessie Ritchie relict of wmquhill William Layng in Castellhill, and George Ronald in Bogheadis her cautioner, ar decerned to pey and delyüer to ye right honorabill William maister of Forbes tuo bollis of ferm meill and tuo firlotis of malt for ye crop j^m vj^c sextie, togither vith tuentie eight pound ten shilling for ye said crop and zeiris preceideing, mair the soum of fortie tuo markis of money, conform to ane band resteing be ye said defunck William Layng, quhilk band beiring dait ye tuentie nynt of Sepr. j^m vj^c feftie sewin zeris, and the affoirsaid baillie hes ordained them to mak peyment of the abowvryttin restis vithin terme of law vnder the pain of poindeing.

The said day the haill tennentis of ye respectivie parishes ar ordained to pey both yair teind victuall and teind silver to ye ministeris of the saidis parishes and the tym

---

[1] Viz. 14 April.

lastis being prescryūed, and that vuer, ar ordained to mak peyment vithin terme of law vndir the paine of poindcing.

The said day John Gordon, George Shand, Elspet Gordon, executoris to the deccised Bessie Duncan yair mother, somtym laborer of ane pleugh in Castellhill [are ordained] to pey and delywer the haill restcing duetics restcing be yair deccised mother both victuall and silver, both multer victuall and kirk victuall, and ye afoirsaid baillie hes ordained them and ilk ane of them to mak peyment yairof vithin terme of laue vnder the pain of poindcing, and that for crop sextic and all zeiris preccidïng.

The said day the wholl tennentis in Edinbanchrie, to wit Patrik and William Maris, John Angus, William Mitchell, ar found gilltie both of the wod of Bithnie and the sepleines of Logie, and ar ordained to hold them selwes frie of ye saidis vodis in all tymes comeing, and that vnder ye pain of tuentie pound for ilk ane of them giue they be not able to purge them selves quhen they ar nixt suited.

The said day the tennentis of Putachic ar ordained no to giue libertie to no person nor persones in vther menes landis to cast nor transport no turffes, peitis, faill, diwit vithin the boundis of Putachie, Glentoun, Keag, and that in no tymes comeing and vnder the pain of tuentie pound *totiens quotiens*, and iff they cannot purge them selffes for tymes bypast, is ordained to pey the foirsaid onlej.

The said day the haill tennentis of Glentoun, to vit John and Robert Reidis, George Burges, James Gleinn, they ar ordained ilk ane of them becaus they ver not able to purge them selves of ye wod of Puttachie is ordained accordeing to former actis to pey tuentie pound *totiens quotiens*.

The said day William Wedderburn, Robert Mitchell, John Glasse, Robert Wright, John Gellan, ar ordained to sight the vodis of Bithnie, Putachie and Bogiesyd and Kirktoun and Balphour and seplenes of Logie.

The haill tenentis of ye affoirsaid parishes ar ordained no to burn no muirburn in forbidin tymes accordeing to ye act of parliament, and yat vnder the pain of ten pound *totiens quotiens.*

The said day accordeing to ane former act maid yairanent the haill tenentis and tenentrie of ye afoirsaid parishes is ordained to send in yair servandis tymoslie to the bondadge accordeing as they ar varned be ye officeris.

The said day John Mitchell in Balfour, William Layng and John Vyr yair, Thomas Layng yair, John Leith in Kirktoun, John Mitchell yair, the affoirsaid baillie hes ordained them and ilk ane of them to pey ten pound *totiens quotiens* becaus they culd not frie them selves of ye bogis and vodis in Forbes.

The said day the wholl absens is ordained to pey ilk ane of them fortie shilling Scotis and that vithin terme of law.

Continues this court vpon 24 horis varneing.

      Arthour Dalgarno, Bailzie.
      J. Thomsone, court clerk.

At ye Miltoun of Ester Tammaidis the coort holdin be the right honnorabill William maister of Forbes, heritable propritour of ye saidis landis, ye court holdin vpon ye tuentie eight day of Jar. j^m vj^c thriscoir tuo zeris. William Garioch in Braidhauch his balzie for ye tym, James Thomsone in Milhill court clerk, James Elmslie officer, [*blank*] damster. The suitis callet ye court laufullie fenssit and affermit.

The said day John Farqr in Craiginheiw, Alexr. Nuckall in Ester Tammaidis, John Carney in Newbiging, James Robertson in Vester Tammaidis, thess four men hes giwin yair oath of fidelitie that they shall be leill and true birlimen throchout the landis of Tammaidis both to maister and tennent so far as yair knowledge serwes them.

The said day Robert Findley, Alexander Smith and lykweyes all the rest of ye tennentis within ye Breass quha peyes not yair ductie according to ye termes conteined within ye assedation, is ordained to pey tuentie shilling for ilk mark, and that within term of law vnder the pain of poindeing.

The said day Alexr. Mercheand is ordained to pey tuentie shilling for ilk mark yat he is resteand for crop sextie, and that within terme of law vnder ye pain of poindeing.

The said day Alexr. Tailliour is ordained to do his duetie to the mill of drawing of ston and trie and vpholding ye mill and in holding mill vatter off Anaytis in all tymes comeing according to his duettie.

The said day John King and James Fergus deponet that John Donaldson cam to ye toun of Wester Tammaidis and his servand and ane trie in his handis, and said he should mak patent doris and tak forth his sheip quhilk they haid takin in yair corn.

The said day John Donaldson hes inacted him selff vnder the pain of ten pound that in all tymes comeing he shall leiwe peiceblie and to be ane guid neightbour in all tymes comeing to ye men of Tammaidis.

The said day the wholl tenentis in Wester Tammaidis ilk ane of them is inacted in ye lyk caice to be guid neightbouris to John Donaldson in all tymes comeing.

The said day William Donaldsone and Alexr. Farqr both in Brom hill ilkane of them in actes them selwes vnder the pain of ten pound that they shall be guid neightbouris to vtheris in al tymes comeing.

The said dey it is inacted that no tenent within the Breass shall haue no foulles to eat yair nightbouris cornes, and that non of them shall dettayn non of yair guid out of ye fauld except it be ane tetherit beast, and vnder the pain of fortie shilling Scotis.

The said day the wholl tenentis both in the suk off Tammadis and ye sukin of Enettis shall do duetie to ye milles in all tymes comeing, and yat vnder the pain of fortie shilling *totiens quotiens*.

The said day ye birlamen is ordained vpon ane call off quhatsomeuer tenentis quhair yair is any controversie either in merches setting or any vther thing that is in oddis in ye said Breass, yat vpon ye said call they shall go and setle ye said bussines.

The said day John Duncan is ordained to keip the

fawld off Torneyvein vith sik guidis as [he] hes, except
they be vpon the tether, and that vnder ye pain of fortie
shilling *totiens quotiens*.

The said day ye Owertoun of Ester Tammadis is
ordained to pey thri stoukis of officer corn, and ye Miltoun
ane threaw of corn out of ye third crop sauld.

The said day it is in acted that no outland man shall
com to ye mosse of Drumlasie to cast peitis in no tym
comeing except they com to the maister of Forbes and
agrie for yair zeiris peitis, and yat vnder ye pain of ten
pound.

The said day the wholl tenentis is ordained to giue
obedience to ye officer in all tymes comeing, and quha-
soeuer refuiss sall pey thrie pound *totiens quotiens*.

The said day the wholl tenentis within the Breass is
ordained to plant yair zardis with timber and vnder ye
pain of [*blank*], and that the growing timber shall be
cairfullie keiped.

The said day it is inacted that no vnfamed person shall
be resset in ye land of Tammadis, nor no skandalous
person shall duell in ye saidis landis without famed testimoniallis, and yat vnder ye pain of ten pound.

The said day James Elmslie is ordained vpon any call
quhatsomeuer to go to ye birlimen, and he and they to
go and mak search quhair yair is any thing amiseing, and
quha does refuiss to go vith ye officer shall pey fyw
pound.

The said day it is in acted yat ye wholl tenentis shall
pey the minister his stipennd and yat at ye termes vsed
and vont, vnder ye pain of poynding of ye double yairoff.

Continues this court vpon 24 horis varning.

       Wm. Gariocii, Ballie.
       J. Thomsone, court clerk.

The Court of ye landis and leiwing of Forbes holdin within
 Castell Forbes vpon the third day of Merch j^m vj^c
 thriscoir tuo zeiris Be William maister of Forbes,
 Arthour Dillagarno baillie, James Thomsou nottar
 publict, clerk of court, John Mill, Patrik Tewidaill and

John Leitch officeris, [blank] damster. The suittis called the court laufullie fenssit and affermit.

The said day it is in acted and ordained that all maillis and dueties for crop and zeir of God j^m vj^c and sextie that all be peyed within term of law, quhilk faillicing of not thankfull peyment as said is, ten pound for ilk boll of meill and tuell pound for ilk boll of malt, and all silver duetie that is resteand for the said crop, the baillie ordaines them to pey ye samen vithin term of law, or vthervayes tuentie shilling for ilk mark, and that according to former actis.

The said day it is ordained that all silver duetie that showld haue bein peyed at Mertimes last for crop sexti ane, that it be peyed within ten dayes, vnder ye pain of poinding, and all silver duetie that should haue bein peyed at Candlemass, the baillie ordaines them to pey the samen vithin term of law, vnder ye pain of poinding, and siklyk all that should be peyed at Lambmass, that it be peyed within term of law, vnder ye pain of poinding, ye termes of peyment first being com and bypast, or vthervayes to pey ane pound for euerie mark.

The said day the wholl tenentis that peyes wictuall duettie, they ar ordained to pey in yair wholl meill ferm against ye last of Merch and ye malt ferm against ye tuentie day off May, vnder ye pain of peying ten pound for ilk boll meill and tuell pound for ilk boll malt.

The said day it [is] in acted and ordained that all tenentis vithin the lordship of Forbes giue obedience to yair ground officeris vpon all laufull charges, and that vnder the pain of tuentie pound *totiens cotiens* to yam quha is able to pey it, and quha is not able to pey it, to sit four dayes in ye stokis.

The said day John Reid, George Burges zonger, Robert Reid, John Reid zounger, James Glein, the affoirsaid persones is found guiltie of cutteing of ye wod of Puttachie, and is vnder the pain of ane merciment accordeing to former actes of court.

The said day William Wedderburn, John Mitchell in

Balphour, William Layng yair, Thomas Layng yair, John
Leyth in Kirktoun of Forbes, William Shireff in Colhey,
John Glass in Barphlet, George Vilson in Castellhill,
John Smith yair, Patrik Marr in Edinbanchrie, William
Mar yair, William Mitchell yair, John Angus yair, William
Taillizour yair, ye haill foirsaid persones ar found guiltie
of cutteing of my lord his wodis, and ar vnder ane merci-
ment according to former actis.

The said day it is inacted and ordained that the haill
tenentis yat is not able to purge yam selwes in tymes
comeing quhen they shalbe requyred of ye maisteris vodis,
shall pey tuentie pound *totiens cotiens*.

James Reind his bill is continued to ye nixt court vpon
his probatione.

The said day it is inacted and ordained that ilk tenent
vithin ye landis and lordshipes of Forbes shall plant
tuentie peice of tumber in yair zardis befor ye last of
Mer., and yat vnder ye pain of ten markis, and quhat is
planted salbe preserved vnder ye said pennaltie.

The said day John Couper in Westhilles is inacted and
ordained to pey fortie shilling for his absence from the
court.

The said day it is inacted that ye wholl tenentis and
croftis qha duellis about ye zardis of Druminour or about
the zardis of Puttachie shall keip ye saidis zardis in all
tymes comeing, and that vnder ye pain of ten markis
totiens cotiens.

Continues this court vpon 24 horis varneing.

ARTHOUR DALGARNO, Bailzie.
J. THOMSONE, court clerk.

[Court at Castell Forbes, 31 Oct. 1662, held by William master
of Forbes, Arthur Dillagarno in Blairndiney his bailie, and
the others as above. Tenants ordained to pay arrears as
above: pounds for merks, 10 merks for each boll of meal
and £8 for each boll of malt.]

The haill tenentis, cotteris, croftis, girss men within ye
parochen of Kern quha cannot cleir them selves of ye

broomes in tymes comeing shall pey ten pound *toticns cotiens*.

The said day the haill tenentis vithin the lord ship off Forbes being conveinit for ye vodis of ye lord ship, vir ar fond gultie, viz. efter following. George Maky and Wm. Reid in Carndaird, John Makie in Bogie syd, John Glas and Wm. Guthrie in Barflet, John Smith, George Vilson and Willyam Touch in Castell hill, Alexr. Garow and Wm. Johnstoun in Balfour, James Varak in Scotis mill, John Leith in Kirktoun of Forbes, quhilk persones ar vnder ye pain of ane merciment.

The said day the haill tenentis, cotteris and girssmen and croftis about ye Maines vez convenit and oppossit vpon yair oath for carr meill, yir ves found guiltie quha could not purge them selves ye persones efter following, John Messer, James Smith, Wm. Hervie, James Shireff, John Allan, quhilk wholl persones ar vnder the pain of ane merciement.

[Court continued on twenty-four hours' warning.]

[Court of the lands and baronies of Tolmadis, held at Newbiging, 14 Nov. 1662, by William, master of Forbes, Wylliam Garioch in Braidhach his bailie, James Thomson notar public clerk of Court, James Elmslie officer, and . . . dempster.]

The said day the baillie ordaines the haill tenentis within the Braes of Tollmadis quha peyes not yair silver ductie for crop sextic ane within term of law to pey tuentie shilling for ilk mark.

The said day the baillie ordaines the haill tenentis as formerlie to pey in yair ducties for crop sextie tuo according to ye termes of yair assedatione, or vthervayes to pey tuentie shilling for ilk mark, and that vithin term of law.

The said day it is inacted that ilk tenent vithin the Breaes of Tolmadis shall plant sextic peice of timber in yair zardis, and yat vpon advertisment, and yat vnder the pain of fyw pound.

The said day it is inacted that ye haill tenentis vithin the sukin of ye mill of Tolmadis shall do yair duetties to ye said mill as neighbour and vther docs and that vnder the pain of ten pound.

The said day James Birss be suited befor the baillie for the blooding of Robert Gray, and yair did confess the blood, and yairfor the baillie ordaines the said James to pey yairfor ten pound, and yat within term of law.

The said day Rober Gray, Robert Marnoch and James Birss, ilk ane of them hes in acted them vnder the pain off tuentie pound that them selves, vyff and bairnes shall be harmles of vtheris in all tymes comeing both in vord, vorke and deid.

The said day the baillie ordaines the haill tenentis in the Breass of Tolmad shall giue the officer due obedience, and that vnder the pain of fortie shilling *totiens cotiens*.

Continues this court vpon 24 horis varneing

Wm. Gariocii, Balley.
J. Thomsone, court clerk.

[Court of same held at the mill of Tomaidis, 24 April 1663, by the same. William Davidson notary public clerk of court.]

The said day anent the complaint givin in be John Watt and William Forbes in Milne off Tammadis against other, that is to say the said William Forbes for oppressing the said John Watt vnder silence of night and the said John Watt for strickeing and abusing the said William Forbes his wyff vnchristianlie and shamfullie and showing and discovering [?] nakedness, quhairfor the bailzie examining and tacking strict notice of the said outrage [?] by witness, after matur deliberation and being ryplie advysed yairin did inact and ordaine the said William Forbes and John Watt to pey everie one of them ten poundis the peice to the maister off Forbes, maister off the ground, within terme off law, vnder the [pain of] poinding.

The said day Jhon Farqhre in Craginhj did become cautioner sovertie and lauborowes for William Forbes at Milne off Tammaddis that John Watt yair sall be harmles and skaithles off him and his wyff and familie and bairnes

and servantis eyther in word, work and deid, and sall not
be troubled nor molested bee the said William Forbes
himselff, his wyff, bairnes and familie, goodis and geer, and
that hee sall not be scolded bee him any way, and that
wnder the paine and failzie off threttie poundis Scotis
money to bee payed to the maister and heritour of the
ground after the breach of the said lauborrowes within
term off lawe wnder the pain off poynding.

Sicklyk the said day William Eddie in Bray slatie did
becom cautioner sowertie and lauborrowes for John Watt
in Milne off Tammadis that William Forbes yair sall be
harmles and skathles himselff, his wyff, bairnes and familie
and goodis and geer off the said William Forbes, his vyff,
bairnes and familie, and in no vayes to be troubled nor
nor [sic] molested bee him and his said spous and forsaidis eyther in work, word or deid or scolding, flytting
and railling or any prejudice quhatsumever, and that
wnder the paine and failzie off threttie poundis Scotis
money to bee peyed to the maister and heritour off the
ground after the breach off the said act within tearme
off law wnder the paine off poynding.

The said day the bailzie did act and ordaine all the
tennantis and sucken off the Milne off Ennetis who pay
any corne, bear or aitis throwe the countrey sall giwe the
prooff theroff to the goodwyff off Ennetis, reliet off Thomas
Farqharsone.

The said day the haill tennantis within the ground off
Tammadis ar ordend to pey ther Candilsmess deuties and
byrinnis resting be them to ther master and his chamberlandis within tearm off lawe, wnder the paine off poynding.

This court continud wpon 24 houris advertizment longer
or shorter if ned beis.

    Wm. Gariocii, Baillie.
    W. Davidsone, court clerk and notter public.

The Court off the landis and baronnie off fforbes, Keig,
  Kearn and vyeris landis and leivingis belonging yairto,
  holdin vithin the great hall off Castle Forbes wpon
  the fourtene day off Maij j^m vj^c sextie and thrie

zeiris be the right honorabill William maister off
fforbes, heretable proprietour off the landis and vyeris
above writtin, Arthour Dilgardno in Blairndinnj his
constitut bailzie, William Davidson notter public
court clerk, Patrick Tevindall ground officer, and
[blank] dempster. The suitis called members creat the
court laufullie fenced and affermed.

The said day the baillzie did dicerne and ordain the haill tennantis and possessouris off Kearne, Keyge, Forbes, Clett and Auchindor, wha ar resting any byrune deuties, to mack peyment off ther malt and meill fermes resting bee them for yair severall occupationes for cropt sextie tuo and anie preceidings, together with their teynd victuall, and yat wnder the pane and failzie sex poundis Scotis money for everie boll off meall and elevein merkis money for everie boll malt, to be peyed within tearm off lawe, wnder the paine of poynding, the tearmes off peyment being first com and by past. *Act anent byrune deuties.*

The said day the haill tennantis in the fornamed parishones belonging to the maister off fforbes is ordand bee the bailzie to mack peyment off their Mertimess and Candlsmess deuties to their maister within tearm off law wnder the paine off poynding, and in caice off faillzie to pey for everie merk money resting bee them to pey tuentie shillings. *Act anent silver deuties.*

The said day the baillzie did statut and ordaine the haill tennantis within the respective paroshines forsaid to macke peyment off their Whytsonday and Lambass deuties, viz. silver deuties, the tearmes off peyment being first come and by past with in tearme off lawe yairafter, wnder the pain off poynding, and wnder the pain and faillzie above sett doune. *Act anent . . .*

The said day the bailzie did decerne and ordaine sufficient wnderstanding men within the landis and paroshines belonging to the maister off fforbes for dicyding contraversies and pryssing off biggings and taicking inspectione off any prejudice done eyther to the maister and tennand with in the respective parishones and presinctis quher they *Act anent birlaymen.*

live or quher they ar ordaind to look over to bee birlay-
men, viz. as after followis, for the parishon off fforbes
James Bonar in Sillavethie, Patrick Jameson in Strath-
lunack. Arthour Mitchell in Cullhay, John Mitchell in
Balfour; ffor the paroshin of Auchindor Robert Mitchell
in Logie, John Angus in Edinbanchrie; ffor Keigge John
Clerihew in Putachie, John Gellen elder in Glentoun,
Patrick Moir in New Keigge; ffor Kearne James Anderson
in Marchmarr, John Glass at Milne off Bertlat, James
Walker in Wasthillis; ffor the paroshin off Clett William
Brebner in Towie, Robert Wright in Tailzach; and did tack
their oathes for faithfull administratione off yeir office
as birlay men to followe and performe the deuties and . . .
off their office exactlie conforme to their comissione, viz.
as after follows, yat is to say first they ar commissioned
and ordanit, . . .

[*A few lines blank in the MS.*]

They with consent and assent did swear and promis to
doe conform to yeir commissione sett wpon yaim conforme
to their knowledge and conscience.

Act anent planting.

The said day the haill tennantis off Keige, Clett, Kearne
and Auchindor paroshines their haill zairdis to bee sighted
bee the birlaymen; who hes not planted yeir zairdis conforme and according to former actis and ordinances off
courtis and who is found difficient and remiss in the said
former actis anent planting sall bee lyable to the failzie
containd in the former actis for yeir contraventione and
contumacies which is ordaind bee the bailzie to bee peyed
bee everie person breaker within tearme off law wnder
the paine off poynding.

Act anent breweris.

The said day the bailzie did statut and ordaine the haill
breweris within the respective landis and in the parishones
before mentioned who constantlie brewes and sellis aill, to
pey to their maister ane stone off sufficient brew tallone
zearlie, and thesse who brewis bot seldom, viz. tuyss or
thrysse in the zear, sall pey halff stone tallon, and this act
to stand in all tym coming wes intimat to them all in face
off court least they sould pretend ignorance.

Anent ane complaint givin in wpon severall tennantis *Act for casting off peitis among ye neighboris.* who when the bondage peitis is dry and pairted in the hall,[1] some doe cast in some off their proportiones which they ought to lead themselves, to the rest of ye tennants yair great prejudice ; quherfor the bailzie did tack this to consideration and did statut ordaine yat whatsomever tennant or person cast in any peitis (of their proportiones vlich they ought to lead yem selves) amongst their neighbouris proportiones, it being clearlie maid out and qualified against them, sall pey to their maisteris ten merkis Scotis money *toties quoties*, and this act to stand in all tym coming and this to be exacted presentlie after contravention and probation yeroff.

The said day the bailzie did statut and ordaine the haill *Act anent milne dutie.* tennantis befor mentioned to doe deutie and dew service to their millis yat they ar bound suecken to in all respectis conforme to vse and wonnt and conforme to their obligmentis wnder the pain off four poundis money quha beis found to contraveine this act, and the goodman off the millis to do the lyk deutie wnder the failzie off ye lyk penalty above sett doune quha beis remiss and difficient in sic caices.

The said day the bailzie did ratifie ane act maid anent *Act anent good neighbourhood.* good neighbourechood amongst the haill tennantis, certifeing yem quha beis remiss sall be lyable to former actis penalties maid formerlie yeranent.

The said day the bailzie did statut and ordaine the ten- *Act anent dutie and obedience to ground officers].* nantis to doe dutie and giwe obedience to ground officeris constitut in everie presinct and parishon befor mentioned, wnder the paines and failzies maid in former actis in former courtis yeranent.

It is statut and ordanit bee the bailzie that all tennantis *Act anent keeping off milnes.* and suecken quhatsomever who peyes not dry moulter and peyes dry moulter (*sic*) sall not goe by their oun millis with grinding yer cornes, bot sall punctuallie keep such millis as they ar bound suecken to and pey their moulter

---

[1] Read 'pairted in the *hail*,' *i e.* equally divided.—Note by Dr. R. M. Wilson.

and knaiship and doe dutie yairto, wnder the paine and
failzie off four merkis for every load of dry cornes yat
goes by in all tym coming, and this act to stand in all
tyme coming.

The said day compeared John Burnett and Georg
Burnett in Towie, and yer in face off court befor the
bailzie did inact yaimselves with consentt and assentt to
keepe good neighbourhood one with another and not harme
nor skaith other neyther bee themselves, yer wyves, bairnes
and familie and servantis, goodis nor geir, and that wnder
the pain and failzie everie one of them off tuentie poundis
money of failzie to be peyed to the maister off fforbes bee
any of them or yem both wha sall bee found to contravein
this act *toties quoties* vithin tearme off lawe, wnder the pain
of poynding after the breach off this act.

The said day compeired John Mitchell in Balfour, John
Wecht ther, Thomas Layng yair, John Leith in Kirktoun
off fforbes, William Wedderburne in Bithnie, John Mureson
yair, James Warrack in Scotis milne, John Angus in Edinbanchrie and Thomas Angus his sone, William Mitchell
yair, James Mitchell yair, Patrick Marr yair, William Marr
yair, James Smith in the Druminnour, Alexander Smith in
Westhillis, John Glasse in Balfour, Georg Mackie in Carndaird, John Mackie and James Mackie his sone in Bogisyd,
William Touch in Castlehill, John Smith yair, Alexander
Tailzour ther, James Duncan in Perselowe, John Smith in
Kirkstyll, Georg Burges zounger in Glentoune; and being
acused bee the bailzie for cutting off greene wood did confess yem selves guiltie; quherfor the bailzie did ordaine
ech and everie person abov named to pey the failzie and
penaltie acted and ordainit in former actis maid for cutting
off grein wood to be peyed to the maister off fforbes within
tearme off lawe, wnder the paine of poynding.

The court continued wpon 24 hores advertizment longer
or shorter if neid beis.

     ARTHOUR DALGARNO, Bailzie,
     W. DAVIDSONE, n. p., court clerk.

The Court of the Barrouny and leiwing of Forbes, holden within ye great hall of Castell Forbes wponn ye auchtein day of July j^m vj^c sextie thric zeiris, be the ryght honorabill Wialliam master of Forbes, heritable proprietor of the landis and vyer abowwritine, Arthour Dilgardno in [blank] his baillye, Alexr. Chalmer notar publict court clark, Patrick Tevindaill grond officer, and [blank] demster. The suitis callit memberis creat the court laufullie feenced and affirmed.

The said day compeired Wialliam Reid in Karndard, and gaif in ane complent wpon Wialliam Black in Cushney for blooding of ye said Wialliam Reid.

The said day the bailzie ordaines Wialliam Black in Cushny for blooding and wounding Wialliam Reid in Karndard to pey fyfty pound within term of law wnder the paine of poynding.

Lykwayes the said day ye bailzie ordaines the said Wialliam Black, and Wialliam Reid in Karnindard. Georg Lang yair, and Georg Mackie in Stondeck and James Mackie yair, yat ye haill forsaid persones sall keip good nightbourheid to each other in all tym comyng, wnder the paine of tuentie pound to be peyit be pairtie braker *toties quities*, and to keip them selff within yair owin boundis ether propertie our comontie.

The said day James Walker in Wastheillis gave ane complent againest Alexr. Smyth his nightbour for not keiping good night[bour]heid yair; it is ordained in all tymes coming yat ye said James Walker and Alexr. Smyth, Patrick Leith and Alexr. Couk, yat the haill forsaid persones sall keip good nightbourheid in all tymes coming to each other, yat non sall if [gif?] offence to wther, wnder the paine of tuentie pound to be peyit be ye pairtie braker *toties quities*.

The said day it was complenit be Alexr. Tailzour in Castellhil yat the rest of his nightbouris keipes not good nightbourheid to him, yairfor it is ordained in all tymes coming that the said Alexr. Tailzour, John Smyth yair, Wialliam Touch yair, Wialliam Mallac yair, Wialliam Ellsmie yair, Georg Wilson yair, John Lang yair, yat the haill forsaid persones sall keip good nichtbourheid to other and not in givin offence or skolding or striking, wnder the paine of tuentie pound to be peyit be the pairtie braker *toties quities*.

[Court continued on twenty-four hours' notice.]

The Court of the landis and barrouny of Forbes, Keig and
 Kearne and vyeris landis belonging yairto, holdin
 within the great hall of Castell Forbes wpon the
 tuentie day of November j^m vj^c sextie thre zeiris be
 the ryght honorabill Wialliam maister of Forbes,
 heritabill propritor of the landis and wyeris abowwritine, Arthour Dallgarno [*blank*] his bailzie, and
 Alexr. Chalmer notar publict, and Patrick Tawindaill
 officer, and John Mill officer for Forbes. The suittis
 callit the court lawfullie fenced and affirmed.

[The tenants of Forbes, Keig, Kearne, Clett and Auchindore,
 to pay their victual duties for crop 1663 and preceding,
 the meal before 20 Mar. 1664 or £8 for each boll, the
 malt before 10 May 1664 or £10 for each boll; also to
 pay their Martinmas silver duties, or 20s. for each merk
 thereof.]

The said day the bailzie ordaines the haill millaris within wholl pariochines forsaid being sworne in wisage of ye court befor the haill tennentis that they sall not grind nether dist nor stone among the maister of Forbes his ferme, and wnder the failzie of ten merk and it be mad out the contrarey or . . .

The said day the bailzie ordanes ye wholl tennentis of ye said barrownies and the said landis tha[t] ye said tennentis sall doe dewtie to yair mill as old wse and wont, wnder the paine of fourtie shilling Scottis for ewry led of corne yat the[y] goe by yair awen mill within term of law, wnder the pain of poynding.

The said day ye bailzie ordaines the guidmans of the saidis millis that they sall give sufficient serwice, yat they sall not bink yair shilling nor brok yair stuff, wnder the paine of four pondis within term of law, wnder ye pain of poynding.

The said day ye bailzie ordaines the haill croftis yat belonges to to the Maines of Druminor yat they sall be oblieged to carie the holl malt yat is brewin within ye hous of Castell Forbes to ye mill and frome the mill to ye said place of Druminnore, wnder the pain of tuall shilling Scottis for ewry boll of malt yat is wnearied within term of law, wnder the paine of poynding.

The said day the bailzie ordaines the haill tenentis of Keirne to giv any of the said tenentis or croftis or grasmen sall not cutt nor puy any of the maister of Forbes brumes in ye parrochin of Kearne, wnder ye failzie of ten merkis to be peyed within terme of law, wnder the paine of poynding.

The said day the bailzie ordaines the haill tenentis of Keig to sett yair yardis with young treis betuixt ye dait of yir presenttis and the last of December j^m vj^c sextie thre yeris, wnder the paine of fourtie pound to be peyed to yair maister within term of lav, wnder the paine of poynding.

The said day the bailzie ordaines the haill tenentis of ye forsaid parrochins of ye lordship of Forbes that they who hes planted yardis or till plant yat they sall plant yair yarndes and sall mak them sufficient dykes and oblieg them selffes to hold the treis wnbrokin, wnder the failzie of fourtie pound, to be peyed within term of lav, wnder the paine of poynding.

The said day the bailzie ordaines who ar found loping ye garding dyckes or orchardes of Drinnor or Putachie ether man or woman sall pey fyw pound within term of law, wnder the paine of poynding.

The said day Wialliam Downy being sourne in the said court depones yat he newir cwtted any of ye maister of Forbes his wood and boges for his awin vs, bot declared yat he did cut for his maisteres ws Wiallm Waderburne ane hundreth tyme of Rot tres and of all sort, and declared yat John Mollson, then servitour to Wm. Waterburne [did cut] a number of grethstinges to ye matter of fourtie and abow.

The said day ye bailye ordaines ye haill tennenttis of ye forsaid ground to mack obedence of servic of bonnage and cariages and all other servic as old ws and wont, wnder ye paine of tuentie pound, to [be] peyed within term of law wnder ye paine of poynding.

The said day it is ordained yat ye haill officeres of ye forsaid land sall give lawfull warning to ye teinnentis, and give it be prowin ye contrie ye said officeres sall be labill for ten merk for elk falt, to be peyed within term of law wnder ye paine of poynding.

The said day John Michell in Logie becomes suriti for James Michell in Logie in all tym coming during his abod in Logie yat he sall nocht trouble nor molest John Lang, officir of ye ground, in all tym coming, wnder the paine of ane hundreth pound to be peyed within term of law wnder the paine of poynding after the brakis be maid out and declared.

The said day the persons wnder named, to wit John Leith in Kirktowne of Forbes, John Weir in Ballfowr, John Michell in Balfour, John Michell in Logie, Georg Burges in Glentoune, Robert Reid yair, John Angus in Edinbanchre, Patrik Mar yair, William Michell yair, all being called and compeired in wisag of ye said court confessed yat they wer gultie of cutting and destrouing the master Forbes his woodes and boges, yair for the ballye does ordaine ewry on of the abow named persones to pey fyfty pound to ye maister of Forbes for wood only within term of law, wnder the paine of poynding.

[Court continued.]

> The Court of the landes and barrowny of Forbes and Keig and Kearne and vyer landes belonging yairto, holdin within the great hall of Castell Forbes vpon the nynt day of Maij j^m vj^c sextie four yeiris, be the ryght honorabill Wialliam maister of Forbes, heritour propritour of the landes and vyeres abowwrittin, Arthour Dallgardno his baillyie, and Alexr. Chalmer notar

publict and court clark, Alexr. Simmer officir, [*blank*] demstar. The suittes callit the court lawfullie fenced and affirmed.

[The tenants to pay for each unpaid boll of meal £7, for each boll of malt £8, and for each merk of unpaid silver duty in all time coming £1.]

The said day it is ordained and decerned yat all the breweres of the respectiwe pariochines abowwrittin yat brewes or yat is in brewcroftes yat is ordinares breweres sall pey zerly ane stone of brew tallan att termes vs and wount, or else four poundes Scottis money for ilk stone, to be peyed within terme of law wnder the paine of poynding.

The said day the bailyie ordaines the haill tenenentis of ye respectiwe pariochines who is lyabill for custumes, yat they sall pey ewry wedder wnder the wooll for yair haill custumes at ye termes wsit and wount, or else four merkes for ilk wedder, and tuentie shilling four ilk lamb and halff ane merk four ilk capon and four shilling for ilk hen, all to be peyed at termes wsit and wount as said is, and the said pryces to be peyit within term of law wnder the paine of poynding.

The said day the haill persons wnderwrittin, to wit John Messer, John Smyth, Wialliam Touch, John Villson, Georg Ma'Inteir, hes confessit themselff and is prowin against tham yat they are gultie of steiling and away taking of yair maisteres peittis out of ye mos belonging to ye maister of Forbes, yairfor they are decerned and ordained ewry one of them for yair falt to pey to yair maister the soume of fyw pownd ilk man, to be peyed within term of law wnder the paine of poynding.

The said day ye haill tenenentis wnderwrittin is fund gultie be the birliemen chossin be thair maister for ye pariochin respectiwe, to witt John Leith in Kirktown of Forbes, Margrett Bonnar yair, the haill tenenentis of Balffour, Patrik Jamsone in Stralonack, Alexr. Garvy, John Cleirchew in Putachie, William Sharp yair, John Geilles, Jean Chalmer, Alexr. Forbes, the haill tenenentis of Glentown, for castin ane haill fold, James Duncan and

James Clark in Perse low, Alexr. Anderson Stonfeidle, John Lang in Castellhill, Georg Mackie in Stondyk, and John Glas and Georg Tailzour, for burning murburnes in forbiddin tym, the haill abowwrittin persons is fund gultie of casting with foot spades and flachter spades in meadow grownd, hyning, corn land, lones, and burning of murburne in forbidding tymes, ewry one of them for yair owin pairtis is decerned and ordained to pey to yair maister for yair faltis the soume of ten poundes for ewry foott spad and fyw pundis for ewry flachter spad, attour [?] ten poundes for ewry murburne, according to former actes, all to be peyed within terme of law, wnder the paine of poynding.

The said day it is ordained and decerned the haill tenenentis of the respectiwe pariochin, they being lawfullie wairnid be ther officeres of each barrownyis, they sall giv obedlence to their officeres for all services, publict dewis, sess or ony other charg, that they sall pretend no ignorance, and who obey not ye officer, they sall pey four poundes within term of law wnder the paine of poynding.

The said day it is staitit and ordained ye haill tenenentis of Putachie yat who ewir sall keip ye greine of Putachie sall not eat the gras of it without leiv askit and given or does [east] vpon the greine of Putachie or lowping ye eard dyk sall pey fyw pound within terme of law, wnder the paine of poynding.

[Court continued.]

> The Court of the landes and barrouny of Forbes, Keig, Clat, Kearne, Auchindore, and vyeres landes belonging yair to, holdin within great hall of Castell Forbes wpon ye sextein day of Maij j^m vj^c sextie four yeiris, be the ryght honnorabill Wialliam maister of Forbes, heritour propritour of ye landes and vyeres abow writtin, and be Arthour Dallgarno his baillyie and Alexr. Chalmer notar publict court clark, Alexr. Simmer oficir, [blank] demster. The suittes callit the court lawfullie fencit and affirmit.
>
> The said day the bill gewin in be Alexr. Reid in Bankheid against Alsiner Anderson in Towie for blooding of ye

said Alexr. Reid, who produced witnes yat did sie him blood and gett ye blood, James Touch in Bankheid and James Christie yair, James Smyth in Towie, they as witnes did declare yat they did sie ye said Alexr. Anderson have ane stone in his hand and did strik ye said Alexr. Reid in ye face and did blood him.

Nomina assisa
WIALLIAM BRABERNER, chanlar.

JOHN GLAS.	JAMES DUNCAN.	GEORG MACKIE.
THOMAS ROTGER.	GEORG DUNCAN.	JOHN BURNET.
JAMES ANDERSON.	WIALLIAM MALICE.	GEORG LANG.
JAMES WALKER.	ALEXR. SMYTH.	WIALLIAM BLACK.
	GEORG WILSON.	ALEXR. COUK.

The haill abow writtin syss in ye moutth of ye said Wialliam Braberner, chossin chanllar, after excamation of ye witnes and consideration, does convict the said Alexr. Anderson for blooding of ye said Alexr. Reid in ane voce.

The said day the baillye decernes and ordaines the said Alexr. Anderson in Towie for blooding of ye said Alex. Reid to pey to the said maister of Forbes yair maister heritour of ye landes abowwrittine the soume of fyftie pound Scottis money, to be peyit within terme of law, wnder the paine of poynding.

The said day the baillye decernes and ordaines the said Alexr. Reid for prowokeation of the said Alexr. Anderson, and persewing him vpon his owin meilling, to pey to yair maister abowwrittin ye sowme of fyw pound, to be peyed within terme of law wnder the paine of poynding.

The said day James Duncan in Bankheid becumes cautioner for ye said Alexr. Reid, wnder ye faillye of fyftie pound, ye said Alexr. Anderson in Towie sall be skaiethles and harmles for himselff, wyff, bairnes, servantis in work, deid and skolding or ony other provokeatione in all tym coming or in goodes or geir; and the said Alexr. Reid obleiges him to keip his said cautioner free of all skaith or damage.

The said day John Olifir became cautioner for ye said Alexr. Anderson in Towie wnder the faillye of fyftie pound yat the said Alexr. Anderson sall keip himselff frie in doeing ye said Alexr. Reid in Bankheid, his wyff, bairnes, servants, guides and geir, any harme or skath or molestatioun or any harme be him selff or his wyff or bairnes, servantes in his nam in word, work or deid; and the said Alexr. Anderson obliges him to warrand his said cautioner of the abowwrittin promiss.

The said day the haill tenementis of Carndard and Stondyk and the Maines [promise] yat they sall not incroch vpon the boundes of ye towne and landes of Cushny disigned to Wialliam Black be ye maister of Forbes, laittle propit and marchit, wnder ye faillye of fourtie shilling Scottis money ewry brak wnder the paine of poynding.

[Court continued.]

The Court[1] off the landes off the barrounie and lord ship off Forbes within the parrochin of Kearne and Clatt, belongeing heretablie to William maister of Forbes, holden within the great hall of Castle Forbes upon the seveinteint day of August j^m vj^c threescoir and four zeires by the right honorable William maister of Forbes, heretable proprietor of the landes and others above writtin, and in name of Francis Gordone off Crage, William Gordone of Tilliangus baylie, James Thomson in Towy noter publict court clerk, Alexr. Simmer officer, [*blank*] dempster. The suites lawfullie called, the court fenced and affirmed as accordes.

The said day compleaned the said William maister of Forbes upon Johne Glass, for causeing burne ane moore upon the landes of Windisey, who compeired and denyed that he had caused doe the same, but that one Robert Boock, a servant of his that tyme, had done the samen without his directioune, who also compeired and declared that James Towie in Barflet had ordored him to burne that moor, who

---

[1] The record of this Court is signed by the Court Clerk at the foot of each page.

being present did confesse the samen, and alleadged that
Johne Glasse directed him to cause doe the samen, but the
said Johne Glasse being lykwyse present did deny that he
had ever given the least warrand for doeing therupon.
quhilk being referred to the said James Towie his oath if
ever he had receved or gottin any ordor or warrand from
Johne Glasse for causeing any of the hirdes doe the samen,
he solemnly gave his oath and therafter declared that he
had only and absolute warrand from Johne Glasse for
doeing thereof, that same night quhilk he caused burne
the samen.

Quharupon the said baylie decerned and ordained the
said Johne Glasse to pay to the said maister of Forbes sixtie
pundes Scots within terme of law under paine of poynding.

The said day Patrik Leith in West hilles, in name of James
Waker ther, gave in a bill upon George Andersone in Newtoune of Auchindore, compleaneing and alleadging that
upon the tent day of August instant the said George
Andersone had come to that ground which the said James
Waker payes dewtie for, and ther did violently and cruellie
beat, blood and martyr him ; the said George Anderson
compeireing did deny the samen, but being constantly
alleadged, for clearing of the samen it is referred to the
probatioune of Johne Gordoune in Newtoune and Patrik
Leith forsaid ; who being solemnely sworne did depone in
presens of the said baylie and the assyse efter nominat for
that effect.

The said Johne Gordone deponed (being interrogat) as
efter followes, to witt that James Waker did first lay handes
upon George Andersone and pulled him be the hair, and so
the said James Waker did gett the blood eftir he was dung
over in the water by a fall upon a stone upon the syd of
his head.

Patrik Leith deponed *ut supra* conforme *in omnibus*.

The names of the assyse :—
WILLIAM GORDONE younger off Tilliangus. Chancellor.
JHON GORDON off Knoke-   JHON MACKY in Carnedard.
    spak.

Patrik Gordon off Reny.
Adam Forbes, tutor of Brux.
William Brebner in Towy.
Thomas Roger in Bogysyd.
William Blak in Cushny.

Johne Glasse in Barflett.
Alexr. Smyth in Westhilles.
George Waker in Bogysyd.
George Mackey in Stonedyk.
James Duncan in Persilew.

The said day the haill assyse forsaid by the mouth of the said William Gordon ther chancellor findes George Anderson guylty of the said James Waker's getting of the blood notwithstanding of the provocatioune by the said James to him, quhich is desyred to be considered be the said baylie, he only stryveing to defend him selfe as is made appeir by the forsaides witness ther depositiones, and referres the modification thereof to the baylie.

The said day the baylie forsaid decernes and ordaines the forsaid George Andersone to pay ten pundes Scots for the blood to the maister of Forbes, and fyve pundes money forsaid to the partie wronged, within terme of law under paine of poynding.

The said day the forsaid George Anderson did give in a bill upon the said Patrik Leith for beating and striking of George Brebner his hird, the last harvest 1663 upon ane Sonday efternoone, and stoped his mouth with sand, and put his head under the water, as also that he promised to oppresse and beat the said George his hirdes in tyme comeing in such sort that he should not get a hird in tyme comeing, quhilk the said Patrik Leith compeireing did referre the samen to be prowen by witness, to witt William Black in Cushny and James Taylour in Windseye, who being admitted as witness by both the saides parties did depon as followes, to witt the said William Black deponed that the said Patrik Leith had confessed to him that he had taken his plaid from George Anderson his hird and putten him in the water, and putt sand in his mouth. James Taylour deponed *ut supra*. Quharfor the said baylie ordaines and decernes the said Patrik Leith to

pay to the maister of Forbes fyve pundes Scots with in
terme of law, under paine of poynding.

The said day Patrik Leith did give in a bill upon George
Anderson forsaid for comeing violently upon him with a
drawen durk in his hand offereing to wound and kill him
upon his owne mailing; quhilk being referred to the
probation of Johne Gordon in Newtoune, who deponed
that his durk was drawen bot that he did not sie him
nether strik him with durk nor hand nor any other thing.

The said day be consent of the maister of Forbes and the
laird of Craige (being both present) it is inacted and ordained that the whole tennentes, subtennentes and others
indwelleres in West hilles and Windseye, and also the
tennents, subtennents, and indwellers within the Newtoune of Achindore belonging to the laird of Craig, shall
every one of them *respectiue* keip good neighbourchood
to other under the faylie of twantie pundes to be payed
be partie breaker to the maister of the ground by and
attour the satisfieing of the skaith done. This is for
tulyeing or beating, and fyve pundes for flitting or scolding, the samen being sufficiently prowen aither be witness
or by aith of partie. It is particularly condescended
upon heirby that the forsaides tennentes shall only keip
ther cornes and grasse but from the twantie day of March
inclusive to the twantie day of October and no wtherwyse,
provyding it be not a late harvest.

The said day William Brebner in Towy in name of
William Oliver his hird did give in a bill upon William
Malice in Bogysyde for striking his hird, the said William
Oliver, upon Sonday, which being referred to the said
William Malisse his oath (being present and denyeing the
samen), did depon that the said day he did not [1] strik the
said boy but only did tak his playd, haveing found as he
alleadged his cattelles in the skaith.

As also the baylie forsaid decernes and ordaines that
the whole tennentes off Towy, Stonniefeild, Castlehill, Taylaches, and Blairdinnie shall everie one of them keip

---

[1] MS. *not not.*

neighbour hood to others under the faylie of twantie pundes Scots for the tulyeing and beating, and fyve pundes money forsaid for scolding and flytting in maner above sett doune already betuixt the laird of Craig his tennentes and the tennents of Westhills and Windseye.

This Court continowed to a new day and tymous advertisment and warneing.

The Court of the barrowny of Tomades within ye pariochin of Kincarne, belonging heritablie to the right honnorabill Wialliam maister of Forbes, holdin at Newbigging wpon ye fourtein day of November j^m vj^c sextie four zeires, be Wialliam Garioch his bailye for ye tyme, and Alexr. Chalmer notar publict court clark, James Elssme officer, [blank] demster. Ye suites callit, ye court lawfullie fenced and affirmed as acordes.

The said day forsameikle as James Fergus and Thomas M'Killive in Waster Tomades did giv ane bill ewry on againest ane other for stricking and wounding, and blooding other, and witnes be[ing] sworne, to vit Georg Dickison and John Lang, did depone yat they both strick each other, and did sic James Fergus his wyff blood at the present tyme.

The said day bailzie ordaines ye said Thomas M'Killavie for blooding ye said James Fergus wyff to pey the some of tuentie poundes Scotis money, to be peyed to the maister of Forbes his maister within term of law, wnder the pane of poynding.

The said day bailzie ordaines ye said James Fergus for stricking ye said Thomas M'Killavie and for his miscarriages to pey the soume of ten poundes Scotis money to be pey[ed] to ye maister of Forbes his maister within term of law, wnder the paine of poynding.

The said day the said James Fergus and the said Thomas M'Kilavie hes in actit them selff for ther wyffes, bairnes, servantes, sall be harmles each of an other in all tymes coming both in yair good names, guides and geir, sall be harmles or hurtfull to any of them, and ewry on of them hes be thir presenttes faithfullie bindes and obliiges them,

yair airis, executores or assignays to pey the soume of
fourtie poundes Scottis money ewry on of them, to be
peyed to yair [maister] ye maister of Forbes immediatlie
after any brak or misbehaviour; and we ye said James
Fergus and Thomas M'Killive hes subscryvit this present
actt with our handes, day and plac forsaid, befor thir
witnes, ye said Wialliam Garoch bailye, and John Forbes
in Wester Tomades.

Wm. Garioch, witnes.	We ye forsaid JAMES FERGUS and THOMAS M'KILLAVE with our handes led be ye notar publik wnderwrittin becaus we can not writ our selff. Ita est ALEXR. CHALMER notarius publicus de mandato dict. scribere nescien. instanter rogatus et requisitus.
JOHN FORBES, witnes.	

ALEXR. CHALMER.

The said day the bailze ordaines that give any of ye
tenentes of Tomades does skold or eros any of the birly
men quhill they goe about disyding controversies, giv
ye birly men tack witnes wpon them or againest them
and being prowin againest, they sall pey fyv poundes
Scotis money to ye maister of Forbes within term of law,
wnder ye pain of poynding.

[The tenants to pay byrun silver duties against 18 Nov.
1664, and Martinmas silver duties before 30 Nov., or 20s.
for each merk.]

The said day ye bailye ordaines the haill tennentes, croft
and gresmen yat they sall hav no foulles after ye cornes
be shawin to eat yair neighbour cornes, wnder ye failzie
of fourtie shilling to be peyed within term of law, wnder ye
pain of poynding.

[Court continued.]

The [Court] of the landes of the barrowny and lordship of
Forbes within ye pariochines of Karne and Clat and
vyeres barownyes belongin yairto, belonging heratabill
to Wialliam maister of Forbes, holdin within ye great

hall of Castell Forbes vpon the tuentie sext of November j^m vj^c sextie four yeres, be the ryght honnorabill Wialliam maister of Forbes, heratabill propritour of the landes and vyeres abow writtin, and in name [?] of Arthur Dallgardno his bailye for the tyme, Alexr. Chalmer notar publict court clark. John Mylne officer, [blank] dempster. The suites callit [etc.]

[The tenants in arrears of meal and malt at Candlemas and Rood-day respectively 1665, to pay £8 for each boll of meal and £10 for each boll of malt; those in arrears at Martinmas silver duties 1663 or 1664, to pay 20s. for each merk thereof.]

The said day the bailzie ordaines the haill tenents of ye said barrowneys that they sall doe dewtie to ye guidman of the severall mylnes, and give they to offer any wrong to ye guidman of ye forsaid mylnes, or to ye peekieman, being mad out be vitnes, the wronger sall pey tuentie poundes *totias quatias.*

Lykwayes giv any of ye guidmanes of ye said mylnes or peekieman sall wrong any of ye tenentis, or gev not guid serwice, being maid out be witnes, they sall pey tuentie poundes *totias quatias.*

The said day the bailzie ordaines birlymen in the respectiwe pariochines as after followis : In ye pariochin Forbes, James Morgan and Patrick Jameson, Arthur Michell, James Bonnar ; In ye pariochin of Keig, John Gellen, Pat Mor, John Clerihew ; In the pariochin of Kearne, James Anderson, Thomas Roger, Wialliam Meall--lace ; In the pariochin of Auchindor, Robert Michell, John Angus ; In the pariochin of Clat, Wialliam Brabner, Robert Wright :

All the abow writtin birlamen being sworn in the court that they sall doe obrichtly betuixt maister and tenentis, or vyer controversies among the tenentis in ye severall pariochins or marches in nighbourheid.

The said day the bailzie ordaines the haill tenentis according to formall act maid yairanent who cast faill or deffiotes either with foot spades or flatteres spades in meadow or lone or in hening, they sall pey ye onlayes sett doune in former actes maid for yat effect.

The said day it is ordained that quhatsumewir tenentis or any man in ye said pariochines who gives not dew obidence to ye ground officires according to ye charg. and the day the said sall be found to brak or disabey the[y] sall pey the soume of teuentie poundes *totias quatias.*

Lykwayes is ordained yat giv anye of ye said officires gives not dew adwertiment to ye tenentis, they sall pey ten pound *totias qutias.*

The said day the bailzie hes statut and ordainet that the haill t[e]nentis in ye said pariochins abow writtin sall not cast neither feall or diffites wpon hes nighboures propritie or hening, and ye braker or transgressoures of this act sall pey ten merkes Scotis money *totias quatias.*

The said day the bailye ordaines ewry croft that is vpon the Manes of Drumminor sall pey tuo shilling Scottis money ewry yer to ye ground officir *totias quatias.*

[Court continued.]

[Court for the parishes of Keirne and Clat, holden in the great hall of Castell Forbes, 22 March 1665. Arthur Dallgarno bailie for the time, Alex. Chalmer court clerk, Alex. Simmer officer. Suits called, etc.]

The said day Robert Wright gav in ane bill aganest James Crukshank, yat vpon the tuentie ane day of March 1665 he did follow ye said Robert Wright with an sword and ane durk, and did persew him for his lyff, and did blood him, quhilk wes refferrit to vitnes.

The said day John Glas and John Macke, John Messer, being solemnly sworne did declare that they did sie ye said James Crukshank did persew ye said Robert with ane drawin durk and swore that give he vold not goe back agane he vold hav his skin, and yairafter did sie ye said Robert Vright blood.

Nomina assissa.

WIALLIAM BRABNER. GEORG DUNCAN.   JAMES VALKER.
GEORG LANG.   WIALLIAM MEINY. GEORG WALLACE.

GEORG MACKIE. JOHN BURNETT. JAMES DUNCAN.
WIALLIAM REID. GEORG BURNET. JOHN NORRY.
WIALLIAM BLACK. ALEXR. CUIK. WIALLIAM VATSON.
WIALLIAME BRABNER, chanller.

The haill assys in ye mouth of ye said chanellcr does convict the said James Crushank for blooding of ye said Robert Vright.

The said day the bailzie ordaines and decernes the said James Crukshank for blooding of ye said Robert Vright to pey to Wialliam maister of Forbes his maister the sowme of thritie poundes Scottis, to be peyit within terme of law wnder the paine of poynding.

Lykwayes the bailzie ordaines ye said James Crushank to pey to ye said Robert Wright for his hurt and harme the soum of fyv poundes Scottis money, to be peyit within terme of law wnder the paine of poynding.

The said day ye said James Crushank, Wialliam Black in Cushny his cautioner for ye said James Crushank, hes bund and obliiged yaim selffes, yair airis, exccutouris and successoures, yat ye said Robert Wright sall be harmles and skaithles in his body and wyff and barnes and servantes, guides and geir quhatsumewir, yat he sall nether molest or trowble him or his for saides either be night or day, vnder the failzie of fyftie poundes Scottis money to be peyed to yair maister, to be peyed within terme of law wnder the paine of poynding; and I ye said James Crushank obliiges me to skaithles keep my said cautioner of ye haill paines abow written.

I ye forsaid Wialliam Black and James Crushank with our handes led be ye notar vnder writtin. Ita est Alexr. Chalmer notarius publicus, in fidem specialiter rogatus et requisitus. ALEXR. CHALMER, N.P.

Lykwayes ye said Robert Vright hes fund Wialliam Wilson, burges in Frasserbrugh, yat ye said James Crushank sall be harmles and skaithles of ye said Robert Vright himselff, his vyff, bairnes and servantes, guides and geir, vnder the paine of ye sowme of fyftie poundes Scottis money, to be peyit within terme of law wnder the paine

of poynding ; and I ye said Robert Wright bindes and
obliiges me and my aires quhatsumeuir to releiv and
skaithles keip my said cautioner of the haill premiss
abow writtin.
WIALLIAM WILSON.
ROBERT WRIGHT vith my hand led be ye notar publict
   at my command becaus I can not write
   my self.
     Ita est ALEXR. CHALMER, N.P.

[Penalties for non-payment of victual, kirk or multure
meal, before 30 Apr. 1665, and of silver duties, as above.]
[Court continued.]

[Court for the parishes of Forbes and Killdrumy, holden at
 Dubstoune, 19 June 1665. John Myln officer.]

 The said day Patrick Jameson and James Adame, both
in Strolonaick, being lawffullie warned to ye said court
and thrys callit and not compeirit for striking and batter-
ing ech on ane othir, ye said baiyllye decernes and ordaines
ewry on of them to ye sowme of fourtie shilling Scotis
money to yair maister for yair absenc, to be peyed within
terme of law wnder ye pane of poynding.
 The said day yair was ane bill gevin in by me ye said
Alexr. Chalmer againest Patrick Mare and Wialliam Mare
in Edinbanchrie for offering violence, skandilize his wyff
and his servantes, quhilk I the said Alexr. Chalmer refferit
to ye probatioun of fyv witnes ; they being callit and
sworne did declare yat the said Patrick Mare and John
Mare did offer no violenc nor did skandilize his wyff so
far as they did heir or sie; quhairvpon the said bailye did
absolwe ye said Patrick and John Mare, provyding all-
wayes that ye said Patrick Mare and John Mare and John
Michell in Logey sall come to Alexr. Chalmer his owin
dewelling hous at Mongarie vpon ye tuentie fourt day of
this instant Junj 1665, and yair sall crav ye said Alexr.
Chalmer and his wyff and Issabill Chrystie, spous to
Alexr. Fullartown in Mongarie, and all whow they did
offend or wrong be yair ewill caryag or misbehaviour, sall

crav them pardone and forgiveines for yair offences and
na vyeres except they performe and keip ye said day.
[Court continued.]

[Court for the same parishes, holden at Collhay, 17 July
1665.]

The said day bailye statit and ordaines yat no tenent
in the said pariochines sall giv no libertie to no nighboures
within yair hening to cast no faill and deveittes without
first they acquaint ye maister of Forbes yair maister
and libertie grantit be him to cast quhair he desyres, wnder
ye failyie of four lib. *totias quotias.*

The said day Alexr. Michell in Wakmyln gav in ane
complent vpon James Bonnar in Siliveth, yat vpon the
[blank] day of [blank] j^{m}vj^{c} sextie fyv James Bonnar
did tack his sheip out of ye said James his corne, and being
dreffing them home to ye said James hous, ye said Alexr.
did follow him and desyred ye said James to lett his sheip
goe with him, and did offir him full satisfactioun ffor the
skaith yat his sheip [had done], and did offir to bring birly
men presentlie to satisfie him accordinglie, quhilk ye said
James Bonnar did confess in jugdment.

The said day the bailze ordaines the said James Bonnar
to pey for the abowwrittin reasones for refussall of satisfaction for his corne and skaith and occasioun of yair
discord and bitting each other ye sowm of [blank] Scottis
money to be peyed to ye maister of Forbes yair maister,
to be peyed within term of law wnder ye paine of
poynding.[1]

The said day ye said Alexr. Michell and ye said James
Bonnar bind and obliiges themselffes and yair airis, exe-
cutoures and successoures inacctes them be thir presenttis
to leiv christane lyk in good nighbourheid, and ewry on
of them sall be harmles each ane of them, yair wyffes,
bairnes, servantes, guides and geir, so far as any of them
can lett or hinder ether be night or day, bot sa far as law

---

[1] This paragraph written and deleted.

A.D. 1665. FORBES BARON COURT BOOK 259

will, wnder the failzie of fourtie poundes Scottis ewry on of them, to [be] peyed to ye maister of Forbes yair maister for ewry falt, to be peyed within term of law wnder ye paine of poynding; and subscrivit with our handes day, place and zere forsaid.

   ALEXR. MICHELL.   JAMES BONNAR.

The said day John Leith in Kirktown of Forbes, Arthur Asone yair, being callit and compeired, and being charged for cutting of ye maister of Forbes his greine wood, who did confess themselffes guiltie of ye said clame.

The bailyie ordaines ewry on of them to pey ye sowm of tuentie poundes Scottis money for ye wood on law, to be peyit within term of law wnder ye paine of poynding.

[Court continued.]

[Court for the parishes of Keirne, Clat, Auchindore, etc., holden within the great hall of Castell Forbes, 19 July 1665. Adam Forbes, tutor of Brux, bailie, Alex. Chalmer n.p. court clerk, Patrick Mylne officer. Suits called, etc.]

The said day it is statit and ordained be the said bailzie with consent of the haill tenentis and indweller in the townes and rowmes wnderwrittin, viz. the Maynes and croftes of Druminoŭr, Persclouy, Bankheid, Stenyfeidle, the town of Towy, the Taylaches, Castelhill, Bogey sid, Bogheid and the croftes nixt Bogysyd, yat all persones quhatsumewir sall keip thair haill nolt, sheip and hors out and from the bog of Drumminoŭr efter the dait of thir presenttis and in all tym cuming simer and vinter, and giv it sall happin them or any of them to lett or doe in ye contrarey of this present act, or giv the froster of ye said bog sall find anie of yair beastes within the dyk of ye said bog of Druminor, then and in yat cais they sall pey thrie shilling for ewry hors, and tuo shilling for ewry ox or cow or nolt beist, and tuall pennies Scottis for ewry sheip *totias quaties*, the on halff to be peyit to ye maister off fforbes and the other halff to be peyed to ye froster for his diligence.

Sicklyk it is staitit and ordained who sall be fownd to sheir or cut gras within ye dyk of ye said bog sall pey four poundes within term of law wnder the paine of poynding.

The said day it is staitit and ordained be the said bailzie with ye consent of the tenentis and indwelleres in ye tounes and rowmes wnderwrittin, viz. Wasthilles, Barffalt, Windiseye, Carndard, Steindyk and Cushny, and the croftes and the Maines of Druminor, that all person or persones dwelling in ye said townes abow writtin sall keip thair haill nolt, hors, sheip quhatsumewir both sumir and winter out and from ye birkes of Windis eye or quhair yair is any apperance of birk or saplenes or any other timber is lyk to grow; giv any be found of ye said indwelleres yair beastes forsaid within ye said Windiseye, then and in yat cais they sall pey thrie shilling for ewry hors, tuo shilling for ewry nolt best, and tuall penies for ewry sheip *tatias quatias*, ye on halff to be peyed to ye maister of Forbes and the other halff to any yat is appoyntit to wait vpon the samen.

The said day yair was ane bill gevin in be Andro Alexander aganest Alexr. Simir for blooding of ye said Andro Alexander his vyff; it being confessit be ye said Andro Alexander and his wyff yat giv she was blood it was in ye said Alexr. Simir his owin defenc; for the quhilk reasones abowwrittin the said bailzie absoyles the said Alexr. Simir for the said blood,[1] the said Andro Alexander having not witnes ye said Andro reffered to ye said Alexr. Simir to his oath, and he being suorne be the said bailzie did sewir yat it was in his owin defence, and yairfor the said bailzie absoyles the said Alexr. Simir.

The said day Alexr. Simir gav in ane bill vpon Andro Alexander in ye Coat town, quhich bill caries that he was goeing abowt his maister imployment charg the said Andro Alexander to goe abowt his maisteris dewtie in the said maister of Forbes his service, and the said Andro did brak fourth in bordes, and yairefter persewed him vith ane

---

[1] These four words repeated in the MS.

knyff and gav him tuo great woundes to ye great effusion of his blood, and yairefter persewed for his lyff, which is both confessed and prowin vpon ye said Andro Alexander by his owin confession. Quhairffor the bailzie ordaines ye said Andro Alexander to pey to wronged tuentie merkis, and fyfty poundes of blood wnlaw, to be taken vp be the said bailzie within term of law to be peyed wnder the paine of poynding.

The said day Alexr. Simir hes fund John Glas at the mylne of Barflat, and they both hes inactit them selff conjunctlie and sewirallie that Andro Alexander in ye Coat town sall be himselff, his wyff, bairnes and servantes, guides and geir sall be harmles and skaithles in yair persones, guides and geir be the said Alexr. Simir sa far as he sall or can stop or lett be night or by day sa far as he sall know, except it be in his owin defence, wnder the failzie of fyfty poundes to be peyed within terme of law wnder ye paine of poynding. And the said Alexr. Simir bindes and obliiges him and his airis, exeeutoures and successoures to fre, releiv and skaithles keip his said catinour of ye haill premiss abow writtin. And we ye abow writtin persones with our hands led be ye notar wnderwrittin at our command becaus we can not writt our selff.

A. C., N.P.

The said day Andro Alexander hes fund Wialliam Brabner in Towy, and they both hes inactit them selff conjunctlie and seivrallie yat Alexr. Simir sall be him selff, his vyff, bairnes and servantes, guides and geir, sall be harmles and skaithles in yair persones, guides and geir be the said Andro Alexander, and be his wyff, servantes sa far as he sall or can stop or lett be night or by day sa far as he sall know, except it be in his owin defence, wnder the failyie of fyfty poundes Scottis money to be peyed with in term of law wnder the paine of poynding. And the said Andro Alexander bindes and obliiges him, his airis, exeeutoures and successoures, to fre, releiv and skaithles keip his said cationar of ye haill premiss abow writtin. We forsaides persones with our handes led

be ye notar vnder writtin at our commandes becaus we
can nocht writt our selfl. A. C., N.P.

The said day wee John Gordon in Castellhill and John
Wilsoun bindes and obliiges vs, our airis, execcutoures and
successoures, wnder the failye of fyfty poundes Scottis
money, that Alexr. Simir sall be skaithles and harmles, his
vyff, bairnes and servantes, in bodies, guides and geir be
vs ye said John Gordon and John Vilson, and be our
vyffes and bairnes and servantes or any yat we may stop
or lett sa far as wee can hinder ether be night or day
wnder the failyie of ye abow writtin sowm. We forsaides
persones with our handes led be ye notar vnderwrittin at
our command be caus we can nocht writt our selff.

A. C., N.P.

[Court continued.]

[Court of the barony of Tomaddes, holden at Newbegging,
26 July 1665. Wil. Garioch in Braytoun bailie for the
time, Alex. Chalmer n.p. court clerk. Jas. Ellssme
officer. Suits called, etc.]

The said day the bailzie ordaines the wholl tenentis
within the said barrowny of Tollmades who is resting yair
silwer dewtie for the crop $j^{m}vj^{c}$ sexte fovr zeires to pey
thair dewtie for ye said zeir within term of law, vyerwayes
they sall pey tuentie shilling Scottis money for elk merk
they rest after the said terme of law wnder the paine of
poynding.

The said day ane bill gevin in be Thomas Adam in Newbegging againest John Watt in Miltown ffor striking and
blooding of him, quhilk he took to prow be witnes, to vit
be Alexr. Smyth in Miltown and Alexr. Mylne yair as vitnes, they being sworn in jugdment did declare they did sie
them steiking in otheres haires, and did sie ye said Thomas
Adam his face strakit and sume blood yairon bot ye said
Thomas Adame had non to produc in this present court;
quhairffor for the said tulying and the said blood the said
bailzie ordaines the said John Watt to pey the sowme of
ten poundes Scottis money to ye maister of Forbes within
term of law, wnder the paine of poynding.

The said day ye said John Watt gav in ane complent vpon the said Thomas Adame yat he did come to his hous, and the said witnes abowwrittin being examined did declar ye said Thomas Adame did offir to strick ye said John Wattes wyff wrongouslie, and did sie the said John Watt and ye said Thomas Adame goe to ye ground togidder ewry on in otheres hair, and did sie the said John Watt his heid blood when they did tack them from other, quhilk blood ye said John Watt did produc in judgment; quhairfor the said bailzie ordaines the said Thomas Adame for offerring to striking ye said John Wattis his wyff to pey the sowm of fyv poundes Scottis money, and the sowm of ten poundes money forsaid for blooding of ye said John Watt, to be peyed to ye maister of Forbes within term of law wnder the paine of poynding.

The said day ye said John Watt hes inactit himselff that ye said Thomas Adame sall be harmles and skaithles in his guides and geir of him and his wyff and bairnes and servant either work or deid either be night or day, neither sall hund out any in his name sa far as he can stop or lett, wnder the failyie of fourtie poundes Scottis money to be peyed to ye maister of Forbes after it sall happin him to brak, to be peyed within term of law wnder the paine of poynding. Thir presentis ar subscrivit with ye said John Watt his owin hand. J. WAT.

The said day the said Thomas Adame hes inactit himselff and found Duncan Adam his father cationer, that John Watt sall be harmles and skaithles in his goodes, geir, wyff, bairnes and servantes, either in work or word or deid either be night or day, sa far as he can stop or lett, neither sall hund out any in his name, wnder the failzie of fourtie poundes Scottis money to be peyed to ye maister of Forbes; and the said Thomas obliiges to warrand the said Duncan Adame of ye haill premiss, and of ye said caution, and subscrivit be ye notar publict wnder writtin at our command becaus we can nocht writt our selff. A. C., N.P.

[Court continued.]

The Court of the landes and barrownyes off Forbes lyand within the pariochins of Forbes, Keig, Keirn, Auchindor and Clat, belonging herytabill to ye ryght honorabill Wialliam maister of Forbes, holdin in ye great hall of Castell Forbes vpon ye sext day of December 1665, be ye ryght honorabill Wialliam maister of Forbes and be Arthur Dallgardno in Blairdeny his baillie, Alexr. Chalmer notar publict court clark, Alex. Simir officir, [blank] demster. The suites callit [etc.]

The said day the haill millares and pikj men of ye said barrowny did swer and giv yair oathes in this present that they sall not suffer any tenentis to put any dust or rey attour thair ferme, and that they sall taik vp the dust and cutting to yair hous till thair feirm be delywerit.

The said day the bailzie ordaines and decernes the haill tenenttis within ye said barrowny who is resting the maister of Forbes yair maister any silwer dewtie for ye crop and zeir of God j^{m}vj^c sextie four zeres to pey tuentie shilling for ewry mark they are rest[ing], and that to be pey[ed] with[in] term of law wnder the paine of poynding.

The said day the haill tenentis are ordained and decerned to pey thair silwer dewtie for ye crop sextie fyv at ye termes continowed in yair assedationes, the terme of peyment be[ing] cum and bygon, with[in] term of law wnder the paine of poynding, and to be poynded tuentie shilling for ewry mark they rest.

The said day the haill tenentis are ordained and decerned to bring in to Druminour the halff of yair malt ferme for ye crop sextie fyv againe ye auchtein day of December 1665 [and the other half against 10 May 1666, or £8 for each boll.]

The said day the haill tenentis are decerned to pey thair haill meill ferm betuixt Zowll and Candillmas conform to yair assedationes, or then they sall be lyabill for ten merkes for ilk boll wndelywerit.

The said day the haill tenentis of ye said barrownyes are ordained and decerned be ye said bailzie yat the tenenttis, said cotteres, gras men and croft sall doe, giv guid dewtie and service both to ye guidman off each mill and to ewry pikj men, and the pikj man sall hav power to poynd in yair owin suckin as the grownd officir sall hav giv they giv not obedene and servic to ye mill as vs and wont.

The said day it is staitit and ordained that [giv] ye haill tenentis, cotteres and gras men or croftes men yat lyvs abowt the bog of Drumminour lett any of thair nolt, hors or sheip within ye said bog, then and in yat cais they sall be lyabill and sall pey for ewry nolt or hors yat sall be fownd within ye bog sall pey tuo shilling [f]or ewry beist and aucht penies for ewry sheip, ye on halff to be peyed to ye froster and the other halff to be peyed to ye maister of Forbes.

The said day it is staitit and ordained that ye haill tenentis of Windes eye and all ye townes adjacent yair abowt sall keip the zoung birkes and vyer timber growing yairon, and ye tenentis of Windis eye sall be compabill for ye said timber and to poynd yair nighboures and exack ye pennaltes continowed within ye former actes.

The said day Wialliam Malice and John Smyth in Castell hill hes inactit them selff be thir presenttes, wnder the faillze of ten poundis for the first brak and tuentie poundis for the secund, that they sall keip guid nightbourheid and sall live lyk Christianes togither, sall not neither flytt or strik ane other nor giv any provokeation wnder the pennalities abowwrittin, and to be poyndit immediatlie after the offenc committit; and wee both hav giv the notar publict wnderwrittin to subscrive this act for vs.

A. C., N.P.

The said day it is staitit and ordained that ye haill tenenttis in ye grownd of Puttiachie and Genltown and the said tenentis sall be ansewerabill for yair cotter and grasmen and servantes and heirdes that they sall neither cutt, peill any of ye wood of Putiachie nor sall burne any murburn within a myll, wnder the failzie of fyfty poundes. Lykwayes giv any sall pull headder within ye wood or pull any peattes within ye wood sall pey thrie poundes, to be peyed within term of law, wnder the paine of poynding.

The said day the haill tenentis is inactit within ye said barrownyes that they sall plant tuentie pece of young birkes within yair zardes and mack sufficient dykes wnder the failzie of ten merkes, and they to [be] plantit againe ye last day of March nixt to cum wnder the said failzie, and ewry trie yat is plantit already and found brokin sall pey thrie merkes for ewry trie or els plant thrie for each trie.

Lykwayes according to former actes it is staitit and ordaind yat no person or persones sall cast any feall or divitt within meadowes or haning, wnder the failzie of ten poundes.

Lykwayes it is stait and ordained yat all brewer within the maister landes yat is l[y]abill for brew tallon sall pey it in tymmoslie, wnder the failzie of four poundes the stone.

The said day it is staitit and ordained yat ye haill tenentis of ye sukin of ye mill of Borflait sall com vpon sex houres warning to ye mill watter, and who cumes nocht being tymmouslie adwertis[it] sall pay ane mark from ewry on that reffuss *totias quatias*.

The said day it is ordained with consent of the haill tenentis yat ewry hundreth merkes peying or a chalder of meilles peying sall giv four horss with handes ane day in hervest a day to Drumminor to sheir cornes.

[Court continued.]

[Court for the parishes of Keirne, Clat and Auchindore, holden in the great hall of Castell Forbes, 27 April 1666. Arthur Dallgardno in Blardine bailie, Alex. Chalmer n.p. court clerk, Alex. Sumer ground officer. Suits called, etc.]

Men assyssa

Thomas Roger.	James Duncan.	Robert Wrighte.
Alsinar Anderson.	John Glas.	Georg Lang.
	Wialliam Watson.	Georg Burnett.
Georg Mackie.	James Mackie.	James Duncan.
Wialliam Reid.	Wialliam Maney.	Georg Nicollsone.
John Burnett.		

Thomas Roger, Chanlleler.

The said day Jeane Wallac, spous to John Norie in Towey, compeirit personallie in ye said Court befoir ye said bailzie, and the said bailzie in ye said maister of Forbes name did accuss hir for blooding of William Norey in Towey; who did deny the blooding of him, and the said Wialliam Norey denyed yat he receaved any blood.

Lykwayes the said day comperit ye said Wialliam Norey personallie, and being accussed be ye said bailzie for blooding of ye said Jeane Wallace, who did deny yat he giv hir any blood be him, and the said Jean Wallace denyed that shee receaved any blood be him.

The said day for cleiring of the matter callit tuo vittnes for examinatione and traell of ye matter, to witt William Maney and Hew Myln, who is witnes, who did declare yat they saw the said Waillicm Norey strik ye said Jeane Wallace on ye moueth and the nose and blood hir; lykwayes did sic ye said Wialliam Norie his blood.

The haill assys abowwrittin in the mouth of ye choncelar convictis and mackis the said Wialliam Norey guiltie for blooding and wounding of ye said Jean Vallace.

Lyk wayes ye haill assyss absolvis and fries the said Jean Wallace, becaus it could not be mad out yat shee did blood ye said Wialliam Norey.

The said day the bailzie decernes and ordaines the said Wialliam Norey for blooding and wounding the said Jane Wallace to pey fourtie poundes Scottis money to Wialliam maister of Forbes, and four poundes to ye pairtie wronged, to be peyed within term of law wnder the paine of poynding.

The said day thair was ane complent gevin in be Wialliam Mainey wpon Georg Burnett in Towey, yat the said Georg Burnett will not help to fie ane comwne heird. Thairfor the said bailzie ordaines the said Georg Burnett to conterbut and help according to his labouring to fie and mantaine his pairt of ane commone heird according to his nighboures, wnder the failzie of fyv poundes, to be peyed within terme of law wnder the paine of poynding.

[Court continued.]

[Court for the parishes of Forbes, Auchindore, Keirne and Clatt, holden in the great hall of Castell Forbes, 2 April 1667. Bailie and court clerk as above, John Lang ground officer. Suits called, etc.]

The said day thair was ane bill givein in be Bassie Murgan in Edinbanchrie againest Patrick Mar thair, quhair shee produced ane bloodie cloth and woundis vpon hir bodey that ye said Patrick Mare did give hir; the said Patrick Mare being acussit vairvpon did confess the blooding of the said Bassie Murgane; thairfor the bailyie forsaid ordaines the said Patrick Mar to pey the sowm of tuentic poundis to be peyit to ye master of Forbes his master within term of law wnder the pain of poynding.

Lykwayes the bailyie forsaid ordaines the said Patrick Mare to pey to the pairtie wronged for hir blood the sowm of fyv poundis, to be peyit within term of law wnder the paine of poynding.

The said day the said Bassie Murgane and Wialliam Tailzour hir husband hes inactit themselff and found Georg Michell in Edinbanchrie sovertie and cautione for and with them, that the said Patrick Mar and his wyff, bairnes, servantis, guidis and gear sall be harmles of them either in bodey or meines, and sall not harm the said Patrik Mar neither be day or be night in skoylding or any kynd of wrong so far as they can stop or lett, wnder the failyie of tuentic poundis to be peyit to vair master immediatlie after the wrong be prowin.

  GEORG MITCHELL. ALEXR. CHALMER, N.P.

Lykwayes the said day the said Patrick Mar hes buind and inactit himselff that the said Bassie Murgan and hir said husband sall be skaithles and harmles of him, his wyff, bairnes, servantis in all tym cuming in yair persones, servantis, guidis and geir sa far as they can stop or lett either be night or be day, wnder the paine of ane hundreth poundis to be peyit immediatlie after the wrong be prowin, to be peyit to ye master of Forbes.

        ALEXR. CHALMER, N.P.

[Tenants owing silver duty for crop 1666 to pay within term of law, or 20s. for each merk; and to pay meal and malt duties for same crop within ten days, that is, the meal to be payed against 10 April and the malt against 10 May, or £8 for each boll of meal and £10 for each boll of malt. ' Murburne ' forbidden after present date under pain of £5. Court continued.]

[Court for parishes of Keirne and Clat, holden within the great hall of Castell Forbes, 10 May 1667. Wil. Garioch bailie for the time. Alex. Chalmer n.p. court clerk, Alex. Simmer ground officer. Dempster blank. Suits called, etc.]

The said day ane bill was gevin in be John Olliphir aganest Robert Wright for wronging and blooding of him, quhilk the said John Olliphir refferit to witnes, viz. Allexr. Anderson in Towey and Georg Smyth.

The said Alleiner Anderson being solemlie suorne did declare that the said Robert Wright did com with ane trie and did strick him and did blood him on the mouth.

Lykwayes the said Georg Smyth being solemlie suorne did declare that the said Robert Wright did strick the said John Olliphir on the mouth, and the said John Olliphir did strick him againe with ane trie.

Thairfor the bailyie forsaid ordaines and decernes the said Robert Wright for blooding and oppressing the said John Olliphir to pey the sowm of fourtie poundis Scottis money, to be peyit to Wialliam master of Forbes his master within term of law wnder the paine of poynding.

Lykwayes the bailyie forsaid ordaines the said Robert Wright to pey to ye said John Oliphir for his blood the sowme of fyv poundis Scottis money, to be peyit within term of law wnder the paine of poynding.

The said day Patrick Lieth in Wasthilles, Alexr. Cooke thair, being lawffullie warned to this present court and being thrie tymes callit and nocht compeirit, the bailzie forsaid ordaines the said Patrick Leith and Alexr. Cook to pey the sowm of thrie mark each on of them for thair absene, to be peyit vithin term of law wnder the paine of poynding.

[Tenants ordained to pay their silver, meal and malt duties for crop 1666, or penalties as above. Court continued.]

[Court of the lands and barony of Forbes, Keig and Achindor, holden at Blackhillock in Wil. Grein his chamber, 28 March 1668. Bailie and court clerk as above. John Myln ground officer. Dempster blank. Suits called, etc.]

The said day it is staitit and ordained be the forsaid bailyie that the haill tenentis in the forsaid landes and borrowny that they sall pey in to the gernell of Forbes all thair meill restand for the crop sextie sevin and cropis preceding within ten dayis after the dait of thir presenttis wnder the failzie of aucht poundis for ewry boll wndelyverit, and to pey in all yair malt for crop sextie sevin and yeires preceding againest the first day of May nixt, wnder the failzie of ten poundis for ilk boll wndelywerit after forsaid day; and it is ordained to be poyndit immediatlie for the forsaides pryces heir insert without failyie.

Lykwayis it is staitit and ordained be the forsaid bailyie that the haill tenentis in the forsaid landes sall pey all yair byrune silwer dewties for crop sextie sex yeires and all yeires and cropis preceding wnder the failyie of tuentie shilling for each mark wnderpeyit, and all byrun costumes foules, weadderes and quhatsumever costumes restand for the crop sextie sewin and cropis and yeires preceding, to be poyndit yairfor vithin term of law, conform to the former actis.

The said day it is ordained be the said bailyie that the haill tenentis of the said landes that they sall pey thair haill customes for the crop sextie sevin and cropis preceding, or fyv markis for each weadder wndelyverit and halff mark for each capon wndelywerit and four shilling for each poualtrie foull wndelywerit, and to [be] poyndit vithin term of law wnder the pain of poynding.

Lykwayis it is ordained be the said bailyie that the guidman of ewry myln within the saides landes sall provyd and pey ane guid myln suyne conform to yair assedationes for crop sextie sevin, or aucht poundis money for ewry suyne yat is wnpeyit, and to be poyndit within term of law.

The said day it is ordained be the said bailyie with consent of the haill tenentis within the saides landes that they sall produc and bring thair dischargis to Alexr. Michellis his hous, or any plac quhair he sall desyr them to bring yaim, dischargis for yair custom weadderes and customes foullis for the crop sextie sex and cropis preceding betuixt the dait of thir presenttis and the aucht day of May nixt, and failyeing yairof they sall be holdin to pey them againe.
[Court continued.]

[Court of the lands and barony of Forbes and Keig and Auchindor, held in the house of William Grein in Blackhillock, 30 March 1668. Bailie, etc., as above. Suits called, etc.]

The said day James Wobster gav in ane bill againest John Michell in Logey for blooding the said James Wobster in Logey, and the said James Wobster producit ane lining cloth of blood yairvpon; the said John Michell being acusit yairvpon denyed the blooding of ye said James Wobster; wpon the quhilk the said John Michell was content to refer himselff to ane asyss. The names of the assysirys :—

        PATRICK JAMESON, chanceller.
ALEXR. MICHELL.   ARTHUR MICHELL.
JAMES BONNAR.   ROBERT ANDERSON.
JOHN JAMESON.   JOHN MICHELL.
JAMES DAVIDSON.

The haill assyss in the mouth of Patrick Jameson, chancellar, convictis the said John Michell for blooding of the said James Wobster. Thairfor the said bailzie ordaines and decernes the said John Michell to pey the sowm of tuentie poundes Scotis money to Wialliam master of Forbes as ane blood weete, and fourtie shilling Scotis money to the pairtie wronged, and to be peyit within term of law wnder the paine of poynding.

The said day the said John Michell in Logey compeirit and producit blood and cleirlie declared that James Smyth in Logey did giv him the said blood, quhilk the said James

Smyth confessit yat he gav him the blood; vpon the confession the forsaid bailyie ordaines the said James Smyth to pey to Wialliam master of Forbes the sowm of fyv poundes Scottis money, to be peyit vithin term of law wnder the paine of poynding.

The said day James Smyth compeirit and producit blood and did declar that the said John Michell gav him the blood, quhilk the said John Michell declarit and confessit that he gav him the blood; quhairvpon the bailzie ordained the said John Michell to pey to Wialliam master of Forbes the sowm of fyv poundes Scotis money, to be peyit within term of law wnder the paine of poynding.

The said day the said James Smyth bindis and obliig himself that the said John Michell sall be harmles, his wyff, bairns and servantes, gudes and ger, of him, his wyff, bairnes, so far as he can stop or lett, wnder the failzie of tuentie poundes.   A. C., N.P.

Lykwayis the said John Michell bindes and obliiges himselff that the said James Smyth sall be harmles, his wyff, bairnes and servantes, guides and ger, of him, his wyff, bairnes, so far as he can stop or lett, wnder the failzie of tuentie poundes.   A. C., N.P.

The said day the said John Michell bindes and obliig himselff that the said James Wobster sall be harmles, his wyff, bairnes, and servantes, guides and geir, of him, his wyff, bairnes, so far as he can stop or lett, wnder the failzie of tuentie poundes.   A. C., N.P.

Lykwayis the said James Wobster bindes and obliiges himselff that the said John Michell sall be harmles, his wyff, bairnes and servantes, guides and ger, of him, his wyff, bairnes, sa far as he can stop or lett, wnder the failyie of tuentie poundes.   A. C., N.P.

[Court continued.]

> The Court of the barrowny of Putachie lyand within the pariochin of Keig and shireffdome of Aberdein, and the landes of Tillikiry lyand vithin the parochin of Touch and shireffdom forsaid, pertining hiratcabill to ye ryght honnorabill Wialliam master of Forbes, holdin

within the maner plac of Putachie vpon the nynt day of Maij j^mvj^csextie aucht yeris, be the said Wialliam master of Forbes heritour propritour of ye saides landes, and be Wialliam Garioch of Archballach his bailzie for the tym, and Alexr. Chalmer notar publict and court clark, John Leith ground officer, [*blank*] demster. [Suits called, etc.]

The said day Wialliam Thomson in Auchgathyll compeirit personallie, gave in ane bill and submittit himselff to this present court,[1] and producit ane cloth with blood, quhair he aleigit that John Jameson in Putachie did giv him the said blood; vpon the which the said John denyed the blood, bot the said John Jameson confessit the striking of the said Wialliam Thomson, quhairvpon the said John Jameson referit to the said Wialliam Thomson his oath giv he gav him the said blood; quhairvpon the said Wialliam Thomson was content to giv his oath vpon the said affeir; the said Wialliam Thomson being soleme sworne in visag of ye court did declare yat John Jameson gav him the said blood vith his owin hand vith ane tric. Thairfor the bailyie forsaid ordaines the said John Jameson to pey for the said blood weete to the said Wialliam master of Forbes the sowm of thritie poundes Scotis money, to be peyit within term of law wnder the paine of poynding.

The said [day] Alexr. Burges, servitour to the said John Jameson, gav in ane complent vpon Alexr. Thomson, son to Wialliam Thomson elder, quhairas he did aleig yat ye said Alexr. Thomson did strik him, quhilk he did confess the samen, and did strik the said Alexr. Burges; for the said oppression and striking the bailyie forsaid ordaines the said Alexr. Thomson to pey ten poundes money, to be peyit to Wialliam master of Forbes vithin term of law wnder the paine of poynding.

The said day John Jameson bindes and obliiges himselff yat Wialliam Thomson elder sall be frie and skaithles, his

---

[1] Auchnagathle, though in Keig parish and only a short distance from Puttachie, did not belong to Lord Forbes; in 1620 it belonged to Leith of Lickleyhead (*Retours Aberdeen*, 167), and in 1696 to Forbes of Leslie.

wyff, bairnes, servantes, guides and geir, of him, his wyff, bairnes, servantes, in all tym coming sa far as he may stop or lett either be night or day, wnder the failyie of fourtie poundes incais it sall be found in conntrer. A. C., N.P.

The said day the said Wialliam Thomson elder in Putachie bindes and obliiges him selff that John Jameson, his wyff, bairnes, servandes, guides and geir, sall be fric and skaithles of him and his wyff, bairnes, servantes in all tym coming sa far as he can stop or lett either be night or be day, wnder the failyie of fourtie poundes incais it be found in the conntrer. A. C., N.P.

[The tenants of Putachie and Tillikiry ordained to pay their meal, malt, and silver duties for crop 1667, or the penalties as above.]

The said day Patrick Hendrie, gardner in Putachie, gav in ane bill againest John Jameson, quhair he did aleiig and did refer the samen to his oath, quhair he did confess that he did kill his dog vithout falt; quhairfor the said bailyie ordained the said John Jameson to pey the sowm of fyv pondes to Wialliam master of Forbes vithin term of law, wnder the paine of poynding.

The said day it is staitit and ordained that the said John Jameson and Wialliam Thomson his nighbores and all wyer tenentis vithin the said landes sall tack poyndis, comprys thair cornes sivilie vithout any stryff or debait in all tym coming vithout brak of ye said laburrous abow writtin, bot presew for the skaith be for ye court or any over jugditorie vithin ye shirefdome.

[Court continued.]

[Court for the parishes of Forbes, Keig, Auchindor, Keirne and Clat, holden within the great hall of Castell Forbes, 17 Oct. 1668. Arthur Dallgardno of Blairdiny bailie. Alex. Chalmer n.p. court clerk. Alex. Jaffray ground officer. Dempster blank. Suits called, etc.]

[The tenants ordained to pay their silver duties for crops 1666 and 1667, or 20s. for each merk if unpaid within fifteen days after they be charged for payment.]

The said day the bailzie forsaid decernes and ordaines the haill tenentis vithin the forsaid lordship that is restand any meill or malt for the crop and zeir of God 1667 and preceiding, is ordained to pey such pryces as the maister of Forbes receaved for his gernell cither for meill or malt in this present zeir j^{m}vj^c thriscor aucht zeres, to be peyit within term of law wnder the paine of poynding.

The said day the haill millares and pickjman of the severall millis of ye said lordship is sworn and gav yair oathis in this present court that they sall not suffer any tennentis to putt anic dust or rey among thair fearm, and that they sall tack vp the dust and cuttingis to yair hous till thar ferm be peyit and delywerit.

The said day the haill tennentis within the said lordship with thair owin consentis hes inactit themselff that they sall keip guid nightbourheid in all conditiones, and sall not mack any truble either be striking vyer or skoldin vyer in all tym comyng, bot incais of any differenc they sall goe to ye birly men in ye severall pariochin ordained for ye vs to desyd questiones, and giv they doe not soe, giv it sall fall out any wrong, the pairtie yat wrongis being prowin, they sall pey tuentie poundes vithin term of law wnder the paine of poynding.

The said day the bailzie forsaid ordaines and decernes the haill tennentis and vyer persones vithin the said lordship that hes or sall be to hav castin either faill or diveittes or any kynd of zeird vithin meadowes, hauchis or haning gras, sall pey sex poundes Scottis to ye maister of Forbes vithin term of law, wnder the paine of poynding.

The said day John Gordon in Castellhill did confess that he did strik and beat John Oliphir his son; yairfor the bailzie ordaines him to pey fyv poundes money to ye maister of Forbes vithin term of law, wnder the paine of poynding.

The said day the haill suckin of the myln of **Barflat** hes inactit themselff vith yair owin consent yat incais yat any of them sall sell beir vith the fodder, then and in yat cais they sall pey multer for ilk boll yat John Glas sall instruct to be sold, and for ilk load of oatis yat he sall find goeing to vyer mylnis, then and in that cais they obliig them selffis to pey thrie poundes for ilk load of dry oatis, and ilk boll of oatis sold vith ye fodder they sall be lybill for ye knaship yairof, reservand yair ferm malt and seid.

The said day James Smyth in Auchtmar hes inactit himselff that he sall bring tuo sufficient prowis in the nixt court yat sall be holdin in this plac of Castell Forbes holdin be ye master of Forbes his nam, that Wialliam Mallice did tack away tuo load of timber out of bog of Drumminnor, quhilk belongit to ye said James Smyth vith [vithout?] leav, and giv he sall happin to failzie of his prowis or probation, he obliigis him selff to pey the sowm of tuentie poundes money to ye master of Forbes.

The said day John Gordon in Castellhill yair was ane complent givin in be John Nilson in Castellhill, yairfor the said John Gordon hes inactit him selff that his wyff, bairnes, servantts yat belongis to him sall doe no harm to ye said John Nillson, his wyff, bairnes, servantes, guides and geir in all tym coming sa far as he can stop or lett derectlie or inderectlie, wnder the failzie of fourtie poundes money   A. C., N.P.

The said day John Nillson hes inactit him selff that John Gordon in Castell hill that ye said John Gordon sall be harmles and skaithles of him, his wyff, bairnes, serwantes in all tym coming sa far as he can stop or lett, wnder the failzie of fourtie poundes money.
                                                A. C., N.P.

The said day the haill tennentis of Glentown and Putachie [inactit themselff] that they sall hold and keip yair haill nolt, sheip and hors out of ye wood of Puttachic both sumer and winter, wnder the failzie of ten poundes money ewry tym the froster sall challang any of yair beast in the said wood.[1]

[Court continued.]

---

[1] A generation earlier, in 1623, Puttauchie was set to three tenants, Andrew Jamesone, Patrick Cairill, and John Aydill. A clause in the lease runs thus : 'Item the wood off Puttauchie is reservit out off ye said tennentis assedationis, except libertie sumtymis to ye tennentis guidis to pastour in ye said wood bot not to maik ane dalie pastour, and in ye tyme off storm and snaw no guidis to

[Court for the parishes of Keirnе, Forbes, Keig and Auchtindor, holden at Castell Forbes within the great hall thereof, 17 October 1669. Bailie and court clerk as above. Alex. Simmer ground officer. Suits called, etc.]

The said day the bailzie forsaid ordaines and decernes the haill tennentis within the saidis landis to mack peyment of thair silwer dewties and few dewties and tynd silwer for the zeir and crop sextie aucht to the said William master of Forbes conform to thair assedationes and termes of peyment yairin containit, wnder the failzie of peying poundes for ilk mark that they are found restand conform to former actes mad yairanent, and to mack peyment yairof vithin fourtie aucht houres after they be chargit, wnder the paine of poynding.

[The tenants ordained to pay in their meal and malt for crop 1669 and preceding to the girnel of Castle Forbes, or to pay £8 Scots for each boll of malt and 10 merks for each boll of meal undelivered.]

The said day the bailzie hes ordained and ordained [*sic*] that no froster in Putachie or keiper of any boges or parkes vith[in] the lordship of Forbes sall sell or giv away any manner of timber grat or small, either wandis or any timber or bark quhatsumewir, als weill wnnamed as name[d]. except thair be leiv askit and obtainet from the maister of Forbes or his ladey and ane warrand wnder thair hand for the samen, wnder the failzie of ten poundes *totias quatias*.

---

cum yerin for distroyinge off ye younge treis, and ye saidis tennentis to be suorne frosteris for keipinge off ye said wood on cuttit, and ye said wood to be comprysit be sex honest men, and giff it be found war be ye aitinge off ye guidis yis tyme tuelff moneth, ye said tennentis guidis to be dischargit and yair takis expyr: and yis to be in my lordis will: and ye saidis tennentis to answer for yeir servantis and bairnis for cuttinge and braikinge off ye said wood and for keipinge off ye halkis nestis.' In the same year 'Alexander Simsone gardner hes ye sett of ye gardyne off Putauchie with ye gardneris croft with ye housis and priviledgis yair off vsit and wont, for ye space off thrie zeris, beginand at Candilmes byiane. . . . Payand yerfoir zeirlie ye sowme off ten markis money of maill, and twa mandis to be maid be him self zeirlie, togidder with ye furnysinge of Putauchie and Fiddes with sic frout and herbis as growis in ye said zaird.'

The said day all breweres within the lordship yat is lyabill for peyment of brew tallan to the ladey Forbes are ordained to pey yair tallan within term of law wnder the paine of poynding four poundes for ilk ston yat they are restand.

The said [day] it is staitit and ordained be the said bailzie that giv any tennent or subtennent sall not obey thair severall ground officires within ye lordship of Forbes, being lawfullie warnit to any court or any servic of the master of Forbes, and who sall be absent or disobey yair officir, sall pey fourtie shilling, and who sall defore any officir in poynding sall pey ten poundes *totias quatias*, and to be poyndit immediatlie after ye prowing of yair disobediane. Lykwayes giv any officir sall neglect or givis not tymmos adwertisment to ye tennentis within ye severall groundes sall pey fourtie shilling *totias quotias*.

The said [day] John Clerihew in Dubston, James Anderson in March mar, Robert Wright in Talliche, Patrick Moir in New Keig, being solemlie sworn to be upryght and honnest birly men in decyding of controversic betuixt nightboures and in prysing of cornes betuixt master and tennentis, lykwayes John Agnes [Angus ?], and John Michell being sworn in ye said court as birly men for ye pariochin of Auchtindor for the reason abowwrittin.

The said day the bailzie ordaines ye haill tennentis in the pariochin of Forbes sall be comptabill to ye master of Forbes for such lym as thair servantes receved at ye lym killis to ye master of Forbes his vs.

[Court continued.]

[Court for the parishes of Kearn, Forbes, Auchtindor and Keag, holden in the great hall of Castell Forbes, 21 March 1670. Arthur Dallgarno bailie, Alex. Chalmer n.p. court clerk. John Chalmer ground officer. Dempster blank. Suits called, etc.]

The said day it is staitit and ordained be the said bailzie and with consent of the haill tennentis in the pariochin of Forbes, that is to say, the said tennentis confessit in presenc of this court yat the[y] war and is obliigit be condishendenc with thair severall shoulderes for this present militia according to yair severall devisiones to pey them zeirly ane constant fie in land and money according to thair condishehance. Thairfor the baillzie forsaid ordaines and decernes ewry tennent yat is lybill for peyment to ye said militia shoulderes to pey in yair severall proportiones to ye said John Donald and William Fyny or any vyer concernit vithin term of law wnder the paine of poynding. Lykwayes it is ordained that ewry shoulder of ye militia within ye pariochin of Forbes sall hav after Witsonday nixt and als long as ye militia sall happin to continow zeirly ten markes money at ye termes after speciffied, viz. fyv markes at Mertimas 1670 and vyer fyv markes at Witsonday yairafter j^{m}vj^c sevintie ane, and sa furth zeirly.

[The tenants ordained to pay their meal duties for crop 1669 and preceding crops against 10 April or 10 merks for each boll then unpaid, and their malt 8 May, or £8 for each boll unpaid, and to pay their silver duties for same crops.]

Lykwayes it is staitit and ordained be the said bailyie yat all tennentis in the pariochin of Forbes yat is restand teynd silwer Forbes [*sic*] and teynd wictuall, the termes of peyment being com and by past, are ordained to pey the samen to ye minister of Forbes and receav his disharg vpon the samen, and who failyies to pey the samen are ordained to be poyndit vithin term of law.

The said day Patrick Leith in Wast hillis is ordained to pey ane mark for ane lock to the myln of Barflat, and thrie markes for braking vp ye said myln dore, and the said William master of Forbes his corn vithin the said myln, and to be peyit vithin term of law wnder the paine of poynding.

The said day John Nillson in Castell hill are ordained to pey to ye said William master of Forbes thrie peckes of meill for car meill; lykwayes John Gordon in Castell hill, James Walker yair, Georg Villson yair, are ordained to pey to William master Forbes four haddish of car meill, ilk ane of them vithin term of law vnder the paine of poynding.

The said day John Reid in Glentown gav in ane bill againest John Gordon in Glentown, quhair he did lybill yat ye said John Gordon did blood and strik him, quhich ye said John Gordon confessit yat he did strik him, and ye said John Reid confessit yat he did strik ye said John Gordon ; thairfor the baillzie forsaid decernes and ordaines ye said John Gordon to pey to his master for stricking and beating ye said John Reid ten libs., and ordaines ye said John Reid to pey fyv libs. for stricking ye said John Gordon, to be peyit vithin term of law wnder the paine of poynding.

Lykwayes it is staitit and ordained yat all tennentis yat is lybill for peyment of custom sheip yat they sall pey them in againe the first of Maij nixt, wnder the failzie of fyv markes ffor ilk custom sheip yat is wnpeyit, and to be poyndit for ye samen.

The said day John Chalmer, servant to ye said William master of Forbes, is installit and ordainit officir for ye landes in ye pariochin of Kearne and Clat. Thairfor according to old vs and wont the haill tennentis, croftis men and gras men is ordainit to pey to ye said John Chalmer as ground officir, viz. ewry tennent yat hes ane pluch labouring ane threff of corn out of ye thrid crop sold zeir, and 3s. 4d. from ewry croft yat peyis tuentie markes, and tuall penies Scotis from ewry gras hous, and who failzies to be peyit [poyndit ?] for ye samen.

The said day it is staitit and ordainit that who is lybill for peyit [peyment ?] of brew tallan for crop sextie nyn are ordained to pey the samen vho is restand the samen againe the last day of March instant, or els to be lybill to pey four libs. for ilk ston yat is restand, and to be poyndit for ye samen vithin term of law, wnder ye paine of poynding.

The said day John Chalmer, greiff and ground officir, gav in ane bill, who desyrit ane act of court againest any tennentis, subtennentis vith[in] ye pariochin of Kearne or any deawling vpon ye Maines of Drumminor yat sall put or villfullie keip any of thair beastes eather hors or nolt vpon ye gras, bogis, orchardes of Drumminor sall pey thrie shilling 4d. for ilk beast yat ye said John Chalmer sall tack vpon ye gras.

The said day the haill tennentis vithin ye said lordship yat is restand any putrie foullis or capones for crop sextic nyn is ordained to pey for ewry putrie four shilling and aucht shilling for ilk capon, and to be poynding for ye samen vithin term of law wnder the paine of poynding.

The said day it is staitit and ordained yat who hes castin or sall happin to cast either faill or divittes within meddow ground or haning sall pey ten libs. *totias quatias*.

The said day John Gordon in Glentown bindes and obliiges him yat John Reid in Glentown sall be harmles of him and his wyff, bairns, servantes, guides and geir in all tyme coming, and yat he sall not molest him neither be night or be day bot sall hender, stop all yat he may wnder the failzie of tuentie libs.

Lykwayes the said John Reid bindes and obliiges him that the said John Gordon sall be harmles, etc.

[William Kallzies in Carndard obliges him that John Thomson there sall be harmless, etc.; and the said John Thomson obliges him that the said William Kayllies shall be harmless, etc., except by order of law.]

[Court continued.]

[Court for the parishes of Forbes, Keig, Kearne, Clat, Auchtindor, etc., holden at Castle Forbes, 2 Feb. 1671. Bailie. etc., as above. Suits called, etc.]

[The tenants ordained to pay in their silver duties for crop 1670, under 'failzie' of paying 20s. for every merk; and those in arrear for crop 1669 to pay according to the 'failzies' of former acts. Also to pay their meal and malt to the girnel of Castell Forbes betuixt and 31 May next, under pain of 10 merks for each boll of meal and £8 for each boll of malt.]

The said day the haill tennentis vithin the said pariochines vithin the lordship of Forbes that alcigis that they hav peyit in yair custom veadderes, lambis, capones, henes for the crop sevintic and preceding cropis are ordained to

produc thair dischargis and receitis vpon the delywer off
thair customes betuixt the dait heirof and the last day of
this in[stant] Februare, and who failzies in so doeing, they
sall be holdin as nocht peyit and to be poyndit for the
restand coustomes immediatlie yairafter; lykwayes it is
ordained that the haill tennentis sall pey in thair haill
customes quhatsumevir at the termes insert in yair
assedationes, wnder the failzie of peying fyv markes for
ilk weadder, aucht shilling for ilk capon and four shilling
for ilk hene yat is restand after the termes containit
vithin yair severall assedationes, and to be poyndit
immediatlie after the term of peyment beis bygon.

The said day it is staitit and ordained vith the consent
of the haill tennentis and millars and master of the seiverall
mylns, that the guid man of ewry myln and peckiman sall
hav ane peck of ground malt meit vith ane meill peck for
ewry four bollis of sell malt for Aberdein, and thus for
ewry four bollis of all that growis them, except thair seid
and and [sic] ferm malt, quhich they most hav frie.

Lykwayes it is staitit and ordained be the said bailzie
vith consent of the haill tennentis, that the tennentis
vithtin thair seyverall suckines sall pey thair kenship of
that samen meill of thair ferm vith the seides of ye keiship
of ye ferm meill allennerallic according to old vs and
wont, and kenship of the rest of thair meill vithout seides
according to old vs and wont, and this act is for ye
pariochin of Forbes and myln thair.

The said day it is staitit and ordained be the said bailzie
that the haill sojoures and tennentis vithin the severall
pariochines of the lordship of Forbes sall be comptabill
for the haill armes according as they reccaved of armes
for the militia they sall be comptabill ane mark thence
furth command for the militia, and incais eather muscat,
pick or suord be away or wrongit, they sall be lybill to pey
ten lbs. for ewry muschat and four lbs. for the pick and
four libs. for ewry sword.

The said day it is staitit and ordained that giv John
Clerihew in Dubston sall lett any nolt, hors in James
Smyth in Logie in his cornes being found to night laires,

the said John Clerihew sall pey sex shilling aucht pennies for ilk beast of nolt, hors and prowin to be all night in his corn or tackin out of his corn in the morning, and ane shilling Scotis for ewry sheip yat sall be found in his corn.

Lykwayes it is staitit and ordained that no nightbouris sall not fold non of thair nightbouris sheip, in speciall hill sheip, wnder the failzie of tuall pennies for ilk beast.

The said day Robert Wright in Tailyee mackes and findes sovertie and lawborrowis that Georg Roger in Tailziachee he him selff, vyff, bairnes, servantes, guides and geir, sall be harmles and hurtles of him in all tym cuming of him, his vyff, bairnes and servantes in all tym coming sa far as he can stop or lett eather be night or be day, wnder the failzie of fourtie libs. Scotis money.

[George Roger finds lawburrows to Robert Wright in Tailziache, ' except be order of law.']

The said day it is staitit and ordained that all tennentis, cotteres or grasmen who is lybill of peyment of sojoures fies, clothing, money or vages for the randiwowes sall pey in thair seiverall proportiones to thair helperes according to thair seiverall proportion within term of law, wnder the paine of poynding.

The said day it is staitit and ordainit that the haill tennentis vithtin the said pariochines abowwrittin sall mack thair fearm of guid cornes of tach and ewall fildis, and be frie of dust or stones.

The said day it is staitit and ordained be the said bailzie that the haill tennentis vithtin the forsaid pariochines sall show in ewry hundretht markes peying or chalder of meill peying tuo peckes of piess, and who failzies or conteines [contraveines?] this act sall pey fourtie shilling Scotis.

[Court continued.]

[Court for the parish of Forbes, etc., holden at Scotismyln, 9 March 1671. William Forbes in Scotismyln bailie for the time. Alex. Chalmer n.p. court clerk. Alex. Jaffray ground officer. Dempster blank. Suits called, etc.]

The said day William Johnston in Ballfour and Agnes

Esson his spous gav in ane bill againest Georg Michell in
Ballfour, quhairas the said Agnes Esson did prow be tuo
vitnes that the said Georg Michell did strick hir, thairfor
the bailzie forsaid ordained the said Georg Michell to pey
fyv poundes Scotis money to William master of Forbes
vithtin term of law, wnder the paine of poynding.

Lykwayes the said Georg Michell brought in tuo witnes,
and the said Aganes Esson confessit judiciallie that shee
callit the said Georg Michell perjurit and miswaron carll,
quhich shee could not mack out the samen. Thairfor the
bailzie forsaid ordaines the said William Johnston and
Agnas Esson to pey the sowm of fyv pound Scotis money
to William master of Forbes within term of law, wnder
the paine of poynding.

The said day Georg Michell bindes and obliiges him selff
that the said William Johnston and his wyff, bairnes and
servantes sall be skaithles, harmles of his wyff and himselff,
servantes and bairnes in all tym coming both of his person,
guides or geir eather in strick or skolding or stayling or
any deid of wrong except be ordour of law, wnder the
failzie of ten pondes *totias quatias.*

[William Johnston obliges himself likewise to Georg
Michell.]

[Court continued.]

[Court for the parishes of Forbes, Kearne, Auchindor, Clat, etc.,
holden within the great hall of Castell Forbes, 19 April 1671.
Arthur Dallgardno of Blerdiny bailie. Alex. Chalmer n.p.
court clerk, John Chalmer ground officer. Dempster
blank. Suits called, etc.]

[Tenants resting any meal or malt for crop 1670 and preceeding, to pay in the rest by 31 May under failzie of 10 merks
for each boll of meal and £8 for each boll of malt. Those resting silver or teind duty for crop 1669 and preceding, and for
Whitsunday 1670, to pay, under failzie of paying 20s. for each
merk.]

The said day it is staitit and ordained, conform to former
actes mad anent castin of faill eather with foot spadis or
flachter spad in the pariochin of Forbes vithtin meadow

gras, hauchis or any pairt of haining of thair severall
possessiones, and who is found to hav transactit or transgressit former actis, to pey ten poundes for the foot spad
and fyv poundes for flachter spades, and this act is genner-
allie for the haill lordship of Forbes, and to be poyndit
for the samen within term of law.

The said day James Bonnar in Silivethic and Georg
Anderson at the mill of Barflat, William Lightown in
Towvie, Arthur Michell in Collhay, James Smyth in Logie
are cossin birlaw men and for the inspecktion of the
former actis mad anent the sigththing of the medow
gras and haugh gras and haning who hes castin cather
vith foot spad or flachter spad or pluchit medow gras,
hes givin thair oath of fedilitie yat they sall trewlie and
reallie mak report to William master of Forbes who is
found guiltie of former actis, and to pey conform to
former actis, yat is to say, ten poundes for ilk man vithtin
the said lordship, and to be poyndit for the samen vithin
term of law wnder the paine of poynding.

The said day Georg Walker in Bogie syd being callit
and persewit be Janet Proctor for strecking and blooding
of the said Janet Proctor, quhich the said Georg Walker
did confessit that he did strik the said Janet, and the said
Janet did produc blood befor the forsaid bailzie, quhair
the said Janet did depon [in] jugdment that the said
Georg Walker did blood hir, quhair it was referit to the
voic of ane syss, and Arthur Michell in Collhay as chanceller in nam of the haill asyss convictit the said Georg
Walker of blooding the said Janet Proctour; thairfor the
bailzie forsaid decernes the said Georg Walker to pey the
sowm of tuentie poundis money to William master of
Forbes as ane blood week, and to be poyndit [peyit?]
vithin term of law wnder the pain of poynding.

The said day Thomas Roger in Bogey syd hes inactit
him selff as principall and William Lang in Drumminor
as cautioner and sovertie for him as lawborrowes, that
Georg Walker in Bog syd, his vyff, bairnes, servantes,
guidis and geir sall be skaithles and hermles or hurtfull
be him, his wyff, bairnes, servantes, guidis and geir in

all tym coming, bot sall stop or lett all dangeres yat he can hinder from him so far as he can cather be night or day, and sall not trouble or molest him except be ordour of law, wnder the failzie of fourtie libs. money.

[The said George Walker, and Alex. Leisk as cautioner, become lawburrows for said Thomas Roger in like manner.]

The said day Patrick Leith in Windis eye being callit in this court for transgressing the master of Forbes his ordour anent the marchis betuixt Windis eye and Barflat, quhairas the said master of Forbes did decyd and apoynt tuo rigis to Windis eye and tuo riges to Barflat, and the said Patrick Leithe out of contemp did ffeid the four rigis, thairfor the bailzie forsaid decernis the said Patrick Leith to pey tuentie libs. money to William master of Forbes for his said contemp, and to be poyndit [peyit] vithin term vnder the paine of poynding.

The said [day] Georg Anderson in myln of Barflatt hes inactit him selff as principall and John Olphir in Steanfeild as cautioner for him bind them selflis law borrowes that Patrick Leith in Vindes eye sall be harmles and skaithles and his wyff, bairnes, servantes, guides and gear in all tym coming of him selff, wyff, bairnes, servantes, except be ordour of law, wnder the failzie of fourtie libs. money.

[Likewise said Patrick Leith, and John Cook cautioner, become lawburrows for said Georg Anderson and the haill neighbouris; no sum specified.]

The said day it is staitit and ordained that the pariochin of Kearn sall keep all beast, hors, nolt, sheip out of the bog of Drumminnor, wnder the failzie of peying halff mark for ilk hors and nolt and thri shilling for ewry sheip that sall be found in the bog or cornes after the 23 day of Apryll, and to be poyndit immediatlie after the[y] be challanged or tackin.

The said day it is staitit and ordained be forsaid that the haill tennentis of the forsaid pariochins sall pey in thair haill custom foullis for crop sevintie on and preceeding cropis, the term of peyment being com and bypast,

wnder the failzie of halff mark for ilk capon and four
shilling for ilk hen, and to be poyndit for the samen
vithin term of law, wnder the paine of poynding.

[Court continued.]

[Court for the parishes of Forbes, Kearn, Clat, Auchtindor and
Keig, etc., holden in the great hall of Castell Forbes
10 Nov. 1671. Bailie, etc., as above. Suits called, etc.]

The said day the bailzie forsaid decernes and ordaines
the haill tennentis within the said lordshipis and pariochines forsaid who is lyabill to pey meill ferm in to the
gernell of Castell Forbes, that they sall pey the samen in
conform to thair termes of thair assedation yairin contcinit, clean bot dust or stones and frie bot heatting or
sweit meill or hunied in any cais, and that incais any
person sall bring any meill to ye gernell that is not
sufficient, they sall carie the meill hom againe to thair
owin vs, and sall be lyabill to pey ten markis for ilk boll
yat the[y] rest for the crop sevintie on and preceding
cropis. And for preventing of not sufficient meill sall not
be maid, the bailzie forsaid ordaines ewry guid man or
master of ewry myln vithin the forsaid landis sall tack
speaciall care of the cornes that sall be brought to the
myln that mack the fearm of that it be not speilt or
hunied cornes, and that they sall tack vp the dust and
keip it till the ferm be delywerit into ye gernell, and that
the guidmanes of each myln sall giv they find any speilt
or hunied cornes to be fearm, then in that cais sall mack
report yairof to the master of Forbes of thair diligenc
and care, and giv tymows adwertisment befor it be brought
or delywerit yat it is not sufficient.

[Tenants liable for malt ferm for crop 1671 and preceding,
shall pay it, under the failzie of £8 for every boll undelivered.]

[Tenants to pay their silver duties for crop 1671 and
preceding; those who faill in payment are to be poinded
20s. for each merk.]

[Tenants resting meal and malt for crop 1670 to pey 10
merks for each boll resting for said crop 1669 (*sic*).]

The said day the bailzie ordaines the haill breweris and
vyer persones who is lyabill for peyment for brew tallan
and butter sall pey in the samen vithin term of law, wnder
the paine of poynding four libs. for ilk ston yat sall be
fund restand.

The said day it is staitit and ordained that all tennentis
vithin the said landis sall bring tadderes with thair hors
in tym of peittes leding be reason that they eat the cornes,
and who sall failzie in so doeing sall hav no gras and sall
pey ten lib. who hes transgressit or who sall transgras in
tymes to com, and to be poyndit immediatlie yairafter.

The said day the bailzie forsaid ordaines the haill suckin
in the pariochin of Forbes sall mack ane suffic[ie]nt mill
dore with lock and key againe the tuentie day of December
nixt, wnder the failzie of fourtie lib. to be poyndit for the
said sowm, wnder the paine of poynding.

The said day the bailzie ordaines Patrick Jameson in
Ballfower, James Murgan in Bithny, are ordained to be
birley men in the pariochin of Forbes, to meitt at any
place in the pariochin of Forbes vpon at adwertessment
to examine and decern vpon all conterversie of pryc cornes
betuixt nighbour and nighbour, and decern conform to
resson and information.

The said day it is staitit and ordained that all gras
men and cotteris and tennentis sall vpon adwertisment
sall com in to the wood of Bithny to dight and clens the
vood, and who sall failzie, the officeires is ordained to
poynd for the samen fourtie shilling *totias quatias*.

[Court continued.]

[Court for same parishes, holden at Castell Forbes, 19 March
1672. Bailie, etc., as above. Suits called, etc.]

[Tenants and others owing silver duties for crop 1671 and
preceding to pay 20s. for each mark; those owing 'ferms'
for crop 1671 and preceding, to pay by 10 April, under
the failzie of peying £8 for each boll unpaid; ferme malt
for same crops to be paid by 30 April, or £10 for each
boll.]

The said day it is staitit and ordained that giv any

tennentis within the said lordship sall brak any arestments
quhatsumewir, that the said William master of Forbes
sall caus his ground officir or shireff officir at his instanc,
and who sall be found guiltie of brak of arestment, eather
be selling cornes, cattell yat is arestit, both the buyer
and seller sall pey ten poundis *totias quatias* byattour the
clame, and to be poyndit immediatlie thairafter.

The said day it is staitit and ordained that all persones
and tennentis within the said lordship sall keip gud
nighbour heid in all respeckis, and in particular James
Michell in Collhay and William Thomson thair sall keip
gud nighbour heid in all tym coming wnder the failzie of
tuentie poundis money, and quhat diffrenc or conterversies is betuixt them. James Murgan in Bithny, Patrik
Jameson in Balfour, John Clerihew in Dubston and James
Bonnar in Silivethie as birlay men or any tuo of them sall
vpon adwertisment sall goe to ye town of Collhay and
decern vpon all conterversies quhatsumewir.

The said day forsameikle as John Mill in Barflat gav in
ane bill againest Georg Walker in Bogisyd, quhair he
aleigis that the said Georg Walker did stolln his beir
shilling in the mill of Barflat, quhich the said John Mill
brought in vitnes, quhich witnes did prow the fact forsaid,
quhich witnes depossitions was reid to fyftein sysseres,
James Murgan in Beithni as chanceller in woic of the haill
assyseres convictit the said Georg Walker of ane poynt
of theifft, quhairfor the bailzie forsaid decernes the said
Georg Walker to pey tuentie poundis money to be peyit
to the said William master of Forbes and ane firlot of
meill to the said John Mill wrongit, and to be peyit
within term of law wnder the pain of poynding.

The said day it is ordained that woodis and bogis
within the said lordships sall be keipit in all tym coming
conform to former actis, wnder the failzie of former actis.

The said day Alexr. Coutis at the Owir mill of Keig
being sworn in former courtis that he should not grind
neither dust or refuss among the master of Forbes his
fearm, and it being collified be John Jamesons fearm in
Putachie yat thair was dust among ye said fearm, and he

found gultie of his office of millart and oath, thair for the
bailzie ordaines the said Alexr. Coutis to pey ten mark,
to be peyit within term of law wnder the paine of poynding
for his forsaid transgression. [Court continued.]

The Court of the lordship of Forbes lyand within the
pariochines of Kearn, Forbes, Keig, Clet, Auchtindor,
pertaining heratibill to the potent William Forbes
lord Forbes, holdin within the great hall of Castell
Forbes be the said lord Forbes vpon the tent day of
October j^{m}vj^{c}sevintie tuo zeires,[1] and be Arthur
Dalgardno of Blairdiny his constitut bailzie, Alexr.
Chalmer nottar publict and court clark, Walter
Michell ground officir, [blank] demster. The suitis
callit, the Court lawfullie fencit and affirmit.

The said day it is staitit and ordained be the said
bailyie that any tennentis within the forsaid lordship who
is restand any silwer dewties for crop sevintie on and
preceiding zeires, the termes of peyment being corn and
bygon, sall pey quhat silwer they are found restand to
my lord Forbes thair master or to his chamberlandis in his
name within term of law, and to be poyndit tuentie
shilling for ilk mark that sall be wnpeyit after term of
law.

The said [day] it is staitit and ordained be the said
bailzie that all tennentis who is restand any meill or malt
for crop sevintie on sall pey in the samen to the gernell
of Castell Forbes vithin term of law wnder the failzie
of peying aucht poundes for ilk boll of meill and nyn
poundes for ilk boll of malt. Lykwayes it is decearned
be the said bailzie that all tennentis sall pey in thair haill
meill and malt for crop sevintie tuo, the term of peyment
being corn and bygon, conform to thair assedationes, and
who failzies of peyment as said is, sall be lyabill for the
failzies of ilk boll abow writtin, and to be poyndit for
the samene conform to ordour of law and to former actis.

---

[1] William, twelfth Lord Forbes, succeeded his father 20 April 1672 (*Scots Peerage*, iv. 62).

The said day it is staitit and ordained be the said bailzie that no car or calffis or stottis sall hav libertie to goe throught or pastour throught the cornes of the Maines of Castell Forbes after the tuentie fourt of June, wnder the failzie of fyv poundis to be peyit for ilk calff that sall be found after the for said day.

The said day it is staitit and decerned be the said bailzie that all tennentis, cotteris or gras men sall keip and preserv thair nolt or any vyer beastis from goeing vithin the wood of Puttachie, Bithny or any vyer parkis or bogis within the forsaid lordship; and in cais of any nolt sall be found be the frosteris, the owneris sall be lybill to pey ane mark of money for ewry beast for the first falt and tuentie shilling for the secund falt and sa furth.

The said day it is staitit and ordained be the said bailzie that the tennentis of the Maines of Putachie sall cook and mack fencabill from thair beast the grein and park of Puttachie within ten dayes after the last of October instant, wnder the failzie of fourtie shilling Scotis for ilk tennent that failzies.

The said day it is found that Alexr. Forbes in Midelmuir and Alexr. Leich hes castin peittis and truffis in forbiddin pairtis and hening vpon the Maines of Puttachie; thairfor the bailzie ordaines the for said persones to pey fyftie shilling each on of them for the first falt and fyv lib. for each person sall be found to cast in hening after wardes.

The said day it is staitit and ordained be the said bailzie that all persones or person that hes burnt any murburnes in forbidd tymes eather them selffis or be thair servantes sall be lybill for such failzeis and onlawis conform to former actis maid theranent.

Lykwayes it is staitit and ordained be the said bailzie that giv any person or persones quhatsumewir sall burn any murburn heirafter except in the month of March, sall be lyabill to pey ten poundes *totias quatias*, and thair masteres sall be lyabill for thair hirdes and servantes, and after prowff sall be poyndit for the samen (except they gett ane debitor who brunt ye murburn).

The said day the bailzie ordaines Margratt Christie, spous to Robert Wright, to pey ten markis money for brewing after shee was inhibitit be the said bailzie, and the said money to be peyit to my lord or the said bailzie vithin term of law, wnder the paine of poynding.

The said day it is staitit and ordained that all tennentis within the forsaid lordship of Forbes sall send in thair servantes with hors and handis conform as they are warned to com in to the Maines of Castell Forbes to the bonnag tymmouslie, wnder the failzie of halff mark for ilk person yat comes not in tymouslie.

The said day it is staitit and ordained be the said bailzie that the haill tennentis of Castellhill and all vyer tennentis vithin the said lordship of Forbes sall keip guid nightbourheid in all respeckis in all tym cuming; and giv thair be any conterversie, then and in that cais they sall goe to the birley men and they sall cognoscik vpon the conterversie, and who does failzie in the counterear sall pey ten poundis, and to be poyndit immediatlie for the samen.

[Court continued.]

The Court of the landis and barouny of the Brey of Tomades, holdin at the Mylntown of Tomadis vpon the fourtein day of November j^{m}vj^{c}sevintie tuo zeires, pertaining heritabill [to William lord Forbes], be William lord Forbes and be Arthur Dalgardno his constitut bailzie, Alexr. Chalmer nottar publict and court clark, James Elssme ground officir, [*blank*] demster. [Suits called, etc.]

The said day the bailzie forsaid decernes and ordaines the haill tennentis within the saidis lands to mack peyment to the said lord Forbes thair haill restand dewties for crop sevintic on and preceding cropis sall mack peyment thairof vithin term of law, wnder the failzie of poynding poundes for markes, the termes of peyment being com and bygon, conform to thair termes of thair assedationes, and to [be] poyndit for the samen who hes failzie[t] in not peyment as

said is. Lykwayes the bailzie forsaid decernes the said
haill tennentis to pey the crop sevintie tuo conform to
thair termes contained with[in] thair severall assedation,
wnder the failzie forsaid.

The said day the bailzie decernes and ordaines the haill
suckin in the mill of Ennettis that they sall keip thair
owin mill with thair haill cornes, oates and malt conform
to old vs and wont, and who failzies or goes to vyer millis
with thair cornes sall pey duble multer, and to be poyndit
vithin the mill dores be the lord Forbes his officir.

[Court continued.]

The Court of the lordship of Forbes lyand within the
  pariochin of Kearn and Clat pertaining heritabillie to
  William lord Forbes, holdin at Kirk styll of Kearn
  vpon the tuentie day of March j^{m}vj^c sevintie thrie
  zeires. [Arthur Dallgardno in Blairndiny bailie.
  Alex. Chalmer n.p. court clerk. Walter Michell ground
  officer. Dempster blank. Suits called, etc.]

The said day Georg Mackey in Steine dyk, John Towch
thair, being somined to this court for wounding and
stricking each other, and blooding other, vitnes being
admittit be the saidis pairties and solemlie suorn for
cleiring of the claim and factis, quhich fact or blood being
referrit to fyftein men chossin for assyss vpon the said fact,
and after the assyss hard thrie vitnes depone, and hard
thair depousitiones; after examination and deliberation
be the assyss, the haill assyss in voic of Georg Androson
in Barflat, chanceller, convictit the said John Touch for
blooding the said Georg Mackey of the sowm of fyftey
pundis money, and lykwayes convictit the said Georg
Mackey for stricking the said John Touch of the sowm of
tuentie pundis money; and the said bailzie interpones
his autithortic hereto and ordaines the said pairtis to
mack peyment thairof of the said respective sowmes to
my said lord Forbes or to his factoures or bailzies vithin
term of law, wnder the paine of poynding.

[Georg Mackey inacted himself as lawburrows to said

John Touch, under failzie of £50 ; and John Touch likewise to Geo. Mackey. Court continued.]

[Court for the parishes of Kearn and Clat. holden within Alex. Sumer's house at the Kirkstyll of Kearn, 17 July 1673. Bailie, etc., as above. Suits called, etc.]

The said day Bassie Thomson in Persellevy gav ane bill againest John Henderson, quhair shee aleigit to prow that the said John Henderson did strick and blood hir, and the witnes being examed did depon that they saw not sic (*sic*) the said John Henderson streik nor blood hir, and confirmit be ye said John Henderson his oath that he did not blood hir nor strick hir. Quhairfor the bailzie forsaid absolues the said John Henderson of the said aleigit blood.

Lykwayes the said John Henderson gav in ane bill againest the said Bassie Thomson, quhairas he did prow be famous vitnes, quhich they did depon that they saw the said Bassie Thomson steik fast in the said John Henderson hair and hardlie could be tackit out of his hair; thair for the bailzie forsaid decernes the said Bassie Thomson to pey the sowm of [fyv poundis][1] money, to be peyit vithin term of law wnder the paine of poynding.

The said Bassie Thomson peyit hir onlaw.

[Lawburrows, John Henderson to Bassie Thomson and her mother, and she to him, under the failzie of £20 each.]
[Court continued.]

[Court for the parishes of Kearn, Forbes, Keig, Auchtindor and Clett, holden within the great hall of Castell Forbes, 31 Oct. 1673. Arthur Dallgardno in Blairdinny bailie. Alex. Chalmer n.p. court clerk. Ground officer and dempster blank. Suits called, etc.]

[Tenants to pay their silver duties for crop 1672 and preceeding, or 20s. for each merk ; and to pay their silver duties for crop 1673; also to pay their meal and malt for crop 1672 and preceeding, or £8 for each boll unpayed;

---

[1] Written and deleted.

also to pay into the girnell of Castell Forbes their meal
and malt for crop 1673, or £8 for each boll of meal and
£10 for each boll of malt.]

[James Bonnar in Siliveth and Alex. Michell in Blackhillock enact themselves lawburrows to each other,
penalty £50 each.]

The said day it is inactit vith consent of the haill
tennentis that giv any persones eather servant or master
sall com to his nighbour bigging and tack out any poyndit
beast vithout leav askit and grantit, the master sall pey
fyv poundis and the servant sall pey thrie mark.

The said day it is staitit and ordained that non of the
tenentis of Putachie and Glentown sall cast no peittis
in my lord Forbes his mos in Bannachie in all tymes
coming vithout leav ask[it] and grantit, vnder the failzie
of fyv poundis *totias quotias*.

The said day it is staitit and ordained that no person
or persones quhatsumevir that dwallis vithin the said
lordship of Forbes sall keip the haill boges, voodis, parkis
and orchardis, that they sall keip thair haill nolt, sheip,
hors from the said voodis and bogis, neither cut, away
tack any of ye timber that growis thairin, neither pull
hedder, vith certificatione any who faillis as said is sall
pey ten poundis *totias quotias*.

The said day the bailzie forsaid decernes James Roger
to pey to my lord Forbes ten pound Scotis money for
stricking and opressing James Duncan servant to James
Christie, and the bailzie decernes the said James Roger
to pey to the pairtie wronged tuentie shilling, and to be
peyit vithin term of law, vnder the pain of poynding.

The said day the said James Roger inactis himselff
that the said James Duncan and his master and all vyer
persones vithin the daach of Towie sall be harmles and
skaithles of him, and thair wyflis, childrein and servantis
in all tym coming sa far as he can stop or lett, except be
ordour of law, vnder the failzie of tuentie poundis.

[Lawburrows, William Thomson in Collhay and James
Michell in Collhay, to each other. Penalty £40 each.]

The said [day] the bailzie forsaid decernes the haill

tennentis that they sall pey in thair custom weadderis
that should hav bein peyit at Rudday sevintie thric,
vnder the failzie of four mark for ilk sheip yat is vnpeyit
after the term of law. Lykwayes the tennentis and
breweris that is lyabill for brew tallan and custom butter
sall pey vithin term of law, vnder the pain of peying of
four poundis for each ston that is restand after the term
of law.

[Court continued.]

[Court of the lordship of Forbes, holden within the great hall
of Castell Forbes, 14 Nov. 1674. Arthur Dallgarno in
Blairdiny bailie for the time. Alex Chalmer n.p. court
clerk. Walt. Michell ground officer. Dempster blank.
Suits called, etc.]

The said day the bailzie forsaid ordaines and decernes
the haill tennentis within the said lordship who is found
be cleir compt restand any meill or malt for crop sevintie
thric, that they sall pey aucht pundis Scotis money for
ilk boll that they sall be found restand, conform to the
pryces of my lordis gernell that he hes receaved from
vyeris for the crop sevintie thric, and that to be peyit
within term of law vnder the paine of poynding.

[Tenants resting silver duties for crop 1673 to pay 20s.
for each merk; and the same for those resting silver
duties for Martinmas 1674 and for crop 1674.]

The said day it is staitit and ordained that the haill
tennentis vithin the said lordship sall pey in thair meill
and malt to the gernell of Castell Forbes conform to the
termes containeit vithin thair severall assedationes, the
termes of peyment being com and bygone, and for the
crop sevintie four, vnder the failzie of peying ten poundis
Scotis money for ilk boll that is found vndelyweʃit as said
is, eather meill or malt, and to be poyndit after the termes
of thair assedation for the said prycis in cais of failzie.

The said day the haill guidmannes of ewry myln within
the said lordship of Forbes sall be answerabill to my lord
Forbes that they sall not suffer the fearm meill be mad
eather of hot or hunied corn or small cornes, bot only of

taieth and cweill corn and in townes cornes, and that thair
sall be neither dust nor stones as they sall be answerabill
to the failzies of former actis ; and the pikimen hes givin
thair oathis that they sall not grein nether duste nor
stones, bot sall informe thair master of the myln incais
they putt any dust among thair fearm, and the dust is
ordained to be taikin be the guidman of ewry myln till
the fearm be peyit to the gernell.

The said day it is staitit and ordained that the wood of
Puttachie sall be keepit in all tym coming conform to
former actis vnder the failzies containit thairin. Lykwayes
compeirit Villiam Moir in Putachie and Patrik Moir thair,
who confessit them selffis that the said Patrick Moir did
pull hedder and cows vithin the wood of Putachie vithout
leive and did cleim the dykis of the said wood; thairfor the
said bailzie decernes the said Villiam Moir to pey ten pundis
as giv varrand to ye said Patrik Moir as his servant.

The said day the bailzie decernes the haill tennentis
vithin ye said lordship that they sall giv obedine to ewry
officir according to the former actis maid thair anent, and
failzies maid thair anent, and to be poyndit yairfor
conform.

The said day compeirit James Zowell and confessit him
selff of killing of somond fish vpon my lord Forbes vatter
vpon the watter of Done both in sumer and in the forbiddin tym ; thairfor the bailzie decernes the said James
Zowell the sowm of fyv pundis Scotis money, to be peyit
vithin term of law vnder the paine of poynding.

The said day it is staitit and ordained that all tennentis
and nighbouris vithin the said lordship sall keip guid
nighbour heid, in speciall for bigging of keill zaird dykis
quhair they are in mein dykis and fold dyk and in all nighbour heid, and in speciall they doe not raiff thair ky in out
feidle, and that they sall hav no beniffiet of any rig that
sall not be reidit conform to thair nighbour, and that no
gras man or thair vyffis or bairnes sall sheir or cutt gras
or cornes vnder the failzie of thric pundis, and peying the
skaith that they sall sustein in defalt of sufficient dykis.

[Court continued.]

The Court off the barronrie off the Breys off Tolmads, holdin in Newbiging wpon the seavint day off Junj J^{m}vj^{c}seavintie fyue yeires. The suitis callit, the court laufullie fensit in our soveran lordis name and authoritie and in name and behalff off the right honnorable William lord Forbes, hearitour off the forsaid landis, William Midlton in Enitis his lordshipis balze, James Ross notar public Court clerk, John Donaldsone officiar and [blank] demstar, Proceiden formerlj as effearis.

[Lord Forbes to have libertie to poind tenants in arrear 20s. Scots for each merk.]

The said day Alexr. Coutis in Tornivein peyit ane leg dollor[1] for the crop j^{m}vj^{c}seavintie thrie yeires.

The said day it is statut and ordeined wpon ane complaint giuen in be George Loch in Barslasie agains the tennantis off Drumlaze for hendering the said George Loch to pastur and cast fogitch wpon thair syd off the burne quhair they haue labort. The said bailze ordeins the chamerlein to tack the birlamen and goe to the controvertit ground quhair Robert Gray and the rest off the tennantis off Drumlazie to haue all probation for instructing thair right, and then hauing hard them the chamerlein and birlamen sall be heirby impourt to decerne in all thair controversies as they sall think fitt, and acording to thair decret both pairties is heirby oblidged to abyd thairon and fulfill wnder the penultie off the peyment off ten poundis Scotis mony.

The said day the wholl tennantis off the sueken off Einitis is heirby ordeind no to goe to ainie other mill with thair stuff, and lykwayes sells thair stuff to others, and that the good wyff off Einitis can gait not count off it, they sall mack peyment off double multer to the said compleaner.

---

[1] A leg dollar was a Dutch coin, 'having the impression of a man in arms with one leg and a shield containing a coat of arms upon the other leg.' By proclamation of the Privy Council, 14 Jan. 1670, its exchange value was reduced from 58s. to 56s. Scots (*P.C.R.*, third series, iii. 126).

The said day it is ordeined incaice that thair be anj who lops the yaird dykes off Enitis and braikes the dykes and planting, that they sall pey fortie shilling Scotis for the first fault and four poundis for the nixt *toties quoties*.

The said day Alexr. Nicoll is for his miscairadgies in the face off the court is amerciat in four poundis Scotis, and is ordeined to pey it within term off lav, wnder the pain off poinding.

The said day anent ane bill giuen in be the chamerlein for eating off my lordis corn then growing in Tornivein, Andrew Din, Alexr. Coutis, Georg Duncan, caurj ane of them thrie is ordeined to pey ane firlot off oatis, as also John Broune, Alexr. Duncan, is ordeined to pey tuo peckis off oatis caurj ane off them, and that within terme off lav, wnder the paine off poinding,

The said day it is statuit and ordeined that no laborer within the forsaid barronrie sall recett nor giue anie hadin to anj soroner nor idle persons nor non quo mack not travill for kaill and fyr but tacks and stealls quhair they can haue them; they who recettis such persons is heirby ordeined to pey ten poundis Scotis.

The said day it is statuit and ordeined that all persons who ar lyable in neightbour hood to other, or anie sub-tennant who is oblidged to fold with his nightbour and maister, sall pey fortie pennies Scotis for each beast nolt for each night they detein them out off the fold, and tuelff penies for each beast sheip, and that the ground officiar sall poind for it, and that within term off lav efter the transgression.

The said day the bailzie interpons his authoritie and ordeins the forsaid actis to be put in execution within term off lav wnder the pain off poinding; and continowis this court wpon tuentie four hours advertisment in form as effears.

Ja: Ross, N:P:, Court clerk.   W. Midtone, Ballie.

[Court for the parishes of Kearn, Forbes, Auchtindor, Clet and Keig, holden within the great hall of Castell Forbes, 16 Oct.

1675. Arthur Dallgardno bailie. Alex. Chalmer n.p. court clerk. Alex. Jaffray ground officer. Dempster blank. Suits called, etc.]

[Tenants ordained to pay their resting silver duties for crop 1674 and 1675, or to be poinded 20s. for each merk; also to pay their resting meal and malt for crop 1674, under failzie of £12 Scots for each boll; also to pay in their meal and malt to the girnell of Castle Forbes for crop 1675, under the like failzie.]

The said day it is staitit and ordained the haill tennentis vithtin the said lordship who is restand any foullis for crop sevintie fyve and preceding crop sall pey them in vithtin terme of lav, vnder the failzie of peying sex shilling aucht penies for ilk capon and four shilling for each restand hene, conform to former actis.

The said day the bailzie forsaid decernies and ordaines the haill guid manes of each mill vithin the said lordship to keip vp the dust and refuss in the mill floor in tym of the fearm grending, that is to say, that yair sall neither be dust or stones rye or any refuss among the fearm greind or mixtit among the fearm in tym of greinding thairof.

The said day the bailzie decernes and ordaines that thair sall not [be] peyit to the vnder millare at the mill of Barflatt bot on moudefow of meill for ilk boll of sheilling.

[Court continued.]

[Court holden at Castell Forbes, 7 Jan. 1676, for parishes of Kearn, Clat, Auchtindor, etc. Arthur Dallgardno in Blairdiny bailie. Alex. Chalmer n.p. court clerk. Wil. Lange ground officer. Dempster blank. Suits called, etc.]

The said day compeirit George Anderson in Barflatt and gave ane bill in aganest John Reiny for striking of his servant, quhich vas prowiit. Thairfor the bailzie forsaid did ordaine the said John Reiny to pey the sowm of fyve poundis Scotis money for his striking the said Georg Anderson servant, to be peyit vithin term of law vnder the paine of poynding.

A.D. 1676] FORBES BARON COURT BOOK 301

[Georg Anderson presented John Oliphir cautioner that John Reiny should be harmless, and John Reiny presented Alex. Simmer cautioner that Georg Anderson should be harmless; each under the failzie of £40 Scots.]
[Court continued.]

[Court for the parishes of Karne, Forbes, Clett, Achendore etc., holden within the dwelling house of Alex. Somer at the Kirkstyll of Kearne, 30 March 1676. Arthur Dalgarno of Blairndynnie bailie. Wil. Gordone n.p. court clerk. Wil. Layng officer. Dempster blank. Suits called, etc.]

The said day anent a complaint given into the cowrt be James Ritchie in Balfowr against Alexr. Ritchie yair, his brother german, for beatting, strickeing, and giveing him blood; and the pairtie complained wpon, to witt Alexr. Ritchie, compeared and confest he wes in handie gripps with his brother, bot denyed the blood. Whervpon the said James Ritchie adduced two wittness to prove the veritie of the thing, viz. William Scott and Georg Weir in Balfowr, against whom ther wes no objectione; who being both solemnlie sworne and examined deponed as followes, to witt the said William deponed that he saw the saides two bretheren hinging in oyeres haires and offering to throw wther to the grownd, and that he heard James Ritchie say he hade gotten blood and called for a nepkyne from his wyfe to keap it, bot did not sie the blood; as also the said Georg Weir deponed that he saw them both in the same maner; and non of them knowes farder. Whervpon the said bailzie ordainit both the saides pairties to suffer the verdict of ane asysse.

Asissores Names

PATRICK JAMESONE in Kirktowne of Forbes.	GEORGE ANDERSONE in Barflett.
WILLIAM LICHTOWNE in Towie.	ALEXR. MITCHELL in Blackhillok.
JAMES ROGDER ther.	ALEXR. SOMER in Kirkstyll.
JOHN OLIVER ther.	WM. BLACK in Cuishney.
GEORG MACKIE in Stondyk.	JOHN TOUCH in Stondyk.

JAMES ANDERSONE in Marchmar.
JAMES CRYSTIE in Bankheid.
JOHN HENDERSONE in Perselciw.
JAMES ANDERSONE yair.
JAMES DUNCANE in Castellhill.

The wholl assysores aforsaid being deeply sworne, be the mouth of Patrick Jamesone aforsaid yair chancellar findis the said Alexr. Ritchie in the wrong to his brother, and referres him to the bailzie, who decerned him to pey to my lord Forbes twentie lib., and yat within terme of law vnder the payne of poynding. And both the saides James and Alexr. Ritchies enacted themselves in the cowrt willingly for good neighbourhood and behaviour in tyme comeing, wnder the payne of ffowrtie lib. Scottis *toties quoties*, to be peyed and exacted in maner forsaid.

[Court continued.]

[Court for the same parishes, held as above, 23 May 1676. Bailie and court clerk as above. Alex. Somer officer. Dempster blank. Suits called, etc.]

The said day anent a complaint given in to the cowrt be James Crystie in Bankheid against Jhon Oliver in Towie and William Oliver his sone, for the said William Oliver his beateing, strickeing and bloodeing of John Malice servitour to the said James Crystie. Whervpon the said William Oliver compeared and confest the strikeing of the said John Malice. Whervpon the said bailzie ordanit the said John Oliver, as being comptable for his said sone, to pay to my lord Forbes the sowme of ten lib. Scottis as a fyne, and twentie shilling to the boy quho wes strucken, and yat within terme of law, vnder the payne of poynding.

As also both the saidis Jhon Oliver and James Crystic doe heirby enact themselves for good neighbourhood as to themselves and for quhom they are be the law comptable in all tyme comeing, wnder the failzie of twentie lib. *toties quoties*, to be exacted incaice of breatche in maner forsaid.

[Court continued.]

A.D. 1676] FORBES BARON COURT BOOK 303

[Court for the parishes of Keirne, Forbes, Clett, Keig and
Achendore, etc., holden within the manor place of Castell
Forbes, 24 Oct. 1676. Bailie and court clerk as above.
Wil. Layng officer. Dempster blank. Suits called, etc.]

The said day the bailzie decernes and ordaines the
wholl tennentis within the grownd lyable in peyment
of maill and dewtie to pay in ther bygone rests for crop
j^{m}vj^{c}sevintie fyve, both money and wictuall, and that
within terme of law, wnder the failzie of the hyest pryces
of the girnall for that year both for malt and meall, and
incaice of not peyment of the silver dewtie within terme
of law, to pay pownds for merkis, and to be poynded
therfor and ther readiest goods and gear to be apprysed
for that effect.

The said day the bailzie decernes the forsaidis tennentis
to pay in ther maillis, fermes, dewties and customes for
this year and cropt j^{m}vj^{c}sevintie sex in maner followeing,
to witt, the wictuall and meall betuixt and Candellmes
nixt preceislie, wnder the failzie of eight lib. for ilk
wndelyvered boll, and the malt payable be the saids
tennents for the said year, ordaines the samen to be peyed
at Dunstane day nixt and the Ruide day imediatlie therefter, be equall halffes; and incaice of failzie, to pey ten
lib. for ilk wndelyvered boll that beis not punctuallie
peyed at the said dayes; and als decernes the silver
dewties the said year to be peyed preceislie at the termes
of peyment vsed and wownt, wnder the payne of poyndeing
and appryseing ther readiest goods and gear at the third
pennie downe; the termes of peyment of the samen
being alweyes being first come and bygone.

The said dey William Rodgie and Alexr. Black at the
Nethermylne of Alfoord compeired and confest them-
selffs guilty of my lords woods, for quhich they are fyned
in tuentie pownds Scotts each of yem, to be peyed within
terme of law, vnder payne of poynding.

The said day it is statute and ordanit that no tennent
nor wther persone within the grownd shall cast wp any
meadow grownd or arable land, wnder the failzie of

twentie merkes the foott spaid and pleuch and ten merkis the flachter spaid; and to be poynded therfor, the fault being prowen and maid appear.

The said day it is ordanit be the said bailzie that no tennent nor wther persone within the grownd that shall happen to be a removeing tennent shall be no meanes tak downe any wallis of houss bot lett them stand wntaken downe, wnder the failzie of double the worth of the samen wallis.

The said day the bailzie decernes fowrtie pennies to be peyed for ilk wndelyvered pultrie fowll efter the terme of peyment wsed and wownt; and als fowr merkis for ilk wndelyvered cwstome wedder; and halff a merk for ilk capone as said is.

The said day it is statute and ordanit that in ewerie mylne belonging to his lordship the mylne peck and the Muttie, quhich is heirby declaired to be fowrt pairt of the said peck, shall be sighted and measured with water and scalled with my lords own scall; and the mylnes and measures aforsaids shall be visited and sighted be John Cleiricheiw and twa birlaemen, all except the mylne of Barflett, quhich is appoynted to be seen be Arthour Dalgarno and the birlaemen heir in this grownd. Sicklyk it is appoynted that ther shall be no more peyed at any of the saidis mylnes for grinding of malt bot only ane meall peck full ffor the fowr bollis and no more, and this to stand in all tyme comeing to all the mylnes payand dry multur to my lords girnell.

The said day it is statute and ordanit that the wholl ground officers belonging to my lord shall be punctuallie and preceislie obeyed be the wholl tennents and wthers in the ground in what they are ordered to doe, and whosoever sall contraveene or disobey sall pey fyve lib. Scotts *toties quoties*.

The said day Thomas Rodger in Bogiesyde compeared and confest him selff guiltie of cutting of the arnes of Bogiesyde, for quhich he is fyned in fiftie lib. Scotts money, to be peyed within terme of law.

[Court continued.]

A.D. 1676] FORBES BARON COURT BOOK 305

[Court for the parishes of Kearne and Clett, holden as above
9 Dec. 1676. Mr. Patrick Andersone of Mylntone bailie
for the time; court clerk and officer as above; dempster
blank. Suits called, etc.]

The said day anent a complaint given in to the cowrt att the instance of Janet Fraser spous to James Clerk in Tailzeach, against Margaret Smith servitrix to John Wricht in Tailzeach, for the allegit bloodeing of her, and efter productione and showeing of the blood in face of the cowrt, and lykwayes efter examinatione of severall famous wittness against whom ther wes no objectione, which wittness being solemlie sworne deponed all that they saw the blood bot knew not that the [said] Margaret Smith gave it, and als deponed yat they saw the said Margaret Smith huele and taw the said Janet Fraser back and fore. Wpon quhich consideratione, and wpon produceing off the blood, the bailzie forsaid hes fyned the said Margaret Smith in the sowme of fyve lib. Scotts, to be peyed within terme of law wnder the payne of poynding.

The said day the said James Clerk wes fyned in the sowm of ten lib. Scotts for the holling of firr without warand in the moss of Tailzeach; and als in respect the said Janet Fraser and her husband are fownd guiltie off the wett of the said blood, and did tost and huele Jean Dalgardno spous to John Wricht, quho being with chyld, wes fyned in the sowme of fyve lib. Scotts, all to be peyed within terme of law.

The said day it is statute and ordanit that in all tyme coming the tennentis and posessoures of the townes and lands of Towie and Tailzeach shall preserve and be comptable for the moss grownd quhich they are in vse to cast in, that ther be no firr nor aik holled therin be no persone nor persones; and incais ther be any holled at any tyme heirefter, the tennent to pey twentie lib. and the servant to pey ten lib. *toties quoties*. And lykwayes what ever firr, aik or trees shall be gotten or fownd be the saids tennentis the tyme of the casteing of ther peitts, they shall

U

have no power to meddle yerwith without speciall ordor fra my lord, and yat wnder the failzie aforsaid ; and thir failzies to be peyed within terme of law vnder the payne of poynding.

The said day William Barron in Stainiefield wes wnlawed in 40 shilling Scotts for his absence, being lawfulie cited.

Wᴍ. Gordowɴe Not: Pub: M. P. Aɴdersoɴe
court clerk.   Baylie.

The Court off the barronrie of Tolmadis with the pertinentis lyand within the parochin off Kincardin and shireiffdome off Aberdein, holden in John Donaldsone hous in Enitis wpon the cleavinth day off December $j^m v j^c$seavintie sex yeires. The suites callit, the court laufuly fensit and affirmit in our soveran lordis name and authoritie, and in name and behalff off the right honnorabill, nobill and potent lord William lord fforbes, hearitour off the forsaid landis, and in name off William Midlton in Enitis his lordship bailzie. James Ross notar public court clerk, John Donaldsone officiar, proceid in forme as effeires, [blank] demster.

The said day John Broune peyit fyue poundis Scotis, quhich compleites the crop $j^m v j^c$seavintie four yeires, As also is found resting ffor the cropts 1675 and 1676 conforme to his assedation.

The said William Donaldson is found resting his Mertimes [deutie for] $j^m v j^c$seavintie sex yeires.

John Farquhar is found resting his Mertimes deutie for the crop $j^m v j^c$seavintie sex yeires, conform to his assedation.

The said day Thomas Adam in Broomhill is found resting his Mertimes deutic for Crop $j^m v j^c$seavintie sex yeires, conforme to his assedation.

The said William Gray is found resting his Mertimes deutie for crop $j^m v j^c$seavintie sex, conform to his assedation.

The said day James Birss is found resting off bygons four poundis sex s. aucht pennies for crop 1675, as also his Mertimes deutie for the crop 1676, conform to his assedation.

George Dickison hes giuen compleit peyment for the crop and yeir off God j^{m}vj^{c}seavintie sex yeires, conforme to his assedation.

The said day James Elsmie and William Tailizur is found resting thair Mertimes deutie for the crop j^{m}vj^c seavintie sex yeires, conforme to thair assedations.

The said day Alexr. Coutis is found resting for the crop 1675 thretein markis, as also is found resting the wholl cropt 1676, conform to his assedation.

The said day Andrew Dun in Tornivein is found resting his wholl deutj for the crop j^{m}vj^{c}seavintie fyue yeires; as also is resting the wholl deuttie for the cropt j^{m}vj^{c}seavintie sex yeires.

The said day it is statuit and ordeined that all the induellers within the forsaid barronrie sall keip neightbourhood each on to other in keiping off foldis with thair goodis and eattin off corns with fouls and calff; that quhatsumewir tenant sall be found guiltie off breach off foldis and eatting off corns to other, that the said breakis and contraveiners sall mack peyment to the keipers for quhat skaith they doe aither in braiking off foldis and eating off cornis, conforme the actis off my lord Forbes courtis maid for that effect.

The said day it is statuit and ordeined that all the forsaid tennantis who ar lyable in peyment off thair ground deutie, the terms off peyment being past conforme to thair assedations, sall mack peyment off thair bygon restis within terme off law wnder the paine off poinding off thair rediest goodis and geir, and mack penic yeroff to overis. The said bailzie interpons his authoritie; and continows this court [etc.].

W. MIDLTONE, ballie.   JA: Ross, court clerk.

[Court for the parishes of Clett and Kearne, holden within the manor place of Castell Forbes, 23 Dec. 1676. Mr. Patrick Anderson of Mylntone of Noth bailie; court clerk, etc., as on 9 Dec. 1676. Suits called, etc.]

The said day Compeared Janet Antone indweller
in Bankheid, and gave in a complaint to the court
against James Crystie and Cristian Lockie his spous,
for strickeing, beating and bloodeing of her, and shee
produced blood in ane cloathe in face of the court. As
also the said James Crystie and his said spous gave in a
complaint against the said Janet Antone for beateing and
streckeing of the said Cristian Lockie and provockeing be
evill words. Whervpon both the saids pairties adduced
the wittness efternamed, to witt Hutcheon Mylne in Bankheid, Cristian Andersone yair and Agnes Hendersone
yair, against whom nor non of them ther wes no objectione;
who being solemly sworne depones vnanimouslie (except
the said Hutcheon Mylne) that they saw the said Janet
Antone her lipp bloodeing and shee kaiping the blood in the
cloath, and also deponed they saw the said Janet Antone
sitteing above the said Cristian Lockie and stickeing in
her hair, and they were pulleing and rugeing wthers haires
and scolding wther with opprobious language. Whervpon
the said bailzie ordanit the saids pairties to pas the verdict
of ane asysse.

Assysores names.

WILLIAM LICHTONE in Towie.   JAMES RODGER in Tailzeach.
JAMES RODGER ther.   JAMES DUNCAN in Castellhill.
JOHN OLIVER ther.   WILLIAM MENIE ther.
GEORG ANDERSONE in   GEORG MENIE ther.
  Barflett.
JOHN HENDERSONE in   JAMES ANDERSONE in Per-
  Perseleiw.   seleiw.
PATRIK LEITH in Windseey.
GEORG MACKIE in Stondyk.
WILLIAM GORDONE in Towie.
ALEXR. CARDES in Barflett.
THOMAS RODGER in Bogiesyde.

The wholl assyssores being solemly sworne all in ane
voyce be the mouth of George Andersone forsaid yair
chancellar, findis the blood prowen, and also the stricking
of the said Cristian Lockie and pulleing of her hair also

prowen, and therfor finds both pairties guiltie, and referres them to the bailzie, who hes fyned them in ten lib. Scotts each of them, to be peyed within terme of law wnder the payne of poynding.

The said day the bailzie decernes and ordaines the within named pairties, to witt James Crystie and his spous and Janet Antone, to keep good neichbourhood and nowayes to scold or abuse wthers with ther tongues in tymes comeing, wnder the payne off fyve lib. *toties quoties*, and also, if they be so fownd doeing, ordaines the officer to tirr the hous above the said Janet Antones head and putt her away wpon a just complaint, and also ordaines the said James Crystie to putt the said Janet Antone away and remove her at Wittsonday nixt, wnder the failzie off twentie lib. Scotts, to be peyed within terme of law wnder the payne of poynding.

The said day William Barron in Towie is fownd guiltj in holleing of firr in the moss of Towie, and yerfor is fyned in fyve lib., to be peyed within terme of law.

[Court continued.][1]

[Court for said parishes, holden as above, 30 Dec. 1676. Bailie, etc., as above. Suits called, etc.]

The said day ther being a mutuall complaint given in to the cowrt be Issobell Rodger dochtter to James Rodger in Towie, and Elspeth Oliver and Elspeth Brabiner her dochter, each of them against wthers, for scolding wthers with base and filthie language; who for proveing of ther complaint adduced the wittness afternamed, to witt John Layng, James Duncan, William Menie, against whom ther wes no objectione; who being solemly sworne de-

---

[1] The following is on a scrap of paper pasted on the *verso* of the last leaf of the MS. : ' I William Clarck in Castelhill humblie means and compleans one James Duncan, who tristed folk to come and brack his hous, and he did steall from him ane kruck sadle with the wholl greath, ane heleren saddell, and ane tedder; he strack his sheep with his foot and ane other tyme with ane corn fork.

'December 23, 1676.

'Continowes this bill to the nixt court day, and ordaines wittness to be adduced and probatione led for that effect.

'WM GORDOWNE N: P: clerk.'

poned all in on voyce that the[y] heard both pairties abovenamed, to witt Elspeth Brebiner and Issobell Rodger, scolding wthers with most base language. For quhich the said bailzie hes fyned each of them in fyve lib. the peice, to be peyed within terme of law wnder the payne of poynding. As also heirby ordained the said James Rodger and William Lichtone and ther wyfes, bairnes and familie and wthers for quhom they are be the law answerable, to keep good neighbourhood in tyme comeing without scolding or such lyk misdemeanour, and that wnder the payne of ten lib. Scottis *toties quoties*, to be peyed within terme of law wnder the payne of poynding.

[Court continued.]

The Court of the lordship of Forbes lyand within the pariochines of Forbes, Keig, Kearne, Clet, Auchtindore, holdin within the plac of Putachie vpon the fourteine day of Junij j^{m}vj^{c}sevintie sevin yeires, holdin be William lord Forbes and be Arthur Dalgarno his constitut bailzie, Alexr. Chalmer nottar publict court clark, Arthur Bunche ground officir, and [*blank*] demster. [Suits called, etc.]

The said day John Clerihew in Duston gave in ane bill againest James Richie in Balfour, Alexr. Mill in Scotismill, that quheras the said James Richie cam violent vpon him to tack the rod out of his hand; quhich was referit to vitnes, viz. Patrick Tailzor in Auchintowll, John Michell in Scotismill, who was solemlie sworne, did depon that they saw the said James Richie com vpon the said John Clerihew to tack the rod out of his hand. Lykwayes the said John Michell did depone that he saw the said James Richie com violentlie vpon the said John Clerihew to clos with him to tack the rod out of his hand. Therfor the bailzie ordained and decerned the said James Richie, for his presuming to persew the said John Clerihew, being in my lordis vice [service ?], to pey the sowm of aucht poundes Scotis money, to be peyit within tearm of law. Lykwayes the said Alexr. Mill confessit that he cam vpon William Lang, on of the greives and onvaitters of my lordis servic, with ane drawin durk, var not the said John Clerihew hinderit him. Yairfor the bailzie decernes the said Alexr. Mill to pey the sowm of sex poundes Scotis money within term of law, vnder the paine of poynding.

The said day Elsspett Richie in Scotismill and Janett Murgone in Silivethie, being lawfullie sumoneit to this court and thrice callit and not compeirit for violentlie vounding and oppressing of George Lang greive in Castell Forbes, and not compeirit, thairfor the bailzie decernes ilk on of them for absenc to pey thrie markis within tearme of law, vnder the paine of poynding vithout modificatione.

The said day forsameikle as Elsspett Richie is fugitive for this court, and her brother James Richie her brother [*sic*] did promissis to produc hir to this court, thairfor the bailzie decernes and ordaines the said James Richie to produce and present the said Elsspett Richie at the plac of Putachie vpon the tuentie day of this instant Junij, and that to William master of Forbes in my lordis absenc; and incais of failzie the said James Richie is ordained to pey the sowm of fyve pundis Scotis money within term of law.

The said day James Bonnar in Silivcithie is ordained and obliiget, conforme abovwrittin, to present Janet Murgane his servant day and place and to ye person forsaid, vnder the failzie forsaid and tearme off law.

The said day forsameikle as thair hes bein sewerall servantis within the lordship of Forbes disobeyis and rebellis and offeris violenc againest my lord Forbes his speciall servantis, greives and owirseires of his vork and millis casting and leiding, and for preventing of the lyk in tym coming, the bailzie forsaid decernnes and ordaines the haill tennentis and tenndrie vithin the lordship of Forbes sall send furth sufficient and peacabill servantis to my lord his servic at quhat tym or tymes they sall be laufullie varnned with them selffis to com vith thair servantis eather to stay vith them the tym of vork or to give thair servic, lawfull command and instructiones to vork peacabill and vnder command of my lordis chamberlaines, officires, greives, the tym of the vork or any vyer

charge quhatsumevir; and incais any of the servantis
failzie of obeying my lord Forbes servantis abovwrittin,
or offer any violenc as said is, or any of the tennentis refuss
or deforce the officires in poynding, sall pey ten poundis
Scotis money, to be peyit conjuctlie and seyveralie be the
master and servantis after the disobedienc or falt be
committ, and the master is ordained to be comptabill
for the servantis onlaw, and to be peyit vithin fourtie
aucht houres after the falt be committit. Lykwayes the
bailzie decernes and ordaines [them] that failzies to send
furth thair servantis to ewry vork, and in specialle to
castin and leading of peittis, mucking and hearring, sall
pey fourtie shilling Scotis for ewry servant that sall be
absent ewrie day of yair absenc, and to be peyit and
poyndit from thair maister immediatlie and to be poyndit
yairfor as effeires.

The said day the bailzie ordaines and decernes James
Davidson, Patrick Moir in New Keig, to mack peyment
to John Clerihew such money as the timber of the mill of
Keig got out of the wood of Puttachie, becaus they cam
debitour for the haill ground and sucking of the Owir
mill of Keig; and John Clerihew is obliigit to find ane
officir with the said James Davidson and ye said Patrick
Moir to poynd for ye proportiones pairtes of the timber
of the said mill.

[Court continued.]

The Cowrt of the lordshippe of Forbes and landis thereto
belonging lyand within the parochens of Kearne,
Forbes, Clett, Achendor, Alfoord and Keig, now
heyretablie belonging to William lord Forbes, holdin
within the great hall of the old towr of Castell Forbes
wpon the twentie third day off October $j^{m}v^{j^{c}}$sevintie
sewen be Arthour Dalgardno in Blairndinnie bailzie,
William Gordowne nottar publict court clerk, William
Layng officer, [blank] dempster. [Suits called, etc.]

The said day it is statute and ordanit be the bailzie
that the wholl tennents and posessouris and wthers who

are lyable in peyment of maill and dewtie within the said lordshippe and parochens abovewritten, to pay in ther bygone rests for cropt j^{m}vj^c sevintie sex and for bygones, and that conforme to the penalties and statutes sett downe in the former acts, viz. for such money as is restand to pay pownds for merks, and for such meill and malt as is restand to pay conforme to the last act for j^{m}vj^{c}sevintie sex, and all wnder the payne off poynding ther readiest goods and gear therfor at the third pennic downe.

The said day it is statute and ordanit be the said bailzy that the wholl tennents and possessoures and wthers lyand within the said lordshippe and parochens abovewritten to pay in ther maills, fermes, dewties, kaynes, customes and wthers quhatsomever payable be them to the said William lord Forbes or his chamberlands, and that [for] cropt and year j^{m}vj^{c}sevintie sewen in maner followeing, to witt the meall betuixt Yule and Candellmes nixt perceisly, wnder the failzie of eight lib. for ilk wndelyverit boll, and the malt payable be the saidis tennents for the said year ordaines the samen to be peyed att Dunstane nixt and the Ruide dey imediatly thereafter be equall halffes; and in caice of failzie to pey ten lib. for ilk wndelyverit boll of the malt yat beis nocht punctuallie peyed at the saids deys; and als decernes the silver dewties for the said year to be peyed perceesly at the termes of peyment vsed and wownt, wnder the payne off poynding and appryseing of ther readiest goods and gear yerfor at the third pennic downe, the termes of payment of the samen being alweys being first come and bygone.

The said day it is statute and ordanit be the said bailzie that eweric tennent haveing ane hundreth merkis pay within the said grownd, shall have for ther own defence and for the good peace and quyet of the covntrey ane sword and ane hagbutt; and eweric fiftie merks pey to have ane sword with ane halbert staff or pitch fork, and all this to be [in] readynes betuixt and the last of Februar nixt, and still yerefter when they sall be called, and that wnder the failzie off fowrtie lib. the hundreth merkis pey and twentie lib. the fiftie merkis pey; as lykwayes for eweric twentj libs. pey to have a sword or pitch fork, wnder the failzie of ten merks Scotts.

The said day it is also statute and ordanit that the wholl tennents and posessouris of the lands of Achentowll, Culfork, Langhauch and Broadhauch and wther pertinents shall pey in ther teend silver to the minister of Alfoord preceisly at the Hallowdey yearlie efter the shearing of the cropt, and to receave and delyver dischairges to my lord yeranent, vnder the failzie of poynding of ther readiest goods yerfor.

The said day it is statute and ordanit that the wholl abovewrittin tennents shall give dew obedience to the greive and severall officers in quhat they are commandit to doe, and yat wnder the failzie of fyve lib. *toties quoties*.

The said day James Andersone in Marchmar, the wholl tennents of Edinbanchrie, Patrick Jamesone in Kirktowne of Forbes, William Thomsone in Cullhay, John Clerk in Walkmill, are fyned in fyve lib. the peice for ther disobedience quher they wer desyred to bring lyme to Balquhen.

The said day James Andersone in Marchmar forsaid is fyned in fyve lib. for disobedience in not goeing for sklaitts to Brux; and als in fyve lib. for not goeing to the Cairne off Mownth with the rest of the tennents at Bartholl dey. All thes fynes to be peyed within terme of law wnder the payne of poynding.

The said dey it is statute and ordanit that the officer be punctualli peyed of his office fie yearly and fowrtie pennies for the old crofts, and that wnder the payne of poynding.

The said dey it is also statute and ordanit that no persone nor persones shall at any tyme heirefter leap the yeard dykes and doe any wrong within or about the yeards of Castell Forbes, and yat aither be yem selves, ther servants, complices or wthers for quhom be the law they are answerable; and this to be punctuallie keeped in tymes comming, wnder the payne of fyve lib. ilk tennent, fowrtie shilling ilk tennentis sone or dochter, and ilk servant on merk of ther fies, all *toties quoties*. This act

A.D. 1677] FORBES BARON COURT BOOK 315

comprehends the yeards of Putachie and Castell Forbes and servants about both the houses.

The said day the former acts of court anent the casteing of meadow grownd aither be foot or flachter spaids or casteing wp of muck faill is at present renewed and ordanit to be putt in executione.

The said dey the bailzie gives libertie to William Gordone in Achentowll to sett such parcellis of his croft at his removealle aither in grais or corne, and to ressave peyment therfor from such persones to quhom he setts.

Absents names the said day

James Parker in Culfork, John Touch in Stondyk, Georg Duncan in Castell hill.

The said day James Smith in Logie confessed the cutteing of a tree in his own yeard, for quhich he is referred to my lord himselff.

[Court continued.]

The Court off barronrie off Tolmadis with the pertinentis, holden within the Enitis wpon the fourtenth dey off December j^{m}vj^{c}seavintie seavin yeires, the suites callit the court laufullj fensit in our soverane lordis name and authoritie and in name and behalff off the right honnorabill and potent lord William lord fforbes hearitor off the said landis, William Midlton his Lordships bailzie, James Ross off Findlarg notar public court clerk, William fforbes officiar and .

[Suits called, etc.]

The said day it is statuit and ordeined that eaurie tennant hawing ane hundreth markis mailing within the forsaid ground sall haue for thair awin defence and good peace and quiet off the countrj ane suord and ane hag bitt, and caurj feiftie markis py to haue ane suord and ane halbert staff or pitch fork, and this to be in readiness betuixt this and the last off Feabruarj nixt to com, and still yairefter quhen they sall be called, and yat wnder the failzie off tuentie poundis for ane hundreth markis pey, [for] each feiftie markis pey ten poundis, as also for cauric tuentie lib. py to haue ane suord or pitch fork, wnder the failzie off ten markis Scotis.

The said day it is statuit that any tennant within the forsaid landis who ar lyable in peyment off multer to the mills [who] goe by the said mill with any off thair corns, bear or oatis, sall mack peyment off double multer to the owner of the mills.

John Broune efter count and reckning is found resting for the cropt 1676 tenn poundis sex shiling aucht pennies.

Moir for the cropt 1677 tuentie four poundis thretein shiling four pennies, besyde cess and teind silver; which soum is to be pyit within terme off law, wnder the paine off poinding off the rediest goodis and gear. To the forsaid acts the said bailzie interpons his authoritie, and ordeins the said actis to be put in execution termes off law being [bypast]; and continowis the court wpon twentie four hours advertisment in forme as effears.

WM. MIDLTONE Ballie.   JA: Ross, N: P: Court clerk.

[Court for the parishes of Kearne, Clett, Forbes, Achendor, Keig and Alfoord, holden within the manor place of Castell Forbes, 23 April 1678. Arthur Dalgardno of Blairndynnie bailie. Wil. Gordone n.p. court clerk. Wil. Layng officer. Dempster blank. Suits called, etc.]

[Tenants liable for mail, duty, customs, etc., due at Martinmas last and Whitsunday now ensuing, to pay pounds for merks, 10 merks the boll of meal and £10 the boll of malt.]

The said day it is statute and ordanit that quhatsomever persone or persones within the lordshipp who is deficient in long cariages, he being requyred, shall pey fowrtie shilling Scotts *toties quoties*.

The said day it is statute and ordanit that quhatsomever persone or persones shall be fownd to transgresse the former acts made anent muireburnings in forbidden tymes shall be punished exactly conforme yerto.

The said day it is statute and ordanit that the wholl tennentis and posessores within the towne and landis of Achentowll, Culfork, Broadhauch and Langhauch, and

A.D. 1678] FORBES BARON COURT BOOK   317

wther pendicles belonging to the barrony of Achentowll, shall pey all publict burdens conforme to the strict meaning and tenor of yair assedationes in all poyntis. Also the saids tennentis sall be lyable to the said act anent long cariages.

The said day it is statute and ordanit that John Cleirichew in Dubstone shall ingather the wholl dischairges and receptis from the tennentis within Keig, Alfoord, Forbes and Achendor, and yat for ther customes of quhatsomever sort and for rest malt, and Arthour Dalgardno for Kearne and Clett, and they both to revise the samen ticketis and report.

The said day Elspeth Thayne servitrix to John Layng in Westhill, being lawfulie warned to this court for abuseing of Patrick Leith in Windsey, and being thrie tymes called and not compeirand, is fyned in fowrtie shilling Scotts.

The said day it is statute and ordanit that ther sall be no hors nor nolt suffered to pasture within the wood off Puitachie aither in the spring or tyme of harvest, and yat wnder the payne of fowr lib. ilk beast, for quhich the forrester hes power to poynd quhen he fiind any goods ther, and if the forrester doe conceill, and beis fownd guiltie, he is to pey the said fyne.

The said day the equivalent act is now also made anent the boag of Castell Forbes, only yer is 40sh. Scotts to be penaltie, and James Robertsone the forrester hes power to poynd yerfor.

The said day anent ane complaint given in be the sucken of Scottsmylne against Alexr. Black mylner at Scottsmylne anent the dimolisheing of the mill door, it is ordanit that the said mylner sall repair the said doore within fyfteen dayes, vnder the failzie of fowr lib. Scotts.

The said day it is statute and ordanit that the mylnehous of Barflett shall be sufficientlie wpholden be Murdo Anderson [1] according to former acts, and the mylner being deficient yerin sall pey fowrtie shilling; and ordaines the sucken to mak a sufficient calsie abefor the mylne dore;

---

[1] 'The mylner' written, and 'Murdo Anderson' substituted.

and generallie ordaines all dewtie to be done to all mylnes be ther sucken, and that within the lordshipp, conforme to the former actts.

The said day it is statute and ordanit that the wholl tennents within the parochens of Kearne, Clett, Forbes and Achendor shall putt ther goods to the hill of Curreyne for pastureing, and every parochen to have ane common hird among them.

The said day it is statute and ordanit that William Menie in Castell Forbes sall stryk oxen in a plewch with James Duncain, and sall bear good neighbourhood with him, wnder the payne of ten libs.

The said day it is statute and ordanit be the said bailzy that no persone nor persones quho leads peatts to my lord shall remove from the moss wntill they give satisfaction to the mossgreiwf both for abuses comitted in the moss and for dighting the lair and gate, and yat wnder the payne off fowr lib. Scotts ilk plewchs laboureing.

The said day it is statute and ordanit that ther sall be ane hors aff everie hundreth merkis pey be sent to Aberdein for carrieing owt goods to the minister, and yat quhenever they sall be requyred, wnder the payne off fowrtie shilling Scotts, and to doe all wther dewtie to him as to peitts, muckeing and wtherwayes, and this tends to the parochen of Kearne.

[Court continued.]

[Court for the parishes of Auchindor, Kearn and Clatt, holden in Alex. Simer's house at the kirk of Kearne, 21 June 1678. Arthur Dalgardno in Blairfinie bailie. James Ross n.p. court clerk. William Lang officer. Dempster blank. Suits called, etc.]

The said day wpon ane bill giuen in be Georg Gairdner in Logie wpon Thomas Straquhan in Edinbanchorie for strickíng, woonding off his bodie and bruissing yeroff, witnessis being callit for prowing off the same, to witt Alexr. Gillespie in Cottoune off Castell Forbes, William Gillespie his sone, and James Adame yer, the forsaid witnessis comperit and nothing could be objectit against them. They wer solemlie suorne and depont; Alexr. Gilespie depont he saw that Alexr. Straquhan servitor to James Smith in Logie did strick the said compleaner Georg Gairdner ane great stroak one the head with ane staff, and tuo great stroaks on the shoulders.

Lykwayes James Adam in Cotton Lon accords with the last witnes.

And William Gilespie declairt he saw Thomas Straquhan cast Georg Gairdners bonit in the myr, and then the said Georg Gairdner took the said Thomas Straquhan his plaid and cast it in the myr and tramplit wpon it with his foot; whairvpo[n] Alexr. Straquhan brother to the said Thomas did cast the said Georg Gairdner in the myr and straik him thrie or four stroaks one the head with ane trie, and pust him yerefter with the point off the trie.

The said bailzie, finding the forsaid complaint and battrj cleir[l]j prowin as said is, decerns the forsaid Alexr. Straquhan to pey to my lord fforbes aucht pundis Scotis, and fortie shiling Scotis to the pairtie compleaner as ane asythment, and that to be peyit within terme off law, wnder the paine off poinding off his rediest goodis and gear.

The said day the bailzie decernt and ordeined the forsaid Georg Gairdner and the forsaid Alexr. Straquhan to sett suirtie each on for other that they sall act nor comit no bodilj harme to other in any tyme heirefter; the said Georg Gairdner sett Johne [corrected from Alexr.] Mitchell in Logie his maister cationer for him that the said Alexr. Straquhan sall be harmlis, skaithlis in all tyme comming full Mertimes nixt to com 1678, and the said Alexr. Straquhan setts James Smith in Logie his maister cationer for him yat George Gairdner sall be frie off any bodilj harme done be him betuixt this and the said terme off Mertimes, and yat wnder the failzie off tuentie poundis Scotis to be peyit be pairties and thair cationers to my lord Forbes imeadiatlj efter the break off lawborrows, and that within terme off law, wnder the paine off poinding off thair rediest goodis and gear, the forsaid pairties and cationers for the mor vearificatione off the same hes subscriuit the samen with thair handis.

Ita est Jacobus Ross notarius publicus de mandatis Georgii Gairdner et Alexr. Straquhan scribere vt asseruearunt nescientium ad hec rogatus et requisitus.

Jo. MITCHELL.   JA. SMYTH.   JA: ROSS, N:P:.

[Court continued].

[Court of the barony of Tolmads held 21 Oct. 1678, in Einits. Alex. Garioch of Litill Indivie bailie. James Ross n.p. court clerk. Wil. Forbes officer. Dempster blank. Suits called, etc.]

The said day it is statuit and ordeined yat all former actis off courts be put in execution aganis all casters in lons, meadoue and suaird ground, yat all contraveiners off the forsaidis acts sall py the peannilties mentioned and conteined in the said acts, wnder the paine off poinding off thair rediest goodis and gear.

The said day it is statuit and ordeined yat all the forsaid tennants and subtennants sall wpon demand [be] redie to mend anj burns or breaches yeroff wpon ane call for the said effect; who refuissis the said call, the tennant sall pey tuentie shiling *per diem*, and the subtennant hawing ane croft ten shilling, and the gras men fyue shiling, and the said sounes to be peyit *toties quoties*.

The said day it is statuit and ordeined that anj off the forsaid tennants who ar lyable in pyment off teind silver for the crope j^{m}vj^{c}seavintie aucht yeires sall mack peyment yeroff conforme to thair proportions to the collector yeroff, wnder the paine off poinding off thair rediest goodis and gear within terme off law.

The said day it is statuit and ordeined yat his majesties new suplie for this term sall be castin proportionalj wpon the wholl tennants lyable in peyment off deutie to yair maister amongest yem; as also that the said tennants sall haue pour to haue ye benefit off thair subtennants, cotters and grasmen, domesticks and all and sindrj quhatsomever; that is to say, tenn shiling for the croft, halff ane mark for the grasmen, and fortie pennies for his domestick servant for this terms suplie; as also the said bailzie ordeins this stent to be onlj for this terme allenarlj and noveyes to be ane preparateiv in tyme coming.

The said day Alexr. Nicoll in Easter Tolmads, John Farquhar in Craginhoe, Duncan Adam in New biging, William Donaldsone in Broomhill, birlamen chossin, gaue thair oath *de fidelj* to decerne acording to thair knowleadge to decerne betuixt maister and tenna[n]t and tenant and tennant in anj thing they ar desyrt to.

The said day the bailzie ordeins all the tenants sall haue all the armes in rediness acording as they ar ordeined in the act off court maid yairanent, wpon the call from thair maister, with this certification, whosoeavir contraveins sall mack peyment off the penulties conteined in the said act, wnder the paine off poinding off thair rediest goodis and gear within terme off law.

The said dey the bailzie ordeins the wholl tennants to plant thair kaill yairds betuixt this and the first off March 1678 [1679?], they gaiting plantins from thair maister, wnder the failzie off tenn pounds Scotis money.

The said day it is statuit and ordeined that all tennants sall send in sufficient servantis to casting and leading off thair peats due to my lord Forbes, and yat no weak persone be send for yat effect, and quhen long carradgies is sent for, as lym or anj other thing, that thair sall goe able men who sall be countable for thair loads and carradgies; and quhair the tennents sall haue no domestick servants off thair awin, that yair cotters and grassmen sall obey yair maister for yat effect.

The said day Patrick Pattersone in Drumlazie, Alexr. Minye in Tornivein, Andro Dun yair, John Broune yair, Alexr. Coutis yair, John Farquhar in Craginhoe, John Ritchie in Miltone crofts, William Forbes, ar ordeined to py thair rest deuties within terme off law, wnder the paine off poinding off thair rediest goodis and gear, and pounds for markis.   ALEXR. GARIOCH.

JA: ROSS: N: publique court clerk.

INDEX

ABERDEEN appoints a public fast on account of the 'distrest estate of the Kirk of Chryst' in 1621, 182.
Aberlady's contribution to the distressed Church of France in 1622, 190-191.
Absence from court, 315; fines for, 229, 233, 269, 306, 311, 317.
Adam, Duncan, in Newbigging, 263, 321.
—— James, in Strolonaick, 257.
—— —— in Cottoune of Castle Forbes, 318-319.
—— Thomas, in Broomhill, 306.
—— —— in Newbigging, 262; fined for 'blooding,' 263.
Adamson, Agnes, 201.
—— Nicoll, baxter, 195.
Aikin, David, in Auchinderg, 218.
Aikman, Richard, 197.
Airlie, James, second earl of, 75 *n*.
—— countess of, 7, 21 and *n*; refusing to allow English soldiers to quarter in Cortachy, her house is entered by force, 21-29; the finding of the court-martial, 30.
Aitkin (*see also* Aikin, Atkine), George, mason, 195.
—— James, 197.
Alane. *See* Allan.
Alexander, Andro, fined for 'blooding,' 260-261.
—— Isabell, 17.
—— James, 196.
Alford, 211, 312, 316, 317; Old Statistical Account of, 212, 214.
Allan (Alane), Barbara, 196.
—— John, 234.
Alured, colonel Matthew, 3.
Ambergris, 148 and *n*.
Anaytis. *See* Ennetis.
Anderson, Alexander, 32.
—— —— in Stonfeidle, 246.
—— —— 266; in Towie, 246, 269; fined for 'blooding,' 246-248.

Anderson, Archibald, belt maker, 196.
—— Cristian, 308.
—— Eliz., 14.
—— George, in Auchindore, fined for 'blooding,' 249-250.
—— —— in Barflat, 285-286, 293, 300-301, 308.
—— —— notary, 224-225, 251.
—— James, 247, 254.
—— —— in Marchmarr, 238, 278, 302, 314.
—— —— in Perselew, 302, 308.
—— Margaret, 14.
—— Mongo, 194.
—— Murdo, 317.
—— Patrick, of Mylntone of Noth, 305, 307.
—— Robert, 271.
Angus, John, 254, 278.
—— —— in Edinbanchrie, 228, 233, 238, 240, 244.
—— Thomas, 240.
Anlaby, Arthur, 166 and *n*.
Annand, Alexander, of Auchterallan, 153 *n*.
—— Jean, wife of Robert Trail, minister of Old Greyfriars, 153 *n*.
—— John, minister of Inverness, 136, *n*.
Antone, Janet, in Bankheid, 308-309.
Arms to be borne by tenants, 217, 313, 315, 321.
Arrestments, breach of, 230, 258, 289, 295.
Arthur, William, minister of the West Kirk, Edinburgh, 193-194, 201.
Ashfield, colonel Richard, 3, 9-11, 66.
Askin, Agnes, 17.
Asone, Arthur, in Kirktoun of Forbes, 259. *See* Eisoun, Esson.
Assaults, 13-17, 214, 235, 250-252, 255, 257, 262, 263, 273, 275, 280, 284, 293, 294, 295, 300, 302, 308, 310, 311, 318-319.

Atkine, Alison, wife of Duncan Robertson, sheriff-clerk of Argyll, 71.
—— James, bishop of Galloway, correspondence, 1679-1685, 69-96; letter from, to Lord Stair, 86; letters to, from Robert Bowis, etc., 93; Alex. Burnet, abp. of St. Andrews, 90; James Colhoun, etc., 92; James Gordon of Carleton, 88 and *n*; Graham of Claverhouse, 85; Archibald Grahame, bp. of the Isles, 82; Thomas Grierson, 78; Hector Maclean, bp. of Argyll, 80; Thomas Naismith, etc., 93-94; Robert Paterson, 83 and *n*; Arthur Ross, abp. of Glasgow, 76-80; James Sharp, abp. of St. Andrews, 74-76; Henry Walker, minister of Whithorn, 84; Alex. Young, bp. of Ross, 89.
—— Lilias, wife of Patrick Smyth, advocate, 71.
—— Marion, wife of William Smith, minister of Moneydie, 71.
Atye, Eleanor, wife of sir William Roberts, 160 *n*.
Auchinderg, 218.
Auchindoir, 237 and *passim*; parish, 210, 225, and *passim*.
Auchintoul, 211 *n*, 216, 314, 316-317.
Auchnagathle, 273 and *n*.
Aydill, John, 276 *n*.
Aytoun, Elizabeth, wife of sir Thomas Hope of Craighall, 156 *n*.
—— Margaret, wife of sir Arch. Hope of Rankeillor, 130 *n*.

BACKE or Barke, Thomas, 43-44.
Bagge, lieut., 60, 66.
Baillie, Grizel, wife of Robert Kirkpatrick of Closeburn, 137 *n*.
—— sir William, of Lamington, 101, 144 and *n*.
Balcanquall, Robert, minister at Tranent, 190-191.
Balcomie, Fife, 106.
Baldwin, Tho., 14.
Balfour, 215, 226, 228, 245.
—— sir James, of Denmylne, lord lyon king of arms, 139 and *n*.
Balquhen, 314.
Bankheid, 259.
Bannachie, 295.
Bar, Adame, 195.
Barbour, Peter, writer, 120, 160 and *n*.
Barebones parliament, 120, 122.

Barflett, 226, 260, 266, 275, 279, 286, 289, 300, 304, 317.
Barilla, 140 and *n*.
Barker or Backer, William, 62-63.
Barnbarroch. *See* Vaus, John.
Baron Bailie, 211. *See* Anderson, Patrick; Dalgarno, Arthur; Forbes, Adam; Forbes, William; Garioch, Alexander; Garioch, William; Gordon, William; Midleton, William.
Baron Court of Camnethan, Lanarkshire, 205; of Carnwath, 205, 209, 214 *n*; of Auchterarder, Drummond, Drymen, and Kincardine in Menteith, 205; of Fowlis, in Gowrie, 205.
Baron Court Book of Corshill, Ayrshire, 206; of Stitchill, 206, 208; of Urie, 206, 208.
Baron Courts, jurisdiction of, 207-209; in England, 206; in Scotland, 220.
Barra's contribution to the distressed Church of France in 1622, 185, 190, 192.
Barron, William, stanman, 199.
—— —— in Stainiefield, 306.
—— —— in Towie, 309.
Bartilmo, George, stanman, 198.
Baskett, Wm., 50-52, 54.
Basnage, Benjamin, receiver of contributions for distressed presbyterians in France, 185, 187-190, 192, 201.
Bathans' contribution to the distressed Church of France in 1622, 190-191.
Baynes, captain Robert, 9-11, 66.
Beang, Andro, 219.
—— George, 219.
Beaton, Margaret, 132 *n*.
Beg, John, 200.
Bell, Anna, wife of sir Alex. Hope of Granton, 131 *n*.
—— Christian, 19, 20.
—— James, provost of Glasgow, 77 and *n*.
—— John, in Bellismill, 196.
—— Robert, 19, 20; to be hanged for robbery, 39-42.
—— Thomas, 199.
—— Walter, 194, 197.
Bellendene, William, 198.
Bennet, Elizabeth, wife of sir Thomas Hope of Craighall, 99, and 131 *n*.
—— Thomas, glaissin-wrycht, 199.

INDEX

Bigar, David, skinner, 198.
—— James, maltman, 196.
Bird, Robert, his evidence as to the plundering of Cortachy, 27-28.
Birlawmen, 212, 226, 229-231, 237, 238, 245, 253-254, 275, 278, 285-288, 292, 298, 304, 321.
Birss, James, 306; fined for assault, 235.
Bischope, Patrick, 201.
Bithny, 215, 226, 228, 288, 291.
Black, Alex., in Scottsmylne, 317.
—— —— at Nethermill of Alford, 303.
—— John, 198.
—— William, 247, 256; in Cushnie, 248, 250, 256, 301; fined for 'blooding,' 241.
—— —— minister of Closeburn, 137 and *n*.
Blackhillock, 226, 270, 271.
Blair, Robert, regent of Glasgow university, 188.
Blaircheillie, 218.
Blairdinnie, 251.
Blantyre, Alexander, fourth lord, 49-51, 58.
Bleaton or Blaiden, Elias, 9.
'Blooding,' 207, 214, 235, 241, 246-247, 249, 250, 252, 255-256, 260, 262-263, 267-269, 271-273, 285, 293-294, 301, 302, 305, 318.
Bloody cloth produced, 268, 271, 273, 301.
Bogheid, 259.
Bogieside, 215, 226, 228, 259, 304.
Bogs. *See* Woods.
Boirland or Boriland, Alane, 197, 200.
Bolter, Richard, to ride the wooden horse and receive thirty stripes for robbery, 59-60.
Bolton's contribution to the distressed Church of France in 1622, 190, 192.
Bonar, James, 254, 271; in Sillavethie, 238, 258, 285, 289, 295, 311.
—— Margrett, in Kirktown, 245.
Bond, Thomas, corporal, 33-34.
Bondage work, 225, 229, 244, 266, 292, 311-312.
Boone, captain, 9, 10, 66.
Booth, Robert, 248.
Borgue kirk, 88-89.
Bowie, Patrik, 197.
Bowis, Robert, minister of Stoneykirk, letters from, to the bishop of Galloway, 93-94.

Bowman, Henry, 43-44.
Bowne, Jane, wife of Alex. Jaffray, 167 *n*.
Boyd, Zachary, 186.
Boynton, Dorothy, wife of John Anlaby, 166 *n*.
Bradie, William, 199.
Braes. *See* Tolmaads.
Braid, the laird of, 195.
Bramston, capt., 66.
Brayne, lieut.-col. William, 9-11, 21, 66.
Brebner (Brabiner), Elspeth, fined for scolding, 309-310.
—— George, his herd, 250.
—— William, 247, 254-256; in Towie, 238, 250-251, 261.
Brewers and brew tallon, 238, 245, 266, 278, 280, 288, 296; brewing, 292.
Bridges, major Tobias, 66.
Brigges, Henry, tried for plundering, 15-16.
Brisbane, Matthew, rector of Glasgow university, 80 and *n*.
Broadhauch, 314, 316.
Broadhurst, capt., William, 62, 64, 66.
Brodie, Alexander, of Brodie, 164 *n*.
Brok, Walter, 196.
Broom, cutting of, 233, 234, 243.
Brown, or Broun, Alexander, 196.
—— George, 193-194.
—— —— minister of Stranraer, 93.
—— James, meilmaker, 197.
—— —— surgeon, 110, 130, 137.
—— —— tailor, 197.
—— John, 33-34.
—— —— elder, in Gorgie mill, 197.
—— —— younger, in Dalrymillis, 195.
—— —— in Tornivein, 299, 306, 316, 321.
—— Margaret, 195.
—— Robert, in Sauchtounhall, 195.
—— William, 199.
Brux, 314.
Buchollie, 152.
Bunche, Arthur, ground officer, 310.
Burges, Alex., 273.
—— George, in Glentoun, 228, 232, 240, 244.
Burnet, Alexander, 201.
—— —— abp. of St. Andrews, 79; letter from, to the bp. of Galloway, 90.

Burnet, sir Alex., of Leys, 76 *n.*
—— George, 256, 266; in Towie, 240, 267.
—— John, 247, 256, 266; in Towie, 240.
Burton, George, 62; punished for straggling and plundering, 42.
Butter, custom, 288-296.
Butter, ensign, 66.

CAIRILL, Patrick, 276 *n.*
Cairn of Mounth, 314.
Cairnis, Alexander, meilmaker, 195.
—— Issobell, 200.
Caldwell, John, minister of Portpatrick, letter from, to the bp. of Galloway, 94.
Calves (Carr), trespassing, 291, 307.
Cameron, James, minister of Inch and Soulseat, letter from, to the bp. of Galloway, 93-94.
Campbell, Elizabeth, second wife of sir John Campbell of Glenurchy, 137 *n.*
—— sir John, of Glenurchy, 137 and *n.*
—— sir Robert, of Glenurchy, minerals on his property, 135 and *n.*
Campfield, captain, 66.
Candle fir, 216.
Cant, John, of the Grange, 201.
—— - Sarah, second wife of Alex. Jaffray, 167 *n.*
Capons, custom, 245, 270, 281-282, 286-287, 296, 300, 304.
Cardes, Alex., in Barflett, 308.
Cardross, David, lord, 116, 131 and *n.*, 150.
Carey, Mary, second wife of Dr. Fraser, 147 *n.*
Carmichael, James, minister of Haddington, 190-191.
Carndard, 248, 260.
Carney, John, in Newbiging, 229.
'Carr meall,' 217, 234, 279.
Carriages, 225, 244, 314, 316-318, 321; for minister, 318.
Carter, Brian, 15.
Cartockwhee. *See* Cortachy.
Castle-Forbes, 224 and *passim*; great hall of, 236 and *passim* (great hall of old tower, 316); mains, 291-292; manor place, 303, 307, 316; place, 234; yards and yard dykes, 314-315. *See* Forbes, and Druminour.
Castlehill, 227-228, 251, 259, 292.

Cattle (nolt), detained out of fold, 299; trespassing, 259, 260, 265, 276, 280, 282, 285-286, 291, 317. *See* Oxen.
Cess, 216, 246, 316.
Chalmers, Alex., in Mongarie, notary, 241-242, 244, 246, 252-257, 259, 261-266, 268, 274, 276, 278, 283-284, 290, 292-294, 296, 300, 310.
—— Jean, 245.
—— John, ground officer, 278, 280-281, 284.
—— —— tailor, 194.
—— William, 198.
Charles II. urged by sir James Hope to mend his ways, 103.
Charlesworth, lieut., 66.
Charteris, Lawrence, prof. of divinity, Edinburgh university, 77 and *n.*
Cheese, lieut. William, 66.
Cheislie, Robert, 194.
Chortawhee. *See* Cortachy.
Christie or Fullartown, Issabill, 257.
—— James, 295; in Bankheid, 247, 302; fined for 'blooding,' 308-309.
—— —— minister of Kirkinner, 85 and *n.*
—— (or Wright), Margaret, 292.
—— Thomas, minister of Wigton, 85 and *n.*
Christison (Crystesoun), John, 196.
Clark or Clerk, Elizabeth, wife of sir William Hope of Granton, 106.
—— James, in Perselow, 246.
—— —— in Tailzeach, fined for 'blooding,' 305.
—— John, 33 *n.*
—— —— in Walkmill, 314.
—— William, in Castlehill, 309 *n.*
Clarkson (Clerkesone), John, carter, 145.
Clatt, Aberdeenshire, 237, and *passim*; parish, 210, 225, and *passim.*
Cleare, capt. Henry, 66.
Cleghorne (Cleghone), William, 196.
Clerihew, John, 254, 304; in Dubston, 278, 282-283, 289, 310-312, 317; in Putachie, 238, 245.
Clerk. *See* Clark.
Clerk of Court. *See* Anderson, George; Chalmers, Alexander; Davidson, William; Gordon,

INDEX

William; Ross, James; Thomson, James.
Clun, lieut. Joseph, 66.
Clyd, Alexander, 199.
Cobbett, colonel Ralph, 66.
Cochrane, James, of Rocksoles, 157 *n*, 159.
—— Rachel, 118.
—— William, of Rocksoles, 118, 128, 157 *n*.
Cockburne, James, 199.
Colquhoun, James, minister of Penninghame, 85 and *n*; letter from, to the bp. of Galloway, 92.
Colvill, Alexander, 187.
Common herds, 267, 318.
Conventicles in Lanarkshire, 77.
Cook (Couk), Alex., 247, 256; in Westhills, 241, 269.
—— Cristian, 200.
—— Daniell, sheithmaker, 197.
—— Janet, 197.
—— John, 286.
Cooper, sir Anthony Ashley, 165 and *n*.
—— Phillipp, 17.
Corn, pasturing in, 226 and *passim*.
Cornelius, Jacob, Dutch skipper, 150.
Corrie, John, tailor, 198.
Corshill baron court, 213.
Cortachy (Cartockwhee), 23-24.
Cosche, Charles, pultriman, 196.
Cotters, 225, and *passim*.
Couper, Alex., in Fiddes, 219.
—— Arthur, in Muttounbrey, 219.
—— John, in Westhillis, 233.
Courtney, col. Hugh, 167 and *n*.
Courts-martial at Dundee in 1651, 1-66; list of officers present, 66-67.
Coutis, Alex., in Keig, 289-290.
—— —— in Tornivein, 298-299, 307, 321.
—— Daniell, in the Deane, 199.
Craig, laird of, 251-252.
—— John, in Dalry, 198.
—— William, 194.
Craighead (Cragehead), Jhon, in Fiddes, 218-219.
Craiginheiw, 229.
Cranstoun, Issobell, 199.
Craw, James, 197.
Crawford, James, in Plesance, 201.
—— John, 77.
—— —— cordiner, 198.
—— —— tailor, 195.
—— —— 17th earl of, 142 and *n*.

Crawford, Margaret, in Brochtoun, 198.
—— —— in West Port, 198.
—— Martin, writer, 132 and *n*.
Crawford Lindsay, 77 and *n*.
Crawfordmuir gold mines, 101.
Cressett, capt., 66.
Crichton, sir David, of Lugton, 139 *n*.
—— Elizabeth, third wife of sir Alexander Hamilton, 139 *n*.
—— James, of Frendraught, 211 *n*.
—— Patrick, 133 and *n*, 134.
Crispe, major Peter, 66.
Croftmen, 225, and *passim*.
Cromwell, Oliver, 158 and *n*, 159, 160, 167; at Musselburgh, 115; addresses the Barebones parliament, 120; lord protector, 124, 129; his Ordinance for the establishment of Baron Courts in Scotland, 208, 220.
Crosse, Henry, 13.
Crukshank, James, fined for ' blooding,' 255-256.
Culfork, 314, 316.
Culhay (Collhay), 258, 259.
Cultercullen, 219.
Cummyng, Thomas, 197.
Cunningham, Dr., 137.
—— Anna, wife of James, marquess of Hamilton, 142 and *n*.
—— Edward, 193, 195, 201.
Curreyne, 318.
Cushnie, Aberdeenshire, 248, 260.
Customs, 303, 313, 317. *See* Butter, Capons, Fowls, Lambs, Sheep, Swine.
Custwick, Wm., 19-20.
Cutter, George, 55-56, 65.
Cutting of green wood, 226, 232-234, 240, 243-244, 259.

Daach of Towie, 295.
Dale or Deale, Robert, 35.
Dalgarno, Arthur, of Tollie, 224-225, 229, 231; in Blairndiney, 233, 237, 240-242, 244, 246, 254-255, 264, 266, 274, 278, 284, 290, 292-294, 296, 300-301, 304, 310, 312, 316-318.
—— or Wright, Jean, 305.
Dalrymple, sir John, yr. of Stair, 87 and *n*, 88 *n*.
Dalzell, Thomas, of Binns, 139 *n*.
Davids, Bernard, 62.
Davidson, Agnes, 201.
—— James, 271, 312.
—— William, notary, 235-237, 240.

Davies, Godfrey, editor of the Dundee Court-Martial Records, 1651, 4-67.
Davieshill, 218.
Davis, captain William, 66.
Dawborne (Daberon), capt. John, 9, 13, 66.
Dean village, 194.
Denholme, Ninianc, 201.
Dennis, adjutant-general, 9-11, 66.
Desborough, major-general, 164 and *n*.
Dewar, George, meilmaker, 195.
Dick or Dickson, David, minister of St. Giles', 152 and *n*.
—— Harry, weaver, 146 *n*.
—— William, 202.
Dickison, George, 252, 307.
—— John, 193-194.
—— William, tailor, 198.
Din. *See* Dun.
Dirk, assaults with, 251, 255, 310-311.
Discharges for customs, 271, 281-282, 317.
Divots. *See* Fail.
Dodd, John, tried for manslaughter, 8 *n*., 55-57, 65.
Dodgin, captain, 66.
Dodgson, captain, 66.
Dog, killing of, 274.
Dollar, 298.
Don, Johne, 196.
Don, water of, 297.
Donald, John, 279.
Donaldson, Alexander, 200.
—— George, shoemaker in Elgin, 58.
—— James, 57-58.
—— John, 230, 298, 306.
—— Marian, 58.
—— William, in Broomhill, 230, 306, 321.
Dores, 147 *n*.
Dorney, major Henry, 9-12, 66.
Dougal (Dowgall), Johne, 196.
Douglas, captain, 66.
—— sir George, of Mordington, 144 *n*.
—— John, in St. Leonards, 199.
—— Martha, second wife of sir James Lockhart of Lee, 144 *n*.
—— Patrik, in the Potterraw, 197.
—— Robert, bp. of Brechin, 80 *n*, 91 and *n*.
—— —— minister of the High Kirk, Edinburgh, 136 and *n*.

Douglas, William, editor of *The Bishop of Galloway's Correspondence*, 1679-1685, 69-96.
Dowchly, Elizabeth, first wife of Dr. Fraser, 147 *n*.
Downis, James, 202.
Downy, William, 243.
Dreams, 108-109, 126, 128-129, 148, 153-156, 160-161.
Druminour, 215, 243, 264, 266; bogs of, 259, 265, 276, 280, 286; dykes and yards, 233, 243, 259; forester of, 259; green of, 246; mains and crofts of, [234], 243, [248], 255, 259-260, 280; mill of, 243; orchards of, 243, 280. *See* Forbes, and Castle-Forbes.
Drumlasic, 231, 298.
Drummond, James, in West Port, 196.
—— Thomas, 200.
Dubstoun, 257.
Dumbreck, 152.
Dun (Din), Andrew, in Tornavein, 299, 307, 321.
Dunbar, sir David, of Baldoon, 84 *n*.
—— David, jun., of Baldoon, 84 *n*.
Duncan, Alexander, 299.
—— Bessie, 228.
—— George, 247, 255, 299; in Castlehill, 315.
—— James, 247, 256, 266, 295, 309 and *n*, 318.
—— —— in Bankheid, 247.
—— —— in Castlehill, 302, 308.
—— —— in Perselew, 240, 245, 250.
—— John, 230.
Dundas, Christian, wife of Charles Erskine, 131 *n*.
Dundee taken by Monck, 3-4 and *n*; *Court-Martial Records,* 1651, 1-67.
Dunlope, Agnes, 199.
Dykes, 243, 266, 297. *See* Druminour, Puttachie.
Dykis, Robert, in Sauchtoun, meilmaker, 195.

Eddie, William, in Bray-slatie, 236.
Edgecouf, Thomas, charged with stealing cows, 9.
Edict of Nantes, 181.
Edinbanchrie, 226, 228, 314.
Edinburgh university and its connection with the Hope family, 139 and *n*.

INDEX

Eisoun, Cuthbert, maltman, 198.
Elder, Alexander, in the Deane, 196.
Ellis, John, advocate, 117, 151 and *n*.
—— Jonet, wife of sir John Smith of Grotehall, 151 *n*.
Elmslie, James, 229, 231, 234, 252, 262, 292, 307.
—— Wm., in Castlehill, 241.
Elphinstone, Margaret, wife of George Norvell, of Boghall, 132 *n*.
Elsinford's contribution to the distressed Church of France in 1622, 190, 192.
Ely, capt., 66.
Ennetis (Anaytis), 230, 236, 293, 298-299, 306, 315, 320.
Erskine (*see* Askin), Alexander, son of John, earl of Mar, 131 *n*.
—— sir Charles, of Cambuskenneth, 116, 131 *n*, 151.
—— Charles, son of sir Charles Erskine of Cambuskenneth, 131 and *n*.
—— David. *See* Cardross, lord.
Esson or Johnston, Agnes, 284. *See* Eisoun, Asone.
Evans, lieut. Peter, 66.
Everard, ensign Richard, 66.
Everett, David, 62.
—— Edward, 62.
—— William, to ride the wooden horse for abusing his officer, 63-64.
Ewes to be tethered, 226.

Fail and divot, 224, and *passim*.
Fairholm, Issobell, 197.
—— Thomas, 195.
Fairlea, George, of Braids, 144.
—— Helen, first wife of sir James Lockhart of Lee, 144 *n*.
Fairlie, sir William, of Bruntsfield, 187, 194.
Falconer (Faulkenor), William, in Fordoun, 58.
Farmer, capt., 66.
Farquhar, Alex., in Broomhill, 230.
—— John, in Craiginhoe, 229, 235, 306, 321.
Farquharson, Thomas, 236.
Fellowes, ensign, 66.
Fergus, James, 230; in Tolmaads, fined for assault, 252-253.
Ferguson, David, bayliff, 47.
—— William, in Dundee, 43-45.

Feu-duties, 277.
Fiddes, 218; rental, 209-211 and *n*. 196.
Fiddesbeag, 218-219, 277 *n*.
Fiennes, Anne, wife of sir Charles Wolseley, 164 *n*.
Fife, Christian, 30, 196.
Findley, Robert, 229.
Finlasoun, John, smyth, 196.
Fir trees embedded in mosses, 215, 216, 305, 309.
Fischer, John, 200.
Fitch, captain William, 66.
Fleming, Alexander, in Benvie, 41.
—— David Hay, editor of *The Scottish Contributions to the Distressed Church of France in* 1622, 179-202.
—— Walter, meilmaker, 197.
Flint, John, 133 and *n*, 134.
Foggage, 298.
Folds, casting of, 245-246; keeping of, 226, 230-231, 283, 299, 307.
Forbes Baron Court Book, 1659-1678, 203-321; description of the MS., 209.
Forbes, 224, and *passim*; girnal prices of, 270, 275, 277, 281, 287, 290, 295-296, 300, 303; orchards and parks of, 295; policies of, 215; woods and bogs of, 215, 229, 234, 295, 317. *See* Castle-Forbes, and Druminour.
—— Adam, tutor of Brux, 250, 259.
—— Alex., 218, 245.
—— —— in Midelmuir, 291.
—— Arthur, in Kinknockie, 218.
—— —— of Auchintoul, 211 *n*.
—— —— lord, 210.
—— John, in Wester Tolmaads, 253.
—— lady, 278.
—— parish, 210, 225, and *passim*; minister of, 224-225, 279.
—— William, master of, 224-289, *passim*; twelfth lord Forbes, 290-321, *passim*.
—— —— master of (son of last), 311.
—— —— fined for assault, 235-236.
—— —— at mill of Tolmaads, 321.
—— —— in Scotismyln, 283.
—— —— officer, 315, 320
Forester, his duties, 259, 265, 276, 277, 291, 317.
Fornication, punishment for, 14, 17.
Forrester, Alexander, 199.
—— William, 196.

Forsyth (Forsye), Robert, in Fiddes, 219.
Foulis, Anna, first wife of sir James Hope of Hopetoun, 101, 104, 130 and *n*, 144 *n*.
—— James, senator of the College of Justice, 99.
—— Robert, of Crawfordmuir, advocate, 101, 117.
—— —— of Leadhills, goldsmith in Edinburgh, 130 *n*.
Fowls (hens, poultry), custom, 245, 270-271, 281-282, 286-287, 296, 300, 304.
—— trespassing, 230, 253, 307.
Fox, lieut., 66.
Fraser, Dr., court physician to Charles II., 147 and *n*.
—— Andrew, minister of Lochgoilhead, 81 and *n*, 82.
—— or Clerk, Janet, fined for 'blooding,' 305.
Fribairne, Alexander, smith, 197.
—— Johne, smith, 197.
Fugitive from court, 311.
Fullarton, Alex., in Mongarie, 257.
—— John. *See* M'Cloy.
Fyny, William, 279. *See* Phinnie.

GAIRDNER, George, in Logie, 318-320.
—— John, 198.
Galbrayth, Alexander, 200.
Galloway, bishop of. *See* Atkine, James.
Gardiner, capt., 31, 66.
Garioch, Alex., of Litill Indivie, 320-321.
—— William, in Braidhauch, 229, 231, 234-236, 252-253; of Archballach, 272; in Braytoun, 262, 269, 270.
Garow, Alex., in Balfour, 234.
Garvald's contribution to the distressed Church of France in 1622, 185, 190, 192.
Garvy, Alex., 245.
Geilles, John, 245.
Gellan, John, 254; in Glentoun, 226, 228, 238.
Gib, John, 199.
Gibson, Bessie, 201.
—— Robert, 199.
Gillespie, Alex., in Cottoune of Castle Forbes, 318, 319.
—— William, 318, 319.
Gillott, captain, 66.

Glass, scheme for its manufacture, 112; glass works at Prestonpans, 127, 139-141.
Glass, John, in Balfour, 228, 238, 240, 246, 247, 255, 266; in Balfour, 240; in Barflat, 226, 233-234, 238, 250, 261, 275; fined for burning heather, 248-249.
Glaze, James, 7, 31.
Gleinn, James, in Glentoun, 228, 232.
Glenluce regality, 87 and *n*.
Glentown, 228, 245, 265, 276, 295.
Glossary of archaic and provincial words in the *Forbes Baron Court Book*, 122.
Gluiffer, Catherine, 200.
Goffe, col. William, 9-11, 66; dissolves the Barebones parliament, 123, 166 and *n*, 167.
Goldsmiths' incorporation, 109, 126, 133-135.
Good neighbourhood, 239, and *passim*. *See* Lawburrows.
Gordon, Clement, 198.
—— Elspet, 228.
—— Francis, of Crage, 248, 251-252.
—— James, of Carleton, letter from, to the bp. of Galloway, 88 and *n*.
—— James, son of Wm. Gordon of Craiglaw, 91 and *n*.
—— John, 228, 246; in Castlehill, 262, 279; fined for assault, 275-276.
—— —— in Glentown, fined for assault, 280-281.
—— —— of Knokespak, 249.
—— —— in Newtoune, 249, 251.
—— Patrick, of Reny, 250.
—— Robert, meilmaker in the Deane, 198.
—— Wm., in Auchentowll, 315.
—— —— of Craiglaw, 91 *n*.
—— —— of Tilliangus, 248-250.
—— —— in Towie, 308.
—— —— notary, 301, 306, 309 *n*, 312, 316.
Gourlay, David, 132 *n*.
Graham, Alison, wife of Gilbert Primrose, 132 *n*.
—— Archibald, bp. of the Isles, letter from, to the bp. of Galloway, 82.
—— David, sheriff of Wigton, third viscount Dundee, 93 and *n*, 94.

INDEX

Graham, James, sentenced to sixty lashes for attempted rape, 33 and *n*.
—— John, 32.
—— —— of Claverhouse, viscount Dundee, letter from, to the bp. of Galloway, 85-88 *n*, 92-93.
—— Mary, wife of sir John Campbell of Glenurchy, 137 *n*.
—— Patrick, abp. of St. Andrews, instructions for his trial, 169-178.
Grass, cutting and pasturing, 226, 259, 280.
Grass house, 280.
Grassmen, 255, and *passim*.
Gray, Alexander, maltman, 194.
—— col. Andrew, of Droneley, 40-41.
—— Archibald, in Fordoun, 58.
—— Robert (St. Cuthbert's), 196.
—— —— 235; in Drumlazie, 298.
—— —— minister of Whithorn, 83 and *n*.
—— Thomas, 196.
—— William, 306.
Green, lieut. Henry, being defied by the countess of Airlie enters her castle by force, 21-30.
—— capt. John, 66.
—— William, in Blakhillok, 226, 270.
Green wood, cutting of, 226, 240, 259. *See* Wood.
Greer, George, minister of Haddington, 190, 191.
Grege, Thomas, in Auchinderg, 218-219.
Greirson, Thomas, letter from, to James Atkine, bp. of Galloway, 78-79.
Grieve, 280. *See* Ground officer.
Groome, capt., 9-11, 66.
Grosvenor, col. Edward, 3, 30, 66.
—— cornet, 66.
Grotehall, Cramond, 151.
Ground officer, appointed, 280; duties of, 244, 255, 265, 278, 288-289; obedience due to, 226, 231-232, 235, 239, 246, 255, 271, 297, 304, 311-312, 314; deforcing of, 278, 312; payments to, 231, 255, 280.
Groves, Edward, quartermaster, 47, 66.
Guderick, James, 18.
Gudfollow, Andro, brouster, 195.
Gullane's contribution to the distressed Church of France in 1622, 190-191.
Gunter, cornet, 66.
Gunthorne, Lawrence, his evidence as to the forcing an entrance into Cortachy, 26-27.
Gurdon, Marian, 17.
—— capt. Peter, 58.
Guthrie, Wm., in Barflet, 234.
Guyld, Jeane, 198.
—— Margaret, 198.
Gypsum found in Maxwellheugh and Burntisland, 135-136.

HADDEN, James, 198.
Haddingtonshire's contribution to the distressed Church of France in 1622, 190-192.
'Haddish' of meal, 217.
Hainings, casting of, 224, and *passim*.
Hainit grass, 224.
Haliburton, James, 39-41.
Hamilton, sir Alexander, general of artillery, 139 and *n*.
—— Anna, marchioness of, 142 and *n*.
—— sir Claud, of Shawfield, 144 *n*.
—— Grizel, wife of sir Wm. Baillie of Lamington, 144 *n*.
—— James, 191-192.
—— John, in Plesance, 199.
—— lady Margaret, wife of John, son of sir James Hope of Hopetoun, 105.
—— Margaret, wife of sir William Lockhart, 164 *n*.
—— Robert, 57.
Hamonds, Wm., 13.
Hancock, John, of Wallyford, 159 *n*.
Hangitsyd, Jonet, 200.
Hanna, John, 200.
—— Marioun, 200.
Hannay, R. K., editor of *Instructions for the Trial of Patrick Graham*, 1476, 169-178.
Harman, ensign, 66.
Harrowing, 312.
Haselwood, Marmaduke, 20-21.
Hastie or Hastings, Patrick, minister of Borgue, 88 and *n*, 89.
—— Thomas, 200.
Hatfield, ensign Robert, 66.
Hatt, capt., 66.
Hauchs, casting of, 226, 275, 285.
Hawey, Wm., 46.

Hawks' nests, 277 *n*.
Hay, sir Charles, of Park, 87 *n*.
—— Robert, in Droneley, 14.
Heather burning, 212, 222, 224, 228, 246, 248-249, 265, 269, 291, 316.
—— pulling, 265, 295, 297.
Henderson (*see also* Henrysoun), Agnes, 308.
—— John, in Perselew, 302, 308 ; tried for ' blooding,' 294.
—— Thomas, advocate, 32, 117, 152.
Hendrie, Patrick, in Puttachie, 274.
Henrysoun (*see also* Henderson), James, 199.
—— John, 199.
Hens. *See* Fowls.
Hepburn, George, bailiff of Haddington, 190-191.
—— Thomas, 136 *n*.
Herd, common, 267, 318.
Heriot, Henrie, 196.
—— James, 198.
Herseman or Huseman, John, papal nuncio, 174-176.
Hervie, Wm., 234.
Heyrick, capt., 9, 10, 66.
Hilderston coal mine, 155 *n*.
Hill of Fiddes, 218-219.
Hill, James, cordiner, 195.
—— John, 199.
Hind, Jo., 18.
Hineschaw, Jeane, 195.
Hislope, Alexander, belt maker, 195.
Hodge, Agnes, 197.
—— David, smith, 197.
—— John, 200.
—— Mathew, 201.
Hog, Charles, 194.
—— John, 198.
Holbrooke, lieut., 66.
Home, Alexander, minister at Aytoun, 188.
—— Mary, countess of, 158 *n*.
Hooper, lieut. William, 66.
Hope, Agnes, daughter of sir John Hope, 130 *n*.
—— —— [*secundus*], 130 *n*.
—— Alexander, son of sir James Hope of Hopetoun, 105.
—— —— son of sir Thomas Hope of Kerse, 138.
—— sir Alex., of Granton, son of sir Thomas Hope of Craighall. 99, 100, 103, 126, 131 *n*.
—— Anna, daughter of lord Craighall, 118.
Hope, Anna, daughter of sir James Hope, 106, 118, 158 and *n*.
—— —— daughter of sir John Hope and wife of William Cochrane of Rocksoles, 130 *n*, 157 and *n*.
—— —— wife of David Erskine, lord Cardross, 120, 127-128, 131 *n*, 138, 159
—— —— daughter of sir Thomas Hope of Kerse, 131 and *n*, 138.
—— Archibald, 129.
—— sir Archibald, of Rankeillor, 108, 130 *n*.
—— Bathia, daughter of sir John Hope, 130 *n*.
—— Elizabeth, daughter of lord Craighall, 117-118, 152-153.
—— —— daughter of sir James Hope, 106, 110, 127 ; her death, 137 and *n*.
—— —— daughter of sir John Hope. 130 *n*.
—— —— daughter of sir Thomas Hope of Kerse, 117, 128, 131 *n*, 138, 151 *n*.
—— George, son of sir James Hope, 105.
—— Helen, daughter of sir John Hope, 130 *n*.
—— Henry, 131 and *n*.
—— James, son of sir James Hope, 105.
—— —— writer, 132 and *n*.
—— sir James, of Hopetoun, his *Diary*, 1646-1654, 97-168 ; description of the *Diary*, 107 ; expenses of his trip to the Continent, 100 ; his marriages, 101, 104 ; works his mines at Crawfordmuir, 101, 102 ; valuation of his Leadhill mines, 112, 142-145 ; a member of parliament, 102, 104 ; interview with Charles II. at Falkland, 102, 113-115, 128 ; urges the king to treat with Cromwell, and generally to mend his ways, 103 ; a lord of session, 104 ; assures the king of his loyal support, 115, 147-148 ; enters into correspondence with Cromwell, 119 ; a member of the Barebones parliament, 104, 120, 160 ; description of its dissolution, 123-124, 163-167 ; his death, 104, 125 ; names of his children, 105.

INDEX 333

Hope, John, son of sir James Hope, drowned in the *Royal Gloucester*, 105, 126.
—— —— son of sir Thomas Hope of Kerse, 138.
—— sir John, of Craighall, 104, 130 and *n*, 147-148, 151 and *n*, 168.
—— Louisa, daughter of sir Thomas Hope of Kerse, 131 *n*.
—— Margaret, daughter of sir John Hope, 130 *n*.
—— Mary, daughter of sir James Hope, 106.
—— —— daughter of sir John Hope, 130 *n*.
—— —— daughter of sir Thomas Hope, and wife of sir Charles Erskine, 131 and *n*, 138.
—— Rachel, daughter of sir James Hope, 106, 128, 158 and *n*.
—— —— wife of lord Craighall, 158 and *n*.
—— Robert, son of sir James Hope, 105, 127, 137-138.
—— Sara, daughter of sir James Hope, 106.
—— Thomas, son of sir James Hope, 105, 110.
—— —— (*secundus*), 105, 110, 136.
—— —— (*tertius*), 105, 110, 121.
—— sir Thomas, of Craighall, lord advocate, 99 and *n*, 116, 124, 126, 129-133.
—— —— (d. 1643), of Kerse, lord justice general, second son of sir Thomas Hope, 104, 109, 111, 131 and *n*, 139, 151 *n*, 156 *n*.
—— William, son of sir James Hope, 106.
—— —— (*secundus*), 106.
Horse-stealing, 46.
Horses trespassing, 259, 260, 265, 276, 280, 282-283, 286, 295.
Howard, ensign Jerome, 66.
—— ensign Thomas, 66.
Howiesone, Johne, 195.
—— Richard, 194.
—— Robert, 194.
Hughes, lieut., 66.
Humphries, John, 12, 13.
Hunter, John, 201.
—— Samuel, apothecary, 110, 137 and *n*.
—— William, 199.
Huntly, George, fourth marquis of, note on, 75 and *n*.

Huntly, Lewis, third marquis, 49.
—— Marie, marchioness-dowager of, 75 *n*.
Hutcheson, George, minister of Tolbooth parish, 157 and *n*.

ILES, ensign Arthur, 66.
Inglis, Archibald, weaver, 194.
Innes, John, minister of Glenluce, letter from, to the bp. of Galloway, 93.
Inverquharity, 22 *n*, 24.
Ireland, Thomas, minister of Twynholm, 84 and *n*.
Ives, Richard, 60-61.

JACKSONE, Robert, 195.
Jaffray, Alexander, 123, 167 and *n*, 274, 283, 300.
—— Arthur, 218.
—— Gilbert, in Cultercullen, 219.
—— Thomas, in Cultercullen, 219.
Jallott, capt., 66.
Jamesone, Andrew, 276 *n*.
—— James, in Puttachie, 226.
—— John, 271; in Puttachie, 289; fined for 'blooding' and for killing a dog, 273-274.
—— Patrick, in Balfour, 288-289.
—— —— in Kirktown of Forbes, 301-302, 314.
—— —— 254, 271; in Stralunak, 226, 238, 245, 257.
—— William, weaver, 197.
Jardine, George, 150 and *n*.
Johnston (Johnesoun), Helen, of the Craighous, 195.
—— —— wife of Sam. Hunter, apothecary, 137 and *n*.
—— James, 193, 195.
—— John, 200.
—— —— soldier, punished for threatening his officer and swearing, 38-39.
—— Robert, brouster, 197.
—— William, in Balfour, 234, 283-284; fined for scolding, 284.
Jones, capt. Thomas, 66.
Jordan, lieut., 66.
Joussie, John, glass manufacturer at Prestonpans, 112, 141 and *n*.
Juries in Baron Courts, 208, 209.

KAILYARDS, 297, 321.
Kains, 313.
Kallzies, William, in Carndard, 281.
Kearn (Keirne), 236, and *passim*; parish, 210, 225, and *passim*.

Kearn (Keirne) kirk, 318; Kirkstyle, 293-294, 301-302; minister, 225, 318.
Keene, Jacob, skipper, 150.
Keig, 236, and *passim*; parish, 210, 225, and *passim*.
—— Overmill of, 312.
Keith, Mary, second wife of sir James Hope of Hopetoun, 104, 105.
Keith - Humbie's contribution to the distressed Church of France, 1622, 185, 190, 192.
Keith Marischall's contribution to the distressed Church of France, 1622, 185, 190, 191.
Kempcarne, laird of. *See* Ogilvie, Alexander.
Kennedy, James, bp. of St. Andrews, 173.
Kennoche, James, 198.
Kent, ensign, 66.
Ker, John, minister of Prestonpans, 190, 191.
—— Thomas, wrycht, 194.
Kid, ensign, 66.
—— Jane, in Dundee, 59.
Kildrummy, 211, 257-258.
Kilmoden, 82.
Kilpatrik, Thomas, 199.
Kincardine (Kincarne) parish, 252, 306.
Kineand, Alexander, doctor of medicine, 130 and *n*.
King, James, 196.
—— John, St. Cuthbert's, 200.
—— —— Tolmaads, 230.
—— Robert, 200.
Kingwell, capt., 21, 67.
Kinknockie, 218.
Kirk victual, 257.
Kirkby, capt., 21, 30, 66.
Kirkcowand kirk, 86 and *n*.
Kirkinner kirk, 86 *n*.
Kirkliston, 106.
Kirkpatrick, Robert, of Closeburn, 137 and *n*.
Kirkton of Forbes, 215, 226, 228.
Knaveship. *See* Mills.
Knife, assault with, 260.
Knight, Adam, 11, 12.
Knowheid, 226.
Knowles, lieut. William, 35-36, 67.

LADY HOME'S YAIRDS, Edinburgh, 158 and *n*.
Laing (Lang, Layng), George, 247, 255, 266; in Carndard, 241, 246; grieve in Castle Forbes, 311.
Laing (Lang, Layng), John, 227, 252, 309; in Castlehill, 242, 246; officer, 244, 268; in Westhill, 317.
—— Thomas, in Balfour, 229, 233, 240.
—— William, in Balfour, 229, 233; in Castlehill, 227; in Druminor, 285; officer, 300, 301, 303, 310, 312, 316, 318.
Lamb, John, 199.
—— William, 57, 58.
Lambs, custom, 245, 281.
Lamer, Thomas, 198.
Langhauch, 314, 316.
Langley, William, imprisoned for robbery, 42.
La Rochelle, siege of, 182.
Law, David, in Sauchtounhall, 197.
Lawburrows, 230, and *passim*.
Lawrie (Lowrie), George, 194.
—— John, maltman, 195.
—— Robert, minister of St. Giles, Edinburgh, 158 and *n*.
—— Thomas, 193.
Lead mines, 127; of Glenlyon, 135, 137.
Leadhill mines, 101-102, 109; valuation, 112, 127.
Leadhills, 101, 130 *n*, 144 *n*.
Leaping dykes, 225, 311.
Leaseris, Robert, in Bonitoun, 194.
Lee, captain, 9-11, 13, 17, 67.
Leg dollar, 222, 298 and *n*.
Leighton (Lichtone), Robert, abp., 77 and *n*.
—— William, in Towie, 285, 301, 308, 310.
Leisk, Alex., 286.
Leitch (Leich), Alex., 291.
—— John, officer, 232, 273.
Leith, John, in Kirktoun of Forbes, 229, 233-234, 240, 244-245, 259.
—— Patrick, in Westhills, 241, 249, 251, 269, 279; fined for assault, 250.
—— —— in Windseye, 308, 317; fined for contempt, 286.
Leslie, yr. of Kincraigie, 211 *n*.
—— sir John [James], 19 and *n*.
Levett, lieut., 67.
Lilburne, col. Robert, 158 and *n*.
Lime, 214 *n*, 278, 314, 321.
Lindsay, James, bp. of Dunkeld, 74.
—— Thomas, a Leith skipper, 127, 141 and *n*.
Lingwood, capt. Livewell, 9, 11, 67.

INDEX

Linlithgow, George, smith, 196.
Listoun, Harie, 197.
Loch, George, in Barslasie, 298.
Lockhart, sir James, of Lee, lord justice clerk, 144 and *n*.
—— sir William, 164 and *n*, 167.
Lockie or Crystie, Christian, fined for ' blooding,' 308-309.
Logie, 215, 228, 244.
Lones, casting, 246, 255, 320.
Lowis, Nicoll, 200.
Lumsdall, John, 20.
Lumsden, sir Robert, governor of Dundee, 3.
Lun, lieut. Edward, 63, 67.
Lyell, John, 199.
Lyoun, Thomas, 200.

M'Cloy or Fullarton, John, 79 and *n*, 82.
M'Culloch, Mr., commissary of Wigton, 78 *n*.
Mace, ensign, 67.
M'Gachan, John, 132.
Machermore, Newton-Stewart, 92.
M'Inteir, George, 245.
Mackgill (Magilgan), Roger, 50, 54.
Mackie, George, 256; in Carndaird, 234, 240.
—— —— 247, 256, 266; in Stondeck, 241, 246, 250, 301, 308; fined for assault, 293-294.
—— James, in Bogisyd, 240.
—— 266; in Stondeck, 241.
—— John, in Bogisyd, 234, 240.
—— —— 255; in Carnedard, 249.
M'Killivie, Thomas, in Wester Tomades, fined for ' blooding,' 252.
Mackintosh, Isabel, wife of sir Robert Campbell of Glenurchy, 135 *n*.
Maclean, Hector, bp. of Argyll, 79; letter from, to James Atkine, bp. of Galloway, 80.
M'Mariage, Elspet, 199.
M'Math, Edward, 192.
—— James, 186, 191-192.
—— John, 187-188, 202.
M'Quorne, Thomas, 194.
Mains. *See* Castle Forbes, Druminour, Puttachie.
Makeney, John O., his evidence as to the taking of Cortachy, 29.
Malice, John, 302.
—— William, 247, 254, 276; in Bogyside, 251; in Castlehill, 241, 265.

Maners, Geo., 13.
Malt, duties, 224, and *passim*; brewed in Castle Forbes, 243.
Maplesden, lieut., 67.
Mar, Bessie, 200.
—— David Erskine, earl of, 131 *n*.
—— Patrick, in Edinbanchrie, 228, 233, 240, 244, 257; fined for ' blooding,' 268.
—— William, in Edinbanchrie, 228, 233, 240, 257.
Marches, keeping of, 248, 286, 298.
Marnoch, Robert, 235.
Marschell, Margaret, 200.
Marsh, lieut. John, 30, 67.
Marteine, George, tailor, 198.
Marvell, capt., 67.
Mason, lieut. Humphrey, 67.
—— Jo., 13.
Mathie, James, meilmaker, 198.
—— William, brouster, 195.
Maule, James, of Melgund, 22 and *n*, 29.
Maurice, Thomas, 31.
Mayor, capt. James, 67.
Meadows (meadow grass, ground or earth), casting, 224, 246, 255, 266, 275, 281, 284-285, 303, 315, 320.
Meal duties, 225, and *passim*.
Mearnes, Katherine, in Dundee, 60-61.
Measures, 217, 304.
Medley, John, quartermaster, his evidence on the forcing an entrance into Cortachy, 24-26.
Meldrum, George, rector of Marischal college, Aberdeen, 77 and *n*.
Melros, John, tailor, 198.
Melville, Andrew, 186.
Mencour, Francis, 13.
Mending burns and breaches, 320.
Menie, Maney or Minye, Alex., in Tornivein, 321.
—— George, in Castlehill, 308.
—— Issobell, 199.
—— William, 255, 266-267, 309; in Castle Forbes, 318; in Castlehill, 308.
Mennere or Munnier, ensign, 67.
Menzeis, James, 196.
Mercheand, Alex., 230.
Messer, John, 234, 245, 255.
Midden erd, 224-226.
Midleton, Wm., in Enitis, 298-299, 306-307, 315-316.
Military punishments in Cromwell's army, 10-21, 33-36, 38, 42-43, 60, 63-65.

Militia, 217, 279, 282, 283.
Mill or Mylne, Alex., in Miltown, 262.
—— —— in Scotismill, fined for assault, 310-311.
—— -- Hew, 267.
— - Hutcheon, in Bankheid, 308.
- — John, 139.
- —— in Barflat, 289.
—— —— officer, 224, 231, 242, 257, 270.
—— Pat., officer, 259.
Mill measures, 304.
—— swine, 270.
Miller, John, 39-40.
—— Thomas, meilmaker, 194.
Millers' duties, 239, 242, 254; to prevent mixing dust, etc., with ferme meal, 242, 264, 275, 283, 287, 296-297, 300; to renew mill door, 317; upkeep of mill house, 317.
Mills, tenant's duties to, 230, 234-235, 239, 242, 254, 264-265; keeping to their own mills, 236, 239-240, 242, 275, 293, 316; knaveship, 240, 276, 282; multures, 225, 228, 239-240, 257, 275, 293, 298, 316; other payments, 282, 300, 304; renewals of mill door, 279-288; repair of mill-lade, 266; timber for mill, 312.
Milton, Laurence, 10.
Miltoun of Easter Tolmaads, 229, 231, 292.
Ministers' stipends, 224, 227-228, 231.
Miscarriages, fine for, 299.
Mitchell, Alex., 271, 319.
—— —— in Blackhillock, 295, 301.
—— —— in Wakmyln, 258.
—— Arthur, 254, 271; in Culhay, 226, 238, 285.
—— - Cristian, 196.
—— - George, in Balfour, fined for assault, 284.
—— —— in Edinbanchrie, 268.
—— James, in Collhay, 289, 295; in Edinbanchrie, 240; in Logie, 244.
—— John, 219, 271.
—— —— in Balfour, 226, 229, 232, 238, 240, 244.
—— —— in Edinbanchrie, 226.
—— —— in Logie, 244, 257, 278, 319; fined for 'blooding,' 271-272.
—— —— in Scotismill, 310.
—— Patrick, in Cullhay, 238.

Mitchell, Robert, 226, 228, 238, 254.
—— Walter, ground officer, 290, 293, 296.
—— William, in Edinbanchrie, 228, 233, 240, 244.
Mitchelson, Elizabeth, 33 n.
Moffet, Peater, in Sauchtounhall, 195.
Moir, Patrick, 254; in New Keig, 238, 278, 312.
—— —— in Puttachie, 297.
—— William, commissary of Wigton, 78 and n.
—— —— in Puttachie, 297.
Mollson, John, 243.
Monck, general George, takes Dundee, 3; casualties, 4 and n; issues a proclamation forbidding plundering, 7.
Money values in 1614, 187.
Mongarie, 257.
Monks, sergeant Christopher, 63-64.
Monymusk in 1716, 215 n.
Moore, Agnes, 200.
—— Alexander, in Multers in the Hill, 197.
—— Quintayne, 48-51, 53.
—— ensign Thomas, 67.
Moray, Margaret, countess of, 158 n.
Morgan (Murgan), capt. Ethelbert, 9-11, 67.
—— or Taylor, Bessie, 268.
—— James, 254; in Bithny, 288-289.
—— Janet, in Silivethie, 311.
Morham's contribution to the distressed Church of France in 1622, 185, 190, 192.
Morris, capt., 67.
Moseley, Edward, commissioner of justice, 154 and n.
Moss-grieve, 318.
Mowat, sir George, of Ingliston, 117-118, 128, 152 and n, 153.
—— Roger, of Dumbreck, 152 and n, 153.
Mowbray, James, smith, 197.
—— Robert, armourer, 196.
Moyer, Samuel, 167 and n.
Muck-fail, 315.
Mucking, 312-318.
Mudie, Robert, 196.
Muirburn. See Heather.
Mullins, Edward, chirurgeon, 162.
Multures. See Mills.
Munkis hill, Fiddes, 219.

INDEX

Murdoche, Bessie, 200.
Mureson, John, in Bithnie, 240.
Murgan. *See* Morgan.
Murray, Agnes, 200.
—— sir Archibald, of Blackbarony, 105.
—— Jean, wife of Thomas Henderson, advocate, 152 *n*.
—— dame Margaret, 133.
—— Marioun, 199.
—— William, 'whipping-boy' to Charles I., 147 and *n*.
Mushet, Christian, third wife of sir John Campbell of Glenurchy, 137*n*.
—— Robert, of Craighead, 137 *n*.
Mutinous conduct among Cromwell's soldiers, 63-64.
Muttie (Moudefow), 300, 304.
Muttounbrey, 219.
Mylne. *See* Mill.

NAISMITH, Thomas, minister of Stranraer, letters from, to the bp. of Galloway, 93, 94.
Napier, sir Archibald, of Edinbellie, 194.
—— John, tailor, 198.
—— Robert, in Merchesoun, 197.
Neaves, sergeant William, 63.
Neilson (Nilson), John, in Castlehill, 276, 279.
—— Jonet, 197.
Newbigging, 202, 298.
Newham, captain, 67.
Newtoun of Auchindoir, 251.
Nicholas, captain, 67.
Nicoll (Nuckall), Alex., in Easter Tolmads, 229, 299, 321.
—— William, tailor, 198.
Nicollsone, George, 266.
Nimok, Bessie, 200.
Nisbit, David, 198.
—— sir William, of the Dean, 187, 194 and *n*.
Nolt. *See* Cattle.
Norie, John, in Towie, 256, 267.
—— William, in Towie, fined for 'blooding,' 267.
Norman, William, 38.
North Berwick's contribution to the distressed Church of France in 1622, 190-191.
Norvell, George, 132 and *n*.
Nuckall. *See* Nicoll.

OAK TREES, embedded in mosses, 215, 216, 305.
Oddey, James, 16.

Officer. *See* Ground officer.
Ogilvie, Alexander, of Kempcarne, 76 and *n*.
—— lady Isabell, 29.
—— lady Margaret, 29.
—— Marion, wife of James Maule of Melgund, 22 *n*.
Okey, colonel John, 3, 30, 67.
Oliver (Olifer), Elspeth, 309.
—— James, in Tollie, 226.
—— John, 247, 269, 275; in Steanfield, 286; in Towie, 301, 308; fined for assault, 302.
—— William, in Towie, 251, 302.
Ormisoun, Jonet, 200.
Overton, Robert, colonel, 67.
Overtoun of Easter Tolmaads, 231.
Owen, Andrew, commissioner of justice, 154 and *n*.
—— Evan, punished for disobeying his officer, 36-38.
—— ensign Richard, 67.
—— ensign Thomas, 67.
Oxen yoked in plough, 318. *See* Cattle.

PACOK, Jonet, brouster, 199.
Padley, Wm., 20.
Painter, ensign John, 67.
Park, Agnes, 200.
—— William, 200.
Parker, captain George, 67.
—— James, in Culfork, 315.
—— John, 35.
—— Phillip, 13.
Parks, 277, 291.
Paterson, Archibald, 50, 53, 54.
—— John, bp. of Galloway, afterwards of Edinburgh, 72, 74 and *n*.
—— John, brouster, 196.
—— Margaret, 33 *n*.
—— Patrick, in Drumlazie, 321.
—— Robert, letter from, to the bp. of Galloway, 83 and *n*.
Patrick, Janet, 19.
Patronages, bill for the abolishing of, 163.
Paul, sir James Balfour, editor of the *Diary of Sir James Hope of Hopetoun*, 1646-1654, 97-168.
Paulett, Francis, 13.
Peacock, Richard, 16.
—— Thomas, 17.
Peas, order to plant, 283.
Peats, 224, and *passim*.
Peirson, ensign, 67.
—— Thomas, 11, 12.

Pencaitland's contribution to the distressed Church of France in 1622, 190, 191.
Penkaven, cornet, 67.
Pennicook, Issobell, 200.
Perselouy, 259.
Petflug or Balfluig, 211 *n.*
Pettibones, ensign, 67.
Pettimucke, 219.
Pew, David, 12, 13.
Phinnie, Robert, in Gorgie, 197. *See* Fyny.
Piggott, Katherine, in Dundee, 60-61.
Pirie, William, 196.
Pitt, Thomas, 48-49.
Plaid, taking of, 250, 251, 319.
Platt, sergeant, 62.
Plundering by Cromwell's army, 11, 13, 15, 16, 19, 20, 31, 32, 42, 45, 59.
Pollock, Gawin, 196.
—— Johne, 196.
Porteous, Gawin, 196.
—— Robert, 199.
Potter, corporal, 14.
Pouncer, Francis, a soldier, punished for disobedience, 35-36.
Powell, lieut. John, 9-11, 67.
—— Philip, 21.
—— ensign Thomas, 67.
—— capt.-lieut. William, 67.
Prestonpans' contribution to the distressed Church of France in 1622, 190, 191.
Price, Thomas, 17, 18.
Primrose, Gilbert, surgeon, 132 *n.*
Pringle (or Dick), Bessie, 146 *n.*
Proctor, Janet, 285.
Provocation. *See* Scolding.
Public burdens, 216, 246, 316-317, 320-321.
'Puir men,' 216 *n.*
Purves, Adame, baxter, 196.
—— Henry, surgeon, 130 and *n*, 137-138.
—— Thomas, baxter, 196.
Puttachie (now Castle Forbes), 210, 215, 228, 265, 272, 274, 276 and *n*, 277, 295; garden of, 277 *n*; garden-dykes, 225, 243; gardener, 274; green, 246, 291; mains, 291; orchards, 243; park, 291; place (manor place), 273, 311; wood, 215, 228, 233, 265, 276 and *n*, 291, 297, 312, 317; wood-dykes, 297; yards, 233, 315; yard dykes, 246, 315.

RAE, Adam, of Pitsindie, 131 *n.*
—— Helen, wife of sir Thomas Hope of Kerse, 111, 131 and *n*, 138-139.
Rakeham, Phillipp, 14.
Ramsay, Andrew, minister of Greyfriars, 101 and *n.*
—— Christian, 19.
—— George, smyth, 195.
Randall, Abraham, to be shot for striking an officer, 33-34.
Rankin, Isabell, 17.
—— Margaret, in Dundee, 60.
Rattray, James, collector, 40, 41.
—— Walter, 40.
Reade, colonel Thomas, 3.
—— ensign, 67.
Reames, cornet John, 30, 67.
Rede, William, collector, 40.
Regality rights, 87.
Reid (Rid), Alex., in Bankheid, 246-248.
—— Elspet, 200.
—— James, tailor, 194.
—— John, in Glentoun, 228, 232; fined for assault, 280-281.
—— Robert, in Glentoune, 228, 232, 244.
—— William, 256, 266; in Carndaird, 234, 241.
Reind, James, 233.
Removing tenants, 224, 284.
Rentals of Kearn, Forbes, Alford, etc., 209.
Reny, John, fined for assault, 300-301.
Richbell, lieutenant, 67.
Rid. *See* Reid.
Riding the wooden horse, a military punishment, 10, 38, 42-43, 60, 63.
Ritchie (Richie), Alex., in Balfour, fined for 'blooding,' 301-302.
—— or Layng, Bessie, 227.
—— Elspet, in Scotismill, 311.
—— James, in Balfour, 301-302, 310, 311.
—— John, in Miltone Crofts, 321.
Robbery, 39-42.
Roberton, Archibald, of Stonehall, 152 *n.*
—— James, regent of Glasgow university, 185.
—— Margaret, wife of David Dickson, prof. of divinity, 153 *n.*
Roberts, Richard, 63.
—— sir William, 160 and *n.*
Robertson (Robesone), Agnes, 199.
—— Alexander, cooper, 197, 200.

INDEX

Robertson, James, forester, 317.
—— —— in Wester Tammaidis, 229.
—— Margaret, 198.
Robins, captain John, 67.
Robinson, captain, 67.
—— Jane, to be whipped for theft, 39.
—— Thomas, to ride the wooden horse for using seditious language, 60-63.
Robson, Thomas, 14.
Rod of office, 310.
Rodger or Roger, George, in Tailziachee, 283.
—— Issobell, fined for scolding, 309, 310.
—— James, in Tailzeach, 308.
—— —— in Towie, 301, 308-310; fined for assault, 295.
—— Robert, 201.
—— Thomas, 247, 254, 266; in Bogieside, 250, 285, 286, 304, 308.
Rodgie, William, 303.
Ronald, George, in Bogheadis, 227.
Rooke, ensign, 67.
—— lieutenant, 67
Ross, Arthur, abp. of Glasgow, letters from, to James Atkine, bp. of Galloway, 76-80.
—— James, of Findlarg, notary, 298-299, 306-307, 315-316, 318, 320-321.
—— John, in Bellismill, 195.
—— —— maltman, 199.
—— Peter, 196.
Running the gauntlet, 10 and *n*.
Russell, Thomas, cordiner, 195.
Rutherford, Alison, wife of James Atkine, bp. of Galloway, 71.
Ryburne, quartermaster, 49.

ST. CUTHBERT'S CHURCH, Edinburgh, its contribution to the distressed Church of France in 1622, 193-202.
St. Nicholas, Thomas, of Aske, 165 and *n*.
Saddle, 309 *n*.
Salmon poaching, 297.
Salton's contribution to the distressed Church of France in 1622, 190, 191.
Samuell, George, 198.
Sandie, Barbara, 198.
Sandilandis, James, baxter, 197.
—— Marion, third wife of John Ellis, advocate, 151 *n*.

Saurle, Robert, in Sauchtounhall, 198.
Sawrey, lieut.-col. Roger, 67.
Scaith, John, 37.
Scandalous persons, 216, 231.
Schevez, William, archdeacon of St. Andrews, 172, 174.
Schoolmasters, 213 *n*.
Scoble, Thomas, 37, 38.
Scolding (abuse, provocation), fines for, 247, 250-251, 253, 275, 284, 308-310, 317.
Scoler, Thomas, 47.
Scotismyln, 283, 317.
Scott, David, in Blakfurd, 199.
—— James, of Clonbeath, 151 *n*.
—— John, 135.
—— Margaret, second wife of John Ellis, advocate, 151 *n*.
—— Rebecca, first wife of John Ellis, advocate, 151 *n*.
—— Richard, 199.
—— Walter, in the Dean, 195.
—— William, 301.
Scottish Contributions to the Distressed Church of France in 1622, 179-202.
Scowlar, William, weaver, 197.
Scupham, Robert, 17.
Scutter, George, 10.
Scuttle, ensign, 67.
Seaton, Alex., of Thornton, 43.
—— Margaret, 132.
—— William, 58.
Sewell, Tho., 17.
Sewster, Robina, second wife of sir William Lockhart, 164 *n*.
Shand, George, 228.
Sharp, captain, 67.
—— James, abp. of St. Andrews, letter from, to James Atkine, bp. of Galloway, 74-76.
—— William, in Putachie, 245.
Shawe, David, 43-44.
Sheep, detained out of fold, 299; trespassing, 230, 258-260, 265, 276, 286, 295. *See* Wedders.
Shipden, capt., 67.
Shireff, James, 234.
—— William, in Colhey, 233.
Shockley, lieutenant, 67.
Sibbett, Dr., 138.
Sillivathie, 226.
Silver duties, 224, and *passim*.
Silver lace workers, 109, 133-135.
—— mines at Hilderston, Linlithgowshire, 155 *n*, 156.

Simmer (Somer), Alex., 245-246, 248, 255, 260-262, 264, 266, 269, 277, 294, 301-302, 318; in Kirkstyle, 301.
Sinclair, William, 197.
Skeldon, Lenox, 58.
Skelton, capt., 30, 67.
Skene, sir John, of Curriehill, 158 *n.*
Slates, 314.
Smaill, George, cordiner, 195.
Smith, Alexander, 229; in Miltown, 262.
—— in Westhills, 240-241, 247, 250.
—— George, 269.
—— James, 234.
—— —— in Auchtmar, 276.
—— —— in Druminnour, 240.
—— —— in Logie, 282, 285, 315, 319-320; fined for 'blooding,' 271-272.
—— —— in Towie, 247.
—— John, 245; in Castlehill, 233-234, 240-241, 265.
—— —— in Kirkstyll, 240.
—— sir John, of Grote Hall, provost of Edinburgh, 117, 151 and *n.*
—— Margaret, fined for 'blooding,' 305.
—— Marioun, 199.
—— Robert, 117, 128.
—— —— of Southfield, Cramond, 151 and *n.*
—— —— son of sir John Smith of Grote Hall, 117.
—— William, 219.
Society Wynd, Edinburgh, 145.
Soldiers. *See* Militia.
Somer. *See* Simmer.
Somervill, Wm., minister of Leswalt, 93 and *n.*
Serners, 216, 299.
Southside, Newbattle, 117 *n.*
Spades, foot and flachter, 246, 254, 284-285, 304, 315.
Sparkes, Henry, 12, 13.
Speir, James, burgess of Edinburgh, 186, 191-192, 202.
—— Rachel, wife of (1) sir James Skene, (2) sir John Hope of Craighall, 118, 130 and *n.*
—— Sara, wife of Robert Foulis, advocate, 101, 118.
—— William, 187.
Squibb, Arthur, 166 and *n.*
Stair, earl of, letter to, from the bp. of Galloway, 86.

Steelhand, a moss-trooper, 48, 50, 54, 58.
Steill, John, 197.
Stephens, Joseph, ensign, 67.
Steuart, A. Francis, note on George, fourth marquis of Huntly, 75 *n.*
Stevinsone, John, 194.
—— Robert, 194.
Stewart, Elizabeth, her sentence of excommunication to be relaxed, 94.
—— lady Margaret, wife of John Swinton, 159 *n.*
—— lieut. Mathew, 49-51, 54.
Stocks, the, 208, 232.
Stondyk, 248, 260.
Stone in the kidneys, 110-111 and *n*, 121, 137, 162.
Stones, carriage of, 225.
Stonniefeild (Stenyfeidle), 251, 259.
Stralunak, 226.
Strapadoe, a military punishment, 10 and *n.*
Straquhan, Alex., fined for assault, 319, 320.
—— Thomas, in Edinbanchrie, 318-319.
Supply, the king's, 320.
Sutton, lieut. Henry, 67.
Sward ground, casting of, 320.
Swearing among Cromwell's soldiers, 12, 21.
Swine, 270.
Swinton, John, 159 and *n*, 167.
Sydenham, col. William, 165 and *n.*
Syme, Thomas, in Sauchtounhall, tailor, 194, 196.
Symonds, lt.-col. William, 67.
Symsoun, Alexander, 193-194, 197, 277 *n.*
—— Andrew, minister of Kirkinner, 85 and *n*; letter from, to the bp. of Galloway, 92.
—— Ewphame, 199.
—— Thomas, tailor, 199.

Tait, Alex., 150.
Tallow. *See* Brewers.
Tammadis. *See* Tolmaads.
Tay, ensign, 67.
Taylaches (Tailzeach), 251, 259, 305.
Taylor (Tailzour), lieutenant, 67.
—— Alexander, 230.
—— —— in Castlehill, 240-241.
—— George, 246.
—— James, in Windseye, 250.
—— Patrick, in Auchintowll, 310.

INDEX

Taylor, William, 307.
—— —— in Edinbanchrie, 233, 268.
Teinds, 211; teind silver, 227, 277, 279, 314, 316, 320; teind victual, 225, 227, 237, 279.
Terry, James, 15.
Tether, 309 *n*.
Tethering of stock, 226, 230, 288.
Teviotdale (Tevindall), Patrick, 224, 231, 237, 241-242.
Tew, lieutenant, 67.
Thayne, Elspeth, 317.
Theft, 15-17, 289, 309 *n*.
Thirlage to mills, 211, 230, 234, 239, 242-243, 254, 264, 275, 282, 287, 293, 298, 300, 316.
Thomson, Alex., fined for assault, 273.
—— Andro, 201.
—— Bassie, in Persellevy, fined for assault, 294.
—— David, of Strackmortin, 42.
—— George, 199.
—— Henry, killed in a brawl, 55, 65.
—— James, notary public, 227, 231, 233-235; in Milhill, 229; in Towie, 248.
—— John, in Carndard, 281.
—— —— Maitland, editor of the *Forbes Baron Court Book*, 203-321.
—— —— Robert, 195.
—— William, capt.-lieut., 67.
—— —— in Auchgathyll, 273, 274
—— —— in Collhay, 289, 295, 314.
—— —— elder in Putachie, 273-274.
Thorne, Peter, 14.
Tichbourne, alderman, 164 and *n*, 166.
Tillykerrie, 211 and *n*, 272, 274.
Timber, 226, 277; carriage of, 225; stealing of, 276, 295. *See* Wood.
Tindall, Andrew, 15.
Tite, Robert, provost marshal, 35-36, 46, 59.
Todd, William, 58.
Tolmaads, Kincardine O'Neil, 211, 230, and *passim*; Easter, 229, 231; Wester, 230; Miltoun, 229, 231, 292; mill, 235; Overton, 231.
Tolson, James, 18.
Tornaveen, 211, 231, 299.
Tott, Jacqueline, 131 *n*.

Touch, James, in Bankheid, 247.
—— John, in Stondyk, 301, 315; fined for 'blooding,' 293-294.
—— William, 245; in Castlehill, 234, 240-241.
Tough (Touch), parish, 211, 272.
Touris, sir George, of Gairnttoun [Garleton], 187, 193.
Towie, 215, 251, 259, 295, 305, 309.
—— James, in Barflett, 248-249.
Trail, Robert, minister of Old Greyfriars, 153 and *n*.
Tranent's contribution to the distressed Church of France in 1622, 190-191.
Traquhane, Jeane, 199.
Tree, assaults with, 269, 273, 319; cutting of, 315; planting, 212, 231, 233-234, 238, 243, 266.
Trenchard, Grace, wife of col. William Sydenham, 165 *n*.
Trespass. *See* Cattle, Fowls, Horses, Sheep.
Tulliallan, 117, 128, 152.
Twynholm church, 84 and *n*.

UDNY, John, of Newburgh, 211 *n*.
Udwart, Nathaniel, 186 *n*.
—— Nicol, 185-186 and *n*.
University of Edinburgh and its connection with the Hope family, 139 and *n*.
Urbino, duke of, 181.

VAGABONDS, 216, 299.
Vandecroone, ensign Peter, 67.
Vanhoght, Mr., 116, 128, 149.
Varak. *See* Warrack.
Vaus, John, of Barnbarroch, 86 and *n*.
—— sir Patrick, 86 *n*.
Vebest, Vincent, skipper of Middleburgh, 150.
Veitch, Thomas, 132 and *n*.
Victual duties, 224, and *passim*.
—— rent, 211 and *n*.
Visitella, Christopher, glass manufacturer, 111, 127, 139 and *n*, 145.
—— Isaac, painter, 112, 139 *n*.
Vyr. *See* Weir.

WAGES in 1622, 187.
Waite, ensign, 67.

Walker, George, in Bogysyd, 250; fined for 'blooding,' 285; for theft, 289.
—— Henry, minister of Whithorn, letter from, to the bp. of Galloway, 84.
—— James, 247, 255.
—— —— in Castlehill, 279.
—— —— in Westhillis, 226, 238, 241, 249-250.
Walkinshaw, John, 50-51, 54.
Walkmylne, 226.
Wallace, George, 255.
—— or Norie, Jean, 267.
—— John, 149.
—— William, kirk-officer, 194.
Walley, captain, 67.
Walton, Richard, a dragoon, punished for being drunk, etc., 43.
Wands, 277.
Warde, Mathew, quartermaster, 46.
Wariston, laird of, 187, 194.
Warne, Jo., 37.
Warrack (Varak), James, in Scotismilne, 234, 240.
Wast, Elspet, 200.
—— George, tailor, 198.
—— Jeallis, 200.
—— Johne, in Sauchtounhall, 195.
Waterhead, near Leadhills, 148 and n.
Watson, James, of Sauchtoun, 195.
—— William, 256, 266.
—— —— minister of Wigton, letter from, to the bp. of Galloway, 92.
Watt, James, at Bonnett Hill, 32-33.
—— John (in Mill of Tolmaads), fined for assault, 235, 236; for 'blooding,' 262-263.
Weaver, lieutenant Richard, 67.
Webster (Wobster), James, 271, 272.
Wecht, John, in Balfour, 240.
Wedderburn, William, in Bithnie, 228, 232, 240, 243.
Wedders (or sheep), custom, 245, 270-271, 280-282, 296, 304. See Sheep.
Weems, Wm., 20.
Weir, Alexander, meilmaker, 198.
—— —— [son], 198.
—— George, in Balfour, 301.
—— James, in Campvere, 150.
—— John, in Balfour, 229, 244.

Wells, William, 13, 17.
Welsh, John, son-in-law of Knox, 182, 186.
Westhills, 226, 251-252, 260.
Westley, Rooke, 37.
Westoe, William, 39.
Wheeler, capt., 13.
White, col., 123, 166 and n.
—— Archibald, 200.
—— Frances, second wife of John Swinton, 159.
—— (Quhyt), William, 197.
Wigton commissary, 78 n.
Wilburne, Wm., 43-44.
Wilkie, George, 200.
—— James, in Sauchtounhall, 194.
Williamsoun, Thomas, cutler, 197.
Wilson, David, brouster, 197.
—— George, 247; in Castlehill, 233-234, 242, 279.
—— John, 245, 262.
—— Robert, belt maker, 198.
—— —— in Sauchtounhall, 194.
—— William, in Fraserburgh, 256-257.
Windseye, 215, 248, 251-252, 260, 265, 286.
Winrame, capt.-lieut., Wigton martyr, 92.
Wishart (Wyshart), John, meilmaker, 196.
—— William, meilmaker, 195.
Wolseley, sir Charles, 164 and n.
Wood, capt.-lieut., 64.
—— sergeant, 33.
—— John, 17, 200.
Woods, cleansing of, 288; cutting of, 226, and passim; sighting of, 228; trespassing in, 260, 265.
Woodward, lieut., 64, 67.
—— James, 62.
Wrenche, captain, 67.
Wright (Wrycht), Alexander, 199.
—— John, in Tailzeach, 305.
—— —— in Thornton, 43.
—— Richard, soldier, 33.
—— Robert, in Tailzeach, 226, 228, 238, 254-257, 266, 278, 283, 292; fined for 'blooding,' 269.
Wylde, Robert, 55-56, 65.
Wynne, Wm., 31.

YARDS, planting of. See Tree.
York, duke and duchess of, visit Oxford university, 91 and n.

INDEX

Young, Alexander, bp. of Ross, letter from, to the bp. of Galloway, 89.
—— major Arthur, 67.
—— George, minister of Kirkmaiden, letter from, to the bp. of Galloway, 93-94.
Young, Johne, in the Deane, 195.
—— Peater, 197.
—— Thomas, 193, 194.
Yule (Zoole, Zowell), Alexander, 194.
—— James, fined for taking salmon, 297.

REPORT OF THE THIRTY-SECOND ANNUAL MEETING OF THE SCOTTISH HISTORY SOCIETY

The Thirty-second Annual Meeting of the Society was held on Saturday, December 21, 1918, in Dowell's Rooms, George Street, Edinburgh,—W. K. Dickson, Esq., LL.D., Advocate, in the Chair.

The Report of the Council was as follows:—

During the past year six members have died, and six have resigned. One member, Captain James Scott, was killed in battle on March 9th last, whilst gallantly leading his company. Twenty-five new members have joined the Society, and the number now on the roll, exclusive of libraries, is 392.

Since last General Meeting one volume has been issued, viz., *The Army of the Covenant*, vol. ii. The other issue for 1917-1918, viz., *Wariston's Diary*, vol. ii., is nearly ready for issue.

For 1918-1919 it is proposed to issue vol. iii. of the Society's *Miscellany*, a great part of which is already in print. It includes the record of Courts Martial held at Dundee during the English occupation in 1651, edited by Mr. G. Davies of Oxford; a number of interesting letters relating to Galloway during the Covenanting period, edited by Mr. William Douglas; extracts from the Baron Court Book of Forbes, A.D. 1659 to 1678, edited by the Secretary; and a Diary of Sir Thomas Hope, A.D. 1646 to 1654, edited by the Lyon King of Arms. For the second issue Mr. Macphail, K.C., has undertaken to edit another volume of Papers relating to the Highlands.

Dr. Maitland Anderson is engaged upon the Pre-Reformation Records of the University of St. Andrews. The

Rev. W. Stephen is editing the Register of the Consultations of the Ministers of Edinburgh.

The Council wishes to impress upon Members of the Society how greatly they can promote its prosperity, both by making its publications and its objects more widely known, and by bringing under the notice of the Council any MSS. suitable for publication with which they may be acquainted.

Mr. Donald Crawford has intimated his resignation of the Chairmanship of Council, which he has held since 1910. The period of his tenure of the office has been, for more reasons than one, a peculiarly difficult period for us; that we have weathered the storm is largely due to his sound judgment and ungrudging assistance. His retirement is deeply regretted, but the state of his health leaves him no option. He and his predecessors have been elected by the Council; hereafter it has been resolved that the election shall be subject to confirmation by the Annual Meeting, and that the tenure of the office shall be limited to four years. The Council recommend that Sir James Balfour Paul be elected Chairman of Council for that period.

The recent death of Professor Hume Brown, a Member of our Council, is deeply regretted by his colleagues, and represents a loss to learning which will be felt not only in Scotland, but wherever Scottish history is seriously studied.

The Members of Council retiring by rotation are Sir James Balfour Paul, Mr. Francis Steuart, and Mr. MacLehose. It is recommended that the two last be re-elected, and that the vacancy created by the election of Sir James Balfour Paul to the Chairmanship be filled by the election of Lord Strathclyde.

The Accounts of the Hon. Treasurer, of which an abstract is appended hereto, show that the balance in the Society's favour on 13th November 1917 was £160, 2s. 9d., the income for 1917-1918 £495, 12s. 5d., the expenditure £346, 1s. 10d., and the credit balance on 13th November 1918 £309, 13s. 4d.

The Annual Subscription of £1, 1s. is now due and payable at the Bank of Scotland, Edinburgh; or to the Honorary Treasurer.

The CHAIRMAN, in moving the adoption of the Report, said :—

LADIES AND GENTLEMEN,—The first thought in our minds as we turn to this year's Report must be our sense of the loss which the Society has sustained by the death of Professor Hume Brown. In this Society words of conventional eulogy would be out of place. We all knew Professor Hume Brown's work. Most of us knew him as a personal friend. He was the foremost worker of his time in Scottish History and Palæography, and the author not only of an excellent general history of Scotland, but of two classical biographies, the *Lives* of John Knox and of George Buchanan, and of collections of documents, *Early Travellers in Scotland* and *Scotland before* 1700, which have done much to illustrate the social life of our forefathers. As editor of the *Privy Council Register* he took a prominent part in the spade work which is the basis of all sound historical research, and in which this Society has been specially concerned.

He was no narrow specialist, but a scholar of wide mental horizons and versatile human sympathies. To the Scottish History Society he rendered valuable services, not only as a member of the Council, but as editor of one of our recent volumes, the *Seafield Correspondence*, issued in 1915.

I should like to refer specially to one aspect of his work which came less prominently before the public—his work in palæography. Palæography appeals chiefly to specialists, but it is the foundation of all trustworthy research in mediæval records. Twenty years ago, in Scotland, beginners in the subject had to pick up their knowledge as best they could. The appointment of Mr. Hume Brown to the Fraser Professorship saw the beginning of what we hope may develop into a Scottish *École des Chartes*. His place in the intellectual life of Scotland will not be easily filled.

We have also to regret the retirement from the Chairmanship of our Council, on grounds of health, of Mr. Donald Crawford. Mr. Crawford has given to the Society ungrudging work, both as a historical scholar and as a man of business. He edited for our series an important volume, *Fountainhall's Journals*, issued in 1900, and as Chairman of the Council his knowledge of men and of affairs, his sound business judgment, and his unfailing tact, have been of great value to the Society.

I am sure that the proposal that Sir James Balfour Paul should succeed Mr. Crawford as Chairman of the Council will receive the unanimous approval of the Society.

Turning to the business aspect of the Report, I have to congratulate the Society on the position in which it finds itself at the end of four years of war. In 1914 our Society was passing through a period of diminished prosperity, and in the early months of the war there was some ground for anxiety as to our future. Happily these forebodings have been disappointed. We are now in a stronger position than we have occupied for years. As to membership, in December 1914 we had thirteen vacancies, in December 1916 there were thirty-four. They have now been reduced to seven, and we hope soon to have our membership full. Our finances are in a sound condition. We begin the new year with a balance in hand of £309, 13s. 4d., and our publications are up to date.

We have every reason, too, to be satisfied with the quality of the work issued during the war. The volumes include the three volumes of *Melrose Regality Records*, edited by the treasurer, Mr. Romanes, a rich store of knowledge as to Border lands and folk. The *Records of the Earldom of Orkney*, edited by Mr. Storer Clouston, have given us much new light on the story of the Northern Isles. Mr. Steuart's *Scots in Poland* appeared opportunely when that country was much in our thoughts. The *Letter-Book of Bailie John Steuart of Inverness*, edited by Dr. William Mackay, has told us much that was new about life and commerce in the Highlands in the eighteenth century. The *Rentale Dunkeldense*, translated and edited by Mr. Hannay, is an important contribution to the records of the pre-Reformation Church. *Lord Seafield's Letters*, edited by Professor Hume Brown, throw fresh light on the negotiations which led to the Union. Mr. Macphail has given us a second volume of *Highland Papers*, of varied interest, edited with his unique knowledge of Highland affairs. We look forward with interest to his projected third volume, which we hope to get next year. In the *Origins of the Forty-Five*, Mr. Blaikie, out of his unrivalled knowledge of the period, has given us another notable addition to the story of the most romantic episode in our history. Professor Terry's volumes on the *Army of the Covenant* have added to the records of the struggle of the seventeenth century, and we shall shortly have another addition to the same period in the new volume of *Johnston of Wariston's Diary*, now in the hands of Dr. Hay Fleming, and almost ready for publication. Lastly, the two volumes of the *Bibliography of Scottish Topography*, edited by Sir Arthur Mitchell and Mr. Cash, have already become an indispensable working tool to students of Scottish local history and affairs. We have every reason to be satisfied with the present position of the Society, and to be hopeful as to its prospects.

The prosperity of such a society as ours must depend in the first instance upon its officials, but every member can help, and I would appeal to every member to do so. He can help in two ways: first, by getting new members to join the Society, and secondly, by keeping a look-out for documents suitable for publication by us and reporting them to the Council. I would specially suggest that *small* documents should be so reported. Documents which are of great historical interest, and which at the same time are large enough to fill a printed volume of 250 or 300 pages, are rarely to be found, but there are plenty of small documents, letters, private diaries, and the like, which are suitable for inclusion in one of our Miscellany volumes. I should like to see more Miscellany volumes, and if we had abundance of material of this kind it would be possible to compile such volumes relating to special periods, or still better to special districts, say to the Borders or the Lothians, which would give a local and personal interest to each volume. The Council will cordially welcome information as to such documents, as well as suggestions of any kind bearing on the Society's work.

In inviting new members to join us, we should remember that a society like ours is not a mere printing club of dilettanti, or dryasdust antiquaries, concerned with curiosities, old muster-rolls and old account-books. It is a company of people brought together by a common interest in the past of our country, and in the great issues of history and of human destiny. Interest in the history of Scotland was never greater and never more widely spread than at this moment. During the war thousands of men from the Overseas Dominions and from the United States have visited Edinburgh. They have visited the Castle and Holyrood and the Parliament House, the scenes of famous events in Scottish history. They have gone home full of interest in that history; those of Scottish descent have realised their ancestry as never before, and they look to us to respond to that new interest.

The events of the last four years have cast a strange new light on all our past. In the old comfortable Victorian days battle and murder and sudden death seemed a long way off. Such things furnished picturesque incident to the pages of Macaulay or of Hill

Burton, but they did not seem to have much to do with us, as we sat reading by the fire. Flodden and Bannockburn have a new interest now to us, who, since we last met in this room, have watched from hour to hour the retreat from St. Quentin, the great attack on the Marne salient, and the breaking of the Hindenburg line. And not only is this true of our Scottish national history. How the war has given new meaning to all the familiar classical stories of our youth! The story of Thermopylæ has a new meaning to us, who have seen the great armies of the Barbarians stayed by a handful of heroes at Liége and at Ypres. The story of Salamis has a new meaning to us, who have seen the ambitions of the greatest military Empire of the world brought to nothing by the power of the sea. The dreadful happenings in the quarries of Syracuse have a new meaning to us, who have had friends and kinsmen in the German prison camps. The speech of Pericles over the Athenian slain, which we knew of old as a model of stately and moving eloquence, has a new appeal and a new poignancy to us, who have known what it is to mourn the youth of the City fallen in battle.

Not only has history thus received a new interest, but I think we have learned to appreciate better the value of historical knowledge and of the historical horizon in steadying the mind in the presence of great events. We have been so near to momentous events that we have been apt to see them out of proportion. In the darkest days of the War it was sometimes good to look back to the equally dark days of the old French War. We were apt to think of the victories of Nelson and of Wellington, and to forget the time that it took to reach them, and the price that had to be paid for them. It was well to look back, for example, to the year 1797, when things were at their worst. Our armies had been defeated on the Continent; our allies had deserted us; the country was within forty-eight hours of bankruptcy; and, worst of all, two great mutinies had broken out in the Fleet, at Spithead and at the Nore. Our forefathers might well have despaired. And yet if they had only known it, they were within a few weeks of Camperdown; they were within a few months of the overwhelming victory of the Nile; and all the triumphs of Trafalgar, of the Peninsula, and of Waterloo lay before them. In the same way it may not be inappropriate, at the present moment, to recall the years which followed the peace. Those were the days of the "Peterloo Massacre" and the Six Acts; there was acute distress throughout the country; political faction had never been more fierce; discontent had never been more bitter. No wonder that our grandfathers had grave forebodings as to the political and social prospects of the kingdom, and yet, if they had only known it, they were on the threshold of the great Victorian era, which, after all deductions have been made, remains the most splendid period of peace and prosperity, security and progress, which the country has ever known.

It is with such reflections as these in one's mind that one looks forward to the future of historical study, and of our Society.

The motion was seconded by Mr. WILLIAM DOUGLAS and adopted.

The death of Professor Hume Brown leaves a vacancy in the Council, which was filled by the election of Dr. William Mackay, Inverness.

The proceedings terminated with a vote of thanks to the Chairman, proposed by Mr. TRAQUAIR DICKSON, and seconded by Dr. W. B. BLAIKIE.

ABSTRACT OF THE HON. TREASURER'S ACCOUNTS

For the Year ending 12*th November* 1918

I. CHARGE.

I. Funds at close of last Account—
    (1) Sum on Deposit Receipt with the Bank
    of Scotland, Edinburgh, dated 6th
    November 1917, ... £125 18 7
    (2) Sum on Account Current with said Bank, 34 4 2
                                                       £160 2 9

II. Subscriptions received—
    (1) 392 Members for 1917-18, . £411 12 0
    Arrears of subscriptions collected—
        For 1915-16 (one), . . 1 1 0
        For 1916-17 (six), . . 6 6 0
    In advance—
        For 1918-19 (forty-two), 44 2 0
                                       £463 1 0
    Less in arrear (51), . £53 11 0
    Paid in advance in
        1916-17 (47), 49 7 0
                                102 18 0
                                £360 3 0
    (2) 97 Libraries, etc., . £101 17 0
    Arrears collected—
        For 1915-16 (one), . 1 1 0
        For 1916-17 (two), . 2 2 0
        Paid in advance, . 5 5 0

        Carry forward . £110 5 0 £360 3 0 £160 2 9

9

Brought forward, £110 5 0	£360 3 0	£160 2 9
Less 9 in arrear, £9, 9s.		
Paid in advance during 1916-17, £4. 4s., 13 13 0		
	96 12 0	
		456 15 0
III. Books sold to Members, .		29 8 6
IV. Bank Interest—		
Nov. 8, 1918. Interest on Deposit Receipt, dated Nov. 6, 1917, for £125. 18s. 7d., . . .	£3 18 0	
Do. Jan. 15, 1918, for £170,	4 2 11	
Do. March 12, 1918, for £50,	0 19 9	
Do. June 15, 1918, for £35,	0 8 3	
		9 8 11
Sum of Charge,	.	£655 15 2

II. DISCHARGE.

I. Printing, Binding, and issue of Publications—

(1) *Papers relating to the Army of the Solemn League and Covenant, Vol. I.*—

T. & A. Constable for Composition, etc., . . .	£171 5 10	
Cutting Binding Stamps, .	1 5 0	
Binding 540 Copies, . .	29 5 0	
Parcelling, ...	6 15 0	
Delivering by Tramway Parcel Express, . . .	1 3 0	
Despatch by Parcel Post, .	8 2 2	
	£217 16 0	
Less paid to account—		
Oct. 1916, . £27 2 6		
Nov. 6, 1917, . 144 3 4		
	171 5 10	
Nov. 8, 1918, Balance paid, . . .		£46 10 2
Carry forward, . .		£46 10 2

Brought forward,				£46 10 2
(2) *Papers relating to the Army of the Solemn League and Covenant, Vol. II.—*					
Composition and Proofs,		£159 13 11			
Photogravure, Earl of Leven, and Tissues,		4 15 0			
Binding,		29 5 0			
Parcelling,		6 15 0			
Delivering by Tramway Express,		1 3 0			
Despatch by Parcel Post,		8 0 11			
		£209 12 10			
Paid to account, Dec. 31, 1917,				95 19 9
Do. Nov. 8, 1918,				113 13 1
(3) *Johnston of Wariston's Diary—*					
Composition,		£53 19 0			
Less paid to account—					
Oct. 1913,	£20 5 0				
Oct. 1915,	5 1 6				
		25 6 6			
		£28 12 6			
Paid to account, Dec. 1917,				27 7 6
Do. Nov. 8, 1918,				1 5 0
(4) *Miscellany, Vol. III.—*					
Composition,		£36 15 0			
Paid to account, Dec. 31, 1917,				16 2 6
Do. Nov. 8, 1918,				20 12 6
(5) General Printing Account,				10 2 3
II. *Assembly Commission Records—*					
Sum paid during year ending Nov. 12, 1912,		£54 15 0			
III. Sum paid for preparing General Index to Society's Publications, November 1916,		£60 0 0			
Carry forward,				£331 12 9

Brought forward,	£331 12 9	
IV. Miscellaneous Expenses—		
A. Dowell for room for Annual Meeting,	£1 6 0	
Bank charges,	1 11 8	
Auditor's outlays,	1 1 0	
Caldwell Bros. account,	0 9 6	
Secretary's posts—three years,	4 10 0	
Treasurer's posts for circulars, and incidents,	3 3 0	
Bank charges,	1 6 11	
		13 8 1
V. Balance due Treasurer at close of last Account,		1 1 0
VI. Funds at close of this Account—		
1. Sum on Deposit Receipt with Bank of Scotland, dated Nov. 8, 1918,	£300 0 0	
2. Sum on Account Current with Do.,	5 3 10	
3. Balance on hand,	4 9 6	
		309 13 4
Sum of Discharge,		£655 15 2

EDINBURGH, 26*th November* 1918.—Having examined the Accounts of the Hon. Treasurer of the Scottish History Society for the year ending 12th November 1918, of which the foregoing is an Abstract, we find the same to be correctly stated, and sufficiently vouched, closing with a sum on Deposit Receipt with the Bank of Scotland of £300, a balance at the credit of the Society's Account Current with the said Bank of £5, 3s. 10d., and a balance on hand of £4, 9s. 6d.

WM. TRAQUAIR DICKSON, *Auditor.*
RALPH RICHARDSON, *Auditor.*

Scottish History Society

LIST OF MEMBERS

1918-1919

Carmichael, Right Hon. Lord, of Skirling, Malleny, Balerno.
Carmichael, Evelyn G. M., Lilleshall Old Hall, Newport, Salop.
Chalmers, Francis, W.S., 13 Riselaw Road, Edinburgh.
Chambers, W. & R., 339 High Street, Edinburgh.
Christie, Rev. George, B.D., 24 Inverleith Terrace, Edinburgh.
Christie, Walter C., of Bedlay, Chryston, Lanarkshire.
Clark, Mrs. James, Ravelston, Blackhall, Midlothian.
Clark, Sir John M., Bart., 17 Rothesay Terrace, Edinburgh.
70 Clarke, Rev. T. E. S., Saltoun Manse, East Lothian.
Conner, Preston Marshall, 447 North 42 Street, Philadelphia, Pa., U.S.A.
Cormack, Donald Stewart, *Daily Record* Office, Edinburgh.
Cowan, George, 1 Gillsland Road, Edinburgh.
Cowan, J. J., 38 West Register Street, Edinburgh.
Cowan, John, W.S., St. Roque, Grange Loan, Edinburgh.
Cowan, William, 47 Braid Avenue, Edinburgh.
Cowie, Charles R., 20 Blythswood Square, Glasgow.
Craig, William, County Clerk, County Buildings, Dumbarton.
Crichton-Stuart, Lord C. E., St. John's Lodge, Regent's Park, London, N.W.
80 Crockett, Rev. W. S., The Manse, Tweedsmuir.
Crole, Gerald L., K.C., 1 Royal Circus, Edinburgh.
Cross, Robert, 13 Moray Place, Edinburgh.
Cross, W. Irvine, B. and O. Buildings, Baltimore, Maryland, U.S.A.
Cunningham, Captain J. Miller, Leithen Lodge, Innerleithen.
Cunningham, Andrew S., 13 Granby Road, Edinburgh.
Cunningham, George, Advocate, The Square, Kingsley Green, Haslemere, Surrey.
Curle, James, W.S., Priorwood, Melrose.

Dalgleish, John J., Brankston Grange, Bogside Station, Stirling.
Dalrymple, Hon. Hew H., M.P., Lochinch, Castle Kennedy, Wigtownshire.
90 Davidson, James, M.D., Ch.B., Physicist to London Missionary Society, 10 Dagnall Park, Selhurst, London, S.E.
Davidson, J. M., County Buildings, Lanark.
Davidson, J., Solicitor, Kirriemuir.

Davies, Godfrey, 21 Saville Road, Oxford.
Davies, J. Mair, C.A., Sheiling, Pollokshields, Glasgow.
De Prée, Mrs. Ruth, Saughton House, Corstorphine.
Dickson, Hope, 5 Lennox Street, Edinburgh.
Dickson, Walter S., Advocate, 6 Circus Gardens, Edinburgh.
Dickson, William K., LL.D., Advocate, 8 Gloucester Place, Edinburgh.
Dickson, Wm. Traquair, W.S., 11 Hill Street, Edinburgh.
100 Doak, Lieut. James K. R., Struan, Carr-Bridge, Inverness-shire.
Dodds, Sir J. M., K.C.B., 11 Nevern Square, London, S.W.
Douglas, William, 9 Castle Street, Edinburgh.
Douglas, W. D. Robinson, Orchardton, Castle Douglas.
Dowden, John W., M.B., C.M., 48 Manor Place, Edinburgh.
Duff, Thomas Gordon, of Drummuir and Park, Drummuir Castle, Keith.
Dumfries, The Earl of, 5 Charlotte Square, Edinburgh.
Duncan, John, 8 Lynedoch Place, Edinburgh.
Dunn, Robert Hunter, 4 Crown Terrace, Glasgow, W.
Dunlop, W. B., Seaton Castle, Longniddry.
110 Edwards, John, 4 Great Western Terrace, Glasgow.
Eguilles, The Marquis of, 7 Rue d'Alençon, Paris (xv^e).
Elliot, Stuart Douglas, S.S.C., 40 Princes Street, Edinburgh.

Fairley, John A., 3 Barnton Gardens, Davidson's Mains, Midlothian.
Ferguson, John, Solicitor, Duns.
Ferguson, J. A., J.P., 78 Inverleith Place, Edinburgh.
Ferguson, Rt. Hon. Sir R. C. Munro, Raith, Kirkcaldy.
Fergusson, Dr. S., Lylestone House, Alloa.
Findlay, Sir John R., 27 Drumsheugh Gardens, Edinburgh.
Firth, Prof. Charles Harding, LL.D., 2 Northmoor Rd., Oxford.
120 Fleming, D. Hay, LL.D., 4 Chamberlain Road, Edinburgh.
Fleming, J. A., K.C., 33 Melville Street, Edinburgh.
Fleming, John, 9 Woodside Crescent, Glasgow.
Fleming, Mrs. Agnes J., 12 Beaufort Gardens, London, S.W.
Forbes, The Dowager Lady, Castle Forbes, Whitehouse, Aberdeenshire.

Foulis, T. N., 91 Great Russell Street, London, W.C.
Fowler, William Hope, M.B., Ch.B., F.R.C.S.E., 21 Walker Street, Edinburgh.
Fraser, Rev. A. Campbell, Bedlington Vicarage, Northumberland.
Fraser, Captain John, M.D., 3 Darnaway Street, Edinburgh.

Gairdner, C. D., Gateside, Blanefield.
130 Galletly, Edwin G., 71 Braid Avenue, Edinburgh.
Gardner, Alexander, Dunrod, Castlehead, Paisley.
Gardyne, Major A. D. Greenhill, of Finavon, Forfarshire.
Garson, James, W.S., 5 Albyn Place, Edinburgh.
Geddie, John, 16 Ann Street, Edinburgh.
Geikie, Sir Archibald, O.M., LL.D., Shepherd's Down, Haslemere, Surrey.
Gibson, Rev. H. W., M.A., LL.B., All Saints' Rectory, Inveraray.
Gibson, James T., LL.B., W.S., 14 Regent Terrace, Edinburgh.
Gilchrist, Miss M. R. R. M'Gilchrist, 86 Inverleith Place, Edinburgh.
Giles, Arthur, 191 Bruntsfield Place, Edinburgh.
140 Gillespie, Mrs. G. R., 5 Darnaway Street, Edinburgh.
Gilmour, Colonel R. G. Gordon, of Craigmillar, The Inch, Liberton.
Gladstone, Sir John R., Fasque, Laurencekirk.
Glen, James, 26 Bothwell Street, Glasgow.
Glenconner, The Lord, The Glen, Innerleithen.
Gow, Murray T., Newfield, Hamilton.
Graham, Captain J. G. B. P., Carphin, Carluke.
Grahame, Lieut.-Col. G. C., Boodles Club, St. James's Street, London.
Grant, Alex., 11 Salford Road, Streatham Hill, London, S.W.
Grant, Francis J., W.S., 30A George Square, Edinburgh.
150 Grant, Major Frank L., Craig Lea, Audley Road, Hendon, London, N.W.
Grant, Major James, LL.B., 23 Castle Street, Banff.
Grant, J. P., Advocate, 31 Northumberland Street, Edinburgh.
Grant, Mrs. Smith, Minmore, Glenlivet.

Green, Charles E., Publisher, St. Giles Street, Edinburgh.
Grierson, Captain Henry J., W.S., Laguna, Murthly, Perthshire.
Guthrie, The Hon. Lord, LL.D., 13 Royal Circus, Edinburgh.
Guthrie, Lieut. Charles, R.N., Carnoustie House, Carnoustie.
Guy, Robert, 120 West Regent Street, Glasgow.

Hannay, Professor R. K., 14 Inverleith Terrace, Edinburgh.
160 Harrison, G. A., Warrender, Murrayfield, Edinburgh.
Harrison, John, Rockville, 3 Napier Road, Edinburgh.
Hay, W. J., John Knox's House, Edinburgh.
Hedderwick, A. W. Holmes, 19 Oakfield Terrace, Glasgow.
Henderson, George, 48 Avenue Street, Bridgeton, Glasgow.
Henderson, J. G. B., Nether Parkley, Linlithgow.
Henderson, John, 207 West Campbell Street, Glasgow.
Henderson, Robert Candlish, Advocate, 64 Northumberland Street, Edinburgh.
Home, The Earl of, The Hirsel, Coldstream.
Hope, Trustees of George E., of Luffness, Aberlady, per Blair & Caddell, W.S., 19 Ainslie Place, Edinburgh.
170 Houston, Hugo, Kerfield, Peebles.
Howden, J. M., C.A., 11 Eton Terrace, Edinburgh.
Hutcheson, Miss Euphemia Gourlay, Herschel House, Broughty Ferry.
Hutchison, George A. Clark, Advocate, 34 Drumsheugh Gardens, Edinburgh.

Inglis, Harry R. G., 10 Dick Place, Edinburgh.
Inglis, John A., Advocate, 13 Randolph Crescent, Edinburgh.
Ingram, W., Advocate, 22 Great King Street, Edinburgh.

Jameson, J. H., W.S., 16 Coates Crescent, Edinburgh.
Johnston, David, 24 Huntly Gardens, Kelvinside, Glasgow.
Johnston, David, C.A., 14 Netherby Road, Leith.
180 Johnston, George Harvey, 22 Garscube Terrace, Edinburgh.
Johnston, George P., 37 George Street, Edinburgh.
Johnstone, David, 5 Dundas Street, Edinburgh.
Johnstone, James F. Kellas, 67 Forest Avenue, Aberdeen.

Keith, Miss Theodora, Auchingramont, Hamilton.

LIST OF MEMBERS

Kemp, D. William, Ivy Lodge, Laverockbank Road, Trinity, Edinburgh.
Kennedy, A. B., 6 Mansfield Place, Edinburgh.
Kessen, J. A., S.S.C., 26 St. Andrew Square, Edinburgh.
Kippen, W. J., Advocate, 17 Melville Street, Edinburgh.
Kirk, A. F. C., University Club, Edinburgh.
190 LAMONT, Sir NORMAN, Brt., of Knockdow, Toward, Argyllshire.
Lang, Miss Margaret, 21 Kelvinside Terrace, Glasgow.
Langwill, Robert B., 7 St. Leonard's Bank, Perth.
Lawson, Rev. Professor Alexander, D.D., 4 Gillespie Terrace, St. Andrews.
Leadbetter, Thomas Greenshields, Spital Tower, Denholm, Roxburghshire.
Lees, John, Pitscottie, Cupar-Fife.
Leigh, Captain J. Hamilton, Bindon, Wellington, Somerset.
Lemon, Miss Ethelwyn, M.A., 35 Lauriston Place, Edinburgh.
Lindsay, Rev. John, St. John's Manse, Bathgate.
Lindsay, W. A., K.C., Windsor Herald, College of Arms, London, E.C.
200 Lodge, Professor Sir R., LL.D., 25 Hope Terrace, Edinburgh.
Lorimer, George, Durrisdeer, Gillsland Road, Edinburgh.
Low, William, Seaview, Monifieth.
Lowe, David F., LL.D., 19 George Square, Edinburgh.
Lowe, W. D., W.S., 11 Randolph Crescent, Edinburgh.
MACADAM, J. H., 37 Shoe Lane, London, E.C.
M'Bain, Norman, 15 Hill Street, Arbroath.
M'Burnie, John, of Nether Laggan, Sheriff-Clerk, Dumfries.
M'Candlish, Captain P. D., Quarter House, Denny.
MacCrae, A., 23 Doune Terrace, Glasgow.
210 MacDonald of the Isles, Lady, Thorpe Hall, Bridlington.
MacDonald, James, W.S., 27 Heriot Row, Edinburgh.
Macdonald, J. R. M., Largie Castle, Tayinloan, Argyllshire.
MacDonald, Kenneth, Town House, Inverness.
Macdonald, W. K., Windmill House, Arbroath.
MacDougall, Alexander, junr., A.M.I.C.E., Oakhurst, Westcombe Park, London, S.E.
MacDougall, Sir Jas. Patten, K.C.B., Advocate, 39 Heriot Row, Edinburgh.

M'Ewen, W. C., W.S., 9 South Charlotte Street, Edinburgh.
Macfarlane-Grieve, R. W., M.A.Oxon, Lieut. 3rd Black Watch, of Penchrise and Edenhall, Impington Park, Cambridgeshire.
Macgeorge, B. B., 19 Woodside Crescent, Glasgow.
220 MacGillivray, Angus C. M., M.D., F.R.S.E., F.S.A.Scot., 23 South Tay Street, Dundee.
MacGregor, John, W.S., 3 Coates Crescent, Edinburgh.
Mackay, A., Glencruitten, Oban.
Mackay, Eneas, 43 Murray Place, Stirling.
Mackay, James F., W.S., Whitehouse, Cramond.
Mackay, John, S.S.C., 37 York Place, Edinburgh.
Mackay, William, LL.D., Solicitor, Inverness.
Mackay, W. Macdonald, 26 Lonsdale Road, Toronto, Canada.
Mackenzie, A. R., 7 Gilmour Street, Paisley.
Mackenzie, Sir Kenneth J., of Gairloch, King's and Lord Treasurer's Remembrancer, 10 Moray Place, Edinburgh.
230 Mackenzie, Colonel J. A. Stewart, of Seaforth, Brahan Castle, Conon Bridge, Ross-shire.
Mackenzie, Dr. M. T., M.O., Scolpaig, Lochmaddy.
Mackenzie, W. M. (Royal Com. Anc. Monuments), 15 Queen Street, Edinburgh.
Mackinnon, Professor James, Ph.D., 12 Lygon Rd., Edinburgh.
Mackintosh, W. F., Procurator-Fiscal, Linreoch, 3 Craigie Terrace, Dundee.
Maclachlan, John, W.S., Castle Lachlan, Strachur, Argyllshire.
Maclagan, Robert Craig, M.D., 5 Coates Crescent, Edinburgh.
MacLaren, Duncan, S.S.C., 62 Frederick Street, Edinburgh.
MacLehose, James, LL.D., 61 St. Vincent Street, Glasgow.
MacLeod, Fred., 36 St. Albans Road, Edinburgh.
240 Macleod, Professor John, Free Church College, Edinburgh.
Macleod, John, 80 Montpelier Park, Edinburgh.
Macmath, William, 16 St. Andrew Square, Edinburgh.
Macmillan, H. P., K.C., 32 Moray Place, Edinburgh.
Macnaughton, W. A., M.D., Medical Officer of Health, Stonehaven.
Macphail, Mrs., Hearnesbrooke, Ballinasloe, Ireland.
Macphail, J. R. N., K.C., 17 Royal Circus, Edinburgh.

LIST OF MEMBERS

Macpherson, D., Postmaster, 57 Forsyth Street, Greenock.
MacRae, Major Colin, of Feoirlinn, Ascog, Bute.
Macrae, Horatio R., W.S., 14 Gloucester Place, Edinburgh.
250 MacRae-Gilstrap, Lieut.-Col. Iain, Newark-on-Trent.
MacRitchie, Lewis A., 40 Princes Street, Edinburgh.
M'Whir, James, M.D., Norham-on-Tweed.
Maddan, William, Silanchia, Norham-on-Tweed.
Main, W. D., 69 Renfield Street, Glasgow.
Mann, James, Castlecraig, Dolphinton.
Mar and Kellie, The Earl of, Alloa.
Marshall, Robert C., Burntshields, Kilbarchan.
Marshall, W. M., Solicitor, 3 Merry Street, Motherwell.
Marwick, David W., W.S., 39 Inverleith Place, Edinburgh.
260 Massie, James, 9 Castle Street, Edinburgh.
Mathers, George Fleming, M.A., LL.B., W.S., 23 Manor Place, Edinburgh.
Meldrum, A. M., Fasganeoin, Pitlochry.
Melles, J. W., Gruline, Aros, Isle of Mull.
Melville, Alex. P., W.S., 8 Northumberland Street, Edinburgh.
Menzies, John R., 3 Grosvenor Crescent, Edinburgh.
Middleton, Mrs. Alfred, 48 Thurloe Square, London, S.W.
Mill, Alex., 9 Dalhousie Terrace, Edinburgh.
Millar, Alexander H., LL.D., Rosslyn House, Clepington Road, Dundee.
Miller, R. Pairman, S.S.C., 50 Queen Street, Edinburgh.
270 Miller, Rev. W., C.I.E., D.D., LL.D., Burgo Park, Bridge of Allan.
Miller, William, Writer, Motherwell.
Milligan, James, W.S., 10 Carlton Terrace, Edinburgh.
Minto, The Earl of, Minto House, Roxburghshire.
Minto, John (Librarian, Signet Library), 83 Comiston Drive, Edinburgh.
Mitchell, James, 14 Knowe Terrace, Pollokshields.
Mitchell, Sydney, The Pleasance, Gullane.
Moffatt, Alexander, Sheriff-Substitute of Stirlingshire, Falkirk.
Moncreiff, Hon. F. R., Marionville, Colinton.
Moncreiffe, William, Bighorn, Sheridan Co., Wyoming, U.S.A.
280 Moncrieff, R. Scott, W.S., 10 Randolph Cliff, Edinburgh.

Moncrieff, W. G. Scott, Whitchurch Rectory, Edgeware, Middlesex.
Morrison, Rev. John, D.D., 6 Hartington Gardens, Edinburgh.
Muir, J. Harold, Windyknowe, Killearn, Stirlingshire.
Muirhead, James, 2 Bowmont Gardens, Kelvinside, Glasgow.
Munro, Sir H. T., Drum Leys, Kirriemuir.
Murdoch, Rev. George C., Rector, St. John's Episcopal Church, Pittenweem.
Murray, David, LL.D., 169 West George Street, Glasgow.
Murray, Rev. James G., Rafford U.F. Manse, Forres.
Murray, P. Keith, W.S., 19 Charlotte Square, Edinburgh.

290 Neilson, George, LL.D., Wellfield, 76 Partickhill Rd., Glasgow.
Nelson, Thomas, *Times* Office, Printing House Square, London, E.C.4.
Nicolson, A. B., W.S., Glenbervie House, Fordoun.
Nightingale, Charles T., Commercial Bank, Portobello.

Ogilvy, Mrs. M. G. C. N. Hamilton, of Belhaven and Dirleton, Biel, East Lothian.
Oliphant, Walter, S.S.C., 21 York Place, Edinburgh.
Orde, Sir Arthur J. Campbell, Auchnascheach, Ardrishaig.
Orr, John, 74 George Street, Edinburgh.
Orrock, Alexander, 15 Victoria Street, Edinburgh.

Paterson, William, S.S.C., 25 Constitution Street, Leith.
300 Paton, Rev. Henry, M.A., Elmswood, Bonnington Road, Peebles.
Paton, Victor A. Noël, W.S., 11 Oxford Terrace, Edinburgh.
Patrick, Joseph, C.A., 247 West George Street, Glasgow.
Paul, Sir G. M., LL.D., D.K.S., 9 Eglinton Crescent, Edinburgh.
Paul, Sir James Balfour, C.V.O., LL.D., Advocate, Lyon King of Arms, 30 Heriot Row, Edinburgh.
Paulin, Sir David, 6 Forres Street, Edinburgh.
Penney, Scott Moncrieff, Advocate, Renfield, Hunter's Quay, Argyllshire.
Pentland, Young J., Duncliffe, Murrayfield, Edinburgh.
Petrie, James A., 31 Rosslyn Crescent, Edinburgh.
Philip, Rev. Andrew, M.A., U.F. Manse, Invergowrie.

310 Porteous, Alexander, Ancaster House, St. Fillans, Perthshire.
Prentice, A. R., Newark Lodge, 28 Newark Street, Greenock.
Rait, Professor Robert S., 31 Lilybank Gardens, Glasgow.
Ramsay, Miss E. Lucy, Stainrigg, Coldstream.
Ramsay, Captain Iain, Bengeo House, Hertford.
Ramsay, William, 32 Frederick Street, Edinburgh.
Rankin, W. B., W.S., 9 Lansdowne Crescent, Edinburgh.
Rankine, Professor John, K.C., LL.D., 23 Ainslie Place, Edinburgh.
Reichel, Sir H. R., Principal, Univ. Coll., Bangor, North Wales.
Reid, R. C., Cleuchbrae Cottage, Ruthwell R.S.O., Dumfriesshire.
320 Rennie, W. J. M., 57 Leamington Terrace, Edinburgh.
Renwick, Robert, Depute Town-Clerk, City Chambers, Glasgow.
Richardson, Ralph, W.S., Commissary Office, 2 Parliament Square, Edinburgh.
Ritchie, David, Hopeville, Dowanhill Gardens, Glasgow.
Ritchie, Professor James, M.A., B.Sc., 10 Succoth Gardens, Edinburgh.
Robb, James, B.D., LL.B., 7 Alvanley Terrace, Edinburgh.
Robbie, John Cameron, 22 York Place, Edinburgh.
Robertson, Stewart A., M.A., Chief Inspector, Education Office, Katharine Street, Croydon.
Rodger, A. B., Balliol College, Oxford.
Romanes, Charles James Lorimer, W.S., 3 Abbotsford Crescent, Edinburgh.
Romanes, Charles S., C.A., 3 Abbotsford Crescent, Edinburgh, *Hon. Treasurer.*
330 Romanes, James Manners, B.Sc., Romanhurst, Levenhall, Musselburgh.
Rosebery, The Earl of, K.G., Dalmeny Park, Linlithgowshire.
Russell, John, 323 Leith Walk, Edinburgh.
Rutherfurd, John (Messrs. Rutherfurd Bros.), Ingram Street, Glasgow.

Sanderson, Kenneth, W.S., 5 Abercromby Place, Edinburgh.
Sands, The Hon. Lord, 4 Heriot Row, Edinburgh.
Saunders, William, 102 Comiston Road, Edinburgh.

Scott, Henry, Milburn House, Moffat.
Scott, Miss Jean Macfarlane, 1 Park Place East, Sunderland.
340 Seton, Col. Sir Bruce, C.B., Bart., Glasgow Street, Hillhead, Glasgow.
Shaw, Right Hon. Lord, 1 Palace Gate, London, W.
Shaw, Mackenzie S., W.S., 1 Thistle Court, Edinburgh.
Shiell, J. G., Cairnie, Cupar-Fife.
Shiells, C. J., 141 George Street, Edinburgh.
Sime, David, 27 Dundas Street, Edinburgh.
Simpson, Professor J. Y., 25 Chester Street, Edinburgh.
Sinclair, Sir J. R. G., Bart., Barrock House, Wick.
Sinclair, Speirs Paton, C.A., 25 Grosvenor Street, Edinburgh.
Sinton, James, Hassendean, Eastfield, Joppa.
350 Skerrington, The Hon. Lord, 12 Randolph Crescent, Edinburgh.
Slater, W. Work, 85 Colinton Road, Edinburgh.
Smart, John, Junr., LL.B., W.S., 19 York Place, Edinburgh.
Smellie, Peter, 16 St. Andrew Square, Edinburgh.
Smith, Mrs., Birkhill, Lesmahagow.
Smith, Campbell, S.S.C., 19 Clarendon Crescent, Edinburgh.
Smith, David Baird, 6 Woodlands Road, Glasgow.
Smith, Prof. G. Gregory, LL.D., 26 Windsor Park, Belfast.
Smith, John Lamb, S.S.C., 58 Polwarth Terrace, Edinburgh.
Smith, J. K., 4 East Hermitage Place, Leith.
360 Smith, Robert, 9 Ward Road, Dundee.
Smythe, Col. David M., Methven Castle, Perth.
Stair, Earl of, Oxenfoord Castle, Dalkeith.
Steel, R. Forrest, S.S.C., 5 Chalmers Crescent, Edinburgh.
Steuart, A. Francis, Advocate, 79 Gt. King St., Edinburgh.
Stewart, Mrs. Angus, Dawyck, Stobo, Peeblesshire
Stewart, R. K., Murdostoun Castle, Newmains, Lanarkshire.
Stirling, Com. G. H. Miller, D.L., Craigbarnet, Campsie Glen.
Strathclyde, The Right Hon. Lord, 31 Heriot Row, Edinburgh.
Strathern, Robert, W.S., 12 South Charlotte St., Edinburgh.
370 Sturrock, Rev. J., 10 Glengyle Terrace, Edinburgh.
Sturrock, John, junr., 8 Trinity Crescent, Leith.

Tait, William, 64 Albert Drive, Pollokshields.
Taylor, Rev. Malcolm C., D.D., 6 Greenhill Park, Edinburgh.
Telford, Rev. W. H., Reston, Berwickshire.

Terry, Professor C. Sanford, Litt.D., Westerton of Pitfodels, Aberdeen.
Thin, George T., 7 Mayfield Terrace, Edinburgh.
Thomson, Col., Kilkenny House, Sion Hill, Bath.
Thomson, Frederick C., Advocate, M.P., 5 Northumberland Street, Edinburgh.
Thomson, J. Albert, Castle Works, Lady Lawson St., Edinburgh.
380 Thomson, John Maitland, LL.D., Advocate, 3 Grosvenor Gardens, Edinburgh, *Hon. Secretary.*
Thomson, Spencer Campbell, 10 Eglinton Crescent, Edinburgh.
Thomson, Thomas S., 18 Rothesay Place, Edinburgh.
Tod, Henry, W.S., 45 North Castle Street, Edinburgh.
Trail, John A., LL.D., W.S., 14 Belgrave Place, Edinburgh.
Trayner, The Hon. Lord, LL.D., Laurelhurst, Burwash, Sussex.

WALKER, ROBERT, LL.D., Tillydrone House, Old Aberdeen.
Wallace, David, C.M.G., F.R.C.S., 29 Charlotte Square, Edinburgh.
Waterston, George, 10 Claremont Crescent, Edinburgh.
Watson, Guthrie F., 20A St. James' Place, London, S.W.
390 Watson, R. W. Seton, 1 Buckingham St., Buckingham Gate, London, S.W. 1.
Watt, James, W.S., 24 Rothesay Terrace, Edinburgh.
Watt, Rev. Lauchlan Maclean, 7 Royal Circus, Edinburgh.
Whamond, David, 28 Spottiswoode Road, Edinburgh.
Whyte, Robert, S.S.C., 7 Laverockbank Terrace, Trinity.
Williamson, Charles, 4 Bayview Road, Aberdeen.
Wilson, Very Rev. Dean, 17 Atholl Crescent, Edinburgh.
Wood, W. A., C.A., 4 Melville Street, Edinburgh.
Wordie, William, 52 Montgomery Drive, Glasgow, W.

YOUNG, A. J., Sheriff-Substitute, Aberdeen.
400 Young, Thomas F., W.S., Auchterarder.

LIST OF LIBRARIES

Aberdeen Free Public Library.
Aberdeen University Library.
Arbroath Public Library.
Ayr, Carnegie Public Library.
Baltimore, Peabody Institute.

LIST OF LIBRARIES

Belfast Public Library, Donegall Square North, Belfast, Ireland.
Belfast, Queen's University.
Berlin Royal Library.
Birmingham Free Library.
10 Boston Athenæum, Mass.
Boston Public Library, Mass.
California University Library.
Cambridge University Library.
Cambridge, Westminster College Library.
Cardiff Free Public Library.
Chicago, Newberry Library.
Chicago University Library.
Copenhagen, Bibliothèque Royale.
Cornell University, Ithaca, Michigan.
20 Dollar Institution.
Dresden Public Library.
Dundee Free Library.
Dundee University College Library.
Dunfermline, Carnegie Free Library.
Edinburgh, Church of Scotland Library.
Edinburgh, Episcopal Church Theological Library, Coates Hall, Rosebery Crescent.
Edinburgh, Hope Trust, 31 Moray Place.
Edinburgh, New Club, Princes Street.
Edinburgh, New College Library.
30 Edinburgh, Philosophical Institution.
Edinburgh Protestant Institution of Scotland.
Edinburgh Public Library.
Edinburgh, Royal College of Physicians.
Edinburgh, St. Mary's Cathedral Library.
Edinburgh, Scottish Liberal Club, Gladstone Memorial Library.
Edinburgh, Signet Library.
Edinburgh, Society of Antiquaries.
Edinburgh, Society of Solicitors before the Supreme Court.
Edinburgh, Speculative Society.
40 Edinburgh, Stationery Office (for Historical Dept., General Register House).
Edinburgh, University Club.
Edinburgh University Library.
Glasgow, Baillie's Institution Free Library.
Glasgow, Faculty of Procurators.
Glasgow, Mitchell Library.
Glasgow, United Free Church College Library.
Glasgow University Library.
Harvard College Library, Cambridge, Mass.
Hove Public Library, Hove, Sussex.
50 Illinois University Library, Urbana, Ill., U.S.A.

LIST OF LIBRARIES

Inverness Free Library.
Ireland, National Library of.
Kilmarnock Public Library.
Leeds Library, Commercial Street, Leeds.
Leland Stanford Junior University, California, U.S.A.
Liverpool Public Library.
London, The Athenæum, S.W.
London Corporation Library, Guildhall.
London Library, St. James Square.
60 London, National Liberal Club.
London, Public Record Office, per Stationery Office, London.
London, Reform Club, Pall Mall, S.W.
London, Royal Institution, W.
London University, South Kensington, S.W
London University College, Gower Street, London.
Manchester, John Rylands Library.
Manchester Public Free Library.
Minneapolis Athenæum Library.
Nairn Literary Institute.
70 Netherlands Royal Library.
Newcastle-upon-Tyne Public Library.
New South Wales Public Library, Sydney.
New York Public Library.
New York State Library.
Nottingham Free Public Library.
Ontario Legislative Library, Toronto, Canada.
Ottawa Parliamentary Library.
Oxford, All Souls College.
Oxford, Bodleian Library.
80 Paisley Philosophical Institution.
Paris, Bibliothèque Nationale.
Pennsylvania Historical Society.
Perth, Sandeman Public Library.
Princeton Theological Seminary, New Jersey, U.S.A.
St. Andrews University Library.
Sheffield Free Public Library.
Stirling Public Library.
Stockholm, Royal Library.
Stonyhurst College, Blackburn, Lancashire.
90 Stornoway Public Library.
Toronto Public Library.
Upsala, Royal University Library, Sweden.
Victoria Public Library, Melbourne.
Vienna, Library of the R. I. University.
Wales, National Library of, Aberystwyth.
Washington, Library of Congress.
Wick, Carnegie Public Library.
Wigan Free Public Library.
Wisconsin State Historical Society.
100 Yale University Library.

Scottish History Society.

THE EXECUTIVE.
1918-1919.

President.
The Earl of Rosebery, K.G., K.T., LL.D.

Chairman of Council.
Sir James Balfour Paul, C.V.O., LL.D., Lyon King of Arms.

Council.
A. Francis Steuart, Advocate.
James MacLehose, LL.D.
The Right Hon. Lord Strathclyde.
William Mackay, LL.D.
Sir G. M. Paul, D.K.S.
R. K. Hannay.
James Curle, W.S.
George Neilson, LL.D.
William K. Dickson, LL.D., Advocate.
J. R. N. Macphail, K.C.
The Hon. Lord Guthrie.
D. Hay Fleming, LL.D.

Corresponding Members of the Council.
Prof. C. H. Firth, LL.D., Oxford; Prof. C. Sanford Terry, Litt.D., Aberdeen.

Hon. Treasurer.
C. S. Romanes, C.A., 3 Abbotsford Crescent, Edinburgh.

Hon. Secretary.
J. Maitland Thomson, LL.D., Advocate, 3 Grosvenor Gardens, Edinburgh.

RULE

1. The object of the Society is the discovery and printing, under selected editorship, of unpublished documents illustrative of the civil, religious, and social history of Scotland. The Society will also undertake, in exceptional cases, to issue translations of printed works of a similar nature, which have not hitherto been accessible in English.

2. The number of Members of the Society shall be limited to 400.

3. The affairs of the Society shall be managed by a Council, consisting of a Chairman, Treasurer, Secretary, and twelve elected Members, five to make a quorum. Three of the twelve elected Members shall retire annually by ballot, but they shall be eligible for re-election.

4. The Annual Subscription to the Society shall be One Guinea. The publications of the Society shall not be delivered to any Member whose Subscription is in arrear, and no Member shall be permitted to receive more than one copy of the Society's publications.

5. The Society will undertake the issue of its own publications, *i.e.* without the intervention of a publisher or any other paid agent.

6. The Society will issue yearly two octavo volumes of about 320 pages each.

7. An Annual General Meeting of the Society shall be held at the end of October, or at an approximate date to be determined by the Council.

8. Two stated Meetings of the Council shall be held each year, one on the last Tuesday of May, the other on the Tuesday preceding the day upon which the Annual General Meeting hall be held. The Secretary, on the request of three Members of the Council, shall call a special meeting of the Council.

9. Editors shall receive 20 copies of each volume they edit for the Society.

10. The owners of Manuscripts published by the Society will also be presented with a certain number of copies.

11. The Annual Balance-Sheet, Rules, and List of Members shall be printed.

12. No alteration shall be made in these Rules except at a General Meeting of the Society. A fortnight's notice of any alteration to be proposed shall be given to the Members of the Council.

PUBLICATIONS

OF THE

SCOTTISH HISTORY SOCIETY

For the year 1886-1887.

1. BISHOP POCOCKE'S TOURS IN SCOTLAND, 1747-1760. Edited by D. W. KEMP.
2. DIARY AND ACCOUNT BOOK OF WILLIAM CUNNINGHAM OF CRAIGENDS, 1673-1680. Edited by the Rev. JAMES DODDS, D.D.

For the year 1887-1888.

3. GRAMEIDOS LIBRI SEX: an heroic poem on the Campaign of 1689, by JAMES PHILIP of Almerieclose. Translated and edited by the Rev. A. D. MURDOCH.
4. THE REGISTER OF THE KIRK-SESSION OF ST. ANDREWS. Part I. 1559-1582. Edited by D. HAY FLEMING.

For the year 1888-1889.

5. DIARY OF THE REV. JOHN MILL, Minister in Shetland, 1740-1803. Edited by GILBERT GOUDIE.
6. NARRATIVE OF MR. JAMES NIMMO, A COVENANTER, 1654-1709. Edited by W. G. SCOTT-MONCRIEFF.
7. THE REGISTER OF THE KIRK-SESSION OF ST. ANDREWS. Part II. 1583-1600. Edited by D. HAY FLEMING.

For the year 1889-1890.

8. A LIST OF PERSONS CONCERNED IN THE REBELLION (1745). With a Preface by the EARL OF ROSEBERY.
   Presented to the Society by the Earl of Rosebery.
9. GLAMIS PAPERS: The 'BOOK OF RECORD,' a Diary written by PATRICK, FIRST EARL OF STRATHMORE, and other documents (1684-89). Edited by A. H. MILLAR.
10. JOHN MAJOR'S HISTORY OF GREATER BRITAIN (1521). Translated and edited by ARCHIBALD CONSTABLE.

For the year 1890-1891.

11. THE RECORDS OF THE COMMISSIONS OF THE GENERAL ASSEMBLIES, 1646-47. Edited by the Rev. Professor MITCHELL, D.D., and the Rev. JAMES CHRISTIE, D.D.
12. COURT-BOOK OF THE BARONY OF URIE, 1604-1747. Edited by the Rev. D. G. BARRON.

For the year 1891-1892.

13. MEMOIRS OF SIR JOHN CLERK OF PENICUIK, Baronet. Extracted by himself from his own Journals, 1676-1755. Edited by JOHN M. GRAY.
14. DIARY OF COL. THE HON. JOHN ERSKINE OF CARNOCK, 1683-1687. Edited by the Rev. WALTER MACLEOD.

For the year 1892-1893.

15. MISCELLANY OF THE SCOTTISH HISTORY SOCIETY, First Volume—THE LIBRARY OF JAMES VI., 1573-83. Edited by G. F. Warner.—DOCUMENTS ILLUSTRATING CATHOLIC POLICY, 1596-98. T. G. Law.—LETTERS OF SIR THOMAS HOPE, 1627-46. Rev. R. Paul.—CIVIL WAR PAPERS, 1643-50. H. F. Morland Simpson.—LAUDERDALE CORRESPONDENCE, 1660-77. Right Rev. John Dowden, D.D.—TURNBULL'S DIARY, 1657-1704. Rev. R. Paul.—MASTERTON PAPERS, 1660-1719. V. A. Noël Paton.—ACCOMPT OF EXPENSES IN EDINBURGH, 1715. A. H. Millar.—REBELLION PAPERS, 1715 and 1745. H. Paton.
16. ACCOUNT BOOK OF SIR JOHN FOULIS OF RAVELSTON (1671-1707). Edited by the Rev. A. W. CORNELIUS HALLEN.

For the year 1893-1894.

17. LETTERS AND PAPERS ILLUSTRATING THE RELATIONS BETWEEN CHARLES II. AND SCOTLAND IN 1650. Edited by SAMUEL RAWSON GARDINER, D.C.L., etc.
18. SCOTLAND AND THE COMMONWEALTH. LETTERS AND PAPERS RELATING TO THE MILITARY GOVERNMENT OF SCOTLAND, Aug. 1651-Dec. 1653. Edited by C. H. FIRTH, M.A.

For the year 1894-1895.

19. THE JACOBITE ATTEMPT OF 1719. LETTERS OF JAMES, SECOND DUKE OF ORMONDE. Edited by W. K. DICKSON.
20, 21. THE LYON IN MOURNING, OR A COLLECTION OF SPEECHES, LETTERS, JOURNALS, ETC., RELATIVE TO THE AFFAIRS OF PRINCE CHARLES EDWARD STUART, by BISHOP FORBES. 1746-1775. Edited by HENRY PATON. Vols. I. and II.

For the year 1895-1896.

22. THE LYON IN MOURNING. Vol. III.
23. ITINERARY OF PRINCE CHARLES EDWARD (Supplement to the Lyon in Mourning). Compiled by W. B. BLAIKIE.
24. EXTRACTS FROM THE PRESBYTERY RECORDS OF INVERNESS AND DINGWALL FROM 1638 TO 1688. Edited by WILLIAM MACKAY.
25. RECORDS OF THE COMMISSIONS OF THE GENERAL ASSEMBLIES (continued) for the years 1648 and 1649. Edited by the Rev. Professor MITCHELL, D.D., and Rev. JAMES CHRISTIE, D.D.

PUBLICATIONS

For the year 1896-1897.

26. Wariston's Diary and other Papers—
Johnston of Wariston's Diary, 1639. Edited by G. M. Paul.—
The Honours of Scotland, 1651-52. C. R. A. Howden.—The
Earl of Mar's Legacies, 1722, 1726. Hon. S. Erskine.—Letters
by Mrs. Grant of Laggan. J. R. N. Macphail.
Presented to the Society by Messrs. T. and A. Constable.
27. Memorials of John Murray of Broughton, 1740-1747.
Edited by R. Fitzroy Bell.
28. The Compt Buik of David Wedderburne, Merchant of
Dundee, 1587-1630. Edited by A. H. Millar.

For the year 1897-1898.

29, 30. The Correspondence of De Montereul and the brothers
De Bellièvre, French Ambassadors in England and Scot-
land, 1645-1648. Edited, with Translation, by J. G.
Fotheringham. 2 vols.

For the year 1898-1899.

31. Scotland and the Protectorate. Letters and Papers
relating to the Military Government of Scotland, from
January 1654 to June 1659. Edited by C. H. Firth, M.A.
32. Papers illustrating the History of the Scots Brigade in
the Service of the United Netherlands, 1572-1782.
Edited by James Ferguson. Vol. i. 1572-1697.
33, 34. Macfarlane's Genealogical Collections concerning
Families in Scotland; Manuscripts in the Advocates' Library.
2 vols. Edited by J. T. Clark, Keeper of the Library.
Presented to the Society by the Trustees of the late Sir William Fraser, K.C.B.

For the year 1899-1900.

35. Papers on the Scots Brigade in Holland. 1572-1782.
Edited by James Ferguson. Vol. ii. 1698-1782.
36. Journal of a Foreign Tour in 1665 and 1666, etc., by Sir John
Lauder, Lord Fountainhall. Edited by Donald Crawford.
37. Papal Negotiations with Mary Queen of Scots during her
Reign in Scotland. Chiefly from the Vatican Archives.
Edited by the Rev. J. Hungerford Pollen, S.J.

For the year 1900-1901.

38. Papers on the Scots Brigade in Holland, 1572-1782.
Edited by James Ferguson. Vol. iii.
39. The Diary of Andrew Hay of Chaignethan, 1659-60.
Edited by A. G. Reid, F.S.A.Scot.

For the year 1901-1902.

40. Negotiations for the Union of England and Scotland in
1651-53. Edited by C. Sanford Terry.
41. The Loyall Dissuasive. Written in 1703 by Sir Æneas
Macpherson. Edited by the Rev. A. D. Murdoch.

PUBLICATIONS

For the year 1902-1903.

42. THE CHARTULARY OF LINDORES, 1195-1479. Edited by the Right Rev. JOHN DOWDEN, D.D., Bishop of Edinburgh.
43. A LETTER FROM MARY QUEEN OF SCOTS TO THE DUKE OF GUISE, Jan. 1562. Reproduced in Facsimile. Edited by the Rev. J. HUNGERFORD POLLEN, S.J.
Presented to the Society by the family of the late Mr. Scott, of Halkshill.
44. MISCELLANY OF THE SCOTTISH HISTORY SOCIETY, Second Volume—THE SCOTTISH KING'S HOUSEHOLD, 14th Century. Edited by Mary Bateson.—THE SCOTTISH NATION IN THE UNIVERSITY OF ORLEANS, 1336-1538. John Kirkpatrick, LL.D.—THE FRENCH GARRISON AT DUNBAR, 1563. Robert S. Rait.—DE ANTIQUITATE RELIGIONIS APUD SCOTOS, 1594. Henry D. G. Law.—APOLOGY FOR WILLIAM MAITLAND OF LETHINGTON, 1610. Andrew Lang.—LETTERS OF BISHOP GEORGE GRÆME, 1602-38. L. G. Græme.—A SCOTTISH JOURNIE, 1641. C. H. Firth.—NARRATIVES ILLUSTRATING THE DUKE OF HAMILTON'S EXPEDITION TO ENGLAND, 1648. C. H. Firth.—BURNET-LEIGHTON PAPERS, 1648-168-. H. C. Foxcroft.—PAPERS OF ROBERT ERSKINE, Physician to Peter the Great, 1677-1720. Rev. Robert Paul.—WILL OF THE DUCHESS OF ALBANY, 1789. A. Francis Steuart.
45. LETTERS OF JOHN COCKBURN OF ORMISTOUN TO HIS GARDENER, 1727-1743. Edited by JAMES COLVILLE, D.Sc.

For the year 1903-1904.

46. MINUTE BOOK OF THE MANAGERS OF THE NEW MILLS CLOTH MANUFACTORY, 1681-1690. Edited by W. R. SCOTT.
47. CHRONICLES OF THE FRASERS; being the Wardlaw Manuscript entitled 'Polichronicon seu Policratica Temporum, or, the true Genealogy of the Frasers.' By Master JAMES FRASER. Edited by WILLIAM MACKAY.
48. PROCEEDINGS OF THE JUSTICIARY COURT FROM 1661 TO 1678. Vol. I. 1661-1669. Edited by Sheriff SCOTT-MONCRIEFF.

For the year 1904-1905.

49. PROCEEDINGS OF THE JUSTICIARY COURT FROM 1661 TO 1678. Vol. II. 1669-1678. Edited by Sheriff SCOTT-MONCRIEFF.
50. RECORDS OF THE BARON COURT OF STITCHILL, 1655-1807. Edited by CLEMENT B. GUNN, M.D., Peebles.
51. MACFARLANE'S GEOGRAPHICAL COLLECTIONS. Vol. I. Edited by Sir ARTHUR MITCHELL, K.C.B.

For the year 1905-1906.

52, 53. MACFARLANE'S GEOGRAPHICAL COLLECTIONS. Vols. II. and III. Edited by Sir ARTHUR MITCHELL, K.C.B.
54. STATUTA ECCLESIÆ SCOTICANÆ, 1225-1559. Translated and edited by DAVID PATRICK, LL.D.

For the year 1906-1907.

55. THE HOUSE BOOKE OF ACCOMPS, OCHTERTYRE, 1737-39. Edited by JAMES COLVILLE, D.Sc.

56. THE CHARTERS OF THE ABBEY OF INCHAFFRAY. Edited by W. A. LINDSAY, K.C., the Right Rev. Bishop DOWDEN, D.D., and J. MAITLAND THOMSON, LL.D.
57. A SELECTION OF THE FORFEITED ESTATES PAPERS PRESERVED IN H.M. GENERAL REGISTER HOUSE AND ELSEWHERE. Edited by A. H. MILLAR, LL.D.

For the year 1907-1908.

58. RECORDS OF THE COMMISSIONS OF THE GENERAL ASSEMBLIES (*continued*), for the years 1650-52. Edited by the Rev. JAMES CHRISTIE, D.D.
59. PAPERS RELATING TO THE SCOTS IN POLAND. Edited by A. FRANCIS STEUART.

For the year 1908-1909.

60. SIR THOMAS CRAIG'S DE UNIONE REGNORUM BRITANNIÆ TRACTATUS. Edited, with an English Translation, by C. SANFORD TERRY.
61. JOHNSTON OF WARISTON'S MEMENTO QUAMDIU VIVAS, AND DIARY FROM 1632 to 1639. Edited by G. M. PAUL, LL.D., D.K.S.

SECOND SERIES.

For the year 1909-1910.

1. THE HOUSEHOLD BOOK OF LADY GRISELL BAILLIE, 1692-1733. Edited by R. SCOTT-MONCRIEFF, W.S.
2. ORIGINS OF THE '45 AND OTHER NARRATIVES. Edited by W. B. BLAIKIE, LL.D.
3. CORRESPONDENCE OF JAMES, FOURTH EARL OF FINDLATER AND FIRST EARL OF SEAFIELD, LORD CHANCELLOR OF SCOTLAND. Edited by JAMES GRANT, M.A., LL.B.

For the year 1910-1911.

4. RENTALE SANCTI ANDREE; BEING CHAMBERLAIN AND GRANITAR ACCOUNTS OF THE ARCHBISHOPRIC IN THE TIME OF CARDINAL BETOUN, 1538-1546. Translated and edited by ROBERT KERR HANNAY.
5. HIGHLAND PAPERS. Vol. I. Edited by J. R. N. MACPHAIL, K.C.

For the year 1911-1912.

6. SELECTIONS FROM THE RECORDS OF THE REGALITY OF MELROSE. Vol. I. Edited by C. S. ROMANES, C.A.
7. RECORDS OF THE EARLDOM OF ORKNEY. Edited by J. S. CLOUSTON.

For the year 1912-1913.

8. SELECTIONS FROM THE RECORDS OF THE REGALITY OF MELROSE. Vol. II. Edited by C. S. ROMANES, C.A.
9. SELECTIONS FROM THE LETTER BOOKS OF JOHN STEUART, BAILIE OF INVERNESS. Edited by WILLIAM MACKAY, LL.D.

For the year 1913-1914.

10. RENTALE DUNKELDENSE; BEING THE ACCOUNTS OF THE CHAMBERLAIN OF THE BISHOPRIC OF DUNKELD, A.D. 1506-1517. Edited by R. K. HANNAY.

11. LETTERS OF THE EARL OF SEAFIELD AND OTHERS, ILLUSTRATIVE OF THE HISTORY OF SCOTLAND DURING THE REIGN OF QUEEN ANNE. Edited by Professor HUME BROWN.

For the year 1914-1915.

12. HIGHLAND PAPERS. Vol. II. Edited by J. R. N. MACPHAIL, K.C. (March 1916.)
(*Note.*—ORIGINS OF THE '45, issued for 1909-1910, is issued also for 1914-1915.)

For the year 1915-1916.

13. SELECTIONS FROM THE RECORDS OF THE REGALITY OF MELROSE. Vol. III. Edited by C. S. ROMANES, C.A. (February 1917.)
14. A CONTRIBUTION TO THE BIBLIOGRAPHY OF SCOTTISH TOPOGRAPHY. Edited by the late Sir ARTHUR MITCHELL and C. G. CASH. Vol. I. (March 1917.)

For the year 1916-1917.

15. BIBLIOGRAPHY OF SCOTTISH TOPOGRAPHY. Vol. II. (May 1917.)
16. PAPERS RELATING TO THE ARMY OF THE SOLEMN LEAGUE AND COVENANT, 1643-1647. Vol. I. Edited by Professor C. SANFORD TERRY. (October 1917.)

For the year 1917-1918.

17. PAPERS RELATING TO THE ARMY OF THE SOLEMN LEAGUE AND COVENANT, 1643-1647. Vol. II. (December 1917.)
18. WARISTON'S DIARY. Vol. II. Edited by D. HAY FLEMING, LL.D. (February 1919.)

For the year 1918-1919.

19. MISCELLANY OF THE SCOTTISH HISTORY SOCIETY. Third Volume.
20. PAPERS RELATING TO THE HIGHLANDS. Edited by J. R. N. MACPHAIL, K.C.

In preparation.

THE EARLY RECORDS OF THE UNIVERSITY OF ST. ANDREWS. Edited by J. MAITLAND ANDERSON, LL.D.

REGISTER OF THE CONSULTATIONS OF THE MINISTERS OF EDINBURGH, AND SOME OTHER BRETHREN OF THE MINISTRY, SINCE THE INTERRUPTION OF THE ASSEMBLY 1653, WITH OTHER PAPERS OF PUBLIC CONCERNMENT. Edited by the Rev. W. STEPHEN, B.D.

SEAFIELD CORRESPONDENCE. Vol. II. Edited by Major JAMES GRANT.

CHARTERS AND DOCUMENTS RELATING TO THE GREY FRIARS AND THE CISTERCIAN NUNNERY OF HADDINGTON.—REGISTER OF INCHCOLM MONASTERY. Edited by J. G. WALLACE-JAMES, M.B.

ANALYTICAL CATALOGUE OF THE WODROW COLLECTION OF MANUSCRIPTS IN THE ADVOCATES' LIBRARY.

A TRANSLATION OF THE HISTORIA ABBATUM DE KYNLOS OF FERRERIUS.

PAPERS RELATING TO THE REBELLIONS OF 1715 AND 1745, with other documents from the Municipal Archives of the City of Perth.

THE BALCARRES PAPERS.

www.ingramcontent.com/pod-product-compliance
Lightning Source LLC
Chambersburg PA
CBHW030346230426
43664CB00007BB/546